My Little Monster

WITHDRAWN

♡ 8 ♡

Robico

CONTENTS

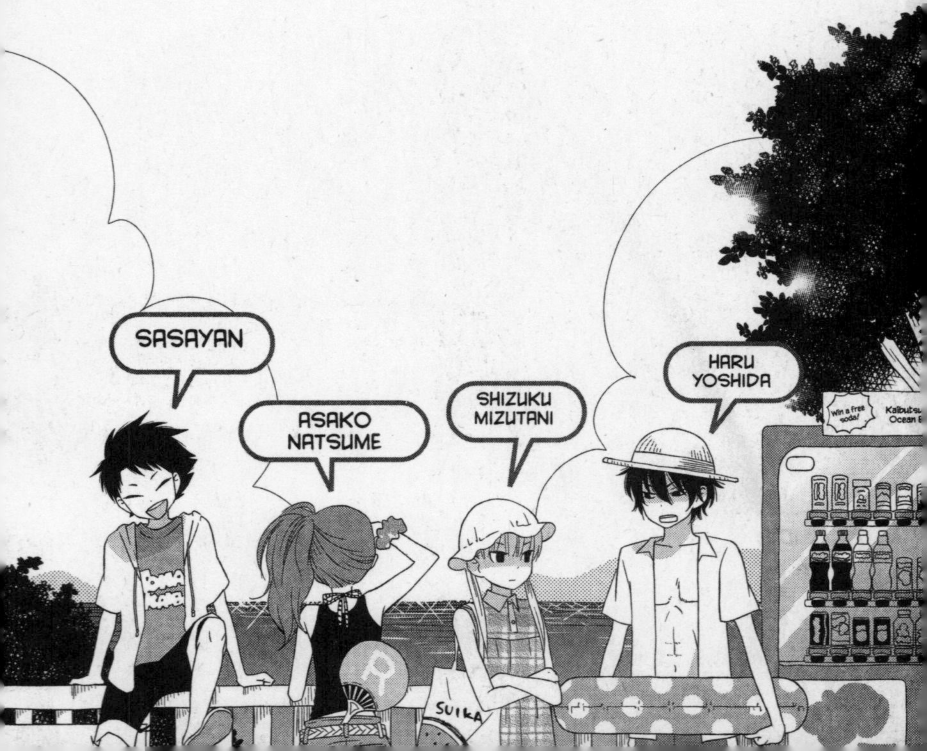

SASAYAN
ASAKO NATSUME
SHIZUKU MIZUTANI
HARU YOSHIDA
Win a free soda!
SUIKA

STORY

When Shizuku Mizutani does a favor for problem child Haru Yoshida, who sat next to her in school, he develops a huge crush on her. Attracted to his innocence, she eventually falls for him, too, but when she asks him out, he inexplicably turns her down. After that, the couple repeatedly fail to find themselves on the same page... until Shizuku boldly confesses her love to Haru for the third time on her birthday, which fell on Valentine's Day. She was sure she got through to him this time, but with everything else going on—Oshima-san confessing her love to Haru, Natsume-san confessing her love to Mitchan-san and getting rejected—Shizuku started her second year of high school with no real answer from Haru. And of all the friends, Haru alone was assigned to the class next door...?

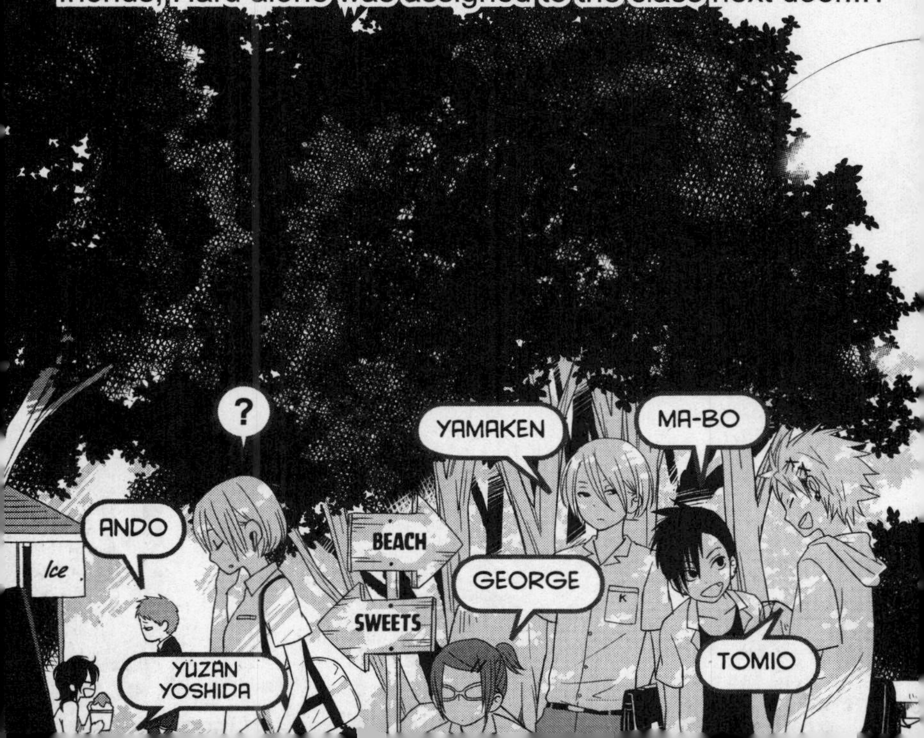
MA-BO
YAMAKEN
?
TOMIO
GEORGE
BEACH
SWEETS
ANDO
Ice
YŪZAN YOSHIDA

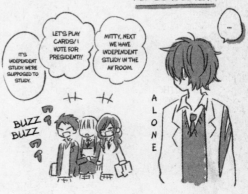

A CERTAIN SCENE FROM THE NEW SCHOOL TERM

...
MITTY, NEXT WE HAVE INDEPENDENT STUDY IN THE AV ROOM.
LET'S PLAY CARDS! I VOTE FOR PRESIDENT!!
IT'S INDEPENDENT STUDY. WE'RE SUPPOSED TO STUDY.
ALONE
BUZZ BUZZ

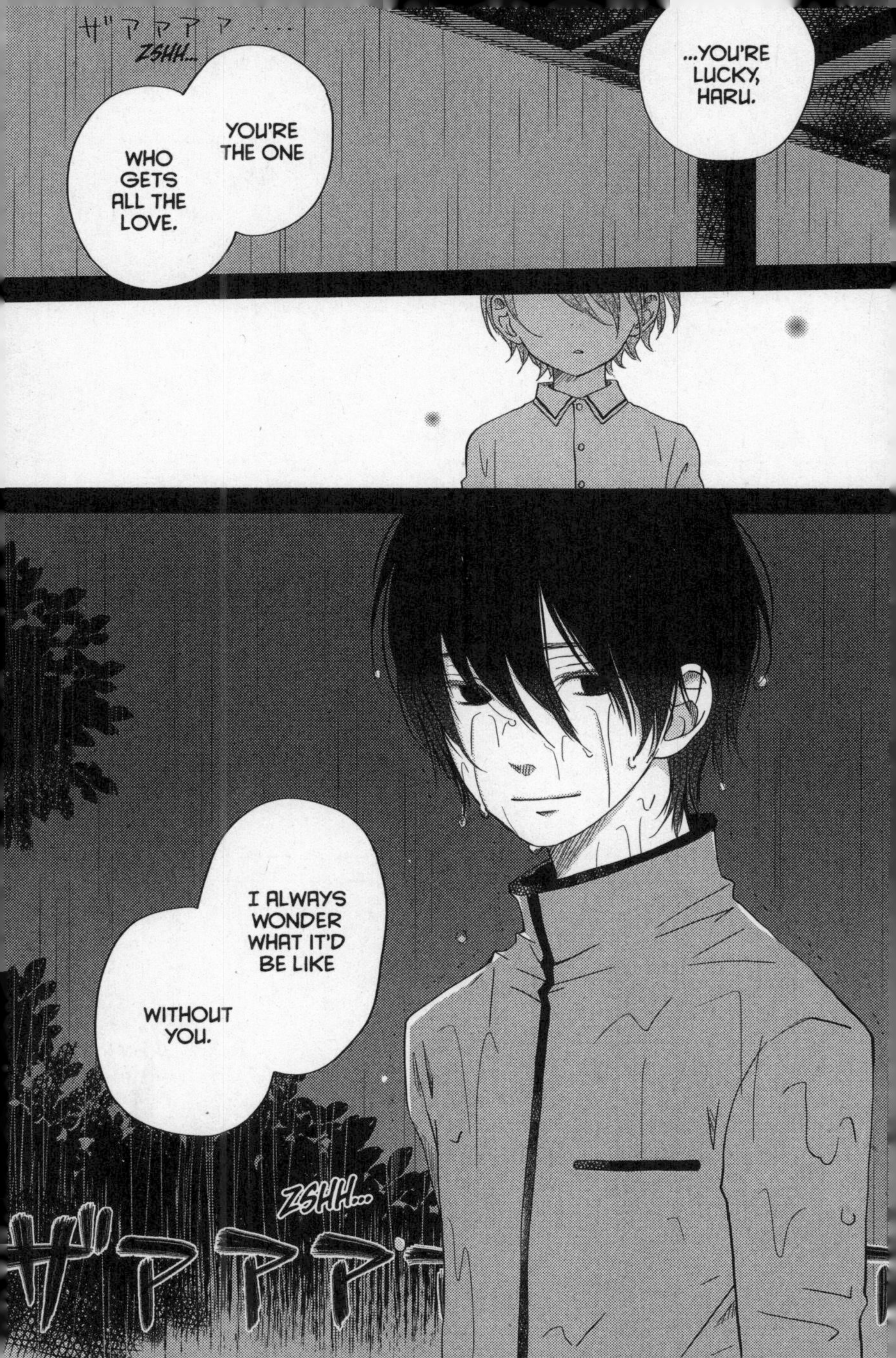
...YOU'RE LUCKY, HARU.
ザァァァ…
ZSHH...
YOU'RE THE ONE WHO GETS ALL THE LOVE.
I ALWAYS WONDER WHAT IT'D BE LIKE WITHOUT YOU.
ZSHH...
ザァァ

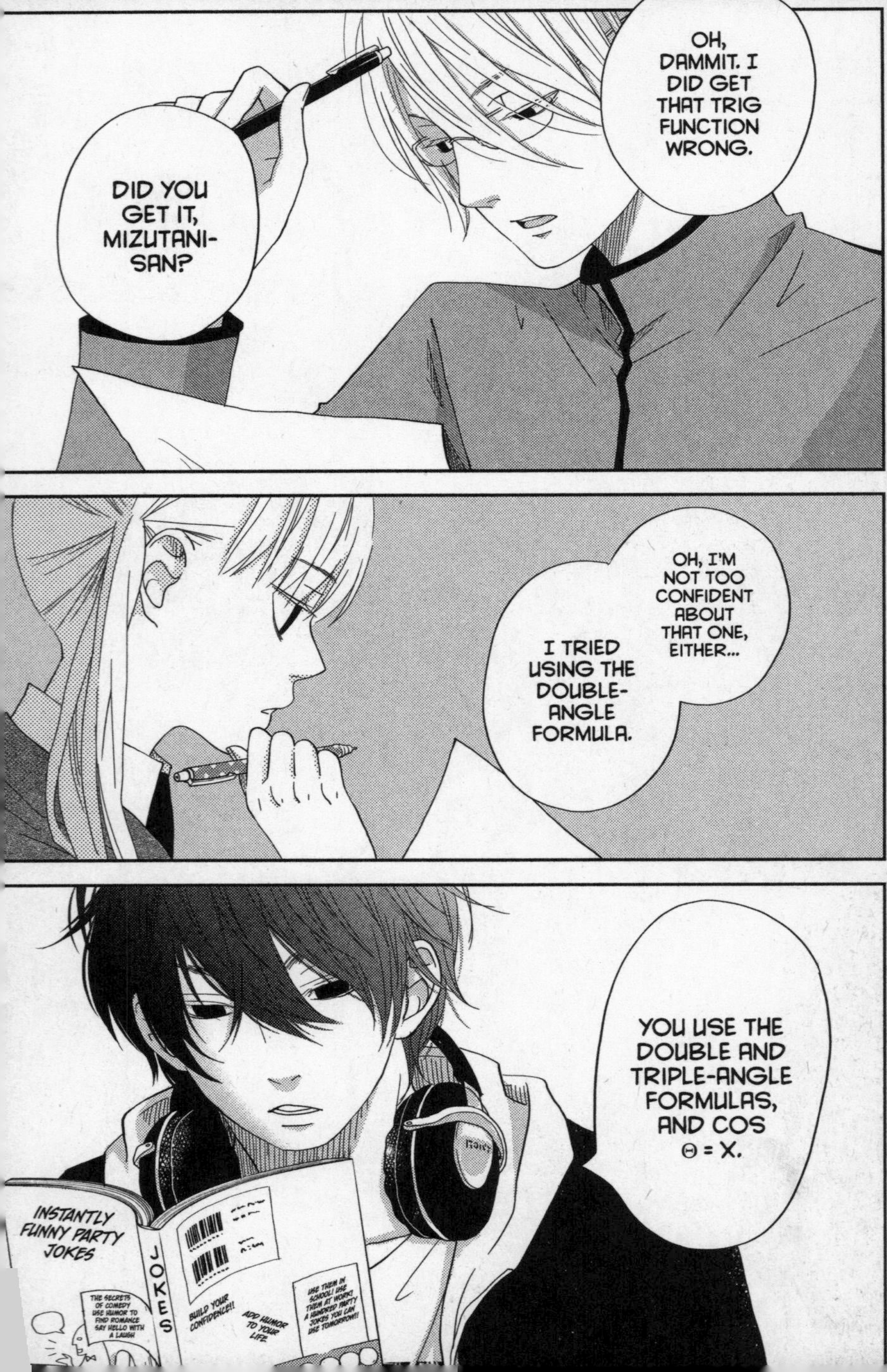
OH, DAMMIT. I DID GET THAT TRIG FUNCTION WRONG.
DID YOU GET IT, MIZUTANI-SAN?
OH, I'M NOT TOO CONFIDENT ABOUT THAT ONE, EITHER...
I TRIED USING THE DOUBLE-ANGLE FORMULA.
YOU USE THE DOUBLE AND TRIPLE-ANGLE FORMULAS, AND COS Θ = X.
INSTANTLY FUNNY PARTY JOKES
JOKES
THE SECRETS OF COMEDY USE HUMOR TO FIND ROMANCE SAY HELLO WITH A LAUGH
BUILD YOUR CONFIDENCE!!
ADD HUMOR TO YOUR LIFE.
USE THEM IN SCHOOL! USE THEM AT WORK! A HUNDRED PARTY JOKES YOU CAN USE TOMORROW!!

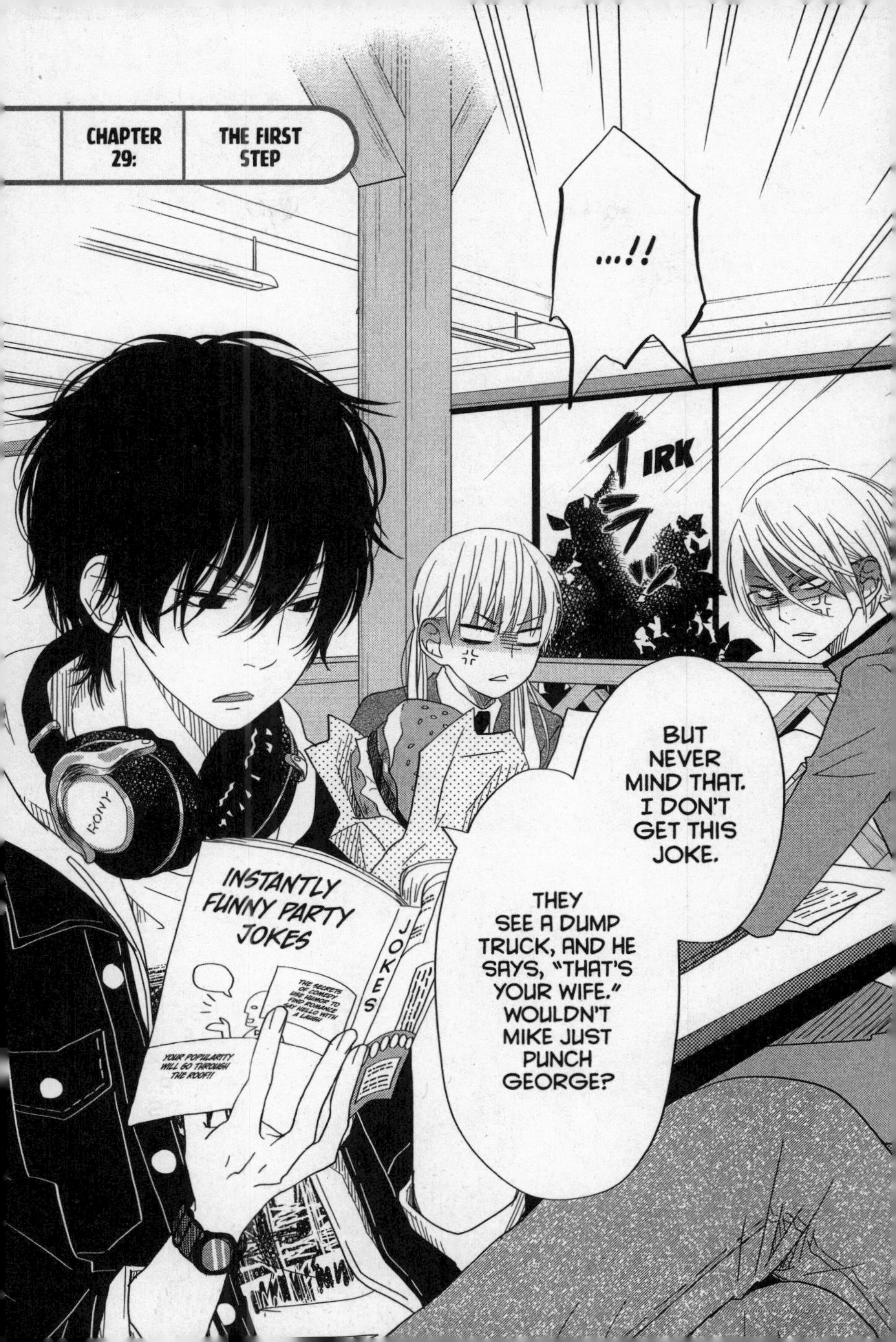
CHAPTER 29: THE FIRST STEP
...!!
IRK
BUT NEVER MIND THAT. I DON'T GET THIS JOKE.
THEY SEE A DUMP TRUCK, AND HE SAYS, "THAT'S YOUR WIFE." WOULDN'T MIKE JUST PUNCH GEORGE?
INSTANTLY FUNNY PARTY JOKES
JOKES
YOUR POPULARITY WILL GO THROUGH THE ROOF!!
RONY

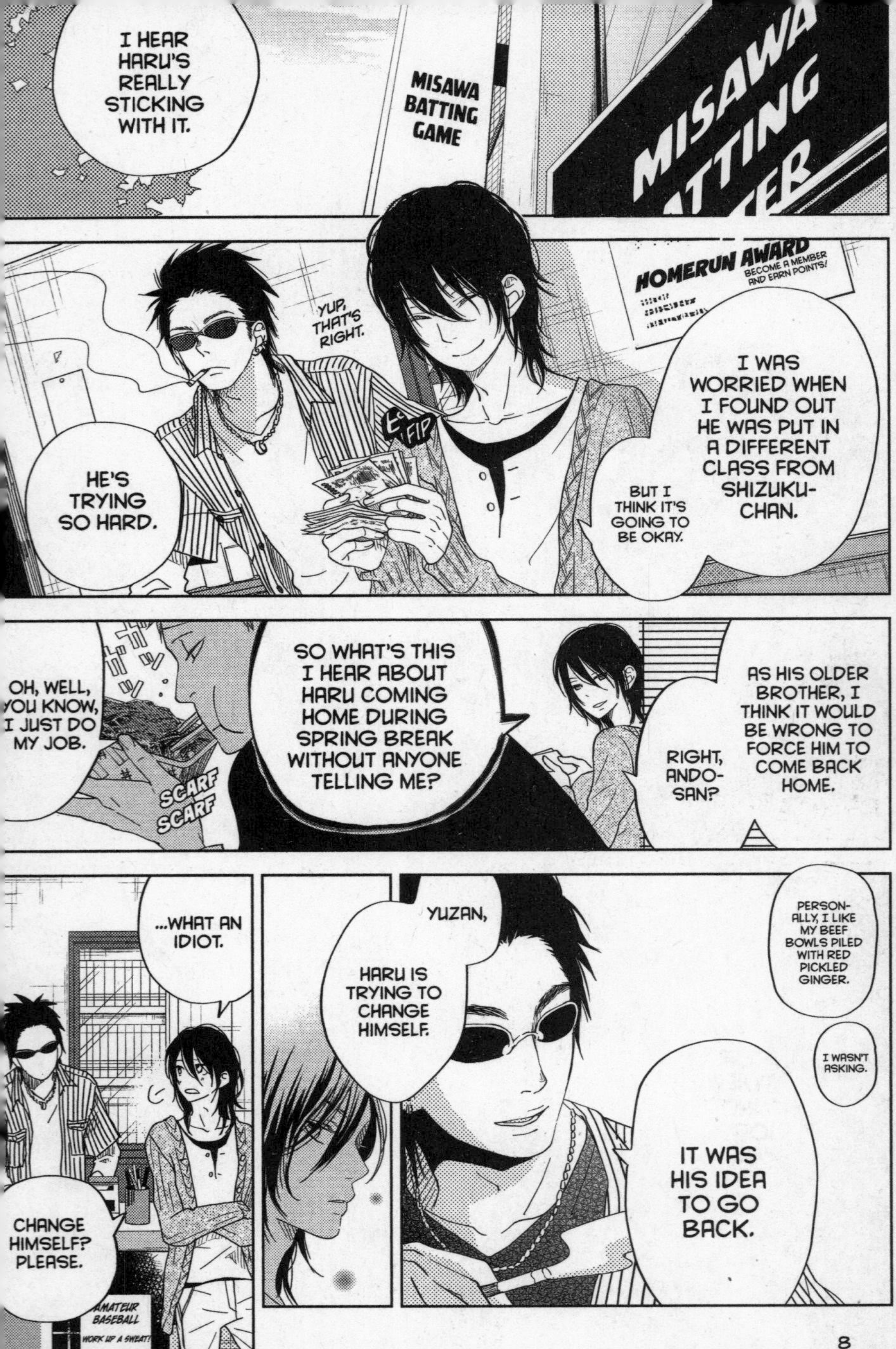
MISAWA
MISAWA BATTING GAME
I HEAR HARU'S REALLY STICKING WITH IT.
HOMERUN AWARD
BECOME A MEMBER AND EARN POINTS!
I WAS WORRIED WHEN I FOUND OUT HE WAS PUT IN A DIFFERENT CLASS FROM SHIZUKU-CHAN.
BUT I THINK IT'S GOING TO BE OKAY.
YUP, THAT'S RIGHT.
HE'S TRYING SO HARD.
AS HIS OLDER BROTHER, I THINK IT WOULD BE WRONG TO FORCE HIM TO COME BACK HOME.
RIGHT, ANDO-SAN?
SO WHAT'S THIS I HEAR ABOUT HARU COMING HOME DURING SPRING BREAK WITHOUT ANYONE TELLING ME?
OH, WELL, YOU KNOW, I JUST DO MY JOB.
SCARF SCARF
YUZAN,
PERSON-ALLY, I LIKE MY BEEF BOWLS PILED WITH RED PICKLED GINGER.
I WASN'T ASKING.
HARU IS TRYING TO CHANGE HIMSELF.
IT WAS HIS IDEA TO GO BACK.
...WHAT AN IDIOT.
CHANGE HIMSELF? PLEASE.
AMATEUR BASEBALL
WORK UP A SWEAT!
NOW

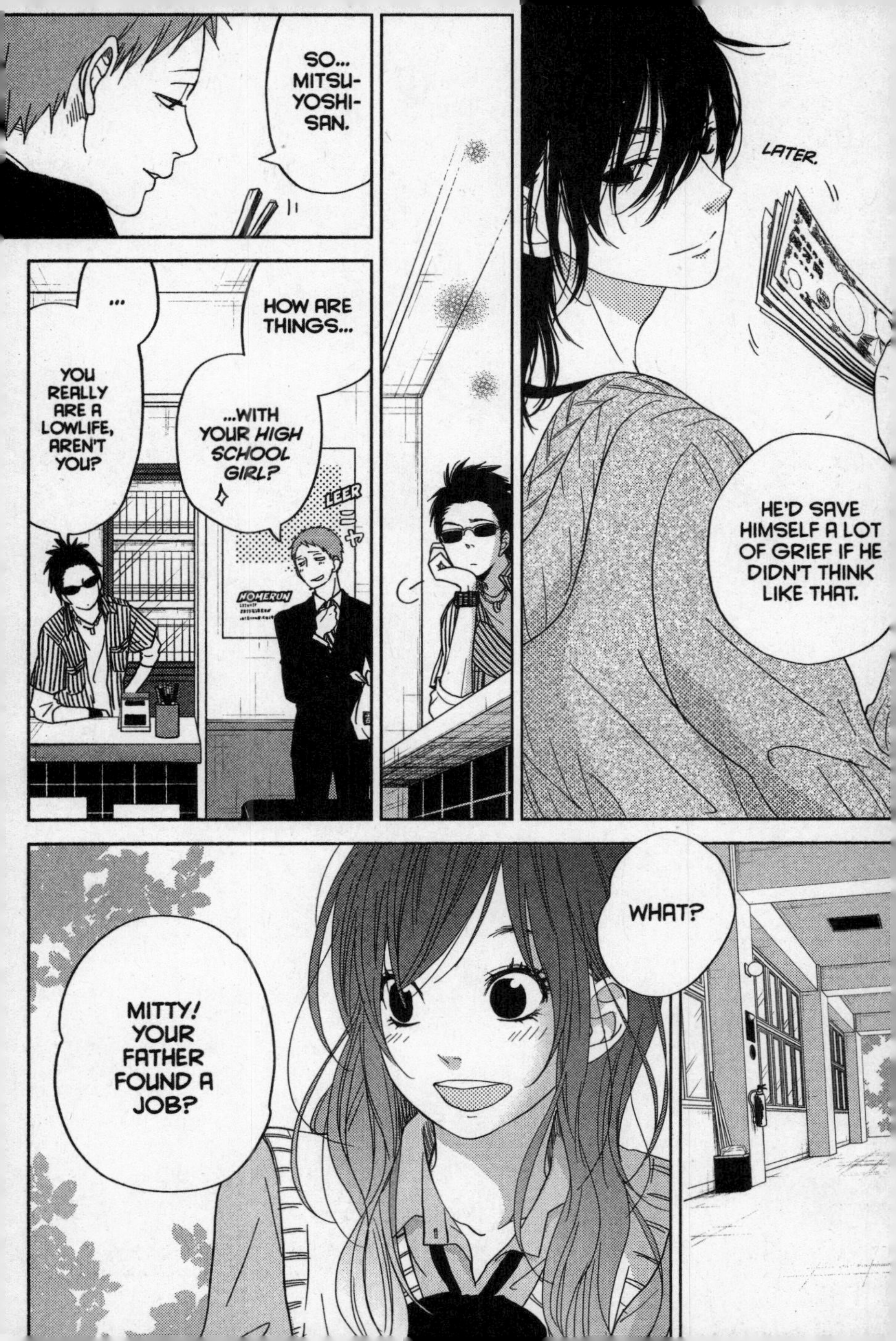
LATER.
HE'D SAVE HIMSELF A LOT OF GRIEF IF HE DIDN'T THINK LIKE THAT.
SO... MITSU-YOSHI-SAN.
HOW ARE THINGS...
...WITH YOUR HIGH SCHOOL GIRL?
LEER
...
YOU REALLY ARE A LOWLIFE, AREN'T YOU?
HOMERUN
WHAT?
MITTY! YOUR FATHER FOUND A JOB?

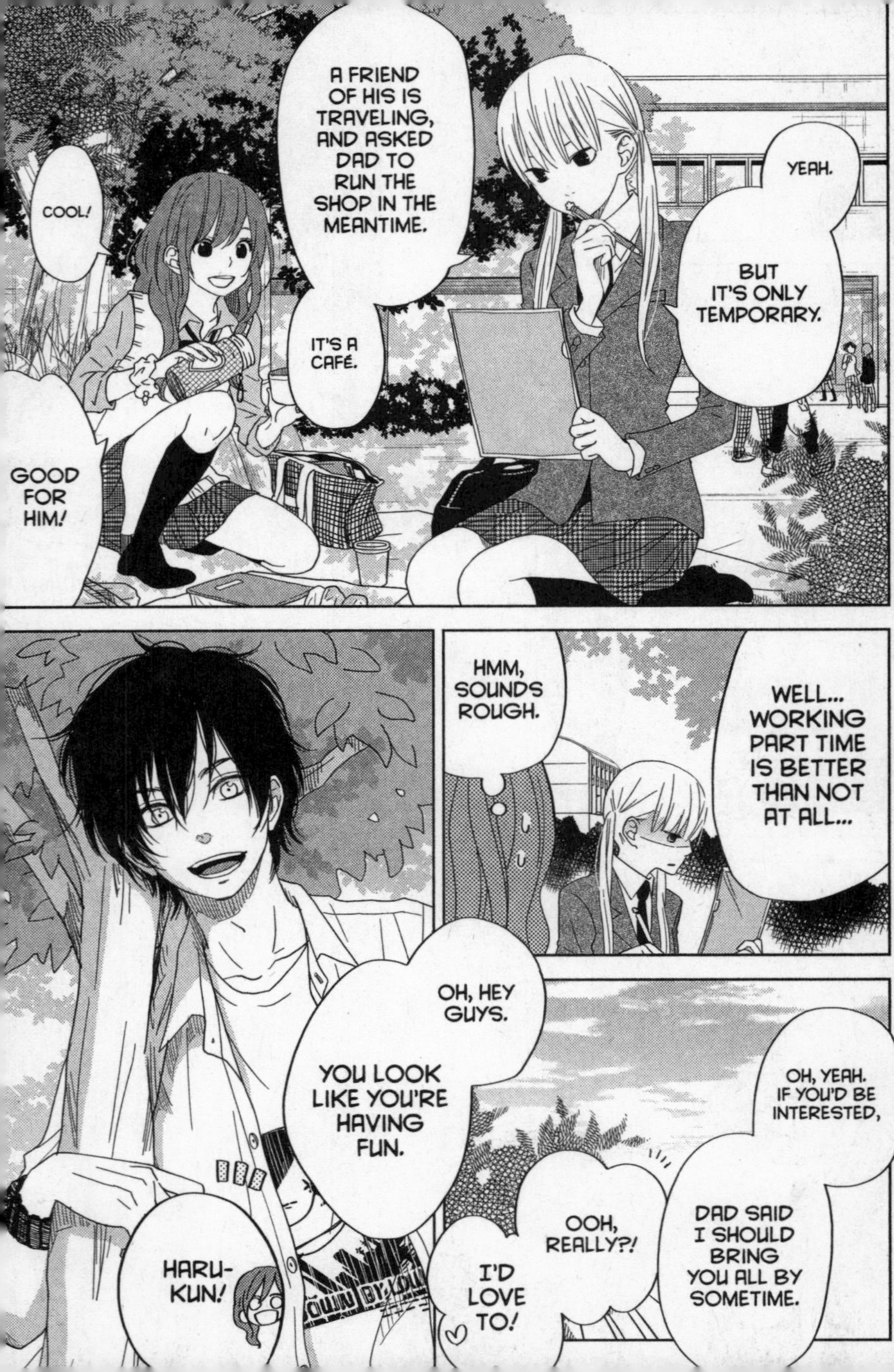
YEAH.
BUT IT'S ONLY TEMPORARY.
A FRIEND OF HIS IS TRAVELING, AND ASKED DAD TO RUN THE SHOP IN THE MEANTIME.
IT'S A CAFÉ.
COOL!
GOOD FOR HIM!
WELL... WORKING PART TIME IS BETTER THAN NOT AT ALL...
HMM, SOUNDS ROUGH.
OH, YEAH. IF YOU'D BE INTERESTED,
DAD SAID I SHOULD BRING YOU ALL BY SOMETIME.
OOH, REALLY?!
I'D LOVE TO!
OH, HEY GUYS.
YOU LOOK LIKE YOU'RE HAVING FUN.
HARU-KUN!

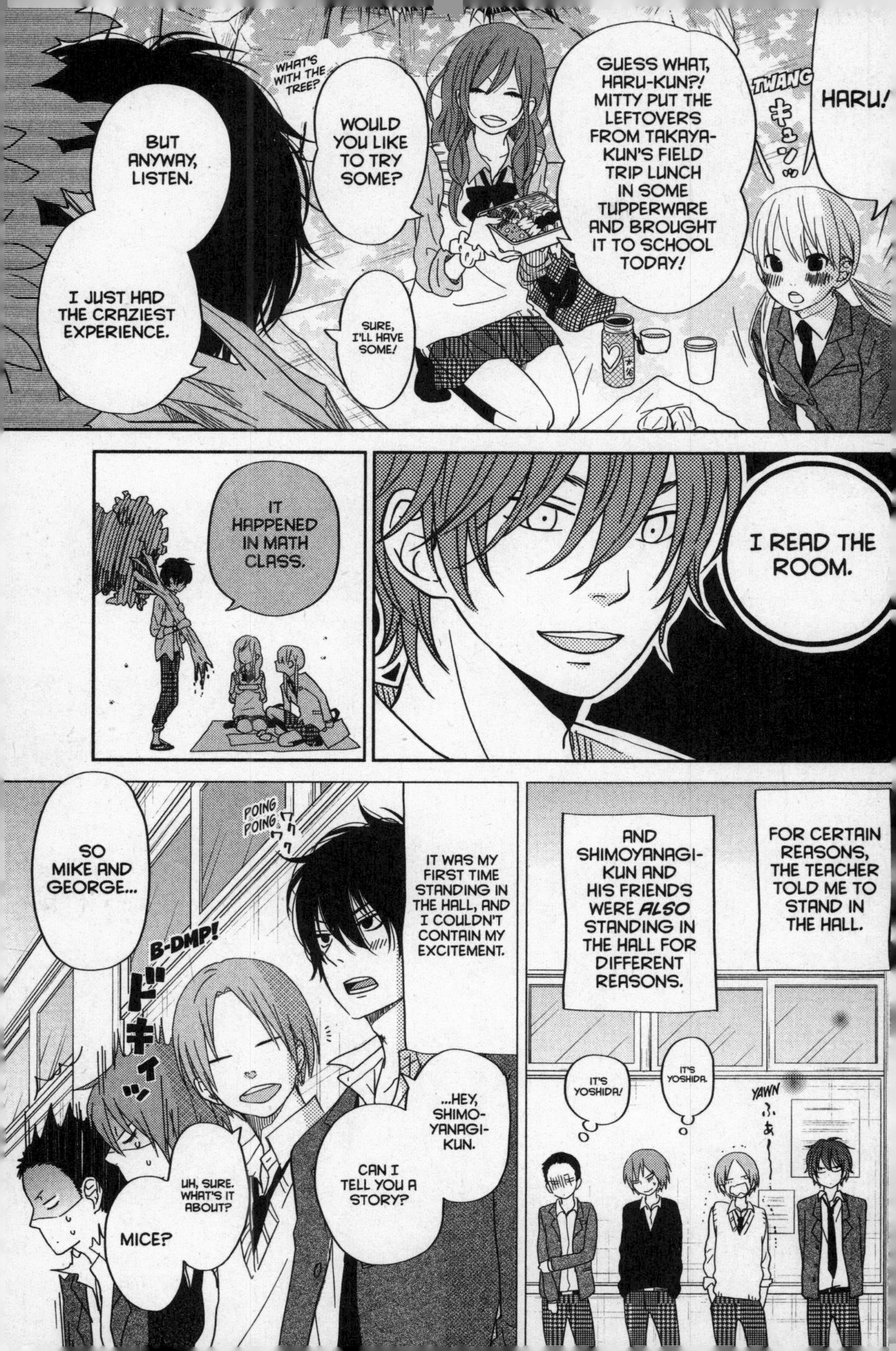
HARU!
TWANG
GUESS WHAT, HARU-KUN?! MITTY PUT THE LEFTOVERS FROM TAKAYA-KUN'S FIELD TRIP LUNCH IN SOME TUPPERWARE AND BROUGHT IT TO SCHOOL TODAY!
WOULD YOU LIKE TO TRY SOME?
WHAT'S WITH THE TREE?
SURE, I'LL HAVE SOME!
BUT ANYWAY, LISTEN.
I JUST HAD THE CRAZIEST EXPERIENCE.
I READ THE ROOM.
IT HAPPENED IN MATH CLASS.
FOR CERTAIN REASONS, THE TEACHER TOLD ME TO STAND IN THE HALL.
AND SHIMOYANAGI-KUN AND HIS FRIENDS WERE ALSO STANDING IN THE HALL FOR DIFFERENT REASONS.
YAWN
IT'S YOSHIDA.
IT'S YOSHIDA!
IT WAS MY FIRST TIME STANDING IN THE HALL, AND I COULDN'T CONTAIN MY EXCITEMENT.
POING POING
...HEY, SHIMOYANAGI-KUN.
CAN I TELL YOU A STORY?
B-DMP!
UH, SURE. WHAT'S IT ABOUT?
MICE?
SO MIKE AND GEORGE...

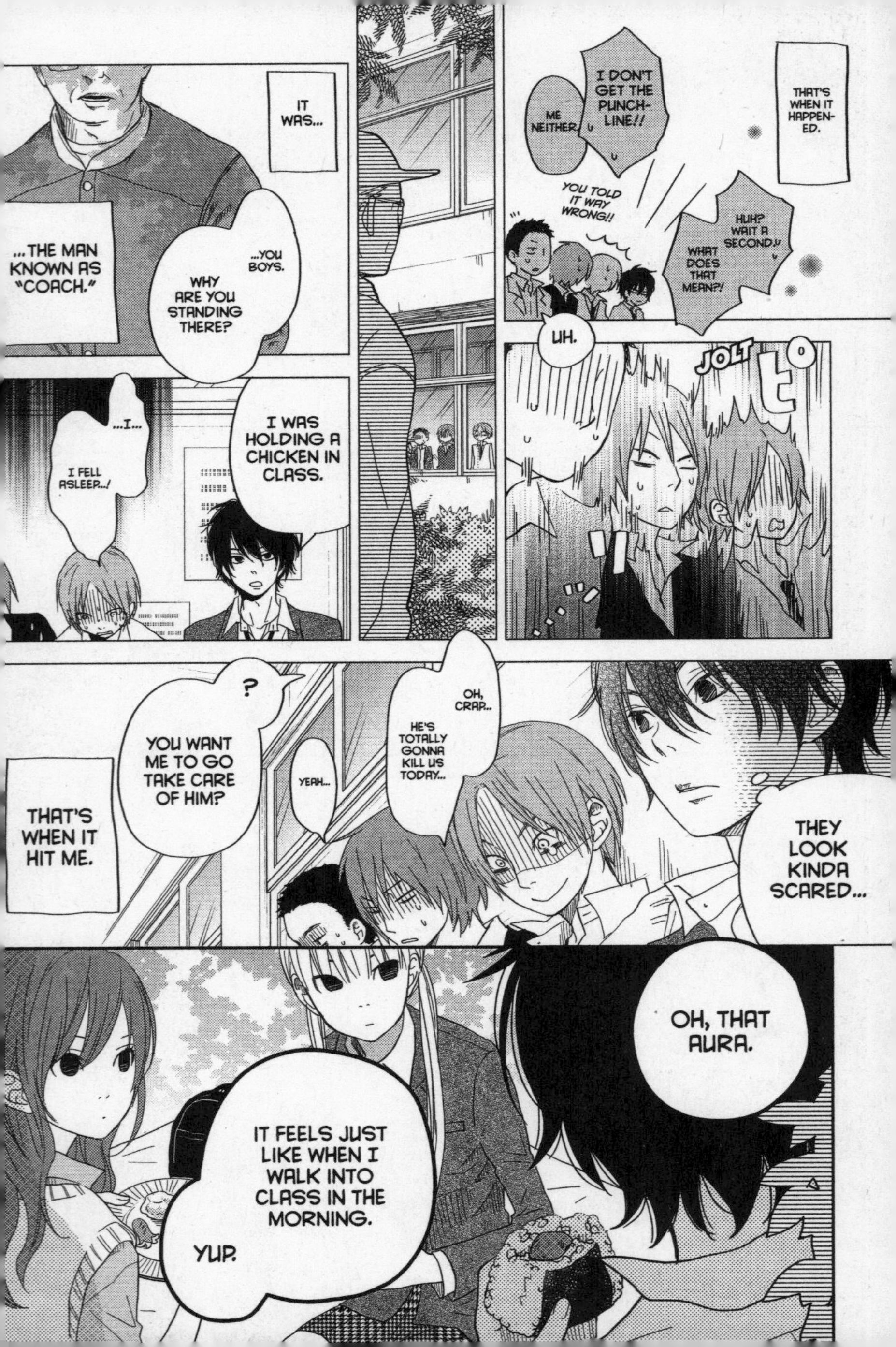
THAT'S WHEN IT HAPPEN-ED.
I DON'T GET THE PUNCH-LINE!!
ME NEITHER.
YOU TOLD IT WAY WRONG!!
HUH? WAIT A SECOND.
WHAT DOES THAT MEAN?!
UH.
JOLT
IT WAS...
...THE MAN KNOWN AS "COACH."
...YOU BOYS.
WHY ARE YOU STANDING THERE?
I WAS HOLDING A CHICKEN IN CLASS.
...I...
I FELL ASLEEP...!
THEY LOOK KINDA SCARED...
OH, CRAP...
HE'S TOTALLY GONNA KILL US TODAY...
YEAH...
?
YOU WANT ME TO GO TAKE CARE OF HIM?
THAT'S WHEN IT HIT ME.
OH, THAT AURA.
IT FEELS JUST LIKE WHEN I WALK INTO CLASS IN THE MORNING.
YUP.

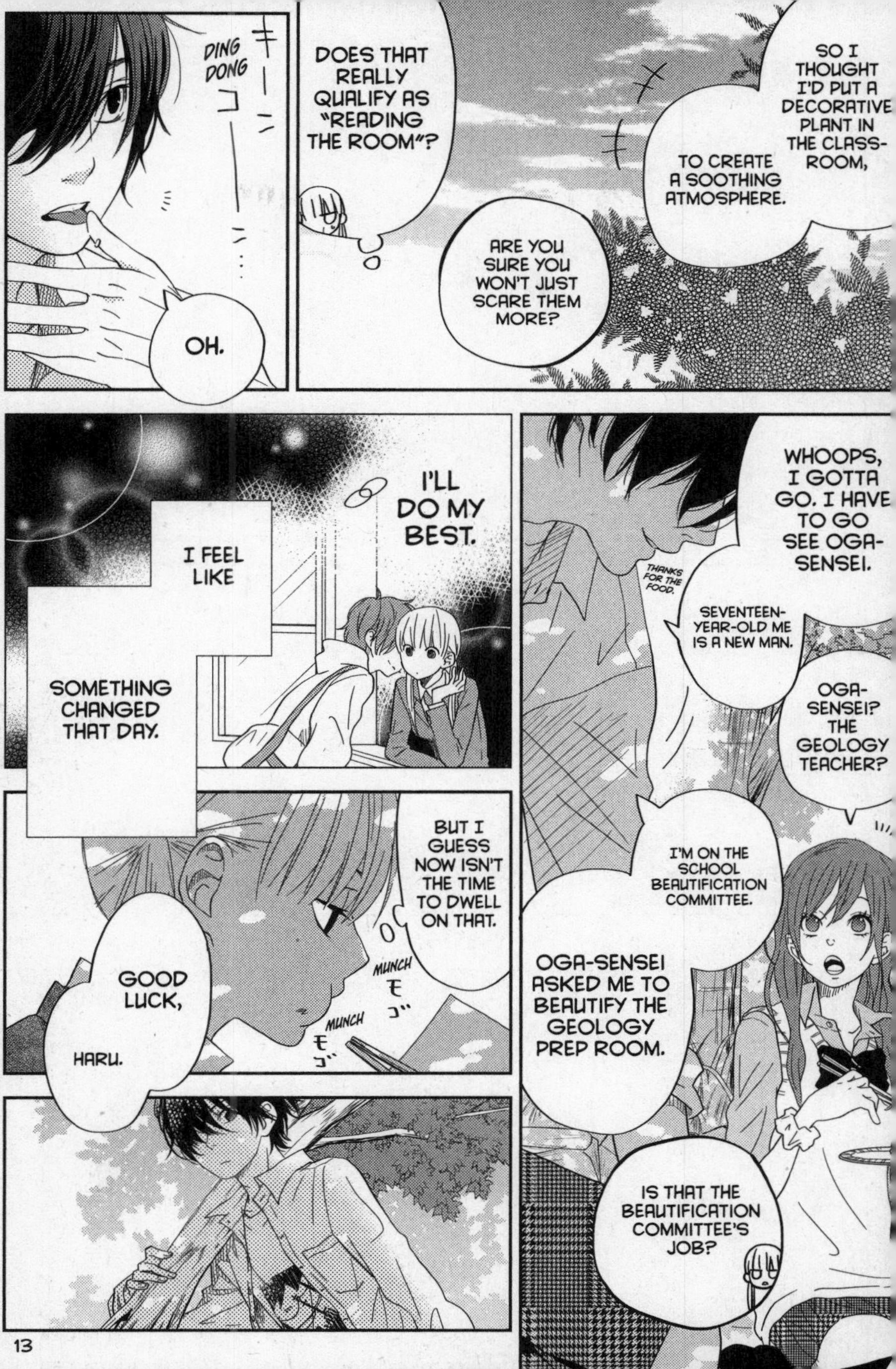
SO I THOUGHT I'D PUT A DECORATIVE PLANT IN THE CLASSROOM,
TO CREATE A SOOTHING ATMOSPHERE.
ARE YOU SURE YOU WON'T JUST SCARE THEM MORE?
DOES THAT REALLY QUALIFY AS "READING THE ROOM"?
DING DONG
OH.
WHOOPS, I GOTTA GO. I HAVE TO GO SEE OGA-SENSEI.
THANKS FOR THE FOOD.
SEVENTEEN-YEAR-OLD ME IS A NEW MAN.
OGA-SENSEI? THE GEOLOGY TEACHER?
I'M ON THE SCHOOL BEAUTIFICATION COMMITTEE.
OGA-SENSEI ASKED ME TO BEAUTIFY THE GEOLOGY PREP ROOM.
IS THAT THE BEAUTIFICATION COMMITTEE'S JOB?
I'LL DO MY BEST.
I FEEL LIKE
SOMETHING CHANGED THAT DAY.
BUT I GUESS NOW ISN'T THE TIME TO DWELL ON THAT.
MUNCH
MUNCH
GOOD LUCK,
HARU.

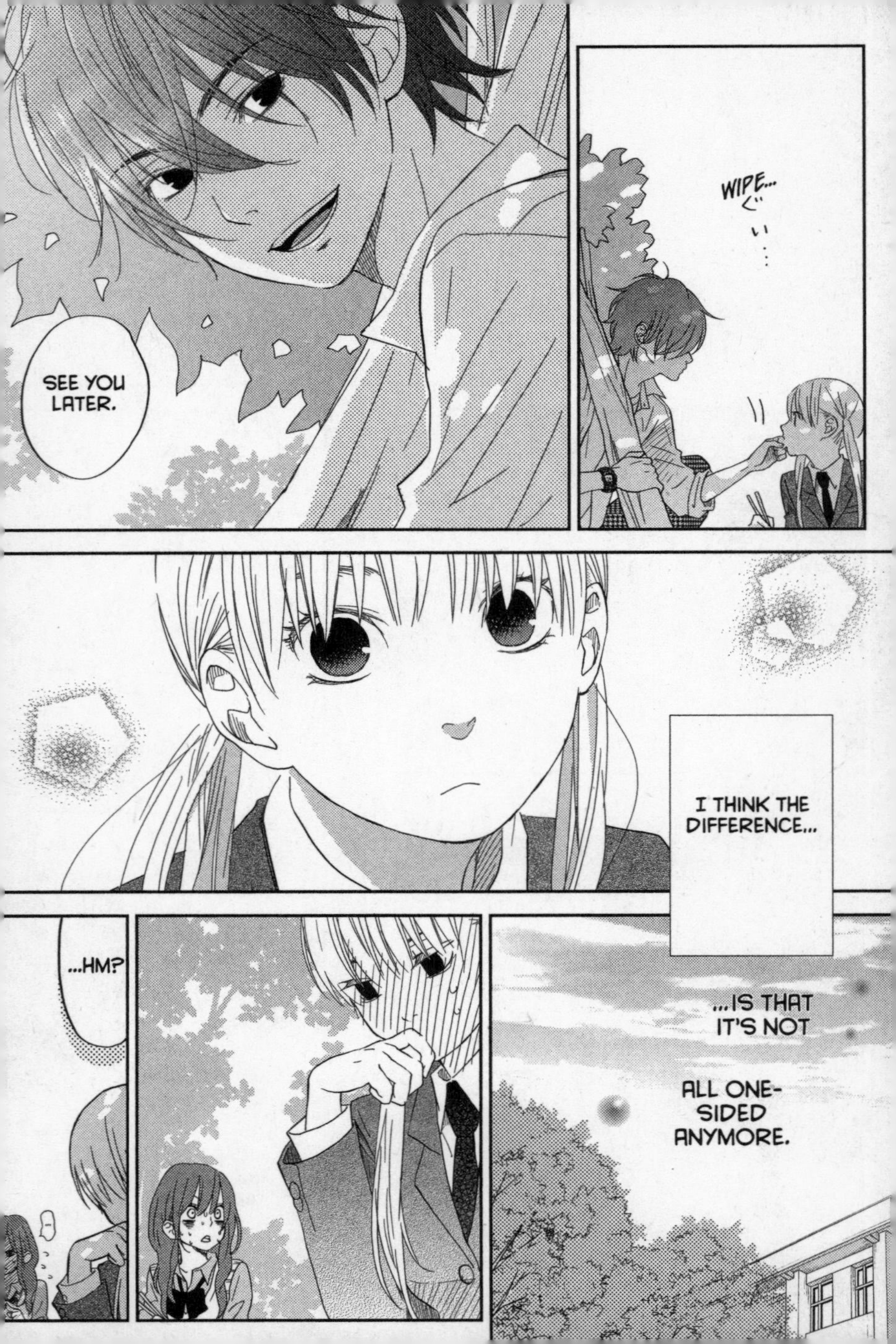
WIPE...
ぐい...
SEE YOU LATER.
I THINK THE DIFFERENCE...
...IS THAT IT'S NOT
ALL ONE-SIDED ANYMORE.
...HM?

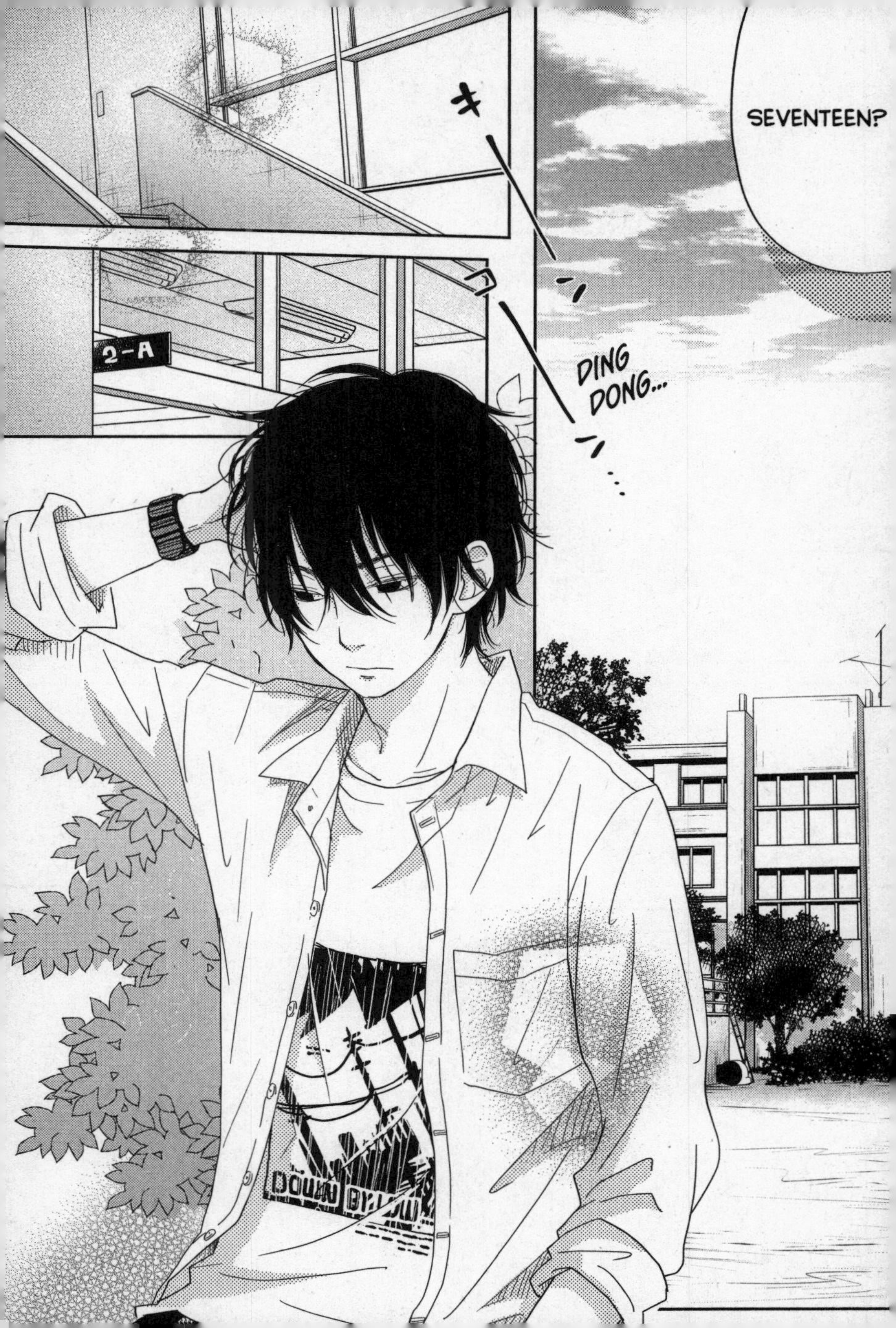
SEVENTEEN?
DING DONG...
2-A

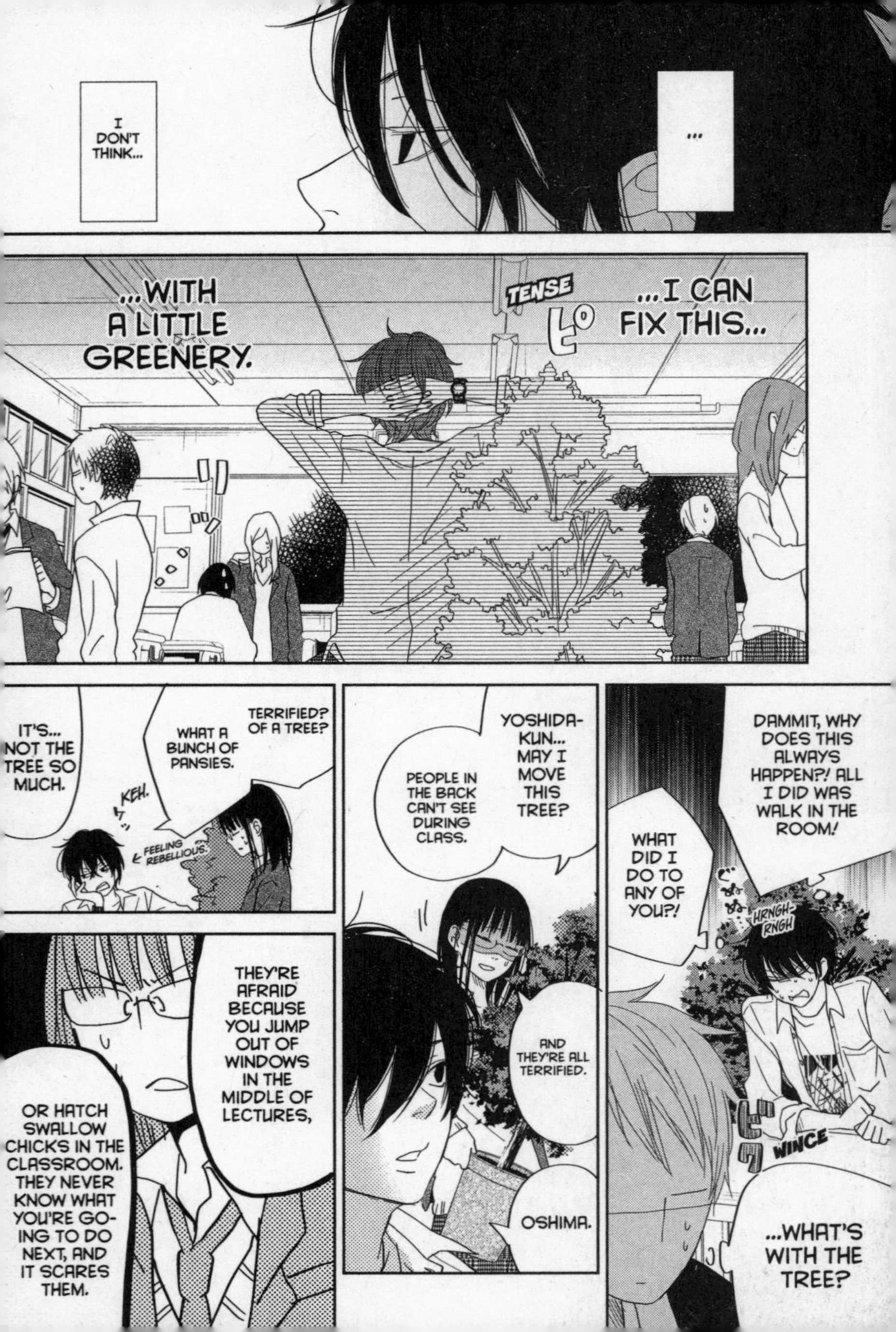
...
I DON'T THINK...
...I CAN FIX THIS...
TENSE
...WITH A LITTLE GREENERY.
DAMMIT, WHY DOES THIS ALWAYS HAPPEN?! ALL I DID WAS WALK IN THE ROOM!
WHAT DID I DO TO ANY OF YOU?!
HRNGH-RNGH
WINCE
...WHAT'S WITH THE TREE?
YOSHIDA-KUN... MAY I MOVE THIS TREE?
PEOPLE IN THE BACK CAN'T SEE DURING CLASS.
AND THEY'RE ALL TERRIFIED.
OSHIMA.
TERRIFIED? OF A TREE?
WHAT A BUNCH OF PANSIES.
KEH.
FEELING REBELLIOUS.
IT'S... NOT THE TREE SO MUCH.
THEY'RE AFRAID BECAUSE YOU JUMP OUT OF WINDOWS IN THE MIDDLE OF LECTURES,
OR HATCH SWALLOW CHICKS IN THE CLASSROOM. THEY NEVER KNOW WHAT YOU'RE GO-ING TO DO NEXT, AND IT SCARES THEM.

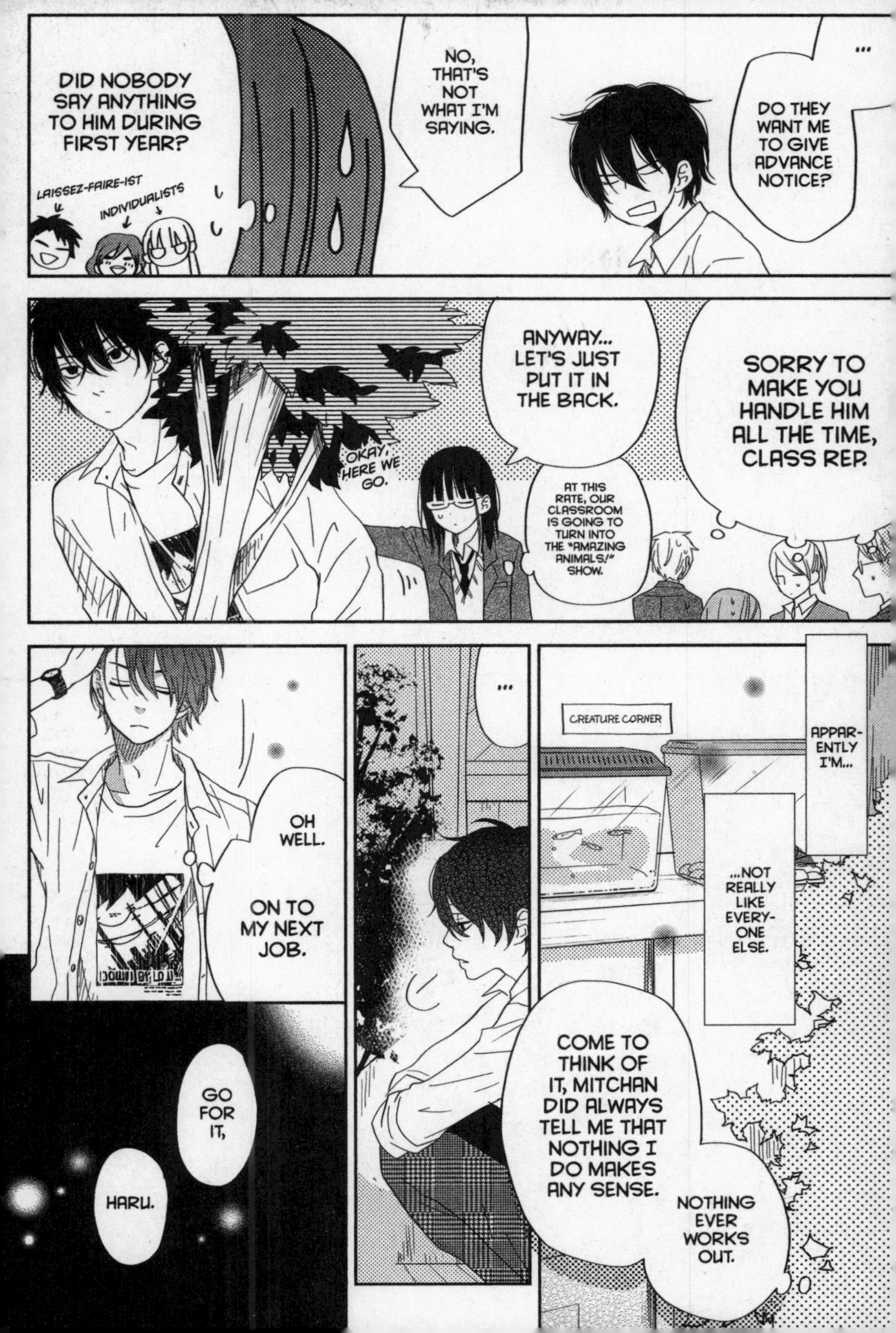
...
DO THEY WANT ME TO GIVE ADVANCE NOTICE?
NO, THAT'S NOT WHAT I'M SAYING.
DID NOBODY SAY ANYTHING TO HIM DURING FIRST YEAR?
LAISSEZ-FAIRE-IST
INDIVIDUALISTS
SORRY TO MAKE YOU HANDLE HIM ALL THE TIME, CLASS REP.
ANYWAY... LET'S JUST PUT IT IN THE BACK.
AT THIS RATE, OUR CLASSROOM IS GOING TO TURN INTO THE "AMAZING ANIMALS!" SHOW.
OKAY, HERE WE GO.
APPARENTLY I'M...
...NOT REALLY LIKE EVERYONE ELSE.
CREATURE CORNER
COME TO THINK OF IT, MITCHAN DID ALWAYS TELL ME THAT NOTHING I DO MAKES ANY SENSE.
NOTHING EVER WORKS OUT.
...
OH WELL.
ON TO MY NEXT JOB.
GO FOR IT,
HARU.

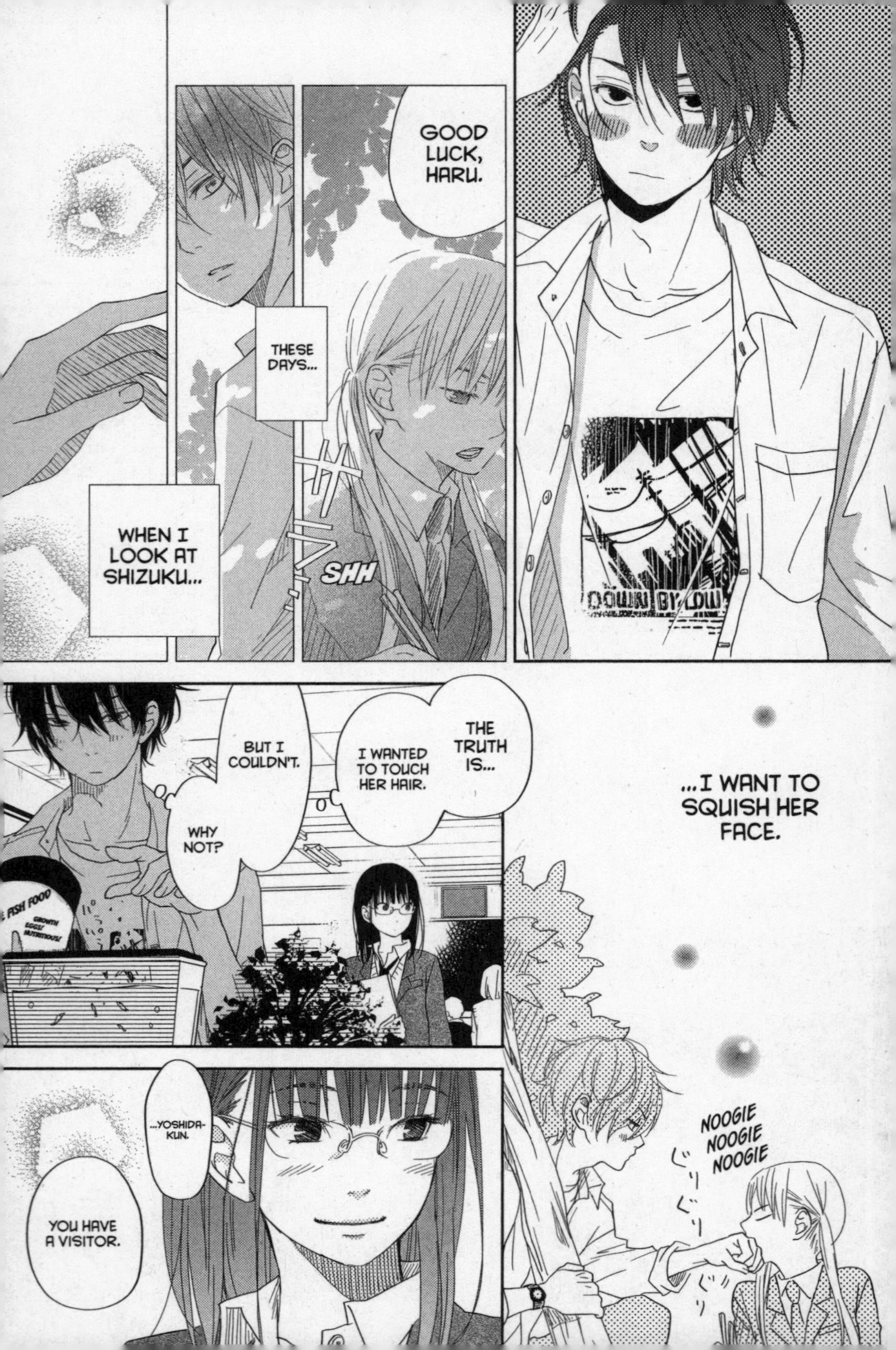
GOOD LUCK, HARU.
THESE DAYS...
SHH
WHEN I LOOK AT SHIZUKU...
...I WANT TO SQUISH HER FACE.
NOOGIE NOOGIE NOOGIE
THE TRUTH IS...
I WANTED TO TOUCH HER HAIR.
BUT I COULDN'T.
WHY NOT?
FISH FOOD
GROWTH EGGS! NUTRITIOUS!
...YOSHIDA-KUN.
YOU HAVE A VISITOR.

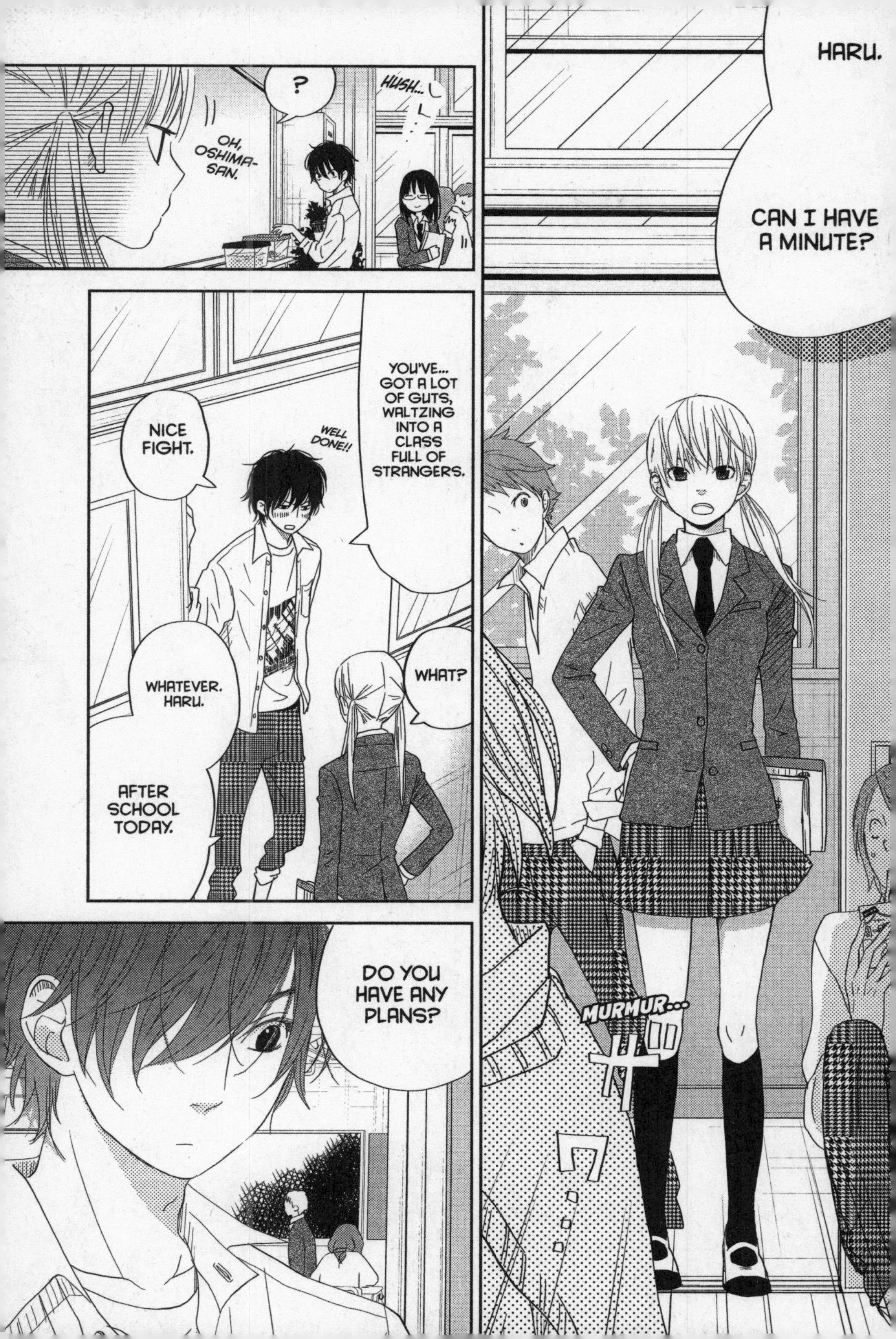
HARU.
CAN I HAVE A MINUTE?
MURMUR...
HUSH...
?
OH, OSHIMA-SAN.
YOU'VE... GOT A LOT OF GUTS, WALTZING INTO A CLASS FULL OF STRANGERS.
WELL DONE!!
NICE FIGHT.
WHAT?
WHATEVER. HARU.
AFTER SCHOOL TODAY.
DO YOU HAVE ANY PLANS?

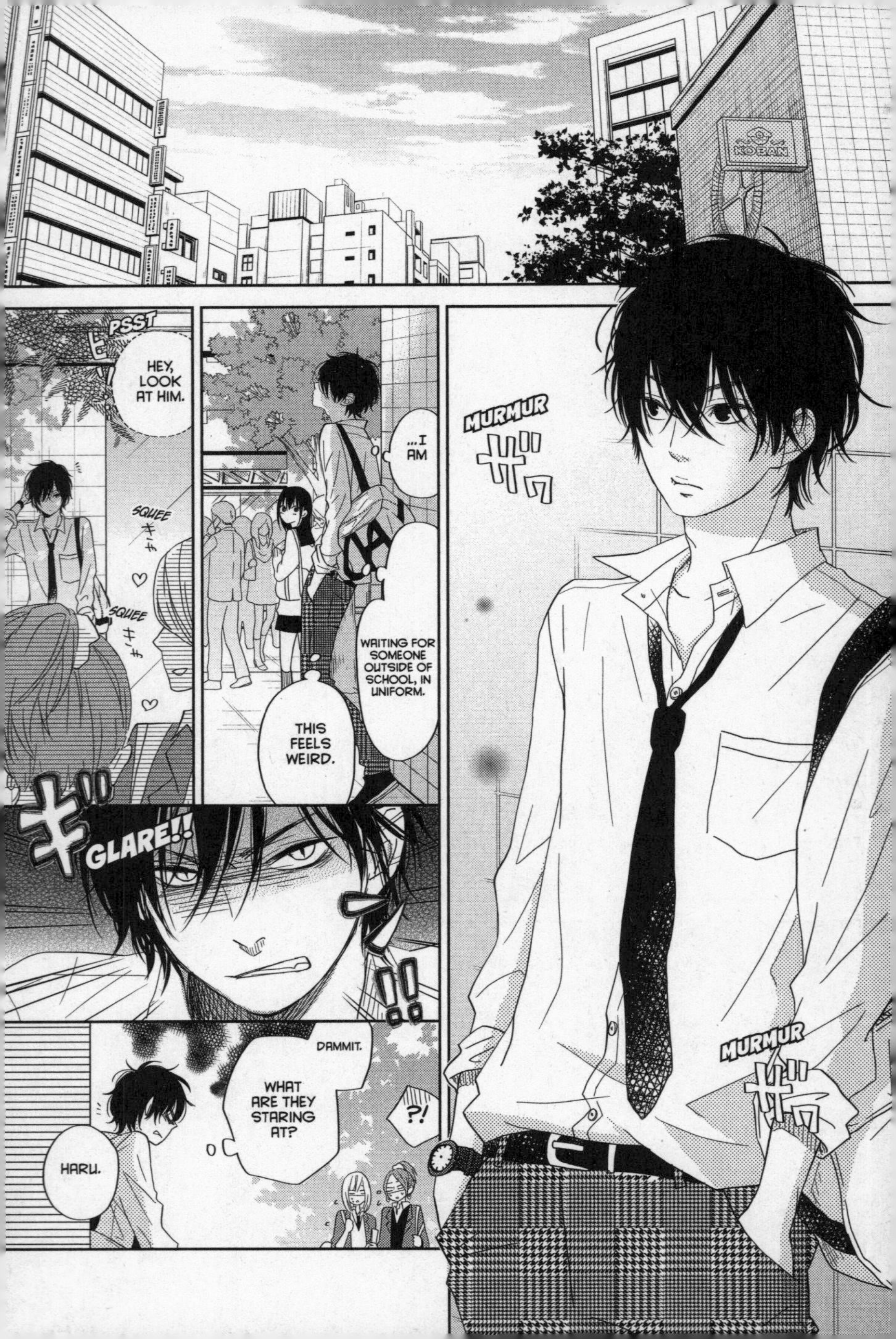
KOBAN
MURMUR
ザワ
MURMUR
ザワ
...I AM
WAITING FOR SOMEONE OUTSIDE OF SCHOOL, IN UNIFORM.
THIS FEELS WEIRD.
PSST
HEY, LOOK AT HIM.
SQUEE
SQUEE
ギッ
GLARE!!
!!
DAMMIT.
WHAT ARE THEY STARING AT?
?!
HARU.

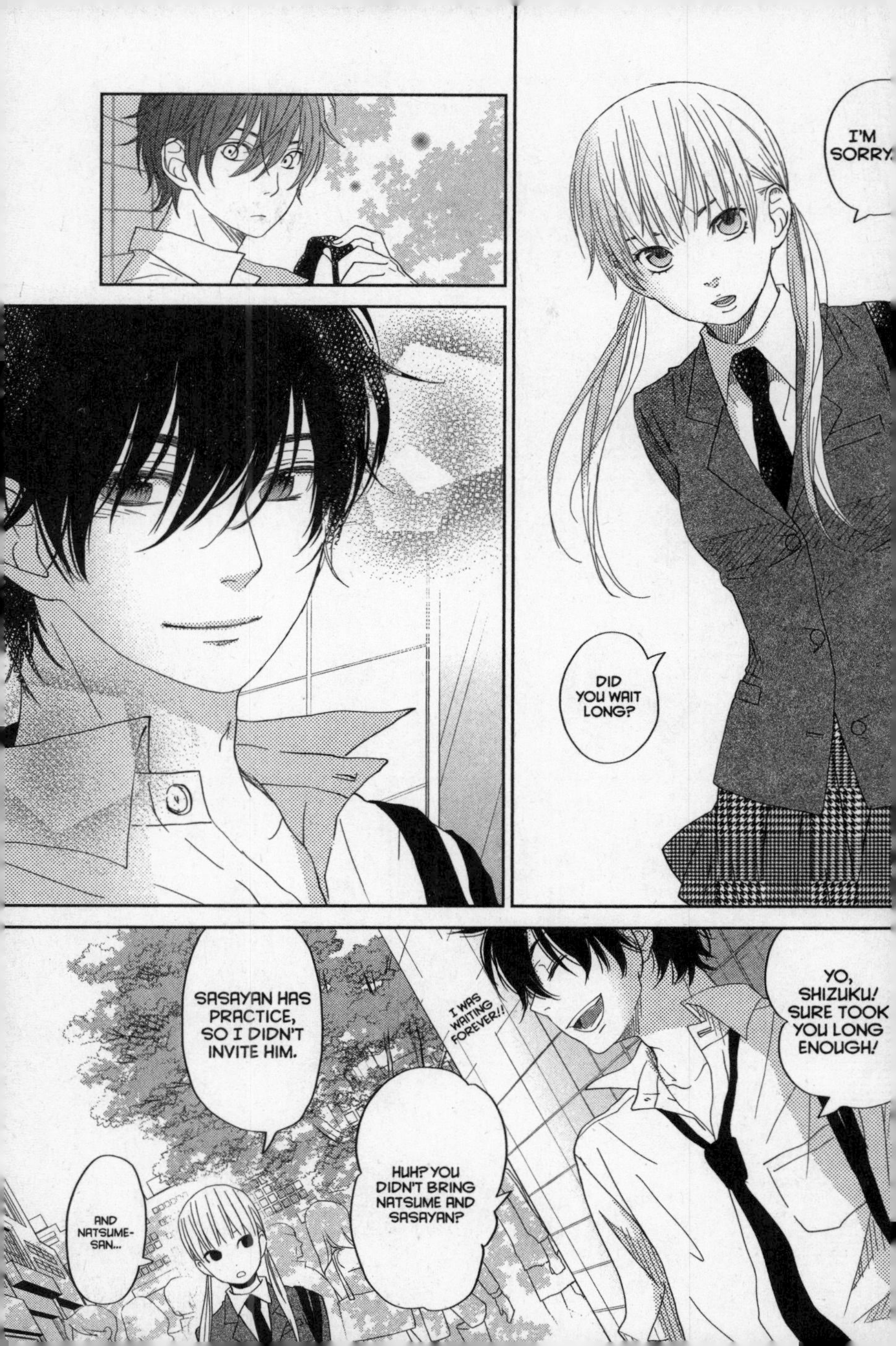
I'M SORRY.
DID YOU WAIT LONG?
YO, SHIZUKU! SURE TOOK YOU LONG ENOUGH!
I WAS WAITING FOREVER!!
HUH? YOU DIDN'T BRING NATSUME AND SASAYAN?
SASAYAN HAS PRACTICE, SO I DIDN'T INVITE HIM.
AND NATSUME-SAN...

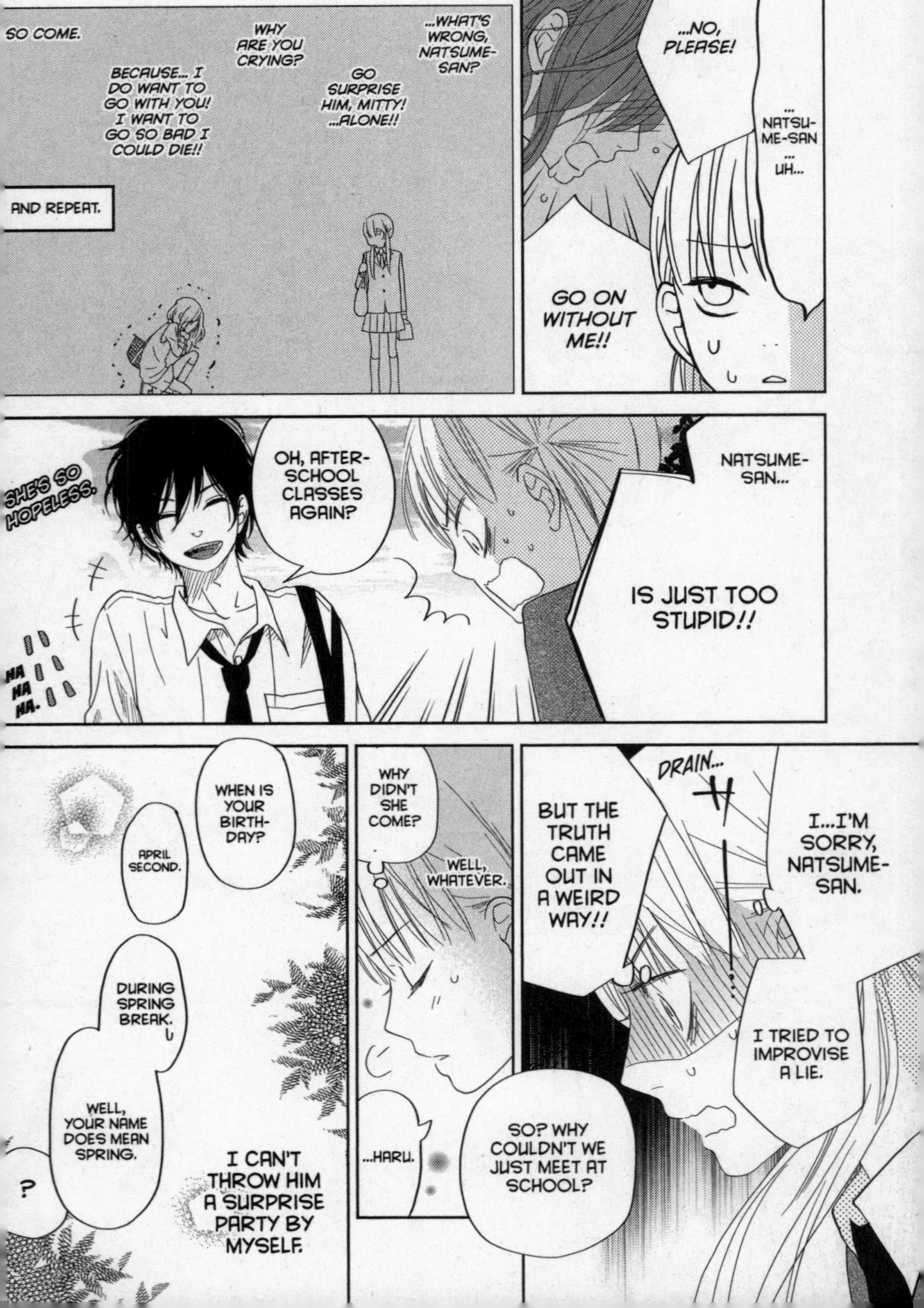
...NO, PLEASE!
... NATSU-ME-SAN ... UH...
GO ON WITHOUT ME!!
...WHAT'S WRONG, NATSUME-SAN?
WHY ARE YOU CRYING?
GO SURPRISE HIM, MITTY! ...ALONE!!
SO COME.
BECAUSE... I DO WANT TO GO WITH YOU! I WANT TO GO SO BAD I COULD DIE!!
AND REPEAT.
NATSUME-SAN...
IS JUST TOO STUPID!!
OH, AFTER-SCHOOL CLASSES AGAIN?
SHE'S SO HOPELESS.
HA HA HA.
DRAIN...
I...I'M SORRY, NATSUME-SAN.
BUT THE TRUTH CAME OUT IN A WEIRD WAY!!
I TRIED TO IMPROVISE A LIE.
SO? WHY COULDN'T WE JUST MEET AT SCHOOL?
WHY DIDN'T SHE COME?
WELL, WHATEVER.
...HARU.
WHEN IS YOUR BIRTHDAY?
APRIL SECOND.
DURING SPRING BREAK.
WELL, YOUR NAME DOES MEAN SPRING.
?
I CAN'T THROW HIM A SURPRISE PARTY BY MYSELF.

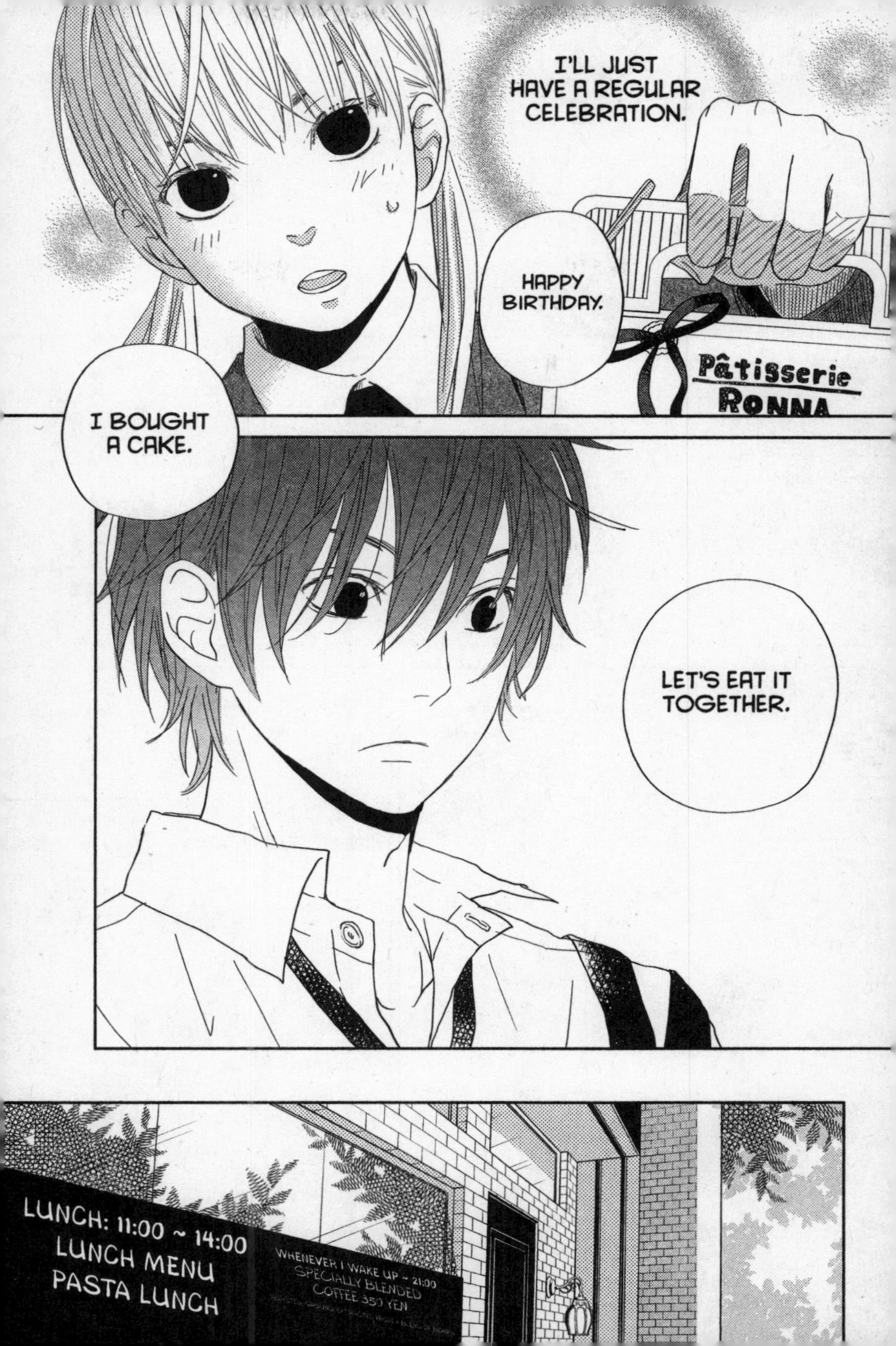
I'LL JUST HAVE A REGULAR CELEBRATION.
HAPPY BIRTHDAY.
Pâtisserie RONNA
I BOUGHT A CAKE.
LET'S EAT IT TOGETHER.
LUNCH: 11:00 ~ 14:00
LUNCH MENU
PASTA LUNCH
WHENEVER I WAKE UP ~ 21:00
SPECIALLY BLENDED
COFFEE 350 YEN

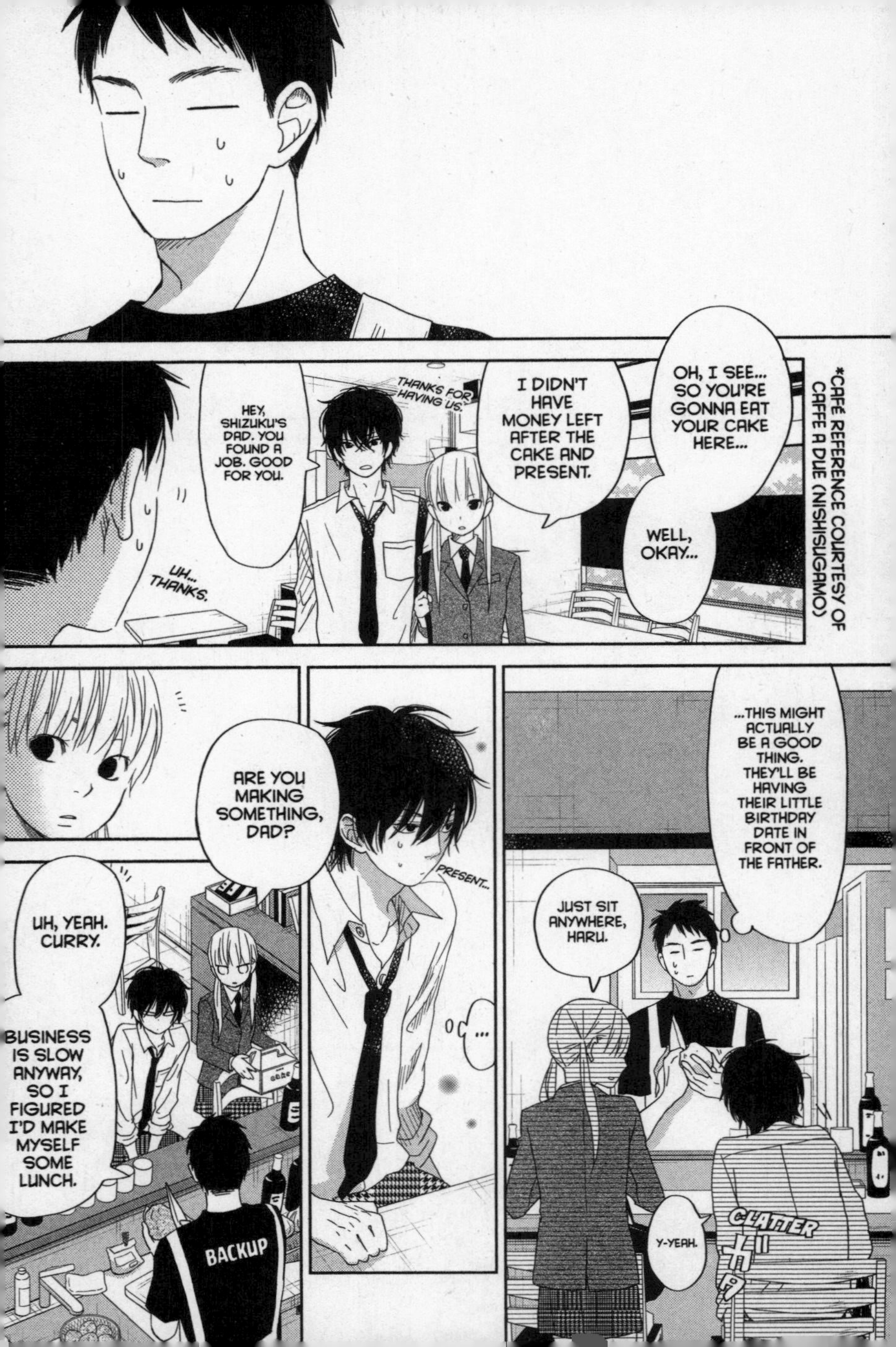
*CAFÉ REFERENCE COURTESY OF CAFFE A DUE (NISHISUGAMO)
OH, I SEE... SO YOU'RE GONNA EAT YOUR CAKE HERE...
WELL, OKAY...
I DIDN'T HAVE MONEY LEFT AFTER THE CAKE AND PRESENT.
THANKS FOR HAVING US.
HEY, SHIZUKU'S DAD. YOU FOUND A JOB. GOOD FOR YOU.
UH... THANKS.
...THIS MIGHT ACTUALLY BE A GOOD THING. THEY'LL BE HAVING THEIR LITTLE BIRTHDAY DATE IN FRONT OF THE FATHER.
JUST SIT ANYWHERE, HARU.
Y-YEAH.
CLATTER
ARE YOU MAKING SOMETHING, DAD?
PRESENT...
...
UH, YEAH. CURRY.
BUSINESS IS SLOW ANYWAY, SO I FIGURED I'D MAKE MYSELF SOME LUNCH.
BACKUP

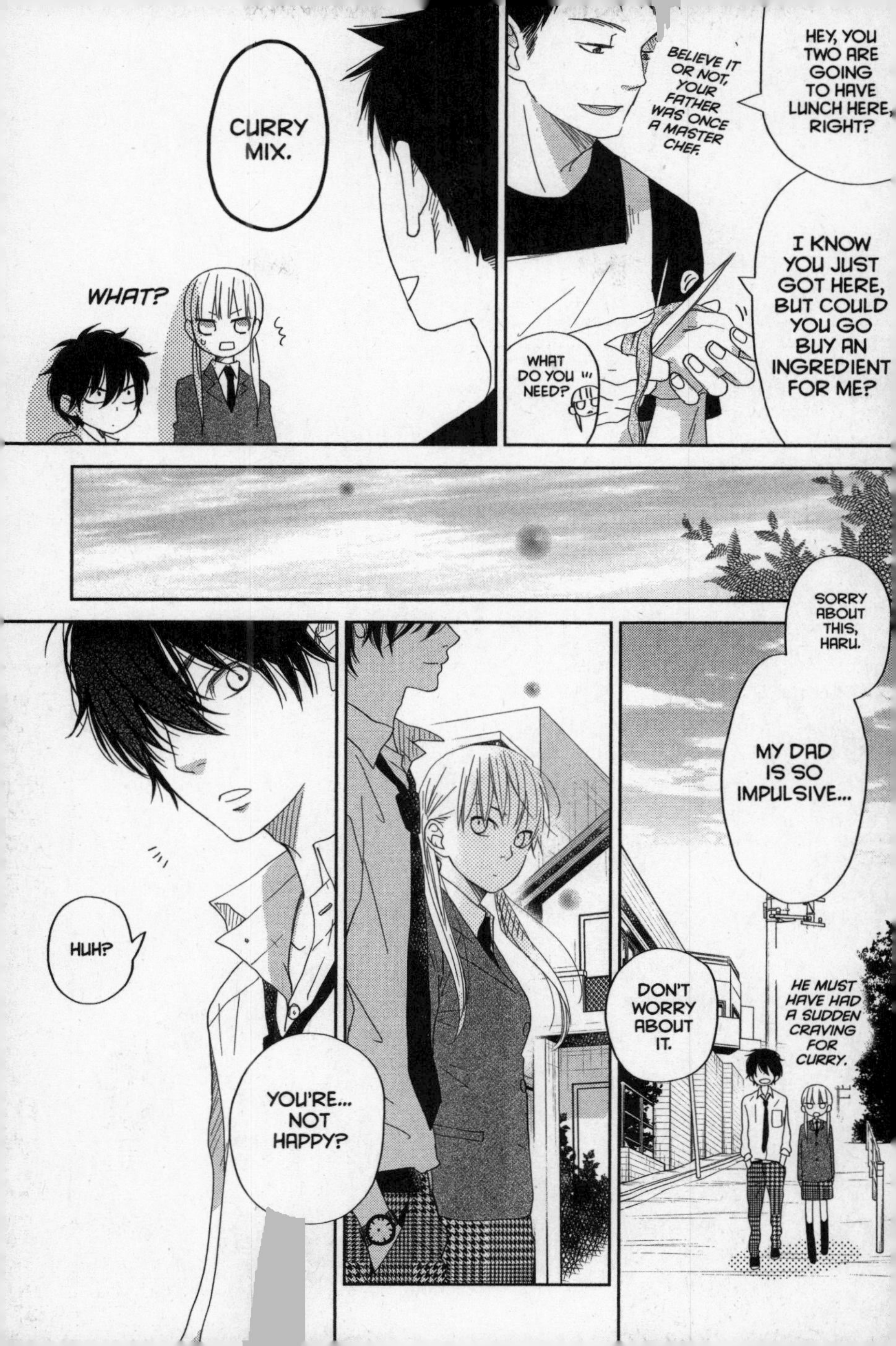
HEY, YOU TWO ARE GOING TO HAVE LUNCH HERE, RIGHT?
BELIEVE IT OR NOT, YOUR FATHER WAS ONCE A MASTER CHEF.
I KNOW YOU JUST GOT HERE, BUT COULD YOU GO BUY AN INGREDIENT FOR ME?
WHAT DO YOU NEED?
CURRY MIX.
WHAT?
SORRY ABOUT THIS, HARU.
MY DAD IS SO IMPULSIVE...
HE MUST HAVE HAD A SUDDEN CRAVING FOR CURRY.
DON'T WORRY ABOUT IT.
HUH?
YOU'RE... NOT HAPPY?

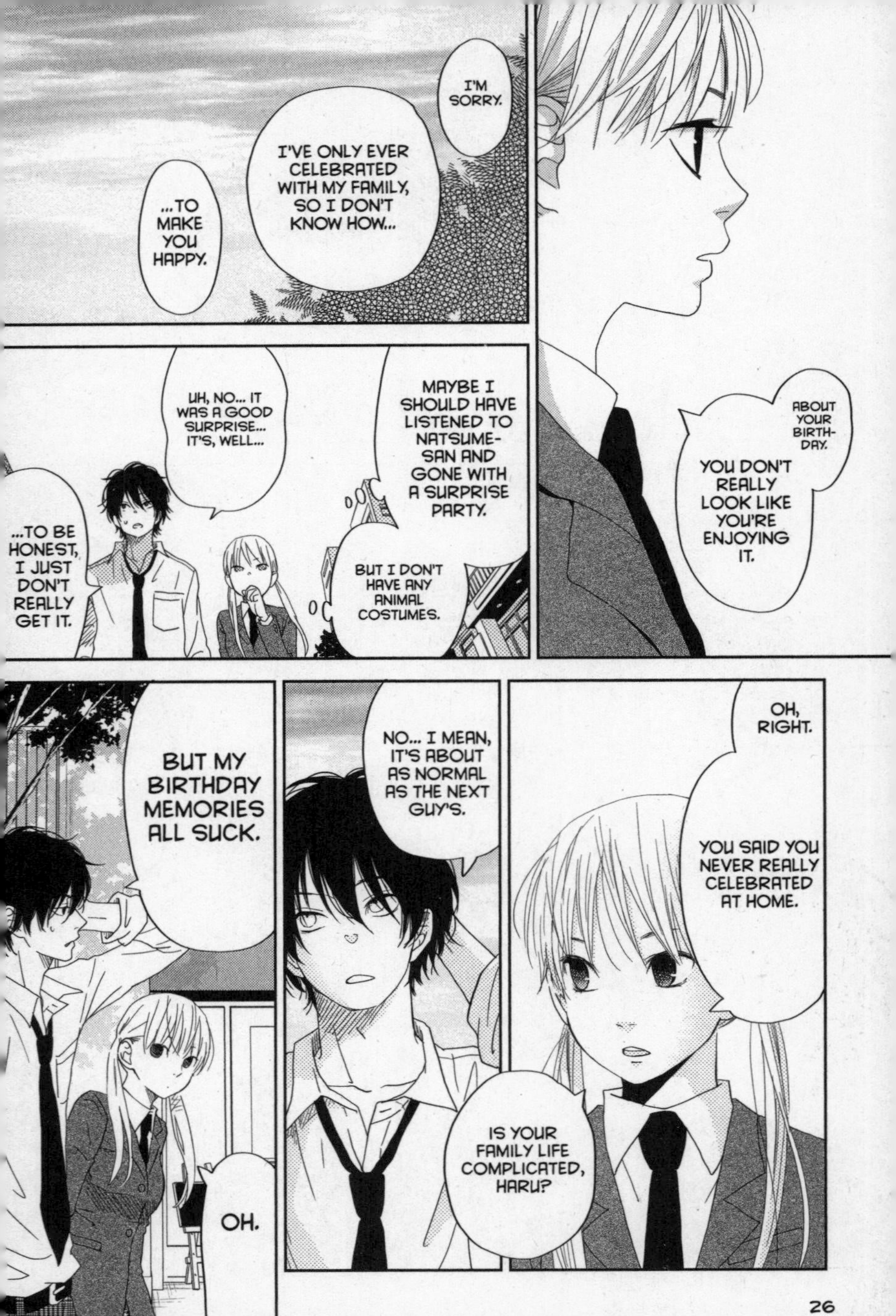
ABOUT YOUR BIRTHDAY.
YOU DON'T REALLY LOOK LIKE YOU'RE ENJOYING IT.
I'M SORRY.
I'VE ONLY EVER CELEBRATED WITH MY FAMILY, SO I DON'T KNOW HOW...
...TO MAKE YOU HAPPY.
MAYBE I SHOULD HAVE LISTENED TO NATSUME-SAN AND GONE WITH A SURPRISE PARTY.
BUT I DON'T HAVE ANY ANIMAL COSTUMES.
UH, NO... IT WAS A GOOD SURPRISE... IT'S, WELL...
...TO BE HONEST, I JUST DON'T REALLY GET IT.
OH, RIGHT.
YOU SAID YOU NEVER REALLY CELEBRATED AT HOME.
IS YOUR FAMILY LIFE COMPLICATED, HARU?
NO... I MEAN, IT'S ABOUT AS NORMAL AS THE NEXT GUY'S.
BUT MY BIRTHDAY MEMORIES ALL SUCK.
OH.

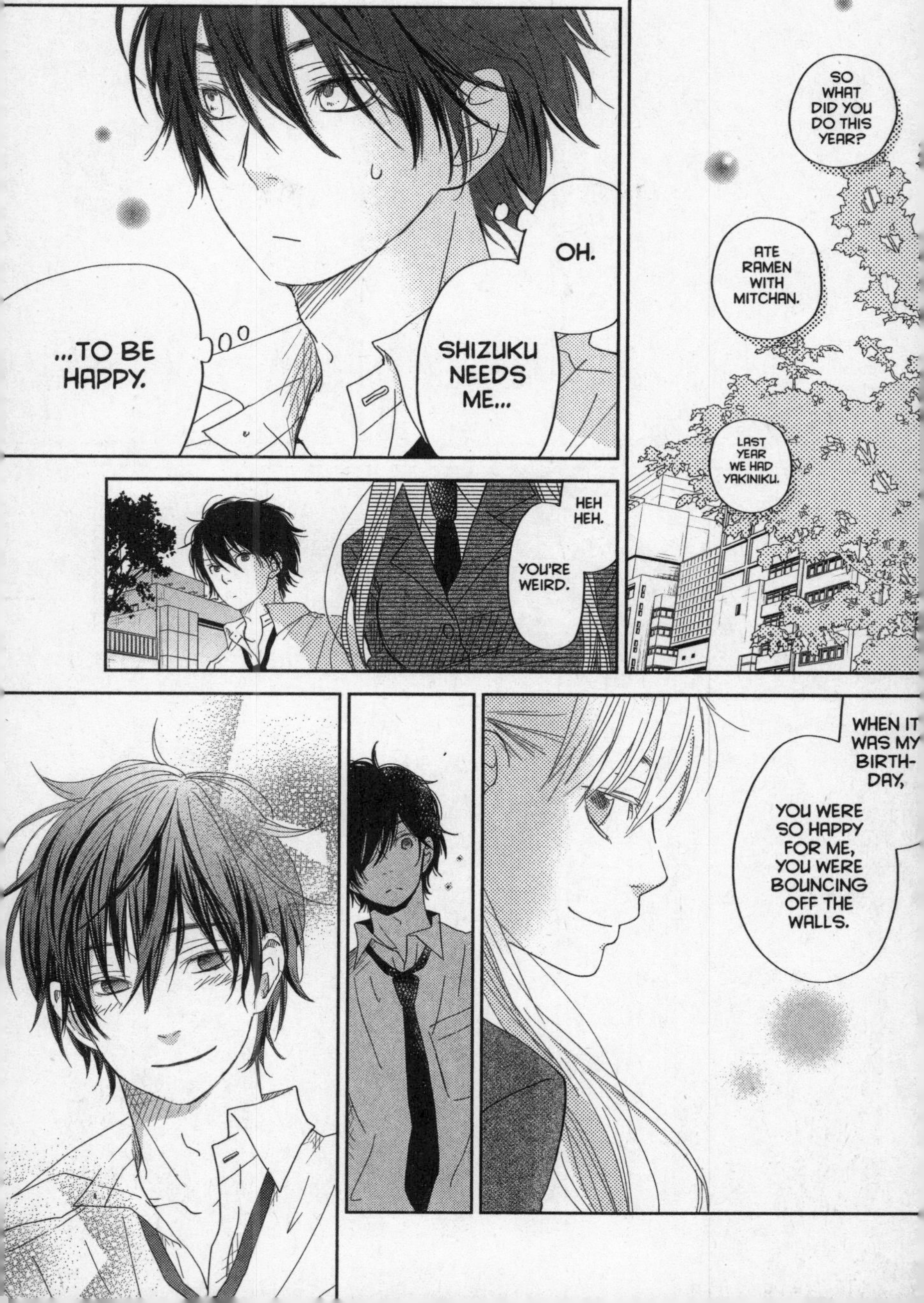
SO WHAT DID YOU DO THIS YEAR?
ATE RAMEN WITH MITCHAN.
LAST YEAR WE HAD YAKINIKU.
OH.
SHIZUKU NEEDS ME...
...TO BE HAPPY.
HEH HEH.
YOU'RE WEIRD.
WHEN IT WAS MY BIRTH-DAY,
YOU WERE SO HAPPY FOR ME, YOU WERE BOUNCING OFF THE WALLS.

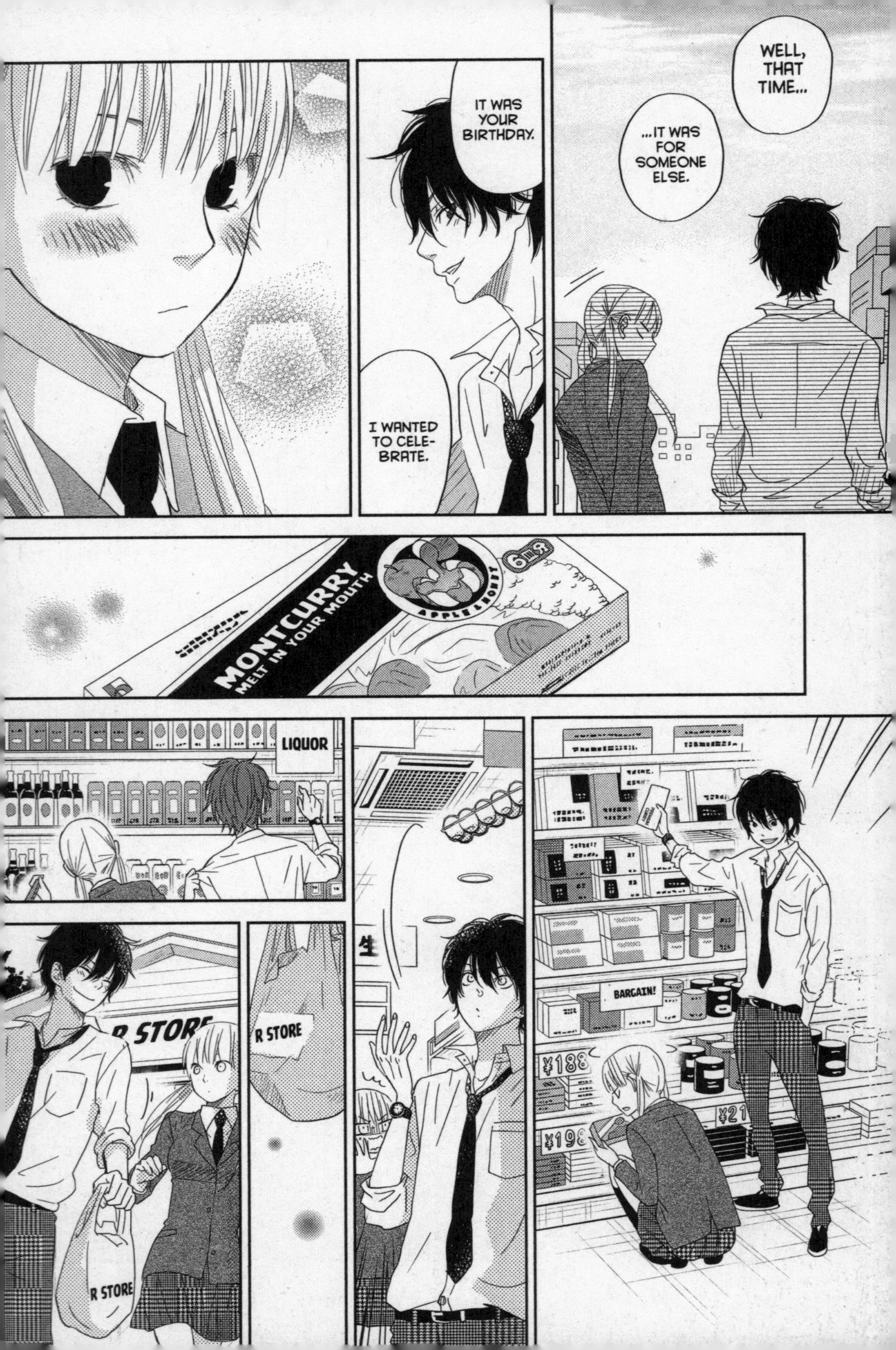
WELL, THAT TIME...
...IT WAS FOR SOMEONE ELSE.
IT WAS YOUR BIRTHDAY.
I WANTED TO CELE-BRATE.
MONTCURRY
MELT IN YOUR MOUTH
APPLE & HONEY
BARGAIN!
¥188
LIQUOR
生
R STORE
R STORE
R STORE

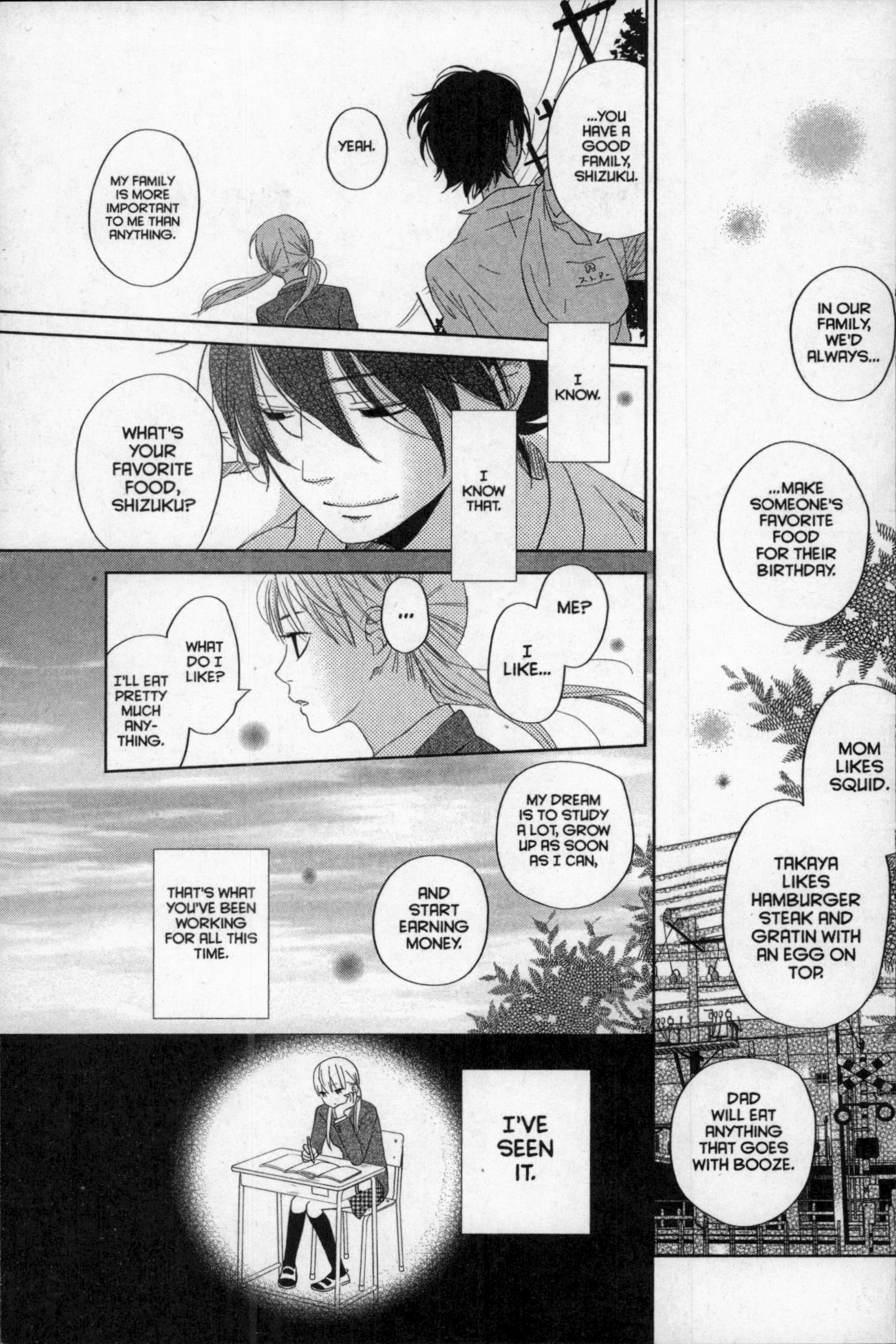
...YOU HAVE A GOOD FAMILY, SHIZUKU.
YEAH.
MY FAMILY IS MORE IMPORTANT TO ME THAN ANYTHING.
I KNOW.
I KNOW THAT.
WHAT'S YOUR FAVORITE FOOD, SHIZUKU?
ME?
I LIKE...
...
WHAT DO I LIKE?
I'LL EAT PRETTY MUCH ANY-THING.
IN OUR FAMILY, WE'D ALWAYS...
...MAKE SOMEONE'S FAVORITE FOOD FOR THEIR BIRTHDAY.
MOM LIKES SQUID.
TAKAYA LIKES HAMBURGER STEAK AND GRATIN WITH AN EGG ON TOP.
DAD WILL EAT ANYTHING THAT GOES WITH BOOZE.
MY DREAM IS TO STUDY A LOT, GROW UP AS SOON AS I CAN,
AND START EARNING MONEY.
THAT'S WHAT YOU'VE BEEN WORKING FOR ALL THIS TIME.
I'VE SEEN IT.

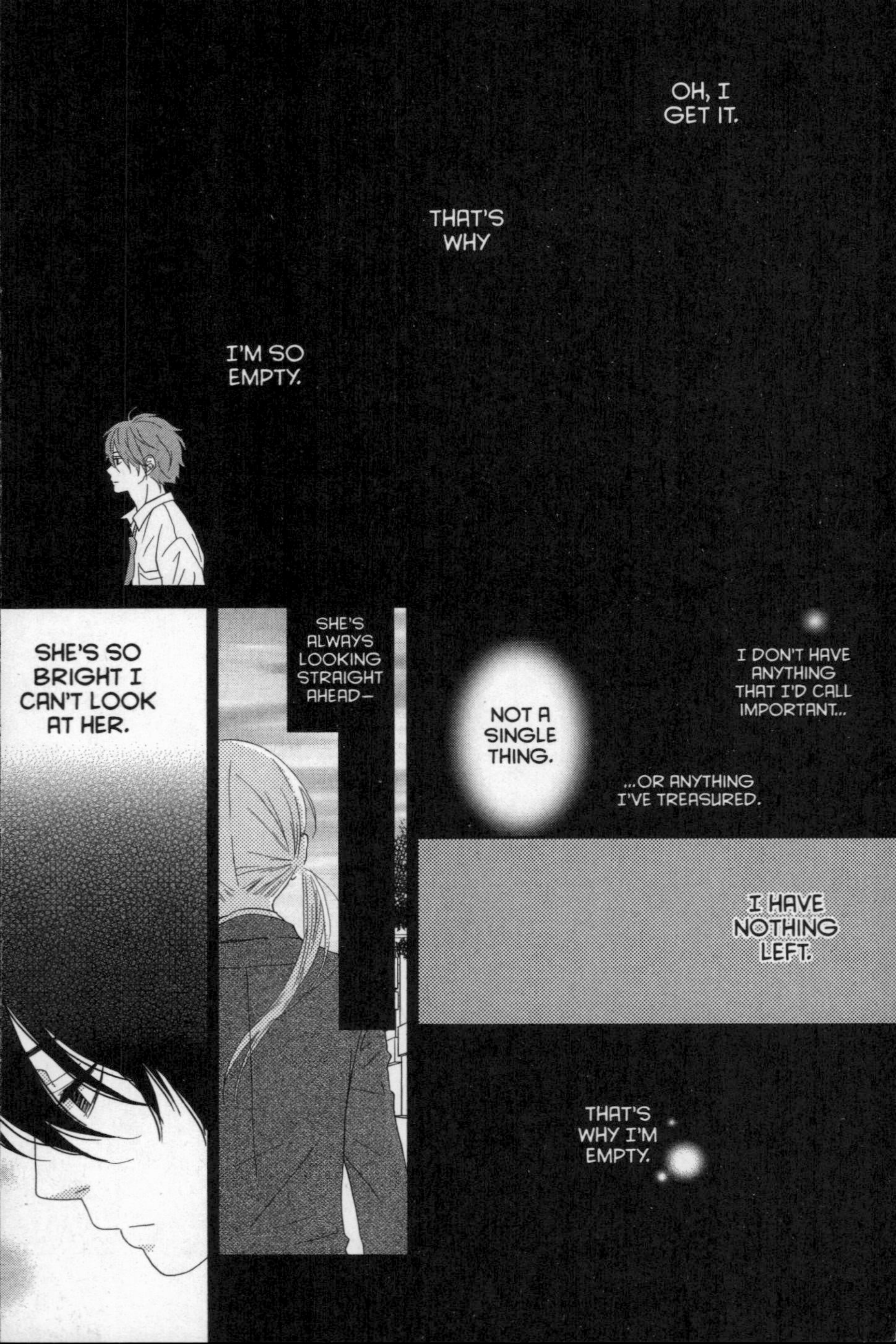
OH, I GET IT.
THAT'S WHY
I'M SO EMPTY.
I DON'T HAVE ANYTHING THAT I'D CALL IMPORTANT...
...OR ANYTHING I'VE TREASURED.
NOT A SINGLE THING.
I HAVE NOTHING LEFT.
THAT'S WHY I'M EMPTY.
SHE'S ALWAYS LOOKING STRAIGHT AHEAD—
SHE'S SO BRIGHT I CAN'T LOOK AT HER.

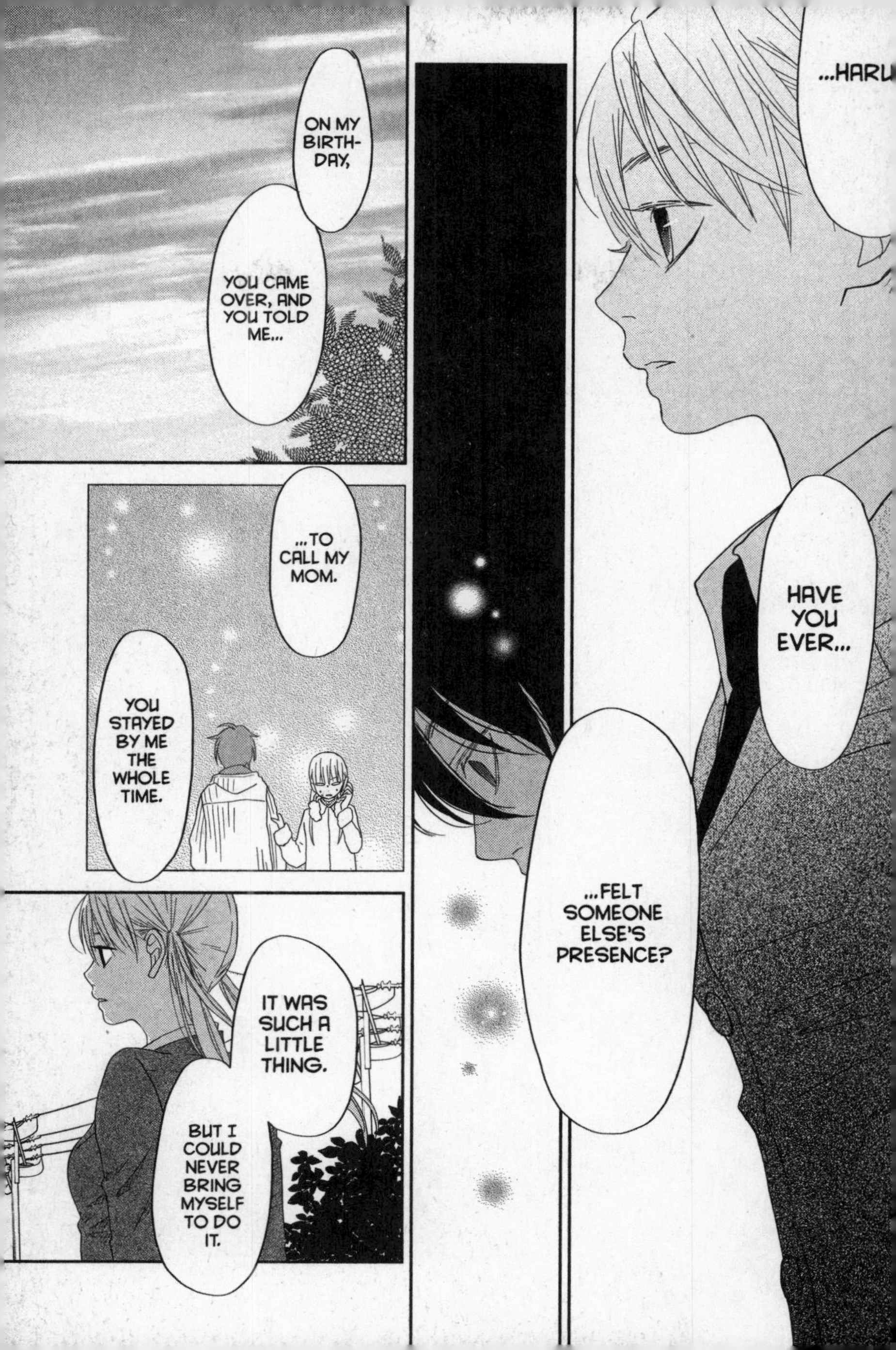
...HARU
HAVE YOU EVER...
...FELT SOMEONE ELSE'S PRESENCE?
ON MY BIRTH-DAY,
YOU CAME OVER, AND YOU TOLD ME...
...TO CALL MY MOM.
YOU STAYED BY ME THE WHOLE TIME.
IT WAS SUCH A LITTLE THING.
BUT I COULD NEVER BRING MYSELF TO DO IT.

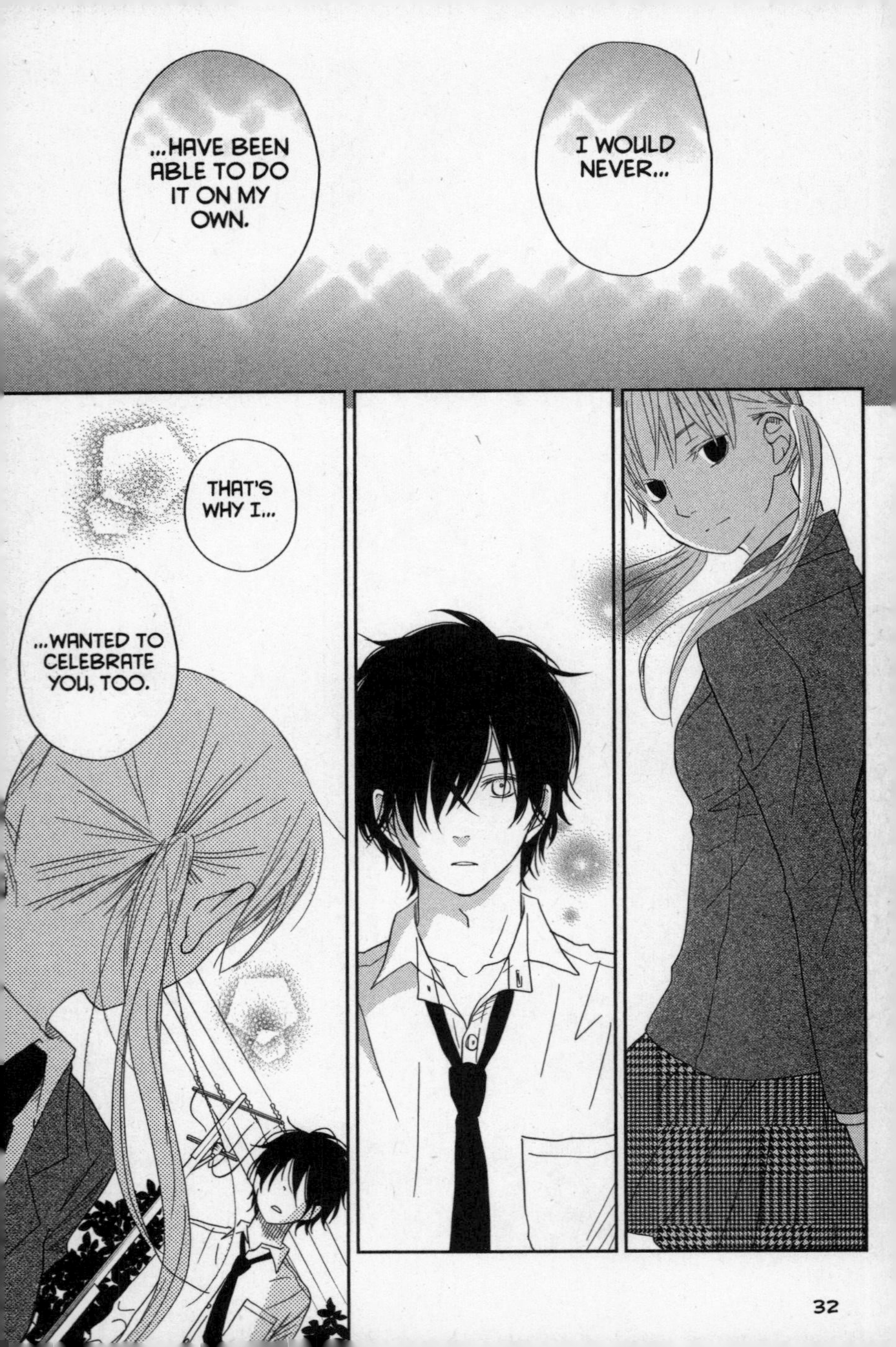
I WOULD NEVER...
...HAVE BEEN ABLE TO DO IT ON MY OWN.
THAT'S WHY I...
...WANTED TO CELEBRATE YOU, TOO.

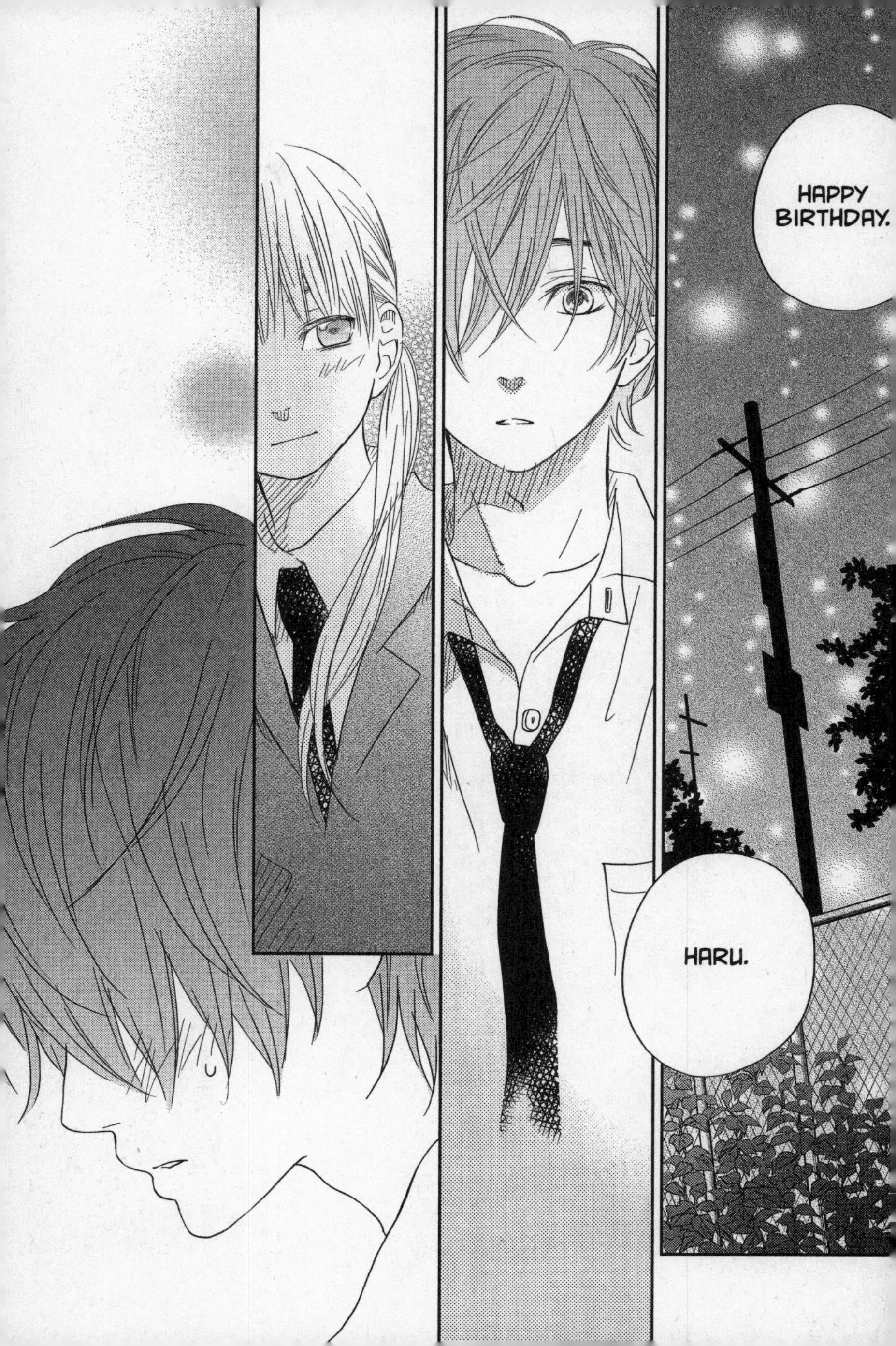
HAPPY BIRTHDAY.
HARU.

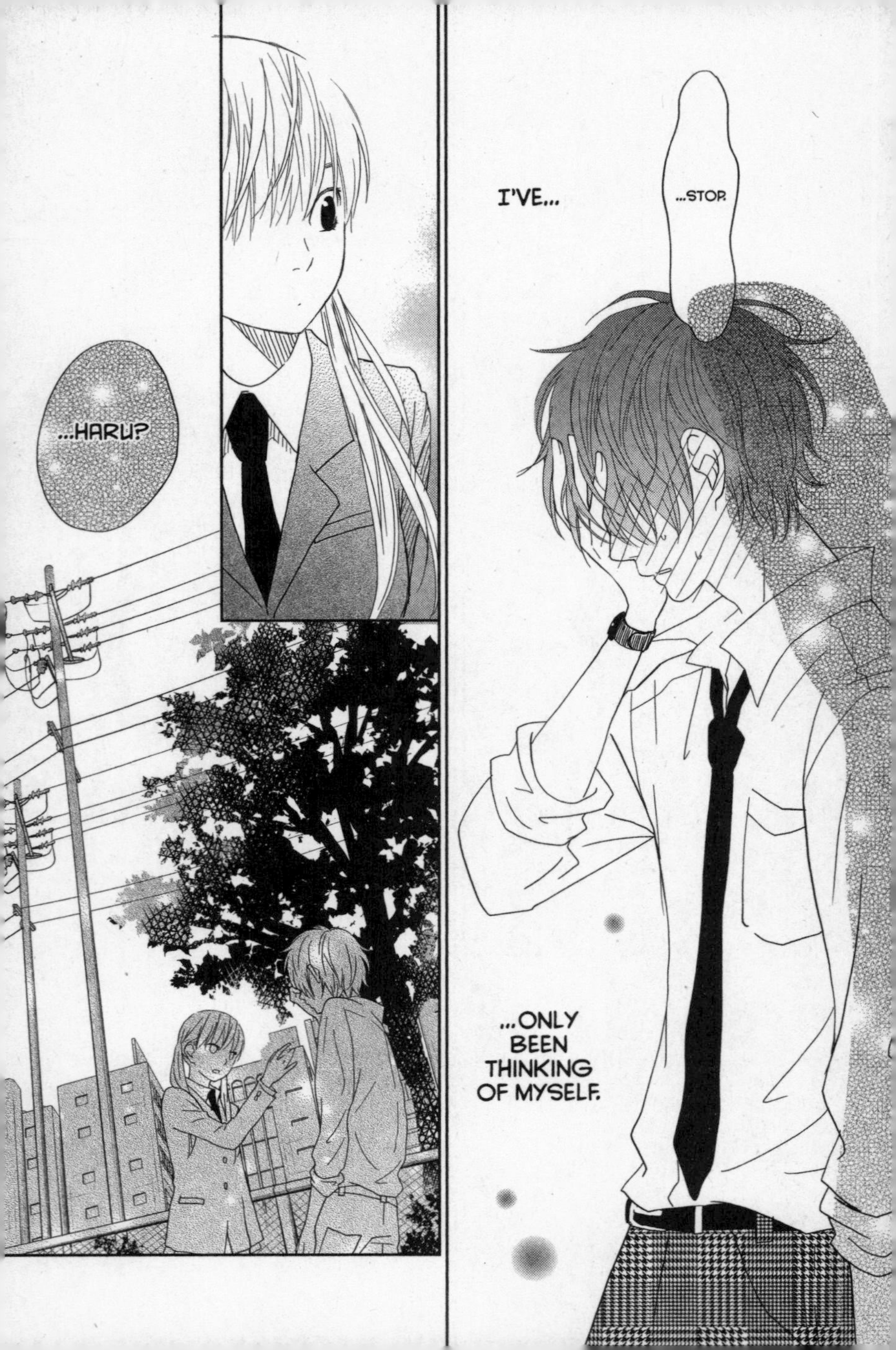
...STOP.
I'VE...
...ONLY BEEN THINKING OF MYSELF.
...HARU?

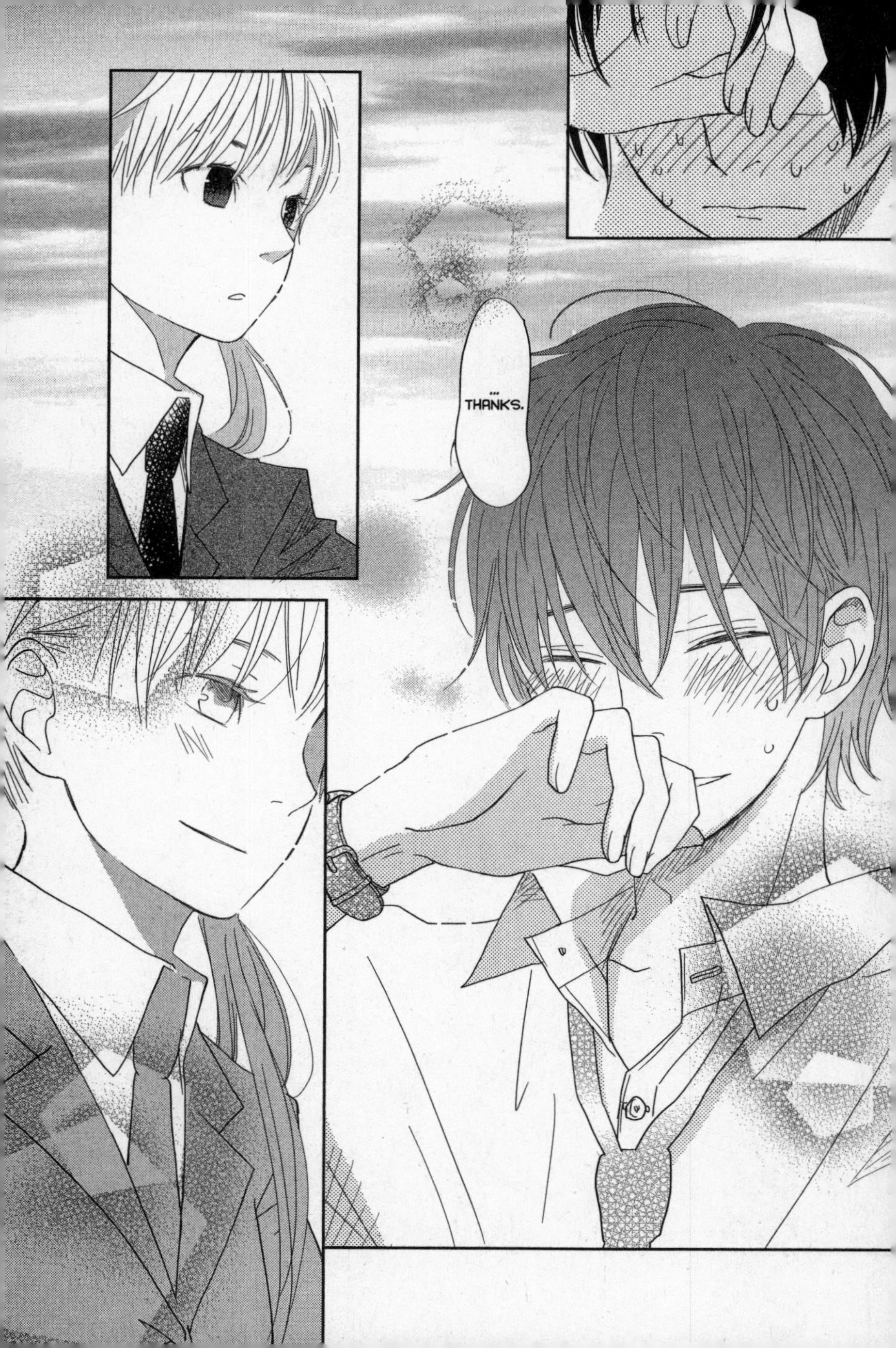
... THANKS.

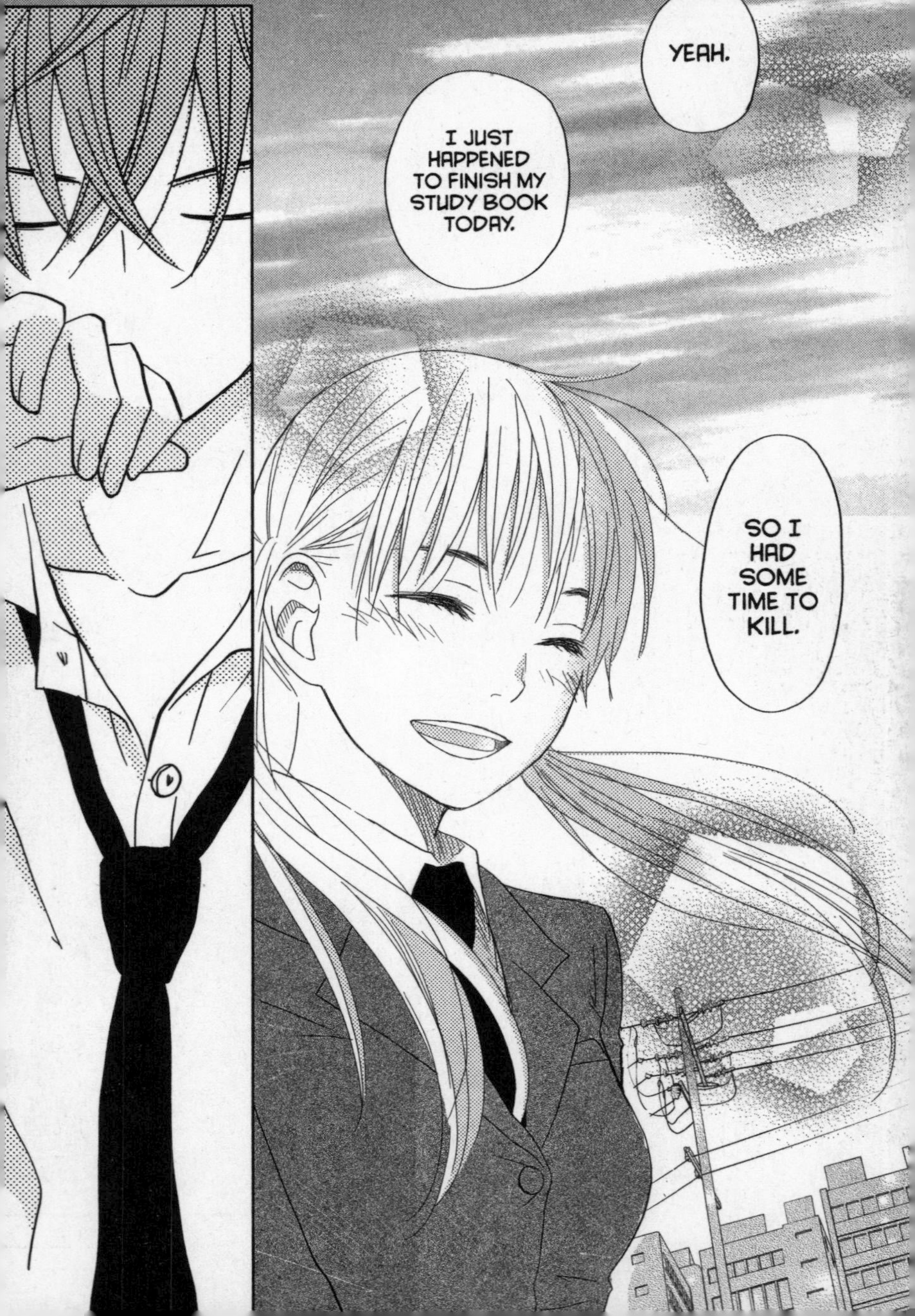
YEAH.
I JUST HAPPENED TO FINISH MY STUDY BOOK TODAY.
SO I HAD SOME TIME TO KILL.

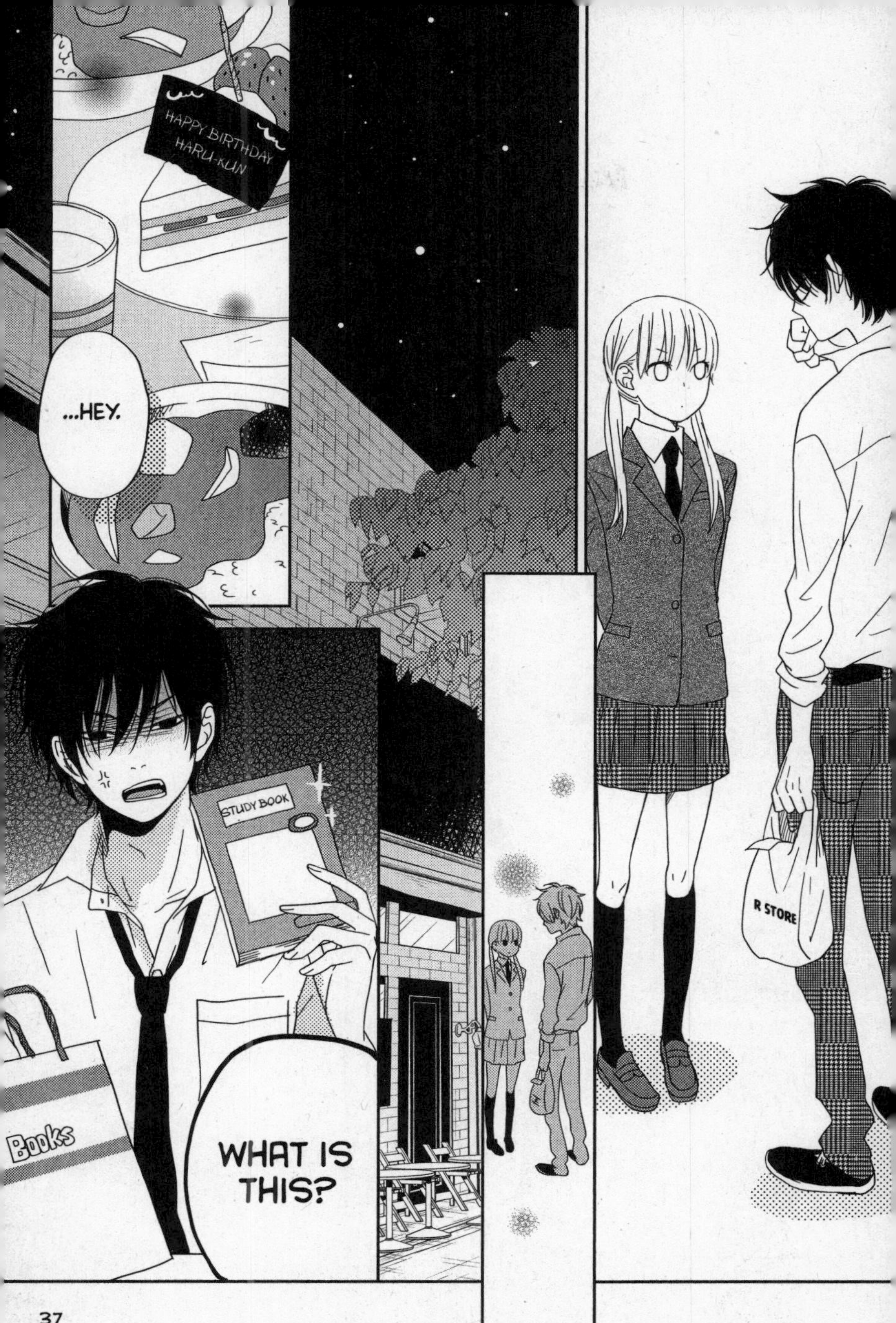
R STORE
HAPPY BIRTHDAY HARU-KUN
...HEY.
STUDY BOOK
Books
WHAT IS THIS?

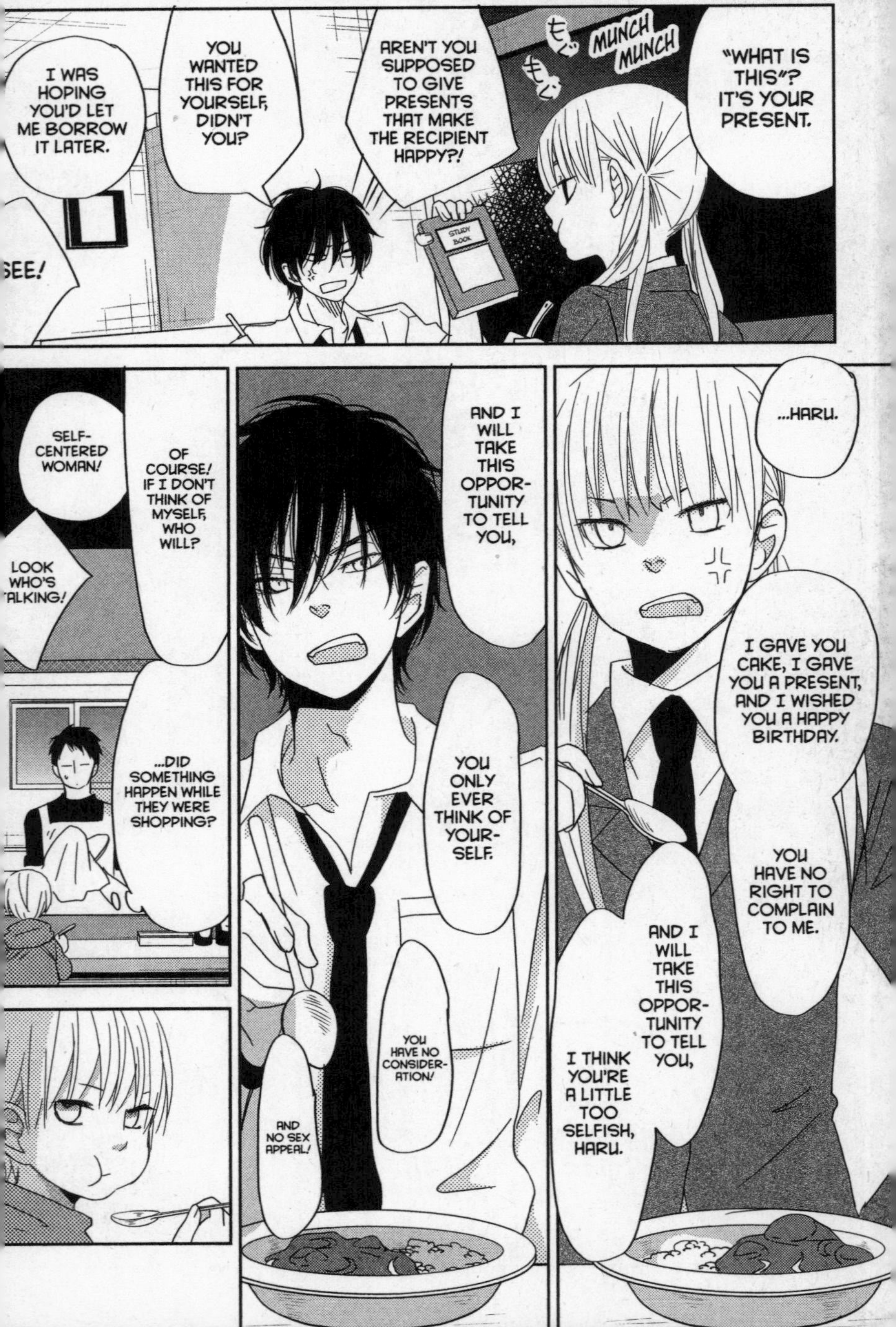
"WHAT IS THIS"? IT'S YOUR PRESENT.
MUNCH MUNCH
AREN'T YOU SUPPOSED TO GIVE PRESENTS THAT MAKE THE RECIPIENT HAPPY?!
STUDY BOOK
YOU WANTED THIS FOR YOURSELF, DIDN'T YOU?
I WAS HOPING YOU'D LET ME BORROW IT LATER.
SEE!
...HARU.
I GAVE YOU CAKE, I GAVE YOU A PRESENT, AND I WISHED YOU A HAPPY BIRTHDAY.
YOU HAVE NO RIGHT TO COMPLAIN TO ME.
AND I WILL TAKE THIS OPPORTUNITY TO TELL YOU,
I THINK YOU'RE A LITTLE TOO SELFISH, HARU.
AND I WILL TAKE THIS OPPORTUNITY TO TELL YOU,
YOU ONLY EVER THINK OF YOURSELF.
YOU HAVE NO CONSIDERATION!
AND NO SEX APPEAL!
OF COURSE! IF I DON'T THINK OF MYSELF, WHO WILL?
SELF-CENTERED WOMAN!
LOOK WHO'S TALKING!
...DID SOMETHING HAPPEN WHILE THEY WERE SHOPPING?

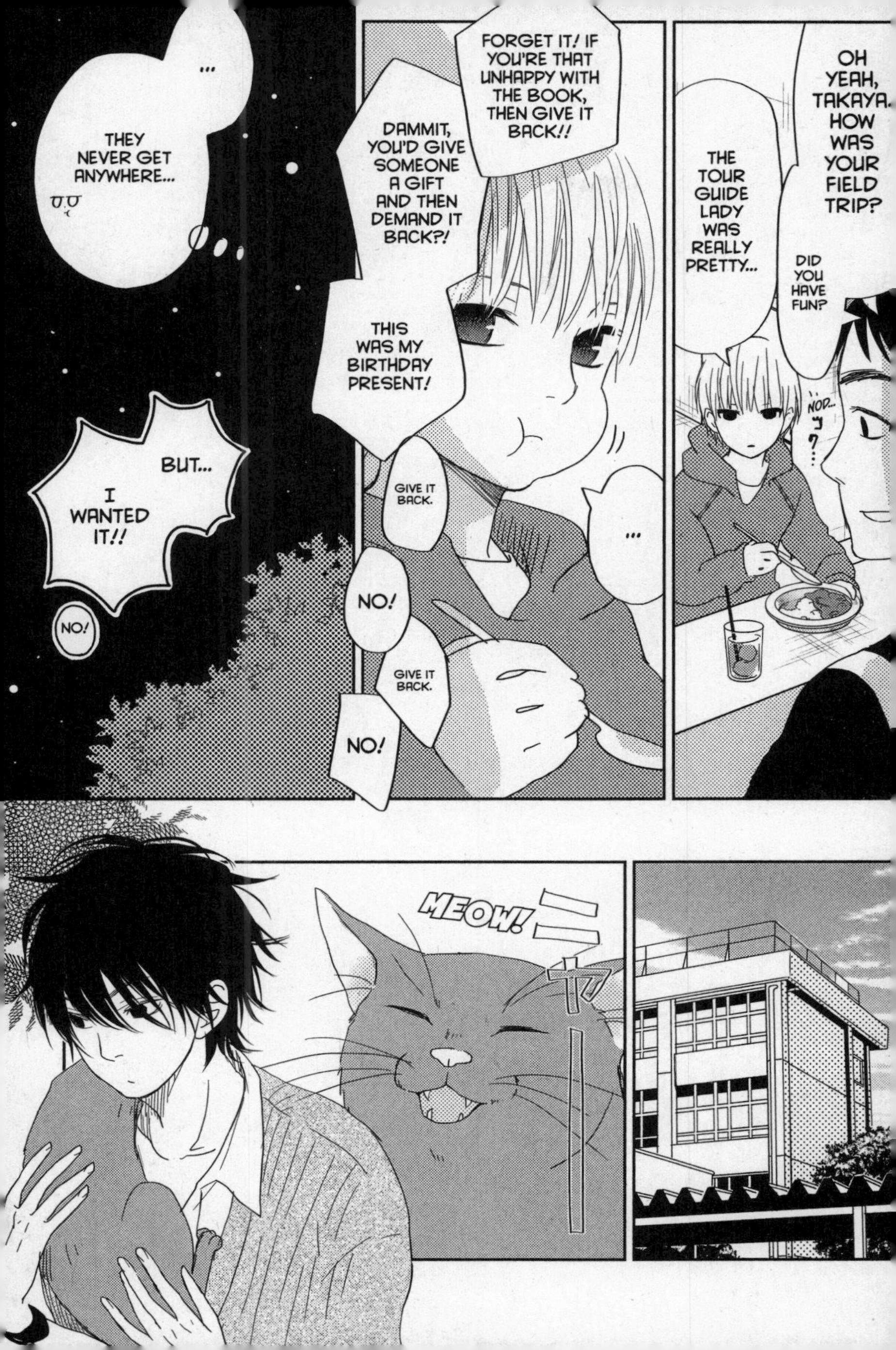
OH YEAH, TAKAYA. HOW WAS YOUR FIELD TRIP?
DID YOU HAVE FUN?
NOD...
THE TOUR GUIDE LADY WAS REALLY PRETTY...
FORGET IT! IF YOU'RE THAT UNHAPPY WITH THE BOOK, THEN GIVE IT BACK!!
DAMMIT, YOU'D GIVE SOMEONE A GIFT AND THEN DEMAND IT BACK?!
THIS WAS MY BIRTHDAY PRESENT!
...
GIVE IT BACK.
NO!
GIVE IT BACK.
NO!
...
THEY NEVER GET ANYWHERE...
BUT... I WANTED IT!!
NO!
MEOW!

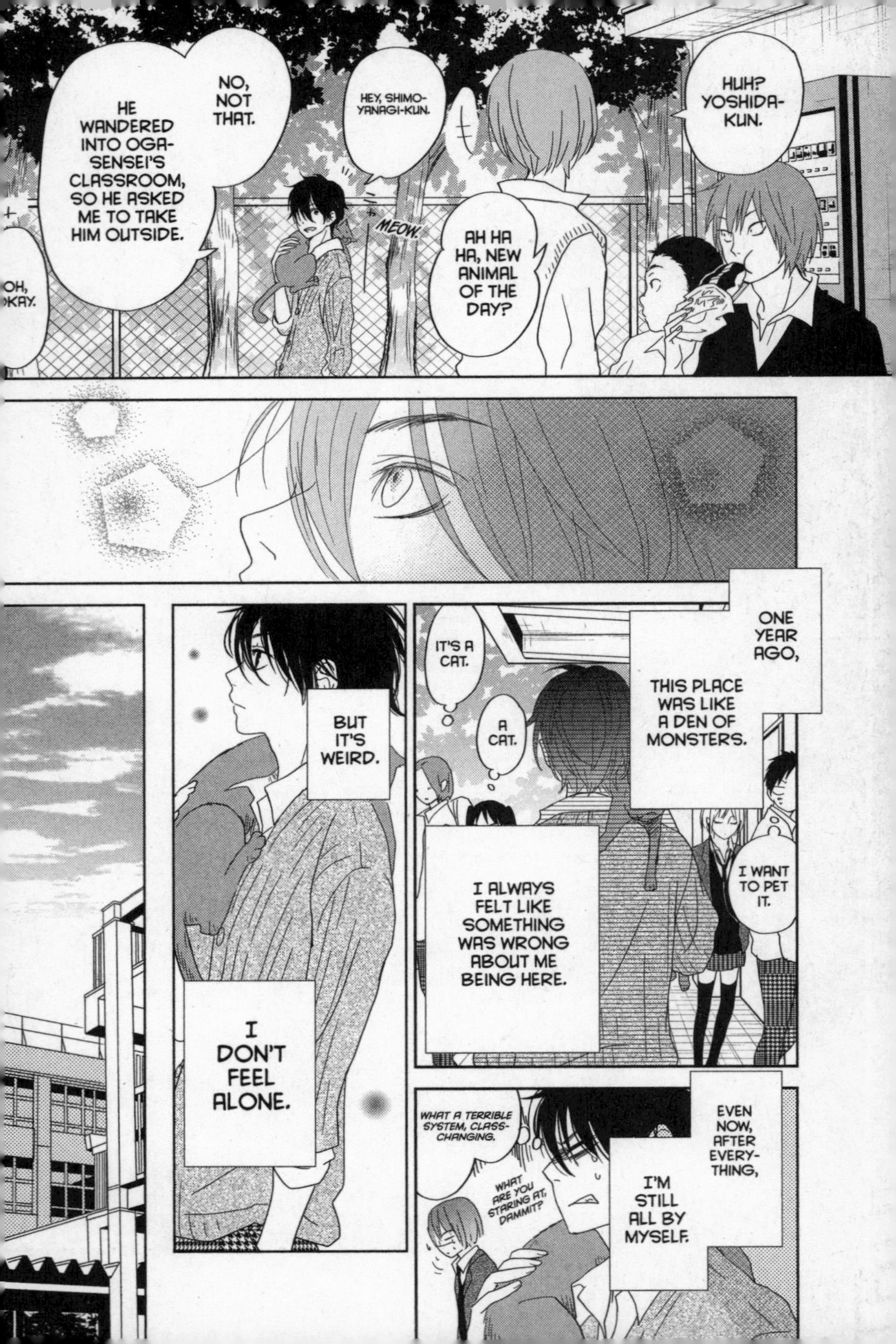
HUH? YOSHIDA-KUN.
HEY, SHIMO-YANAGI-KUN.
AH HA HA, NEW ANIMAL OF THE DAY?
MEOW
NO, NOT THAT.
HE WANDERED INTO OGA-SENSEI'S CLASSROOM, SO HE ASKED ME TO TAKE HIM OUTSIDE.
OH, OKAY.
ONE YEAR AGO,
THIS PLACE WAS LIKE A DEN OF MONSTERS.
IT'S A CAT.
A CAT.
I WANT TO PET IT.
I ALWAYS FELT LIKE SOMETHING WAS WRONG ABOUT ME BEING HERE.
EVEN NOW, AFTER EVERYTHING,
I'M STILL ALL BY MYSELF.
WHAT A TERRIBLE SYSTEM, CLASS-CHANGING.
WHAT ARE YOU STARING AT, DAMMIT?
BUT IT'S WEIRD.
I DON'T FEEL ALONE.

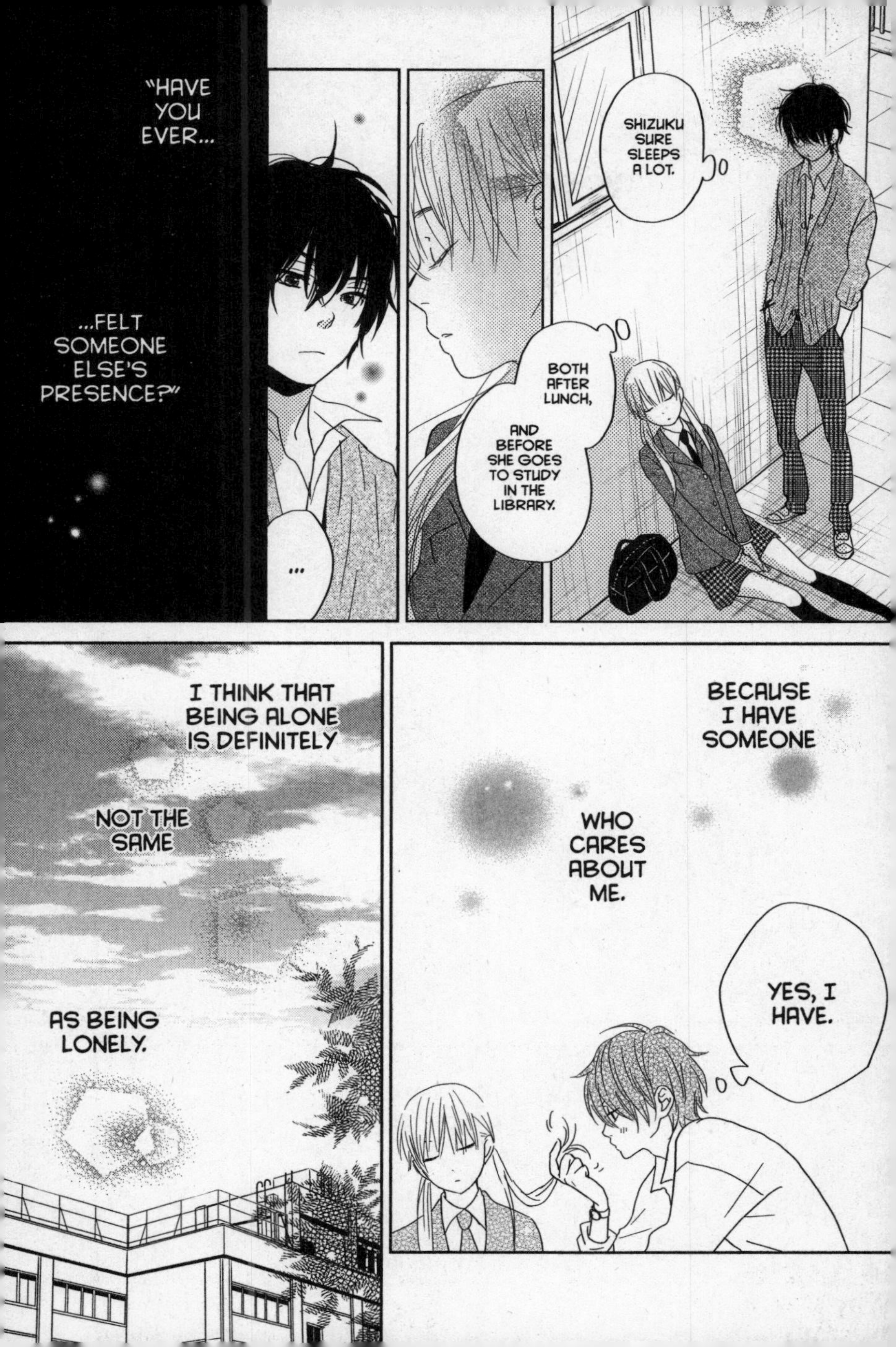
SHIZUKU SURE SLEEPS A LOT.
BOTH AFTER LUNCH,
AND BEFORE SHE GOES TO STUDY IN THE LIBRARY.
...
"HAVE YOU EVER...
...FELT SOMEONE ELSE'S PRESENCE?"
BECAUSE I HAVE SOMEONE
WHO CARES ABOUT ME.
YES, I HAVE.
I THINK THAT BEING ALONE IS DEFINITELY
NOT THE SAME
AS BEING LONELY.

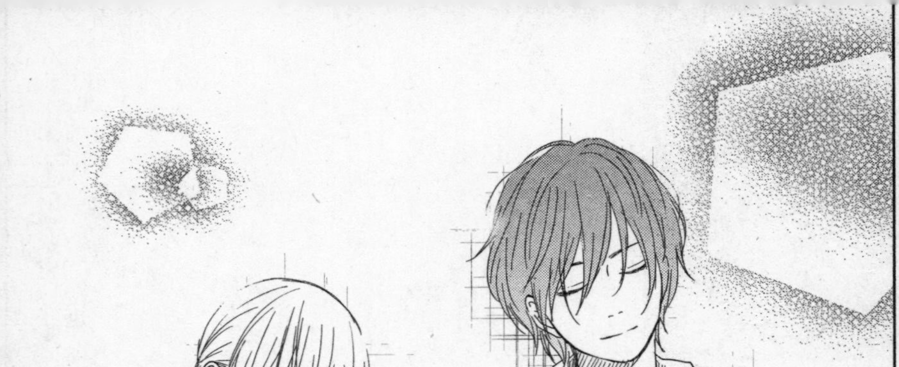

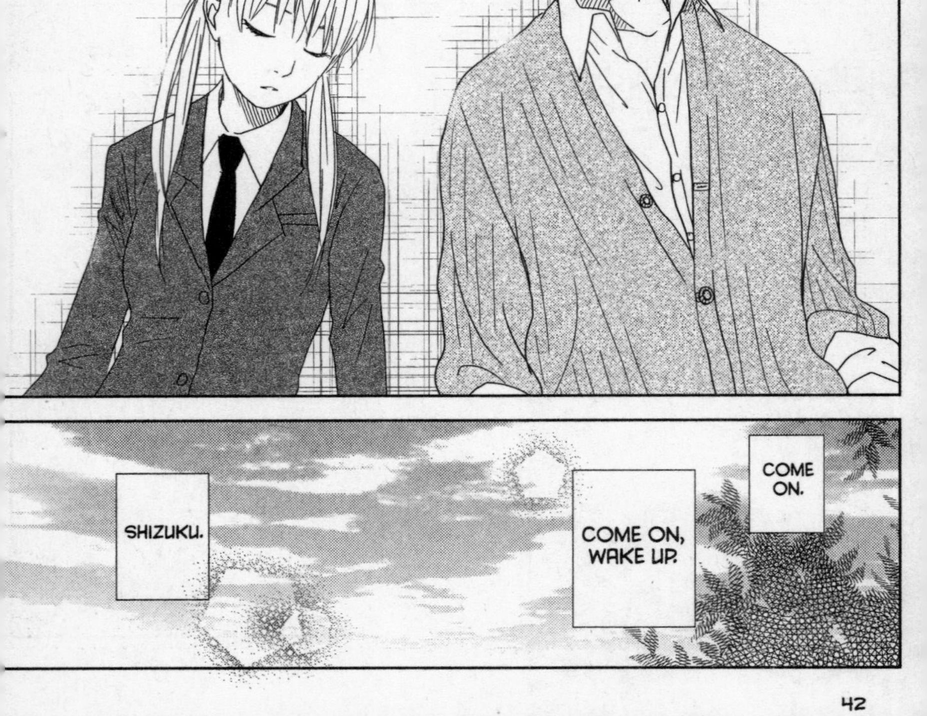
COME ON.
COME ON, WAKE UP.
SHIZUKU.

SHIZUKU AND HARU

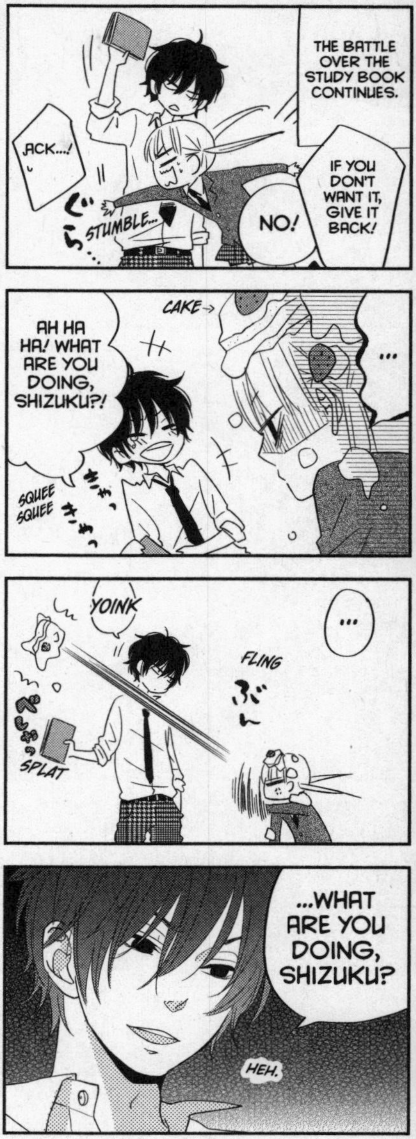
THE BATTLE OVER THE STUDY BOOK CONTINUES.
IF YOU DON'T WANT IT, GIVE IT BACK!
NO!
ACK...!
ぐら
STUMBLE...
CAKE→
...
AH HA HA! WHAT ARE YOU DOING, SHIZUKU?!
きゃっきゃっ
SQUEE SQUEE
...
FLING
ぶん
YOINK
べしゃっ
SPLAT
...WHAT ARE YOU DOING, SHIZUKU?
HEH.

SHIZUKU AND HARU, PART 2

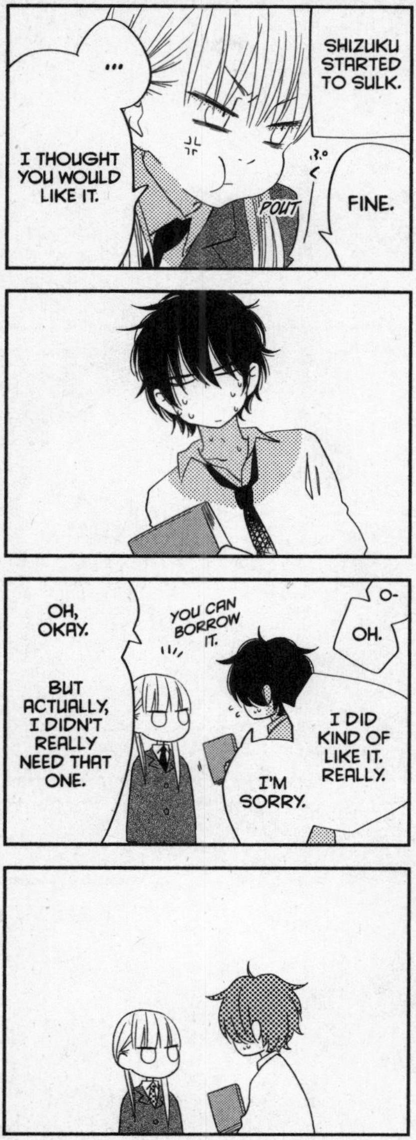
SHIZUKU STARTED TO SULK.
FINE.
ぷく
POUT
...
I THOUGHT YOU WOULD LIKE IT.
O- OH.
I DID KIND OF LIKE IT. REALLY.
I'M SORRY.
YOU CAN BORROW IT.
OH, OKAY.
BUT ACTUALLY, I DIDN'T REALLY NEED THAT ONE.

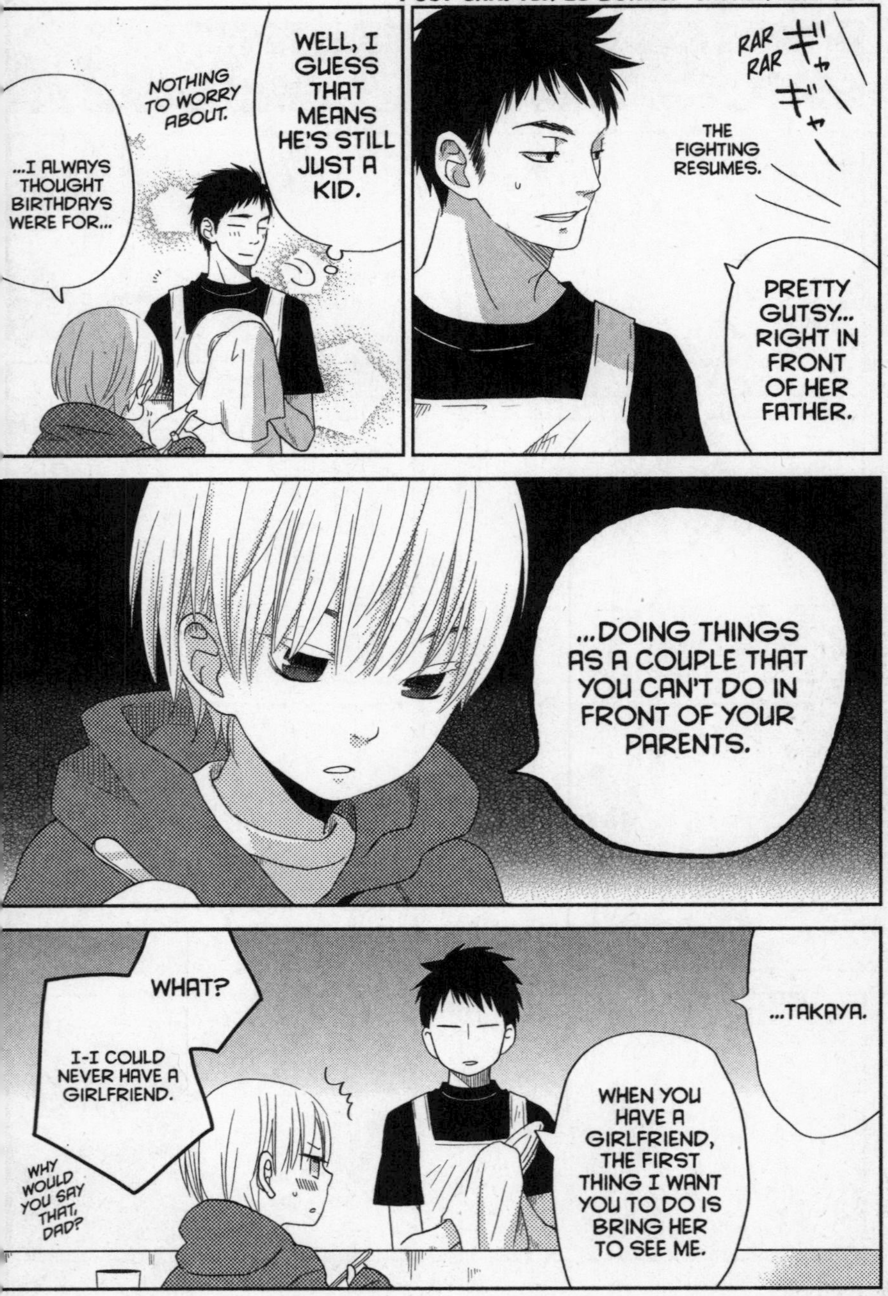
RAR RAR
ギャ ギャ
THE FIGHTING RESUMES.
PRETTY GUTSY... RIGHT IN FRONT OF HER FATHER.
WELL, I GUESS THAT MEANS HE'S STILL JUST A KID.
NOTHING TO WORRY ABOUT.
...I ALWAYS THOUGHT BIRTHDAYS WERE FOR...
...DOING THINGS AS A COUPLE THAT YOU CAN'T DO IN FRONT OF YOUR PARENTS.
...TAKAYA.
WHEN YOU HAVE A GIRLFRIEND, THE FIRST THING I WANT YOU TO DO IS BRING HER TO SEE ME.
WHAT?
I-I COULD NEVER HAVE A GIRLFRIEND.
WHY WOULD YOU SAY THAT, DAD?

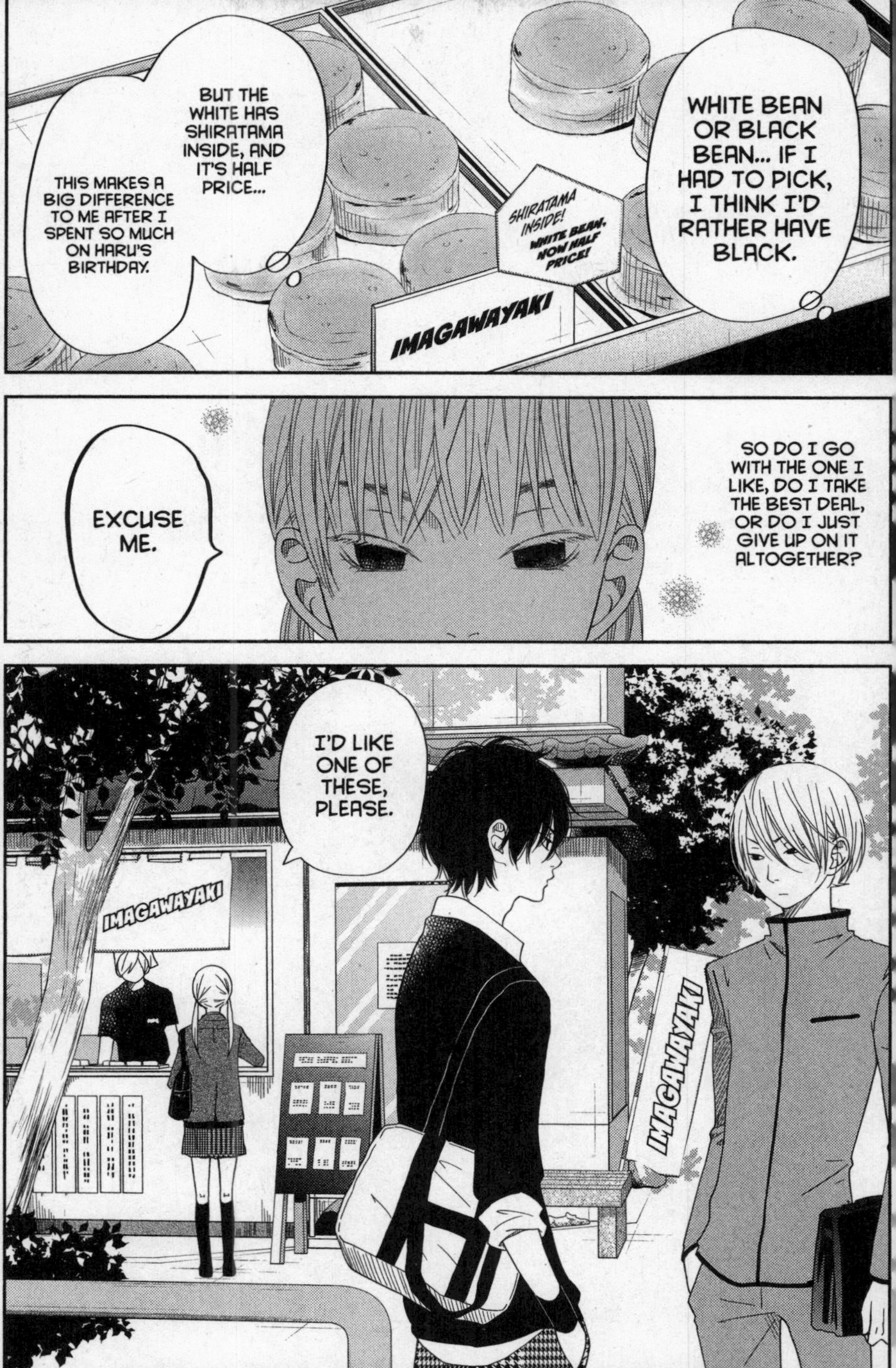
WHITE BEAN OR BLACK BEAN... IF I HAD TO PICK, I THINK I'D RATHER HAVE BLACK.
SHIRATAMA INSIDE! WHITE BEAN, NOW HALF PRICE!
IMAGAWAYAKI
BUT THE WHITE HAS SHIRATAMA INSIDE, AND IT'S HALF PRICE...
THIS MAKES A BIG DIFFERENCE TO ME AFTER I SPENT SO MUCH ON HARU'S BIRTHDAY.
SO DO I GO WITH THE ONE I LIKE, DO I TAKE THE BEST DEAL, OR DO I JUST GIVE UP ON IT ALTOGETHER?
EXCUSE ME.
IMAGAWAYAKI
I'D LIKE ONE OF THESE, PLEASE.
IMAGAWAYAKI

CHAPTER 30: GETTING SOMEWHERE

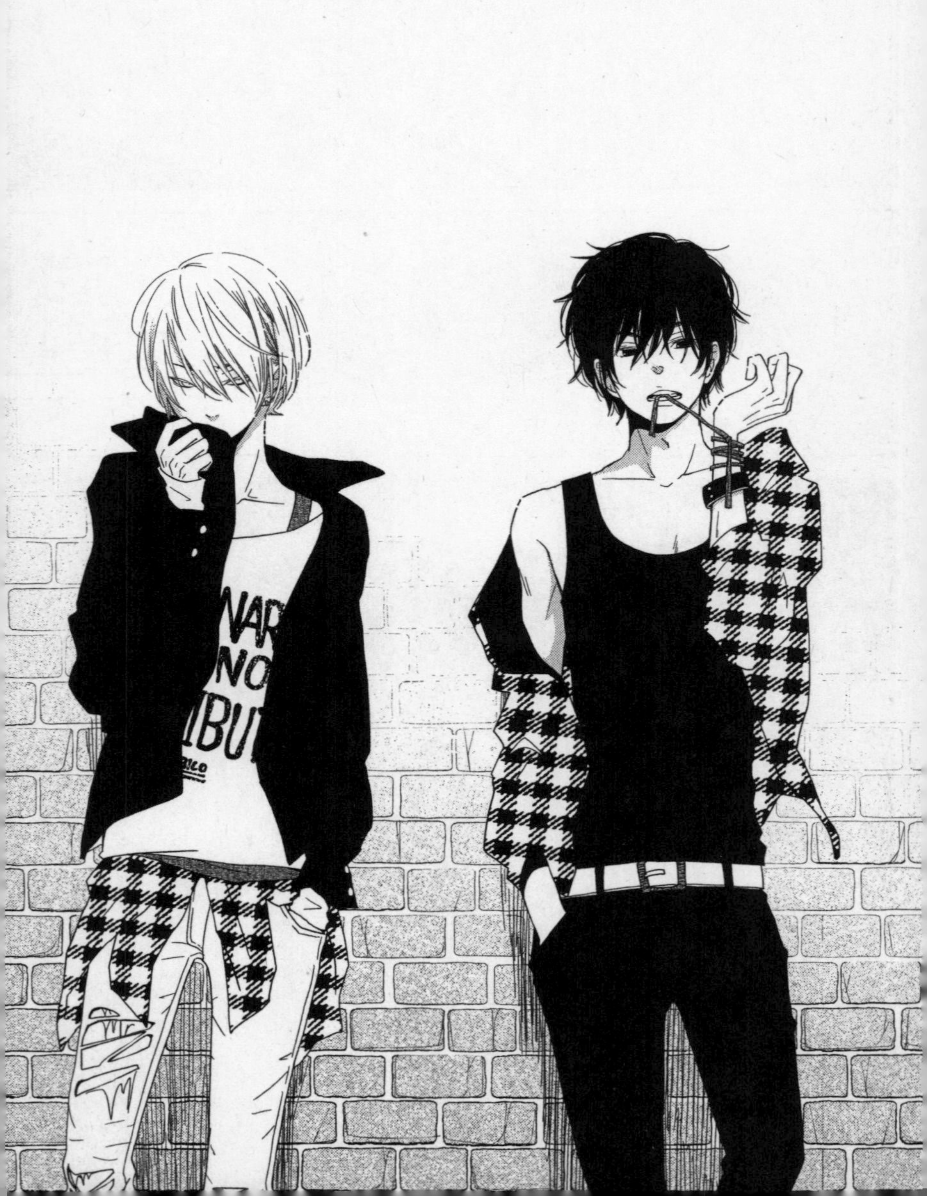

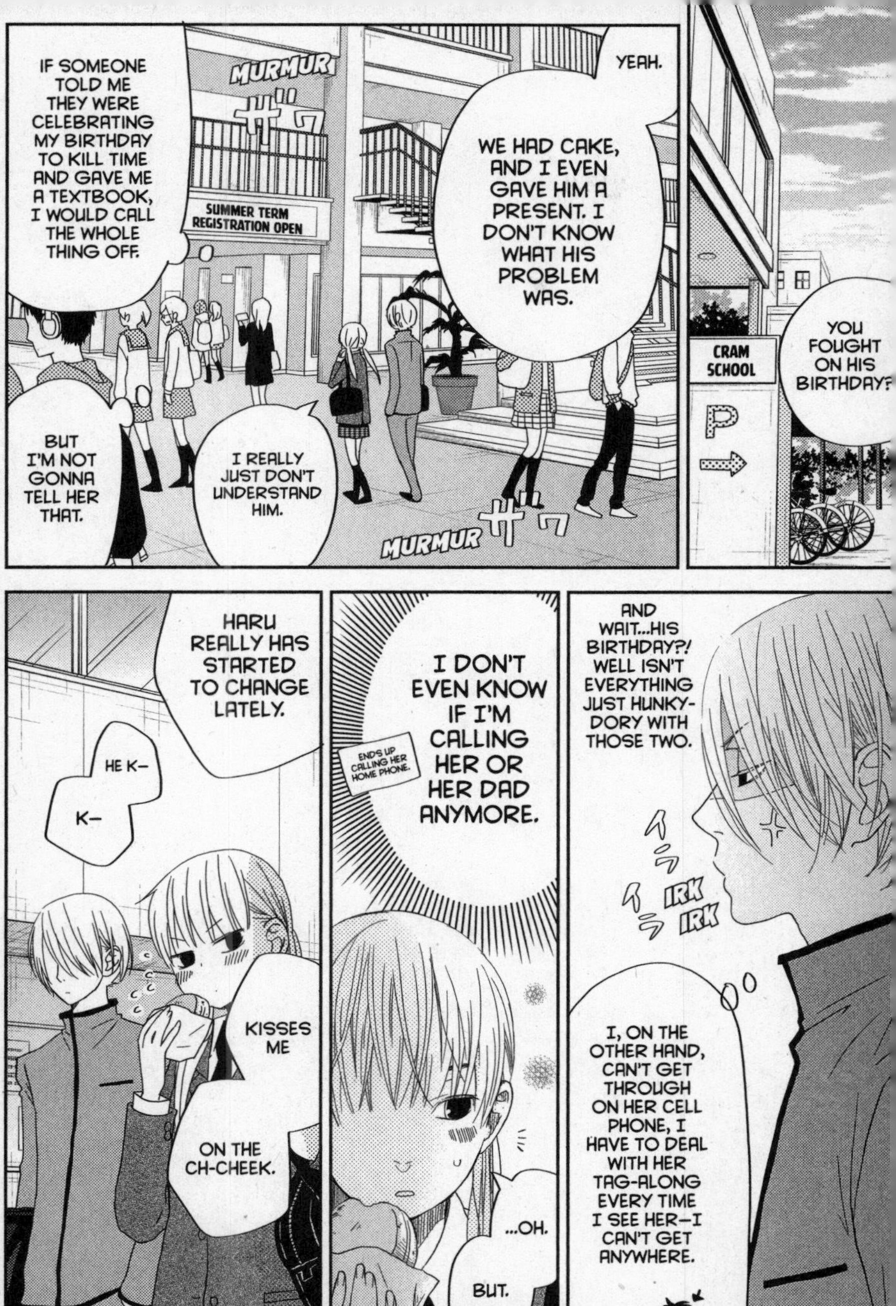
CRAM SCHOOL
YOU FOUGHT ON HIS BIRTHDAY?
YEAH.
WE HAD CAKE, AND I EVEN GAVE HIM A PRESENT. I DON'T KNOW WHAT HIS PROBLEM WAS.
SUMMER TERM REGISTRATION OPEN
MURMUR
IF SOMEONE TOLD ME THEY WERE CELEBRATING MY BIRTHDAY TO KILL TIME AND GAVE ME A TEXTBOOK, I WOULD CALL THE WHOLE THING OFF.
I REALLY JUST DON'T UNDERSTAND HIM.
BUT I'M NOT GONNA TELL HER THAT.
MURMUR
AND WAIT...HIS BIRTHDAY?! WELL ISN'T EVERYTHING JUST HUNKY-DORY WITH THOSE TWO.
IRK IRK
I, ON THE OTHER HAND, CAN'T GET THROUGH ON HER CELL PHONE, I HAVE TO DEAL WITH HER TAG-ALONG EVERY TIME I SEE HER—I CAN'T GET ANYWHERE.
I DON'T EVEN KNOW IF I'M CALLING HER OR HER DAD ANYMORE.
ENDS UP CALLING HER HOME PHONE.
...OH.
BUT.
HARU REALLY HAS STARTED TO CHANGE LATELY.
HE K—
K—
KISSES ME
ON THE CH-CHEEK.

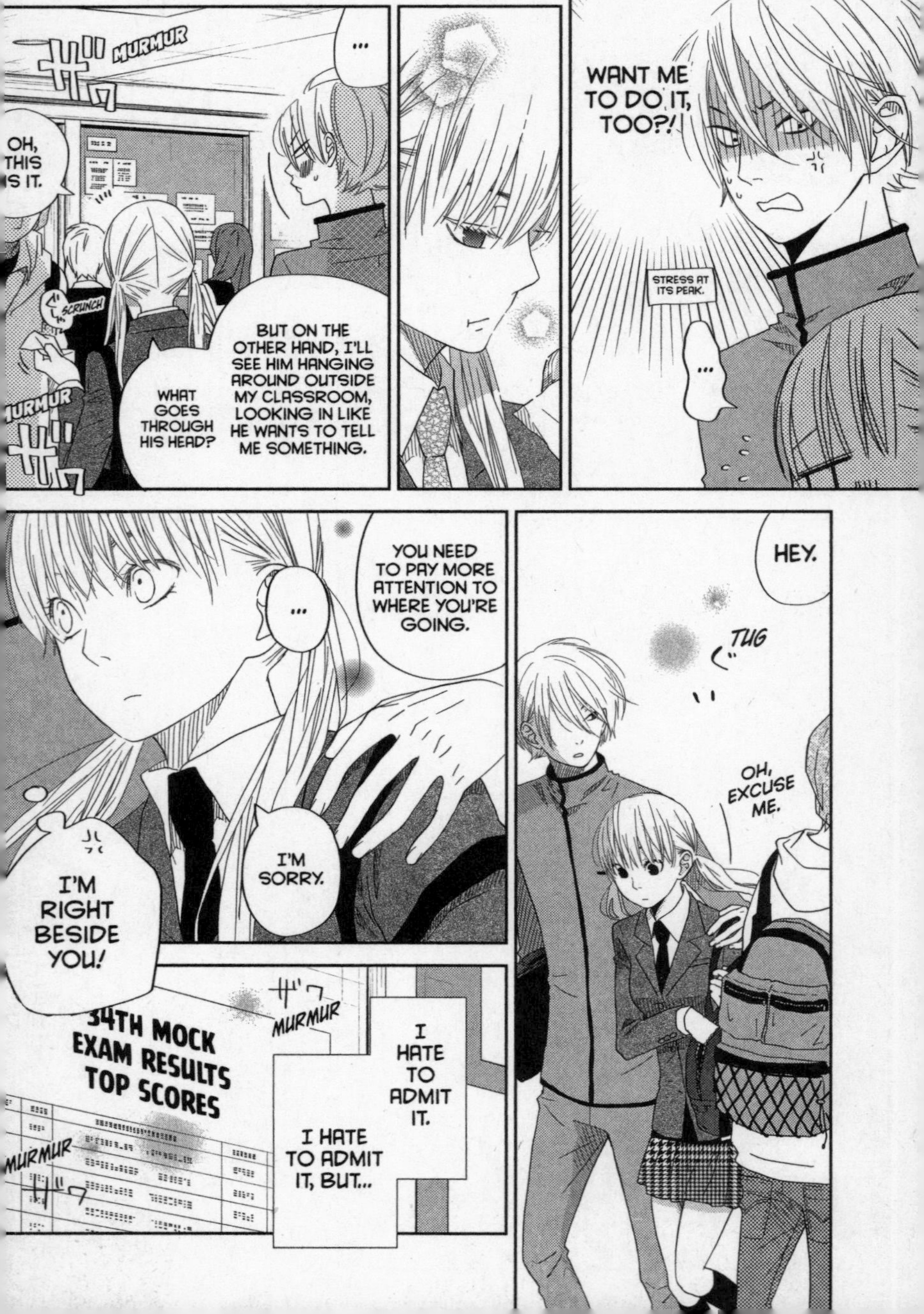
WANT ME TO DO IT, TOO?!
STRESS AT ITS PEAK.
...
...
BUT ON THE OTHER HAND, I'LL SEE HIM HANGING AROUND OUTSIDE MY CLASSROOM, LOOKING IN LIKE HE WANTS TO TELL ME SOMETHING.
WHAT GOES THROUGH HIS HEAD?
MURMUR
OH, THIS S IT.
SCRUNCH
MURMUR
HEY.
TUG
OH, EXCUSE ME.
...
YOU NEED TO PAY MORE ATTENTION TO WHERE YOU'RE GOING.
I'M SORRY.
I'M RIGHT BESIDE YOU!
MURMUR
I HATE TO ADMIT IT.
I HATE TO ADMIT IT, BUT...
34TH MOCK EXAM RESULTS TOP SCORES
MURMUR

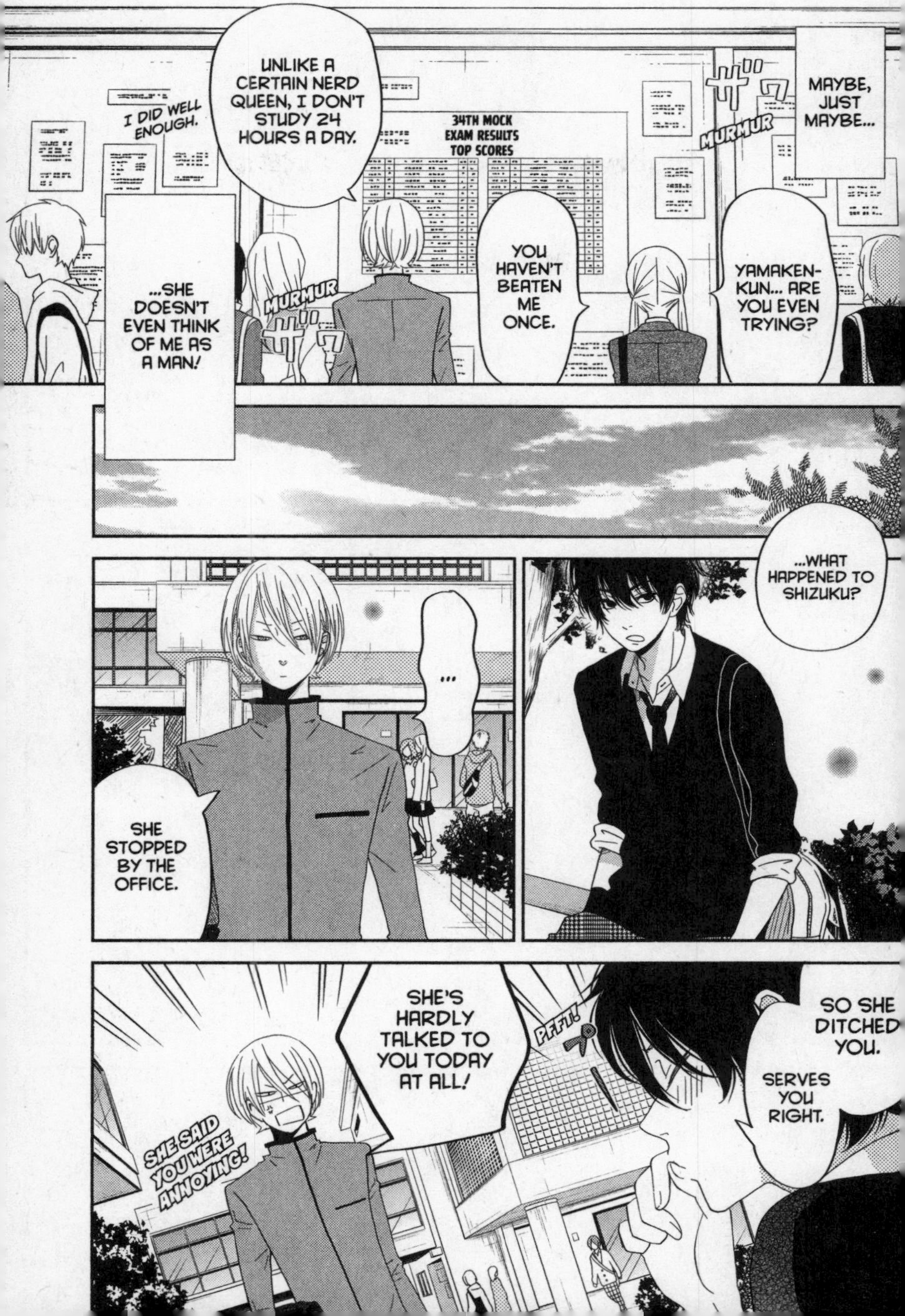
MAYBE, JUST MAYBE...
ザワ
MURMUR
YAMAKEN-KUN... ARE YOU EVEN TRYING?
YOU HAVEN'T BEATEN ME ONCE.
34TH MOCK EXAM RESULTS TOP SCORES
UNLIKE A CERTAIN NERD QUEEN, I DON'T STUDY 24 HOURS A DAY.
I DID WELL ENOUGH.
MURMUR
ザワ
...SHE DOESN'T EVEN THINK OF ME AS A MAN!
...WHAT HAPPENED TO SHIZUKU?
...
SHE STOPPED BY THE OFFICE.
SO SHE DITCHED YOU.
SERVES YOU RIGHT.
PFFT!
SHE'S HARDLY TALKED TO YOU TODAY AT ALL!
SHE SAID YOU WERE ANNOYING!

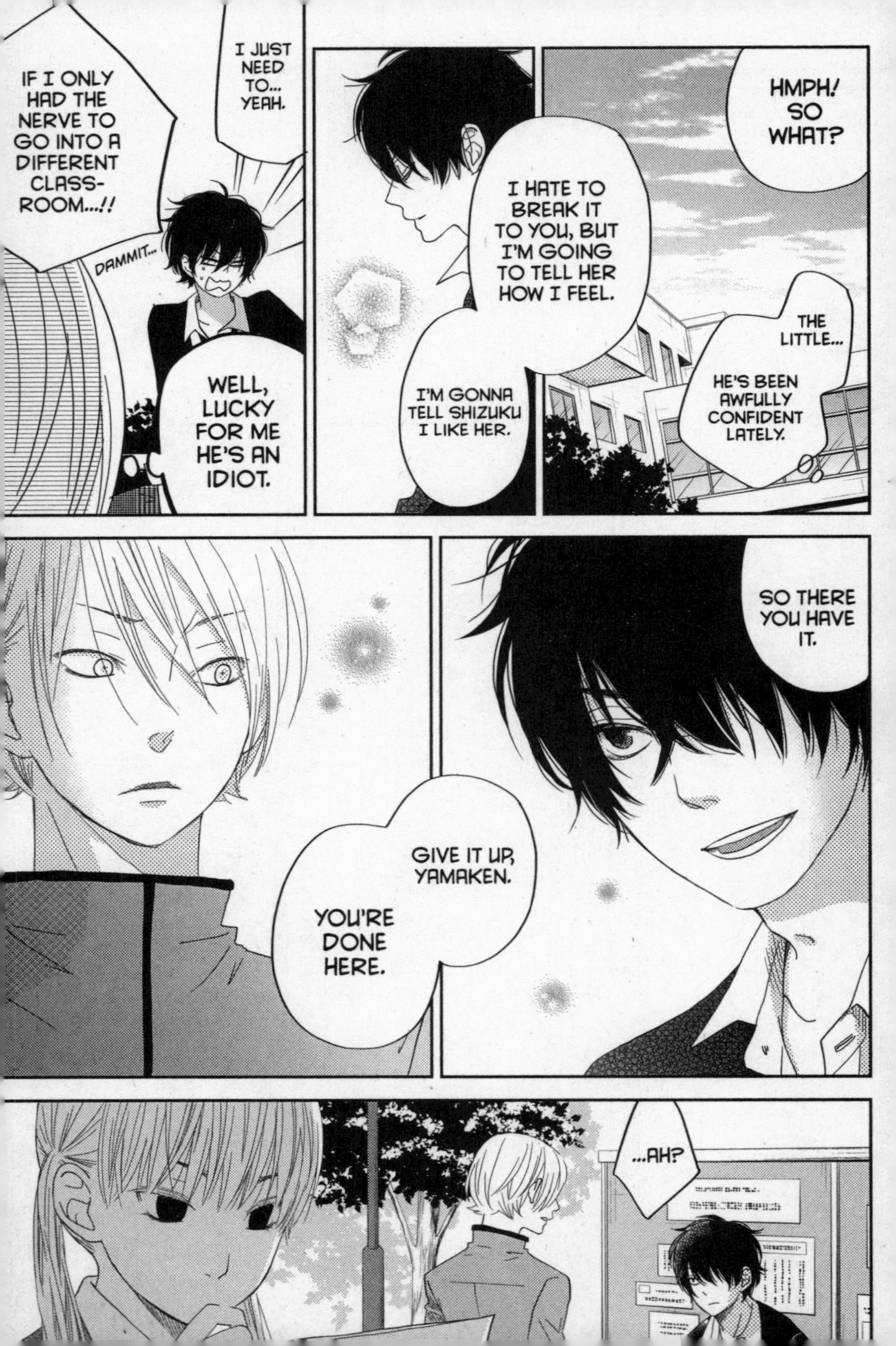
HMPH! SO WHAT?
THE LITTLE...
HE'S BEEN AWFULLY CONFIDENT LATELY.
I HATE TO BREAK IT TO YOU, BUT I'M GOING TO TELL HER HOW I FEEL.
I'M GONNA TELL SHIZUKU I LIKE HER.
I JUST NEED TO... YEAH.
IF I ONLY HAD THE NERVE TO GO INTO A DIFFERENT CLASS-ROOM...!!
DAMMIT...
WELL, LUCKY FOR ME HE'S AN IDIOT.
SO THERE YOU HAVE IT.
GIVE IT UP, YAMAKEN.
YOU'RE DONE HERE.
...AH?

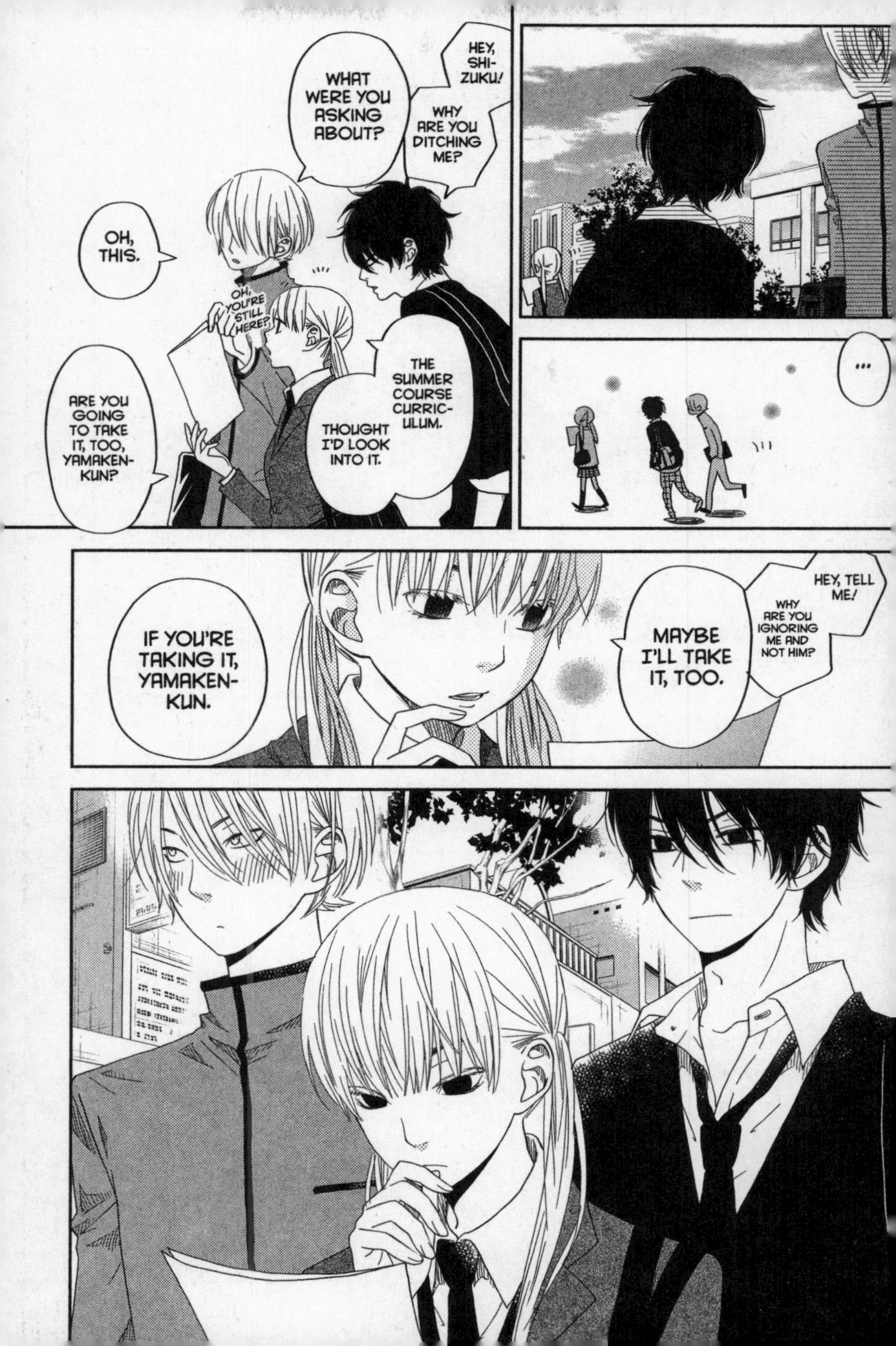
...
HEY, SHIZUKU!
WHY ARE YOU DITCHING ME?
WHAT WERE YOU ASKING ABOUT?
OH, THIS.
OH, YOU'RE STILL HERE?
THE SUMMER COURSE CURRICULUM.
THOUGHT I'D LOOK INTO IT.
ARE YOU GOING TO TAKE IT, TOO, YAMAKEN-KUN?
HEY, TELL ME!
WHY ARE YOU IGNORING ME AND NOT HIM?
MAYBE I'LL TAKE IT, TOO.
IF YOU'RE TAKING IT, YAMAKEN-KUN.

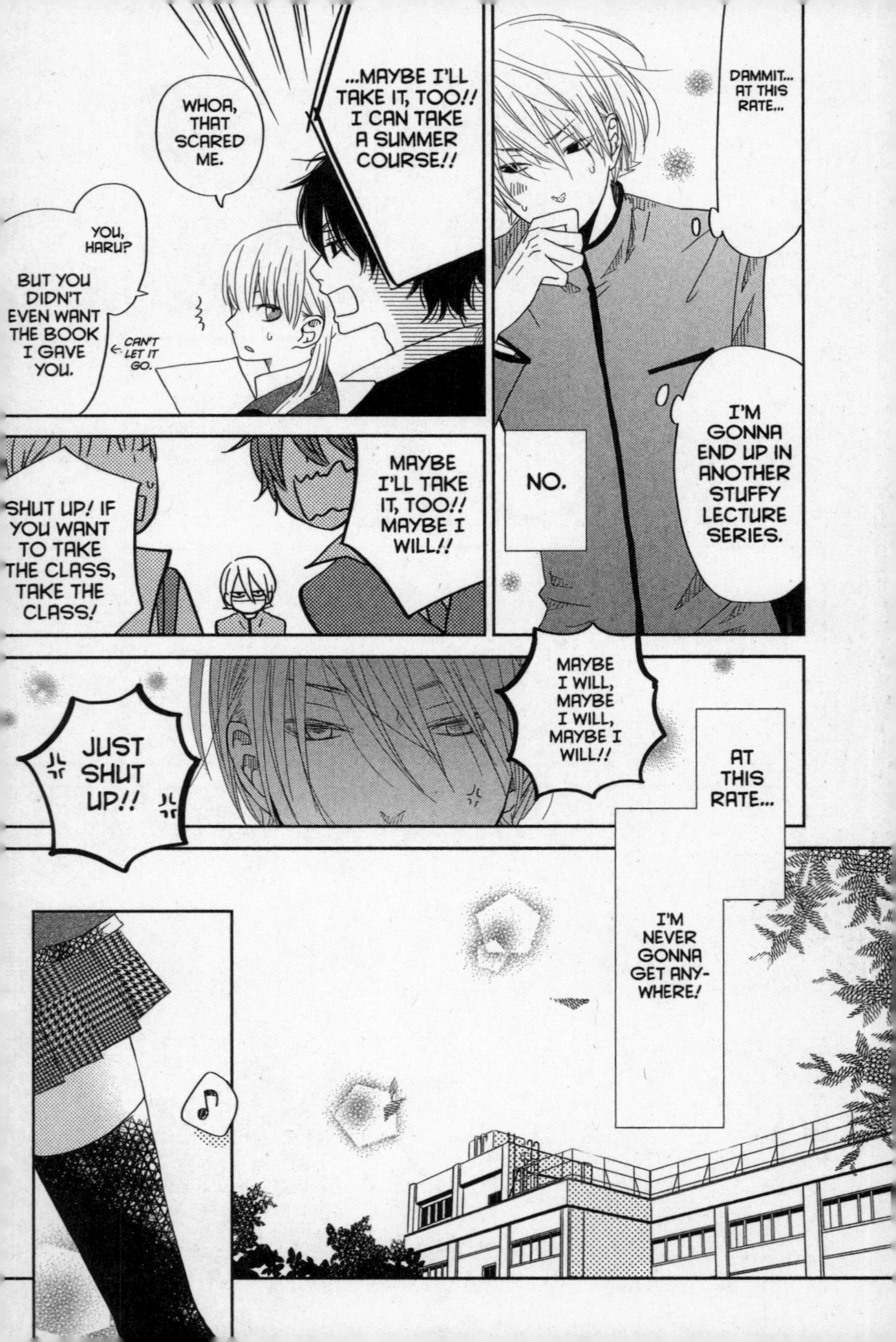
DAMMIT... AT THIS RATE...
I'M GONNA END UP IN ANOTHER STUFFY LECTURE SERIES.
NO.
...MAYBE I'LL TAKE IT, TOO!! I CAN TAKE A SUMMER COURSE!!
WHOA, THAT SCARED ME.
YOU, HARU?
BUT YOU DIDN'T EVEN WANT THE BOOK I GAVE YOU.
← CAN'T LET IT GO.
MAYBE I'LL TAKE IT, TOO!! MAYBE I WILL!!
SHUT UP! IF YOU WANT TO TAKE THE CLASS, TAKE THE CLASS!
MAYBE I WILL, MAYBE I WILL, MAYBE I WILL!!
JUST SHUT UP!!
AT THIS RATE...
I'M NEVER GONNA GET ANY-WHERE!

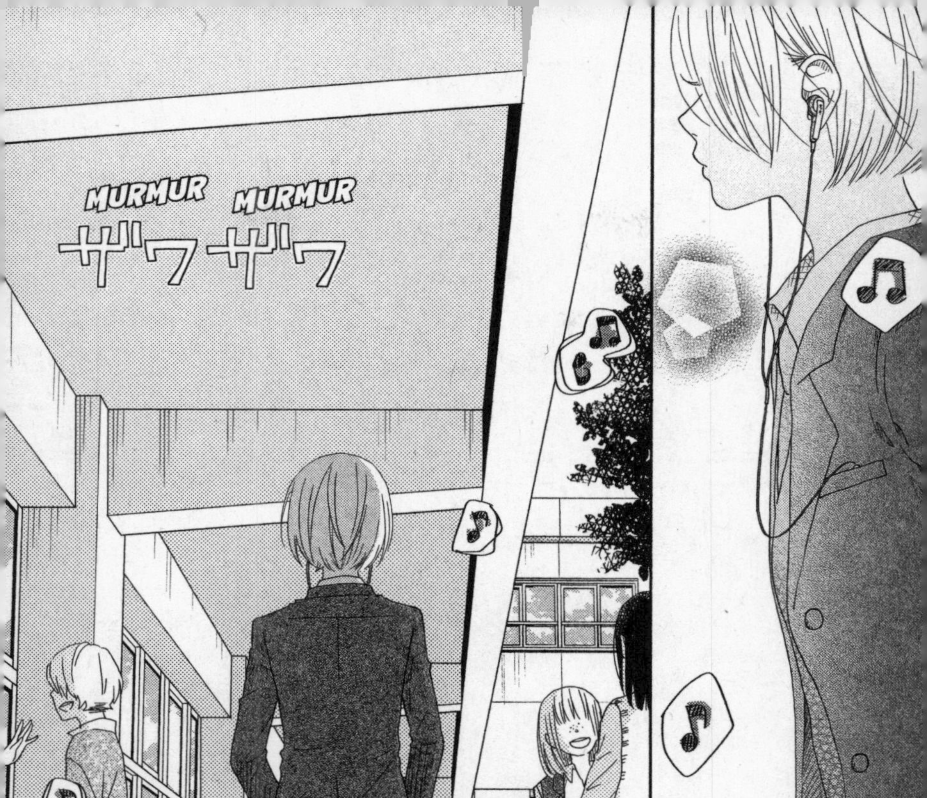
MURMUR MURMUR
ザワザワ
MURMUR
ザワ
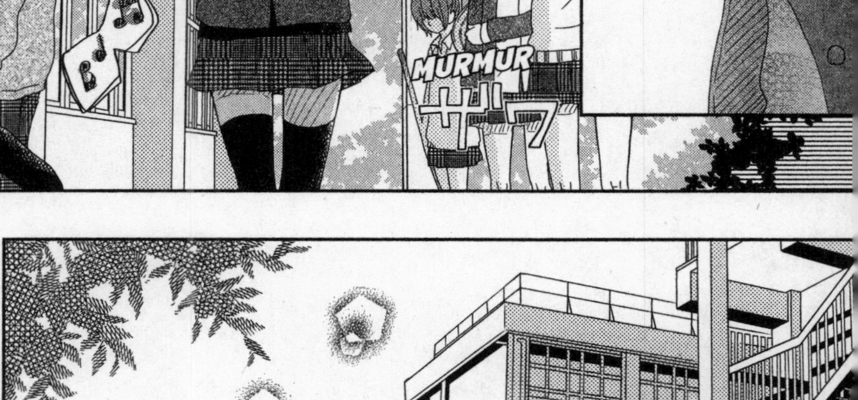

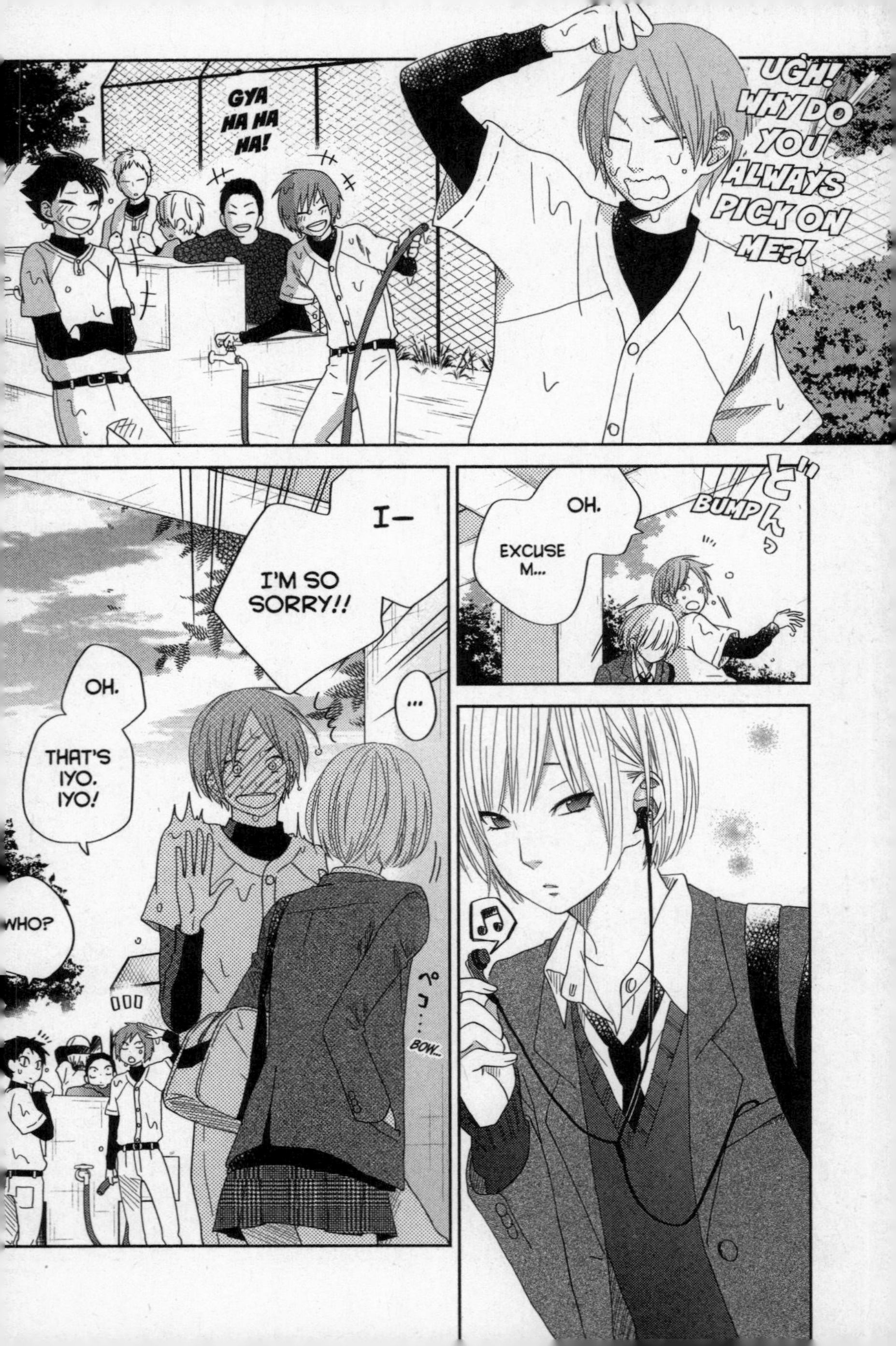
UGH! WHY DO YOU ALWAYS PICK ON ME?!
GYA HA HA HA!
BUMP
OH.
EXCUSE M...
I—
I'M SO SORRY!!
...
BOW...
OH.
THAT'S IYO. IYO!
WHO?

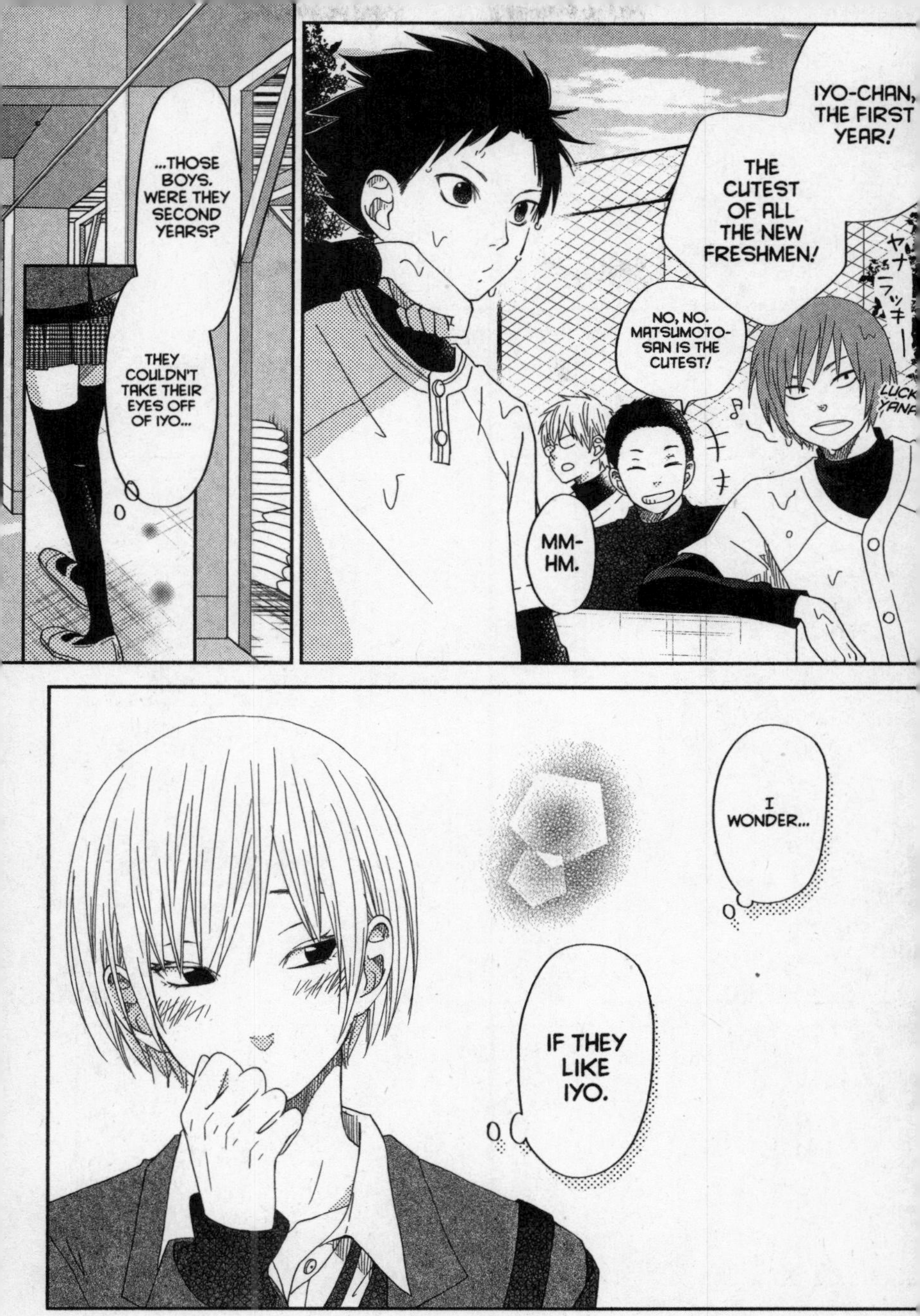
IYO-CHAN, THE FIRST YEAR!
THE CUTEST OF ALL THE NEW FRESHMEN!
ヤナラッキー
NO, NO. MATSUMOTO-SAN IS THE CUTEST!
MM-HM.
...THOSE BOYS. WERE THEY SECOND YEARS?
THEY COULDN'T TAKE THEIR EYES OFF OF IYO...
I WONDER...
IF THEY LIKE IYO.

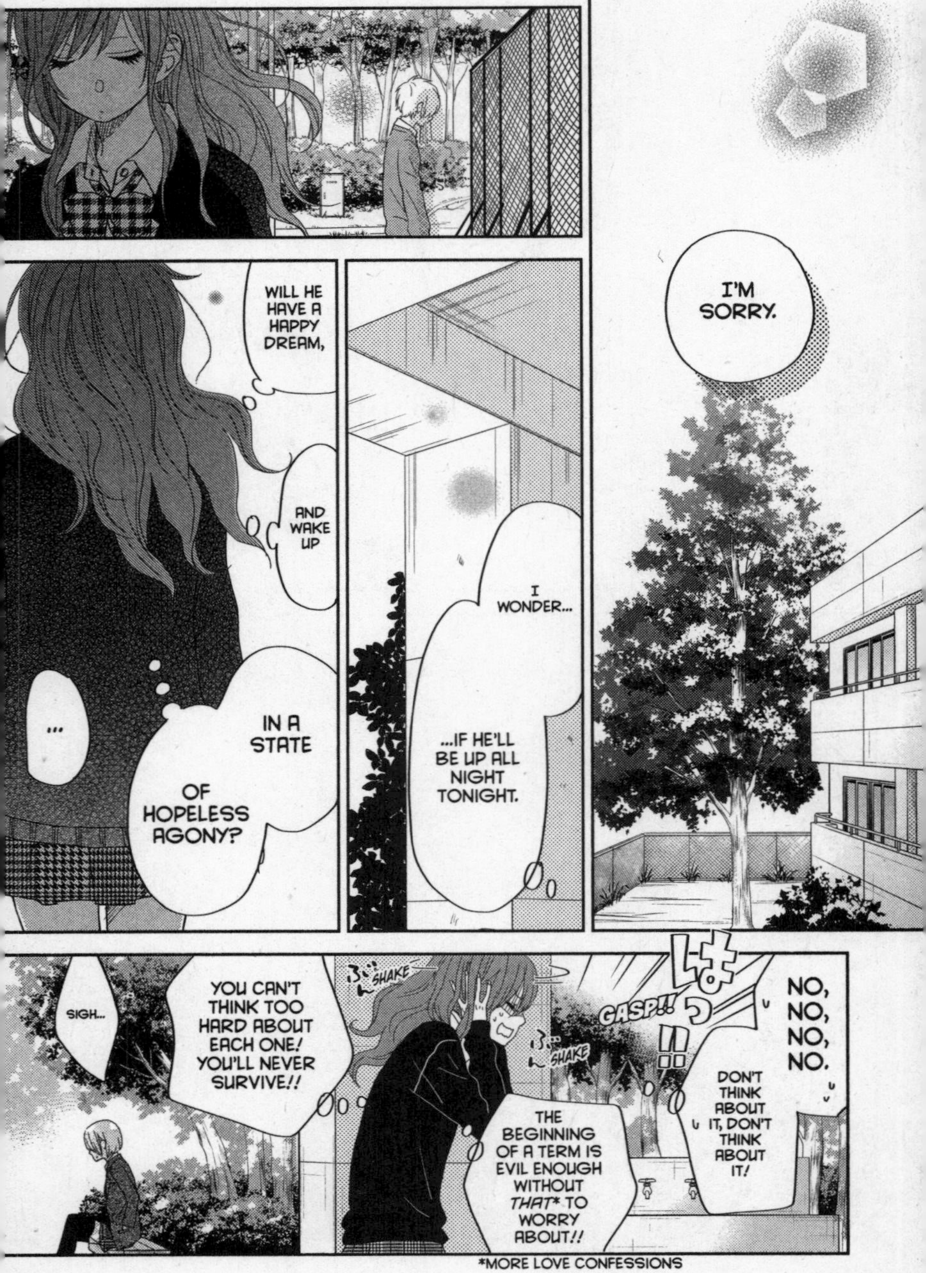
I'M SORRY.
I WONDER...
...IF HE'LL BE UP ALL NIGHT TONIGHT.
WILL HE HAVE A HAPPY DREAM,
AND WAKE UP
IN A STATE OF HOPELESS AGONY?
...
GASP!!
NO, NO, NO, NO.
DON'T THINK ABOUT IT, DON'T THINK ABOUT IT!
THE BEGINNING OF A TERM IS EVIL ENOUGH WITHOUT *THAT** TO WORRY ABOUT!!
SHAKE
SHAKE
YOU CAN'T THINK TOO HARD ABOUT EACH ONE! YOU'LL NEVER SURVIVE!!
SIGH...

*MORE LOVE CONFESSIONS

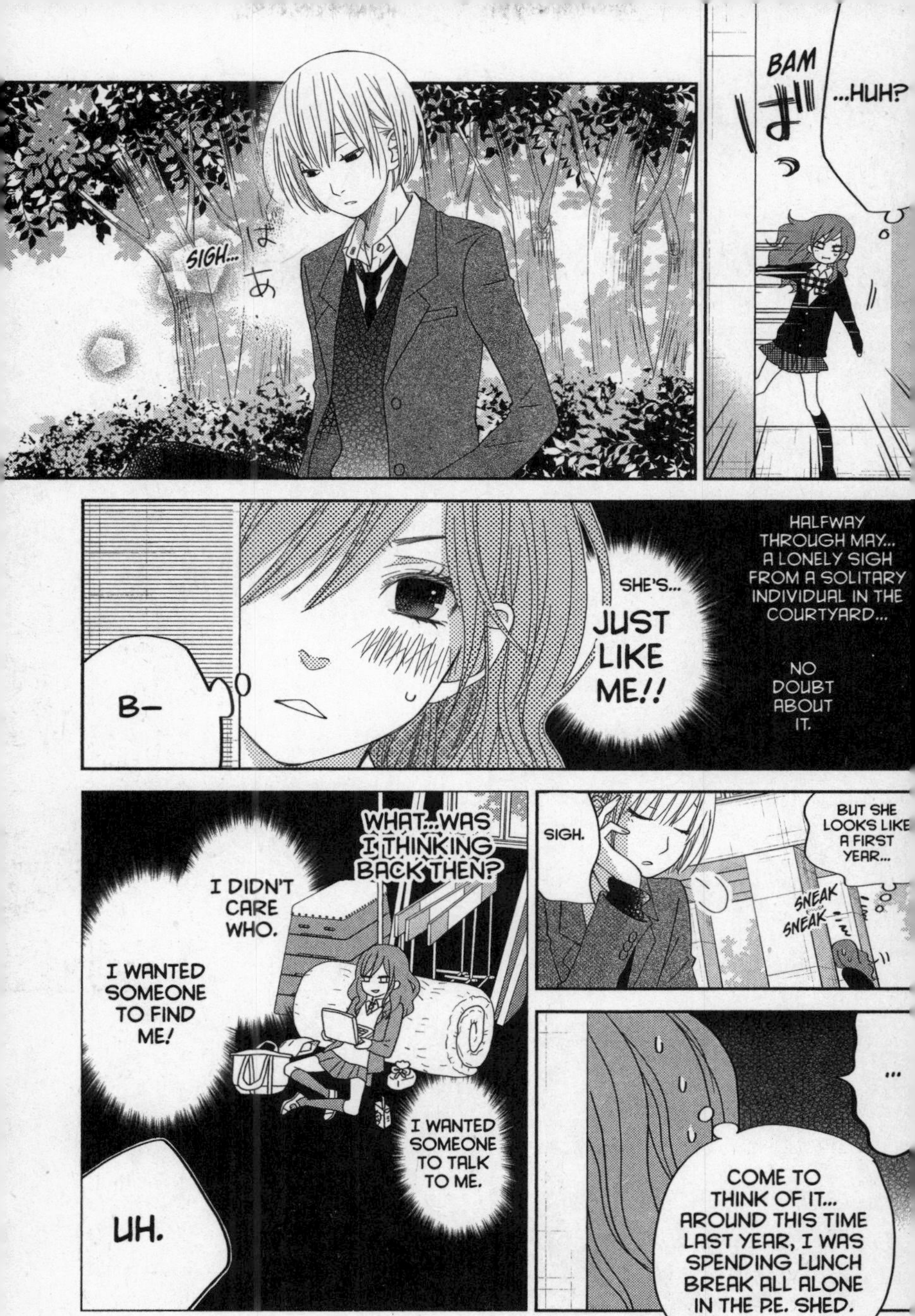
BAM
...HUH?
SIGH...
HALFWAY THROUGH MAY... A LONELY SIGH FROM A SOLITARY INDIVIDUAL IN THE COURTYARD...
NO DOUBT ABOUT IT.
SHE'S...
JUST LIKE ME!!
B-
BUT SHE LOOKS LIKE A FIRST YEAR...
SNEAK SNEAK
SIGH.
...
COME TO THINK OF IT... AROUND THIS TIME LAST YEAR, I WAS SPENDING LUNCH BREAK ALL ALONE IN THE P.E. SHED.
WHAT...WAS I THINKING BACK THEN?
I DIDN'T CARE WHO.
I WANTED SOMEONE TO FIND ME!
I WANTED SOMEONE TO TALK TO ME.
UH.

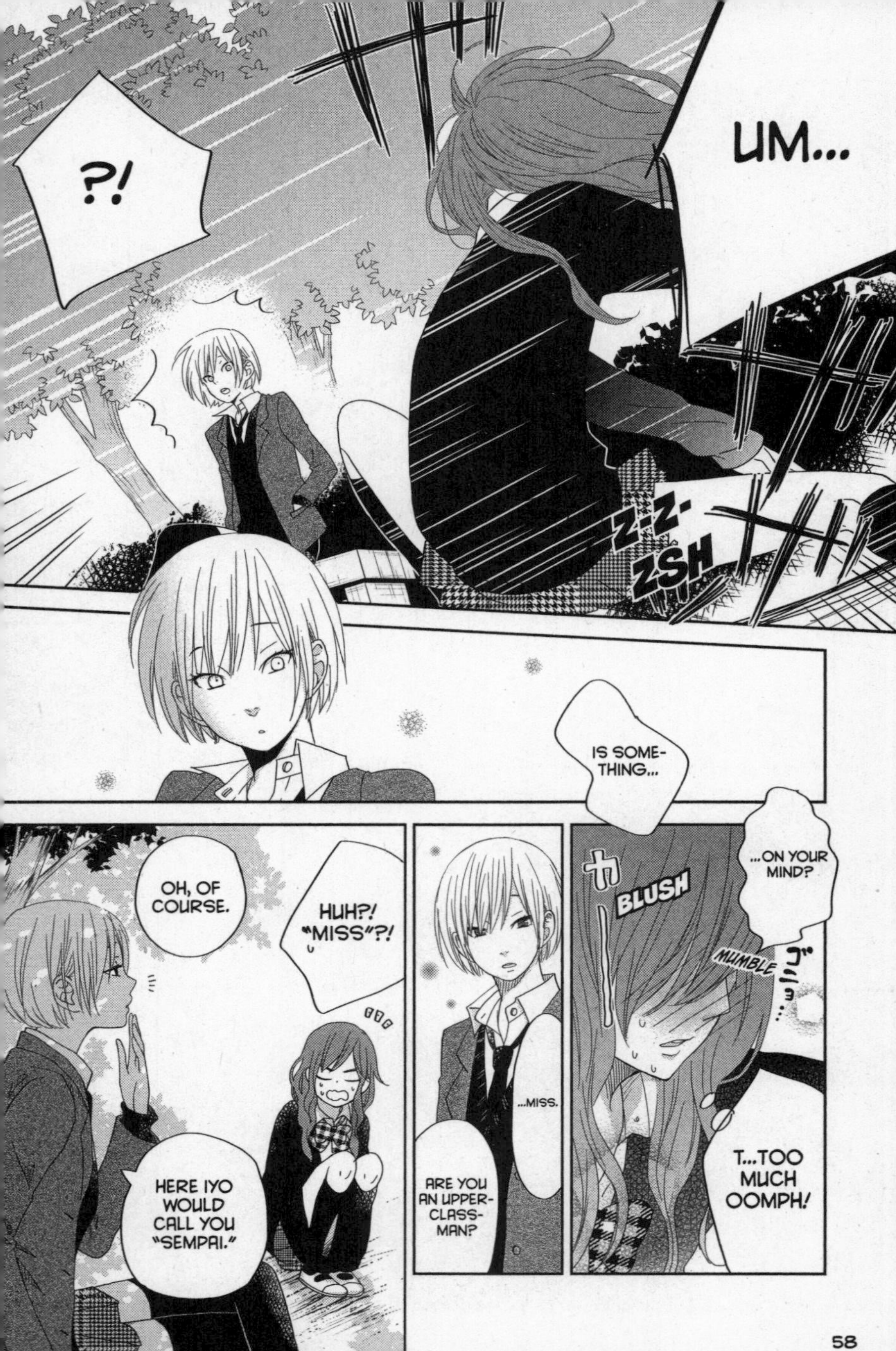
UM...
?!
Z-Z-
ZSH
IS SOME-THING...
...ON YOUR MIND?
BLUSH
MUMBLE
T...TOO MUCH OOMPH!
...MISS.
ARE YOU AN UPPER-CLASS-MAN?
HUH?! "MISS"?!
OH, OF COURSE.
HERE IYO WOULD CALL YOU "SEMPAI."

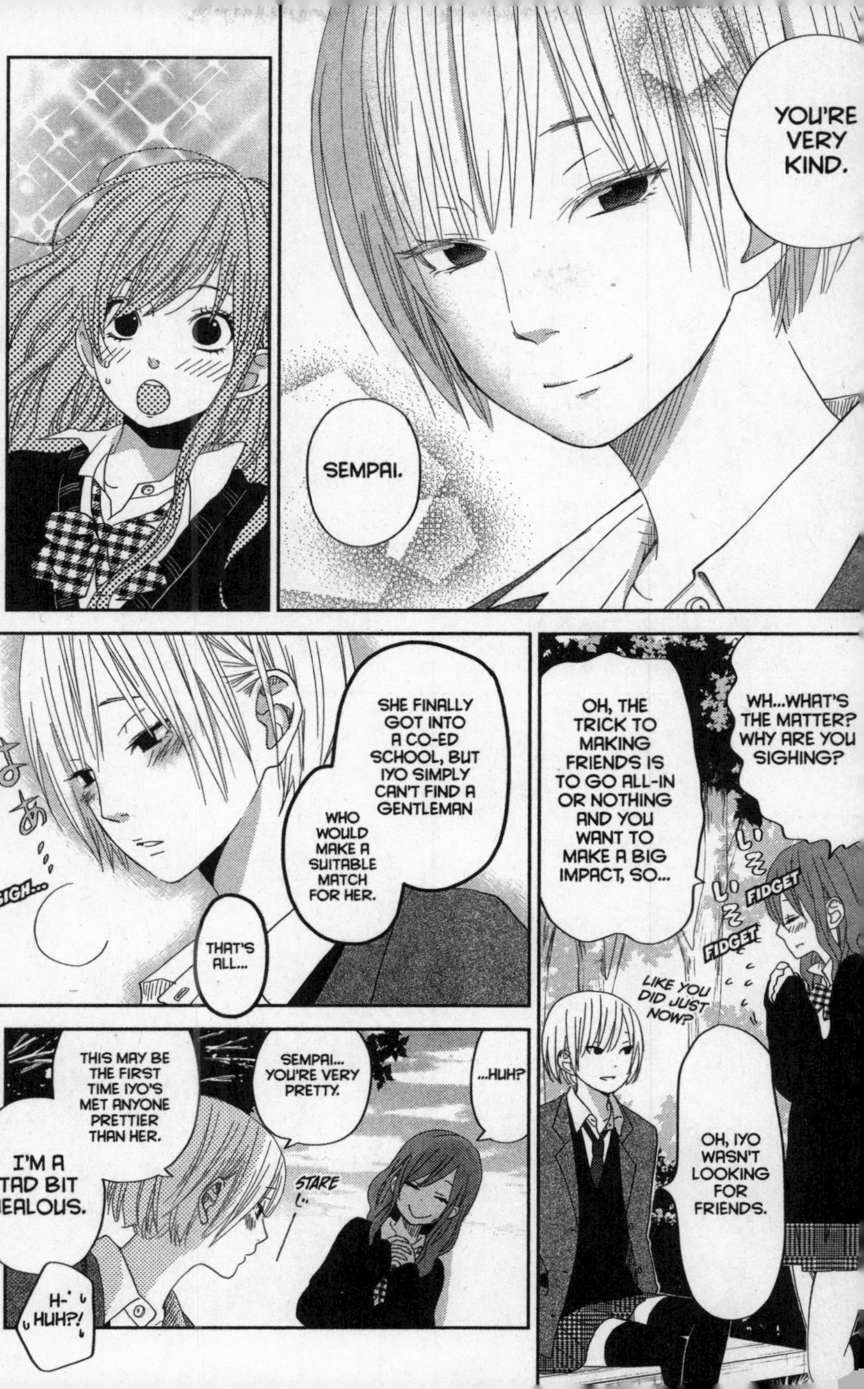
YOU'RE VERY KIND.
SEMPAI.
WH...WHAT'S THE MATTER? WHY ARE YOU SIGHING?
OH, THE TRICK TO MAKING FRIENDS IS TO GO ALL-IN OR NOTHING AND YOU WANT TO MAKE A BIG IMPACT, SO...
FIDGET
FIDGET
LIKE YOU DID JUST NOW?
OH, IYO WASN'T LOOKING FOR FRIENDS.
SHE FINALLY GOT INTO A CO-ED SCHOOL, BUT IYO SIMPLY CAN'T FIND A GENTLEMAN
WHO WOULD MAKE A SUITABLE MATCH FOR HER.
はあ
SIGH...
THAT'S ALL...
...HUH?
SEMPAI... YOU'RE VERY PRETTY.
STARE
THIS MAY BE THE FIRST TIME IYO'S MET ANYONE PRETTIER THAN HER.
I'M A TAD BIT JEALOUS.
H-HUH?!

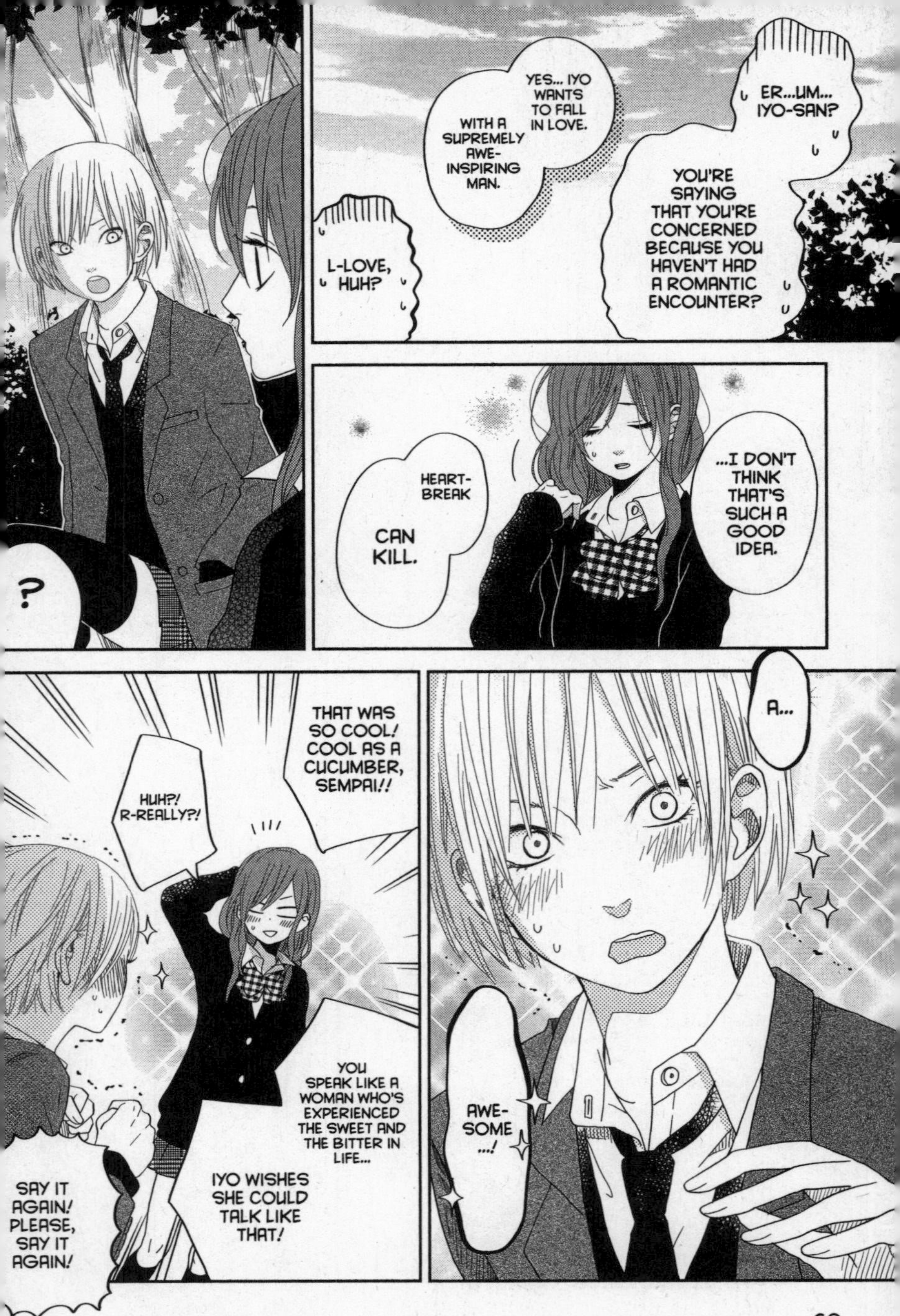
ER...UM... IYO-SAN?
YOU'RE SAYING THAT YOU'RE CONCERNED BECAUSE YOU HAVEN'T HAD A ROMANTIC ENCOUNTER?
YES... IYO WANTS TO FALL IN LOVE.
WITH A SUPREMELY AWE-INSPIRING MAN.
L-LOVE, HUH?
...I DON'T THINK THAT'S SUCH A GOOD IDEA.
HEART-BREAK
CAN KILL.
?
A...
AWE-SOME ...!
THAT WAS SO COOL! COOL AS A CUCUMBER, SEMPAI!!
HUH?! R-REALLY?!
YOU SPEAK LIKE A WOMAN WHO'S EXPERIENCED THE SWEET AND THE BITTER IN LIFE...
IYO WISHES SHE COULD TALK LIKE THAT!
SAY IT AGAIN! PLEASE, SAY IT AGAIN!

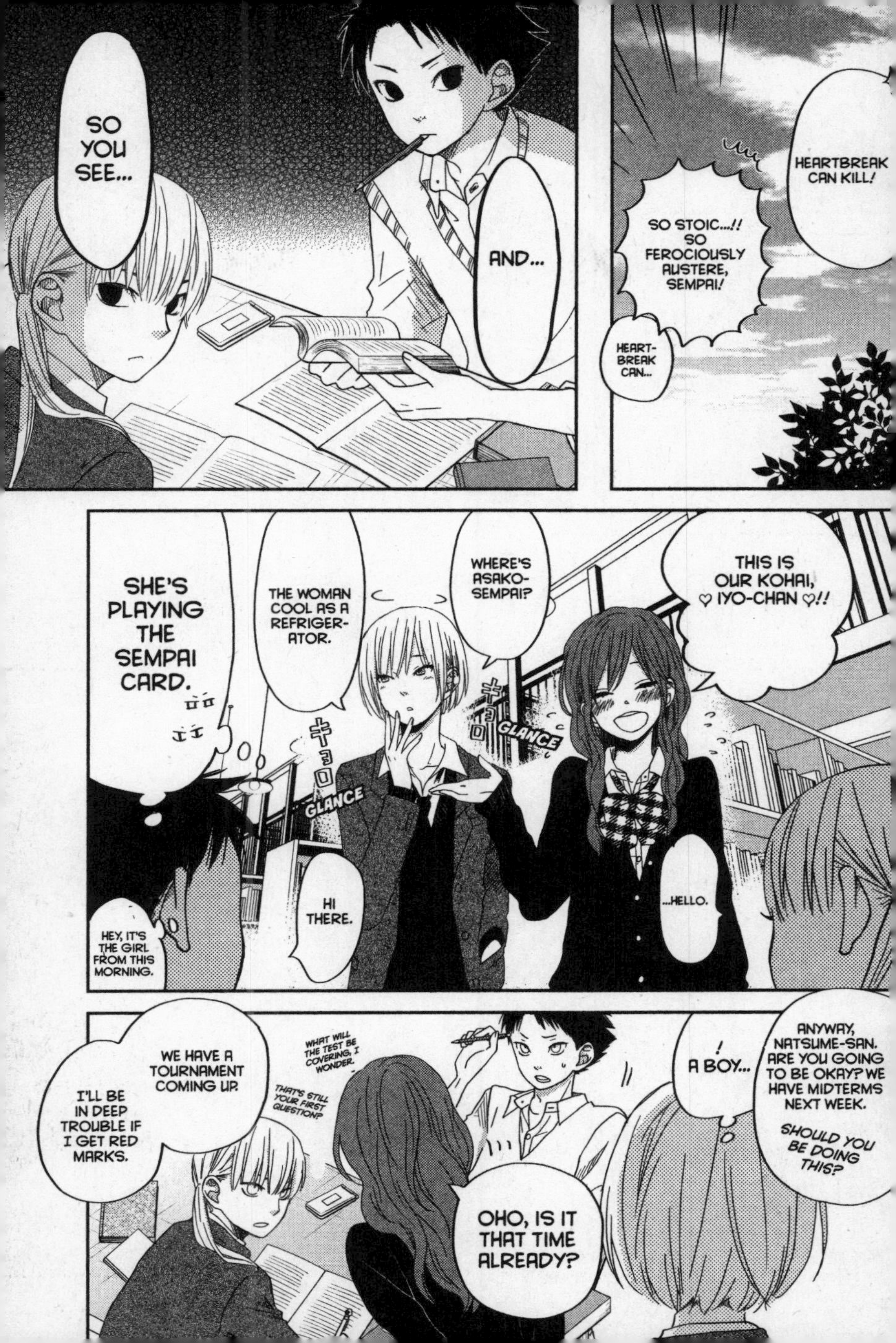
HEARTBREAK CAN KILL!
SO STOIC...!! SO FEROCIOUSLY AUSTERE, SEMPAI!
HEART-BREAK CAN...
AND...
SO YOU SEE...
THIS IS OUR KOHAI, ♡ IYO-CHAN ♡!!
WHERE'S ASAKO-SEMPAI?
キョロ
GLANCE
THE WOMAN COOL AS A REFRIGERATOR.
SHE'S PLAYING THE SEMPAI CARD.
キョロ
GLANCE
...HELLO.
HI THERE.
HEY, IT'S THE GIRL FROM THIS MORNING.
ANYWAY, NATSUME-SAN. ARE YOU GOING TO BE OKAY? WE HAVE MIDTERMS NEXT WEEK.
SHOULD YOU BE DOING THIS?
!
A BOY...
WHAT WILL THE TEST BE COVERING, I WONDER.
THAT'S STILL YOUR FIRST QUESTION?
WE HAVE A TOURNAMENT COMING UP.
I'LL BE IN DEEP TROUBLE IF I GET RED MARKS.
OHO, IS IT THAT TIME ALREADY?

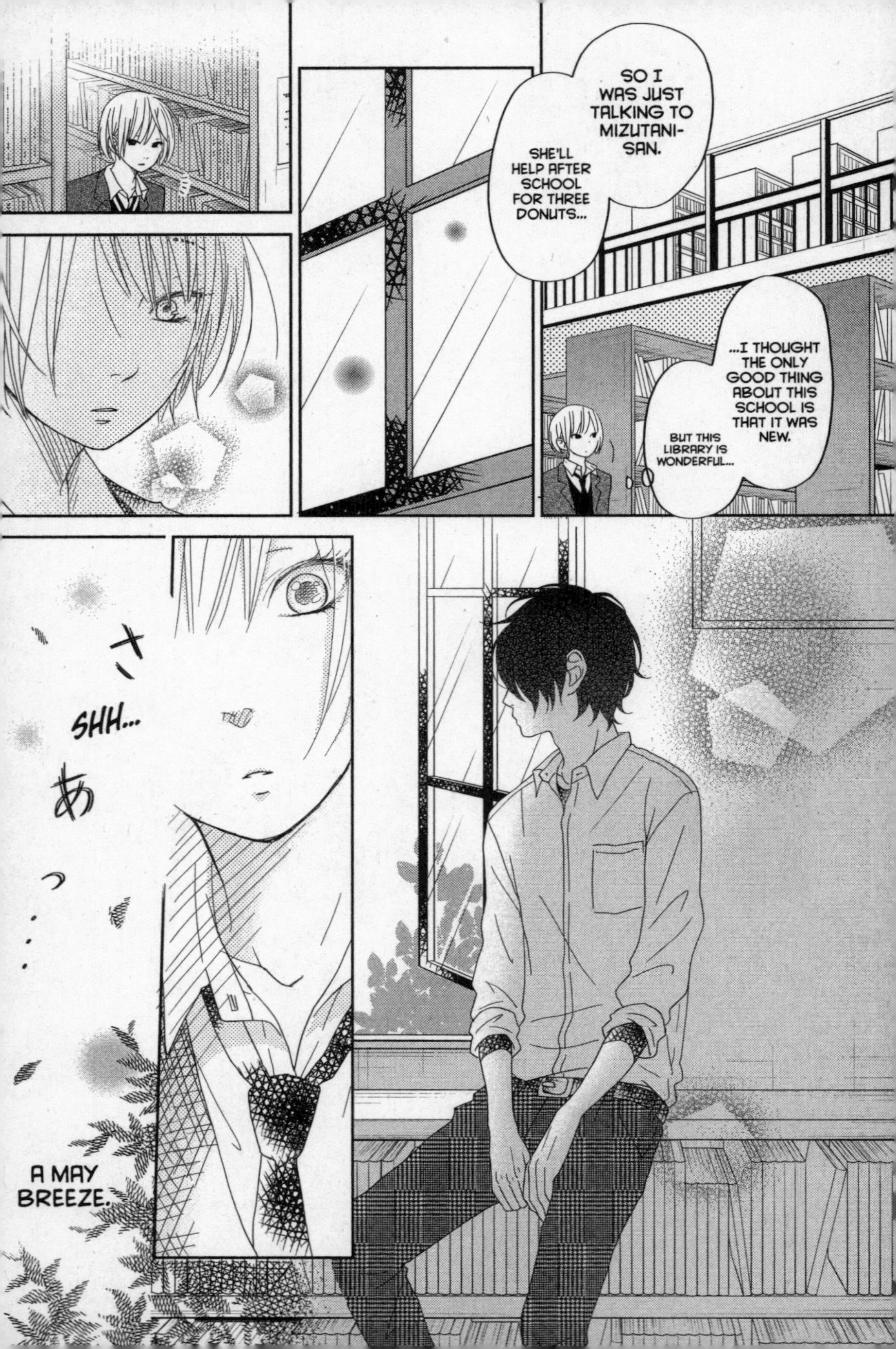
SO I WAS JUST TALKING TO MIZUTANI-SAN.
SHE'LL HELP AFTER SCHOOL FOR THREE DONUTS...
...I THOUGHT THE ONLY GOOD THING ABOUT THIS SCHOOL IS THAT IT WAS NEW.
BUT THIS LIBRARY IS WONDERFUL...
さぁっ…
SHH...
A MAY BREEZE.

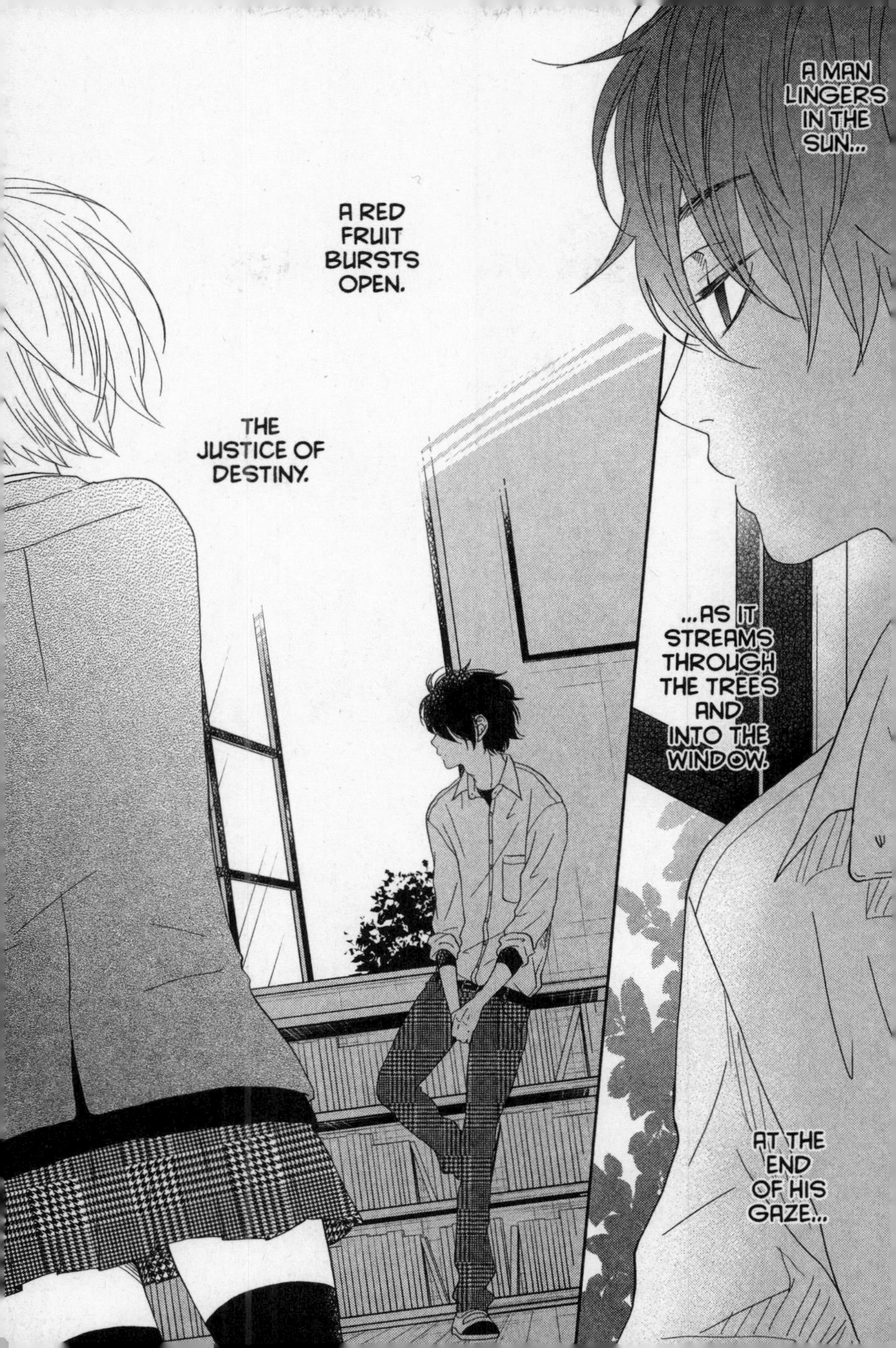
A MAN LINGERS IN THE SUN...
...AS IT STREAMS THROUGH THE TREES AND INTO THE WINDOW.
AT THE END OF HIS GAZE...
A RED FRUIT BURSTS OPEN.
THE JUSTICE OF DESTINY.

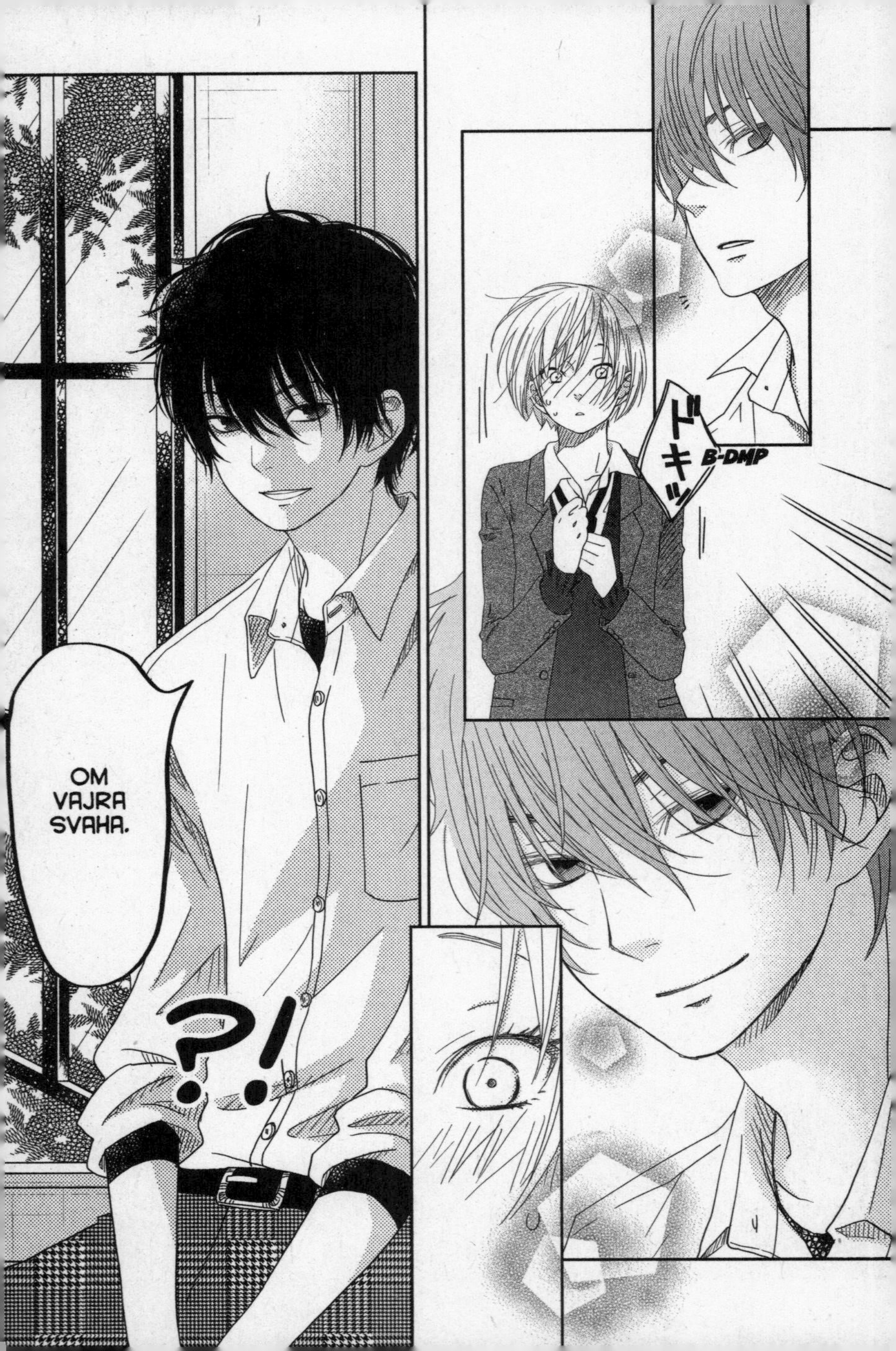

ドキッ
B-DMP
OM VAJRA SVAHA.
?!

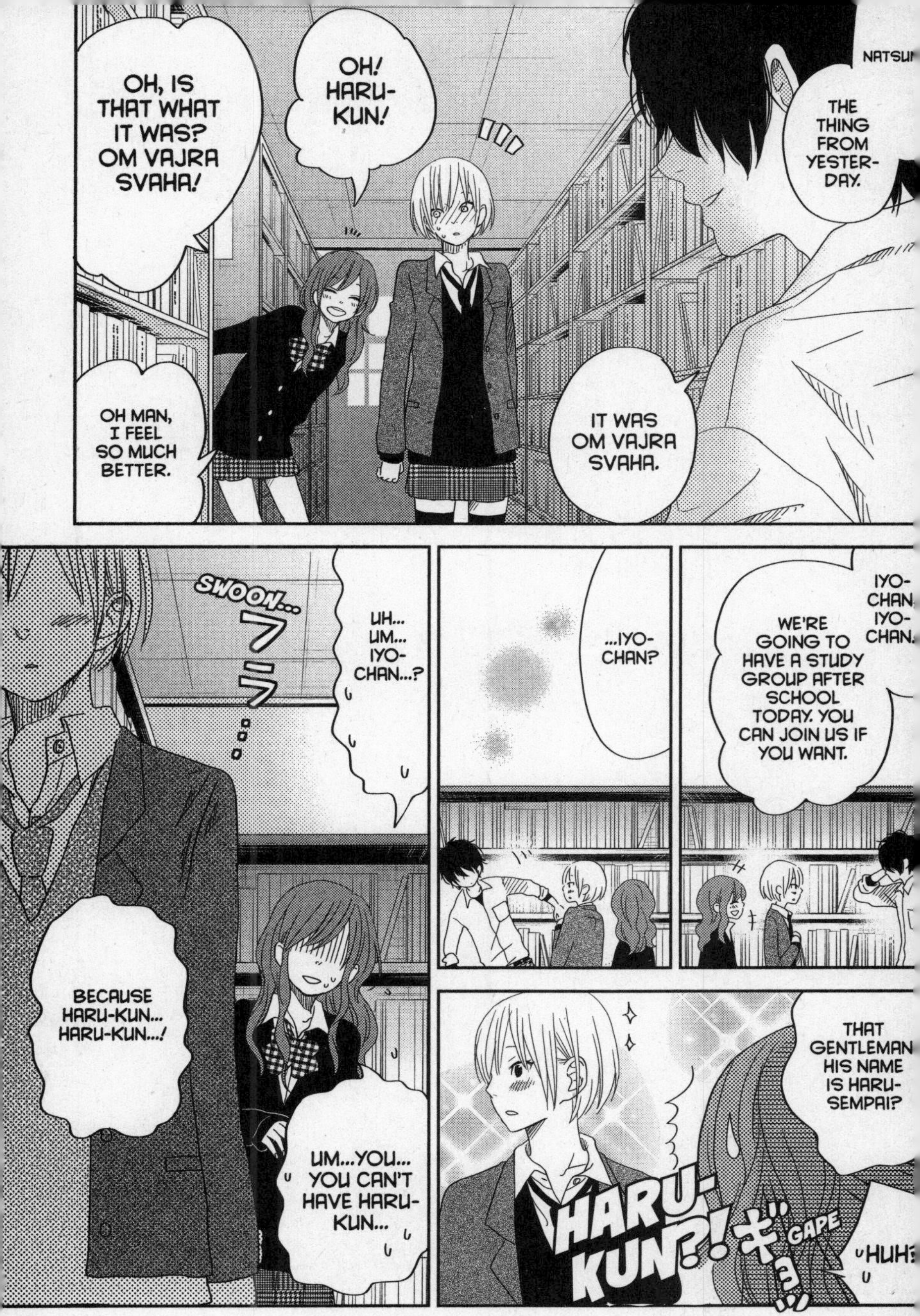
NATSU
THE THING FROM YESTERDAY.
IT WAS OM VAJRA SVAHA.
OH! HARU-KUN!
OH, IS THAT WHAT IT WAS? OM VAJRA SVAHA!
OH MAN, I FEEL SO MUCH BETTER.
IYO-CHAN, IYO-CHAN.
WE'RE GOING TO HAVE A STUDY GROUP AFTER SCHOOL TODAY. YOU CAN JOIN US IF YOU WANT.
...IYO-CHAN?
THAT GENTLEMAN HIS NAME IS HARU-SEMPAI?
HUH?
HARU-KUN?!
ギョッ
GAPE
UH... UM... IYO-CHAN...?
SWOON...
フラ...
BECAUSE HARU-KUN... HARU-KUN...!
UM...YOU... YOU CAN'T HAVE HARU-KUN...

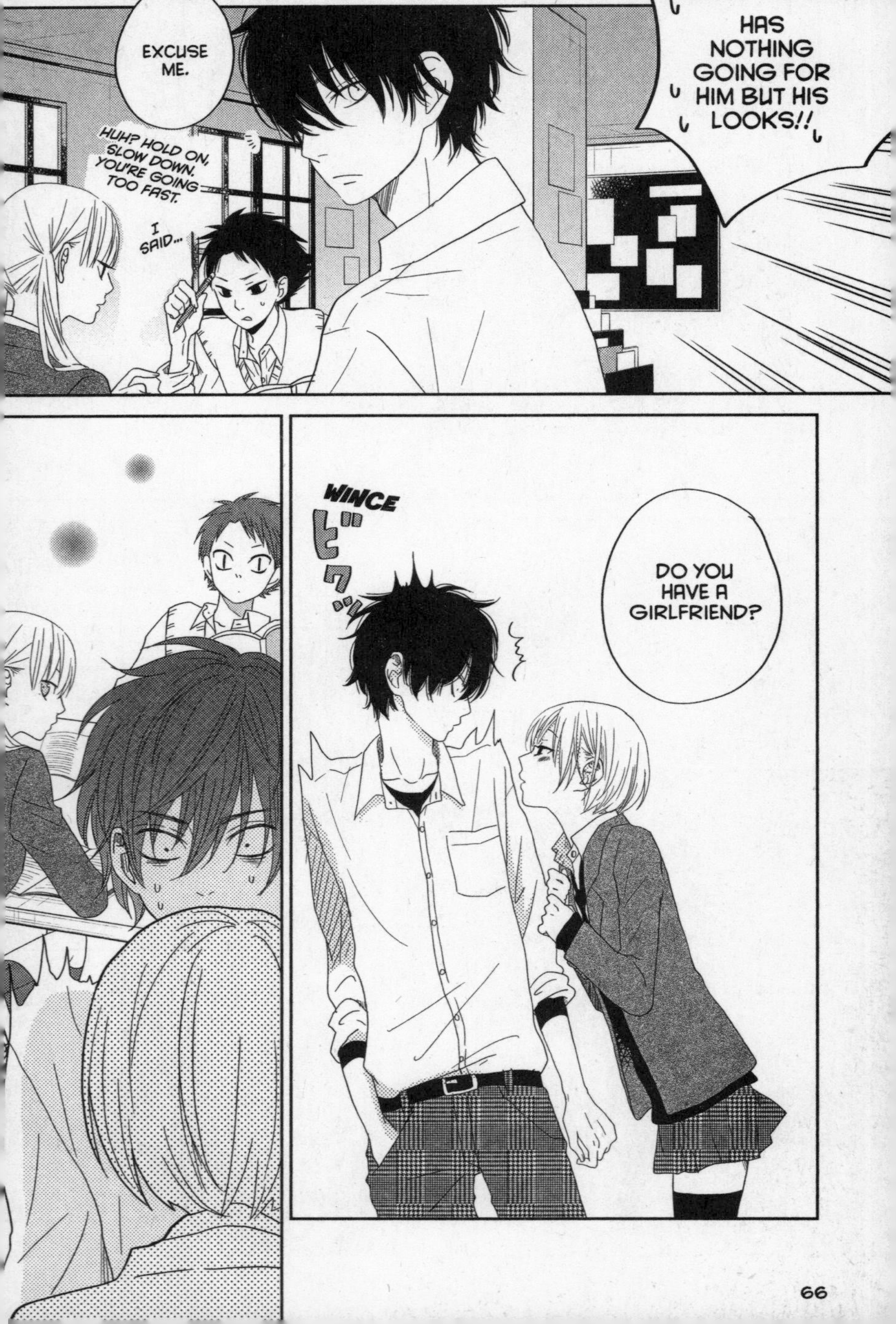
HAS NOTHING GOING FOR HIM BUT HIS LOOKS!!
EXCUSE ME.
HUH? HOLD ON, SLOW DOWN. YOU'RE GOING TOO FAST.
I SAID...
WINCE
ビクッ
DO YOU HAVE A GIRLFRIEND?

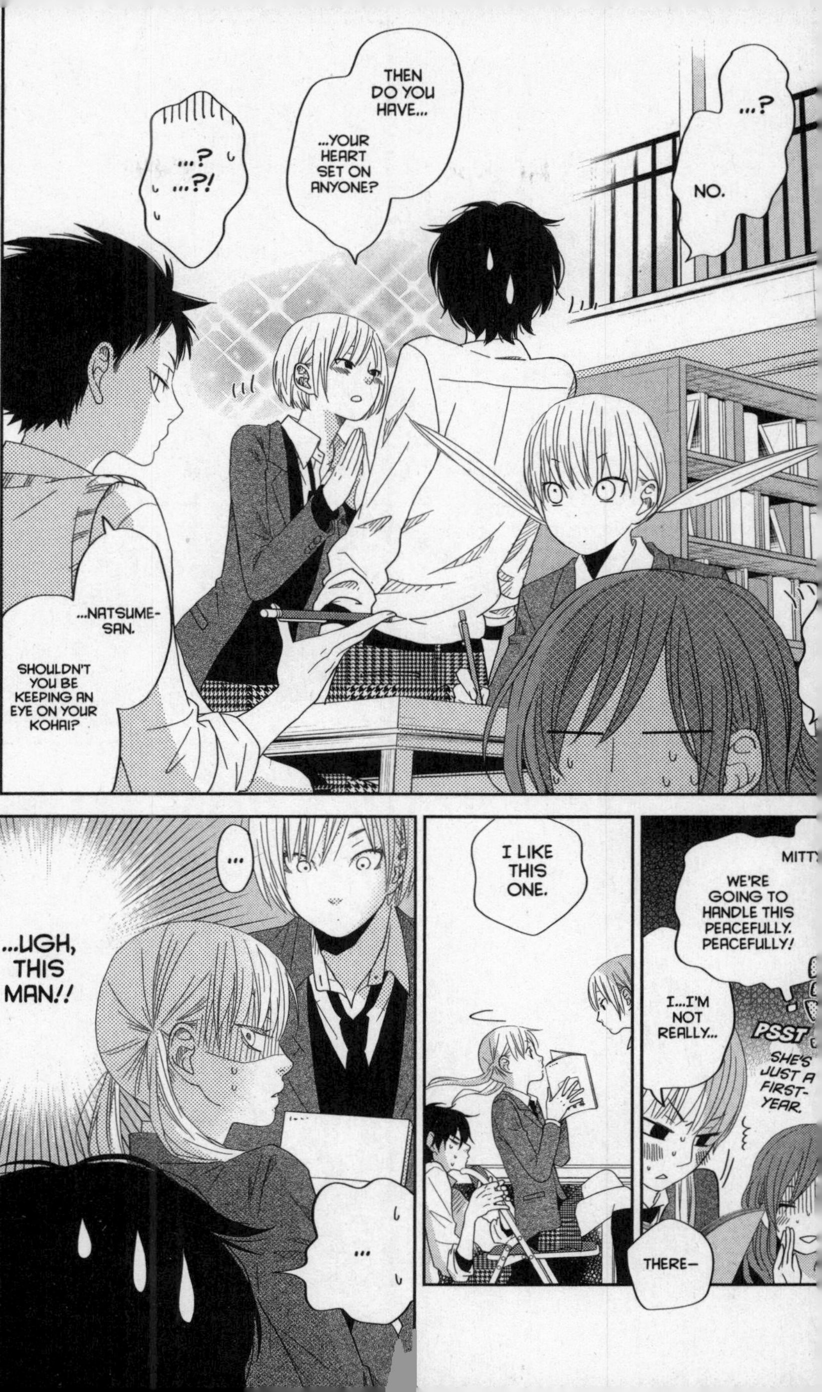
...?
NO.
THEN DO YOU HAVE...
...YOUR HEART SET ON ANYONE?
...?
...?!
...NATSUME-SAN.
SHOULDN'T YOU BE KEEPING AN EYE ON YOUR KOHAI?
MITT
WE'RE GOING TO HANDLE THIS PEACEFULLY. PEACEFULLY!
PSST
SHE'S JUST A FIRST-YEAR.
I...I'M NOT REALLY...
THERE—
I LIKE THIS ONE.
...
...UGH, THIS MAN!!
...

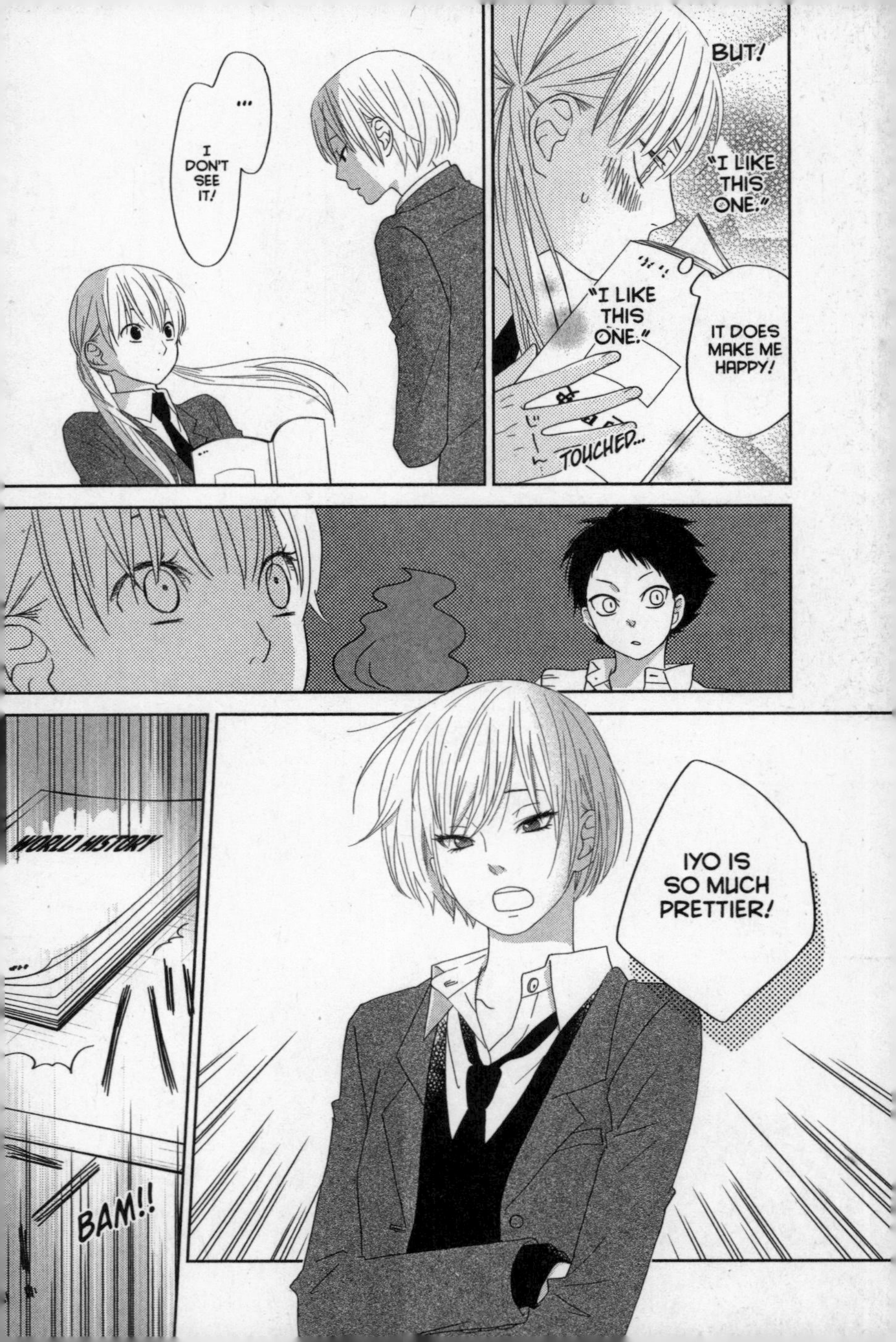
BUT!
"I LIKE THIS ONE."
"I LIKE THIS ONE."
IT DOES MAKE ME HAPPY!
TOUCHED...
...
I DON'T SEE IT!
IYO IS SO MUCH PRETTIER!
WORLD HISTORY
BAM!!

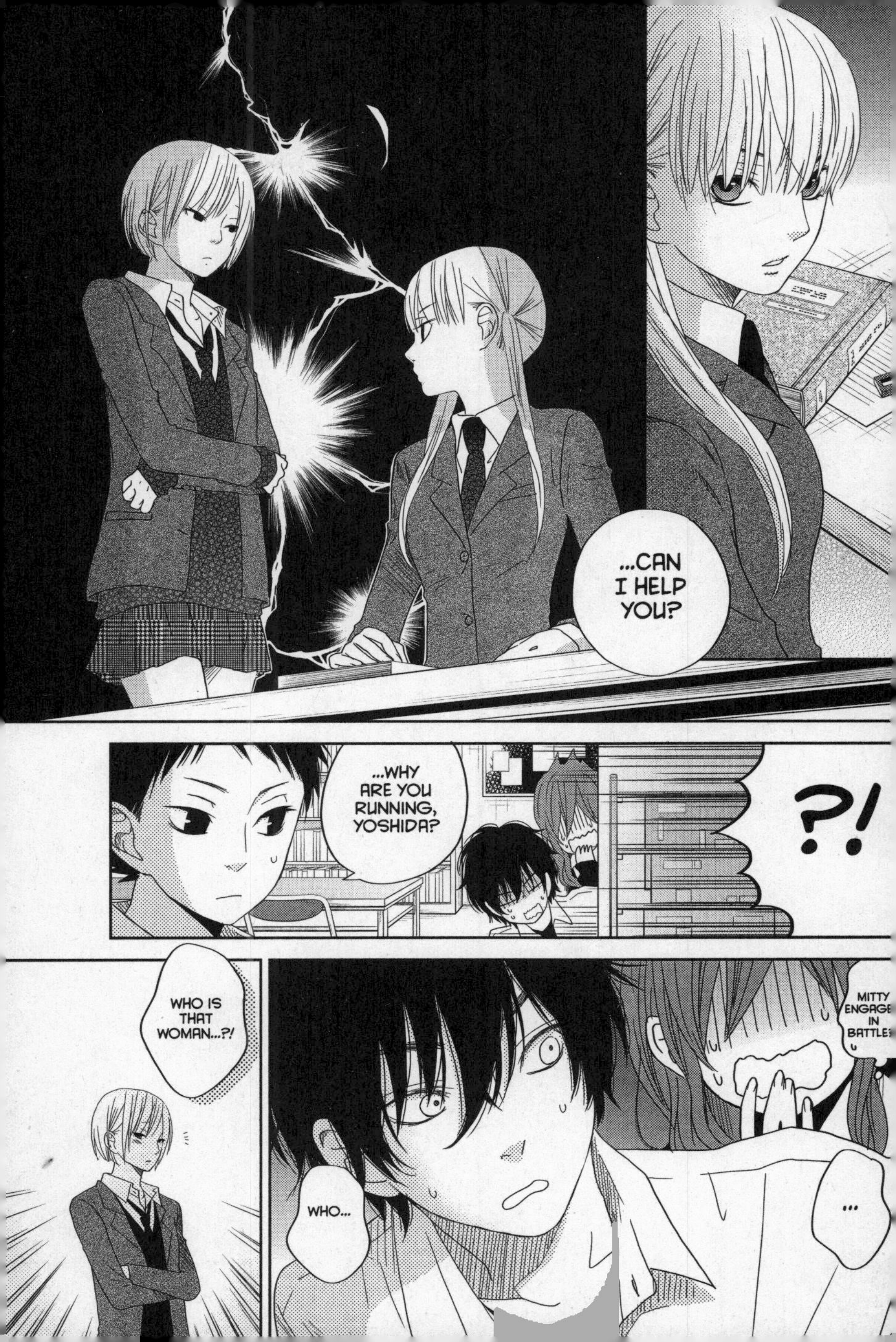
...CAN I HELP YOU?
?!
...WHY ARE YOU RUNNING, YOSHIDA?
MITTY ENGAGE IN BATTLE
...
WHO...
WHO IS THAT WOMAN...?!

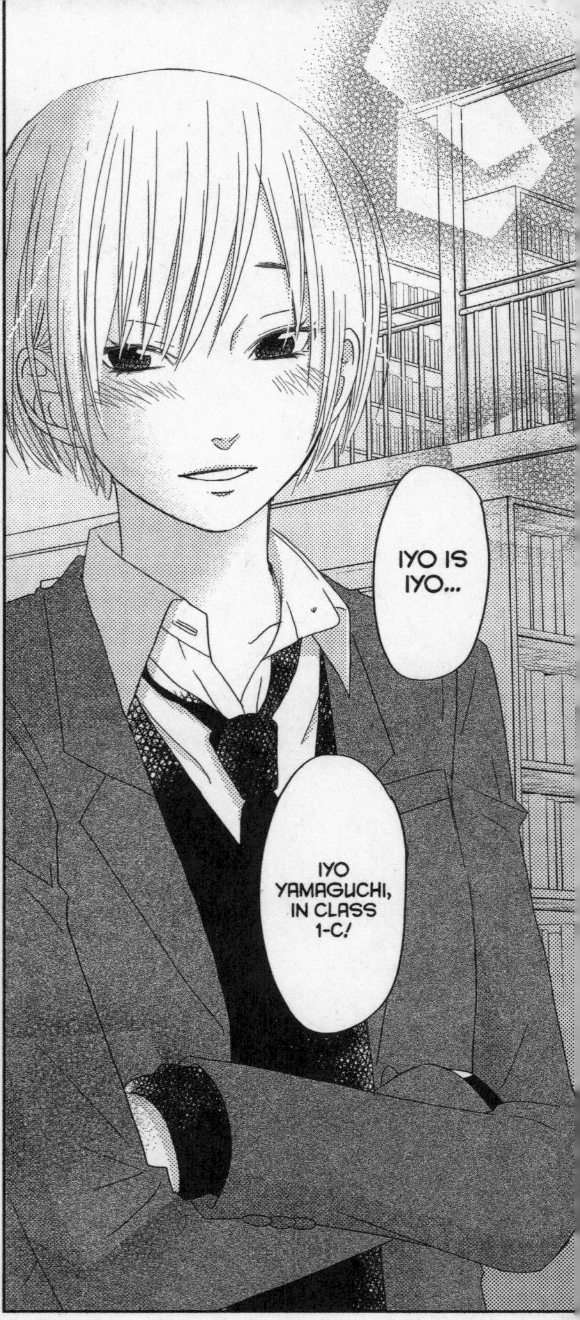
IYO IS IYO...
IYO YAMAGUCHI, IN CLASS 1-C!

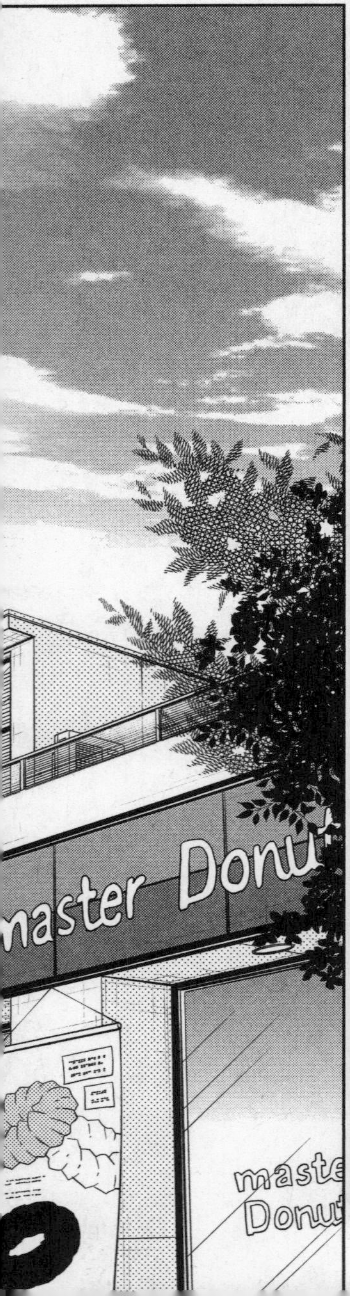
master Donu

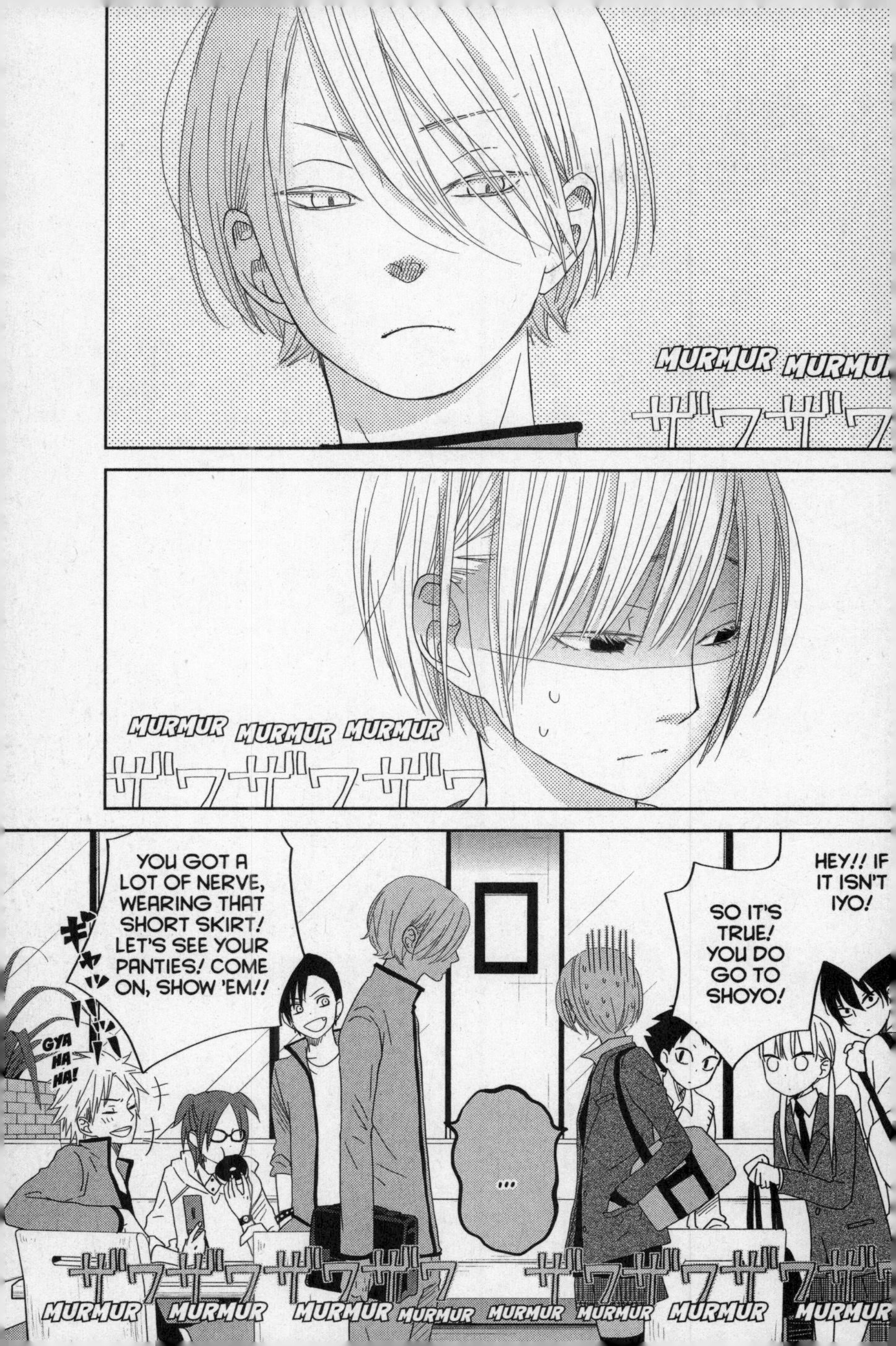
MURMUR MURMU
ザワザワ
MURMUR MURMUR MURMUR
ザワザワザワ
HEY!! IF IT ISN'T IYO!
SO IT'S TRUE! YOU DO GO TO SHOYO!
...
YOU GOT A LOT OF NERVE, WEARING THAT SHORT SKIRT! LET'S SEE YOUR PANTIES! COME ON, SHOW 'EM!!
ギャッ!!
GYA HA HA!
ザワザワザワザワザワザワザワ
MURMUR MURMUR MURMUR MURMUR MURMUR MURMUR MURMUR MURMUR

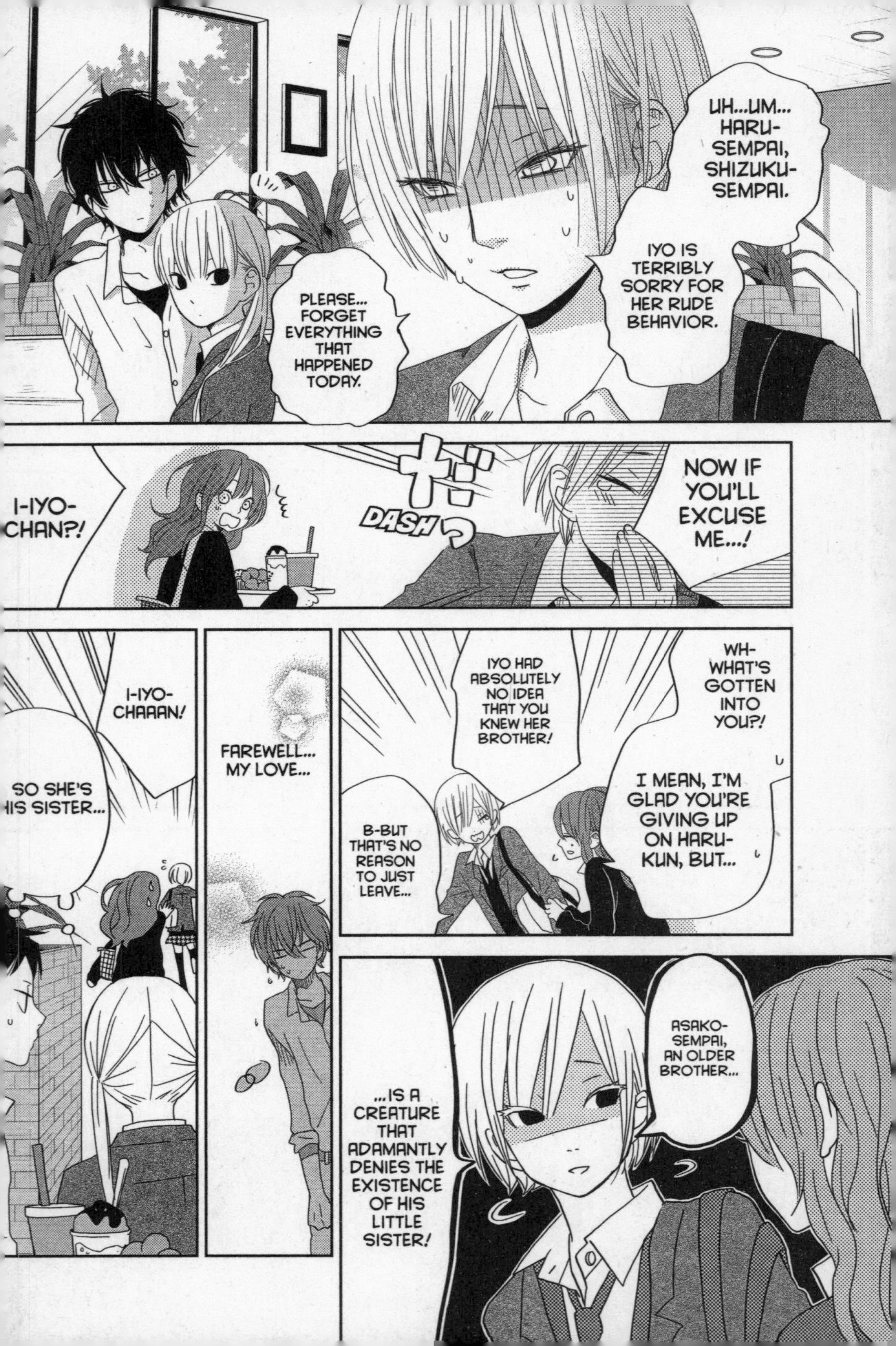

UH...UM... HARU-SEMPAI, SHIZUKU-SEMPAI.
IYO IS TERRIBLY SORRY FOR HER RUDE BEHAVIOR.
PLEASE... FORGET EVERYTHING THAT HAPPENED TODAY.
NOW IF YOU'LL EXCUSE ME...!
DASH
I-IYO-CHAN?!
WH-WHAT'S GOTTEN INTO YOU?!
IYO HAD ABSOLUTELY NO IDEA THAT YOU KNEW HER BROTHER!
I MEAN, I'M GLAD YOU'RE GIVING UP ON HARU-KUN, BUT...
B-BUT THAT'S NO REASON TO JUST LEAVE...
ASAKO-SEMPAI, AN OLDER BROTHER...
...IS A CREATURE THAT ADAMANTLY DENIES THE EXISTENCE OF HIS LITTLE SISTER!
FAREWELL... MY LOVE...
I-IYO-CHAAAN!
SO SHE'S HIS SISTER...

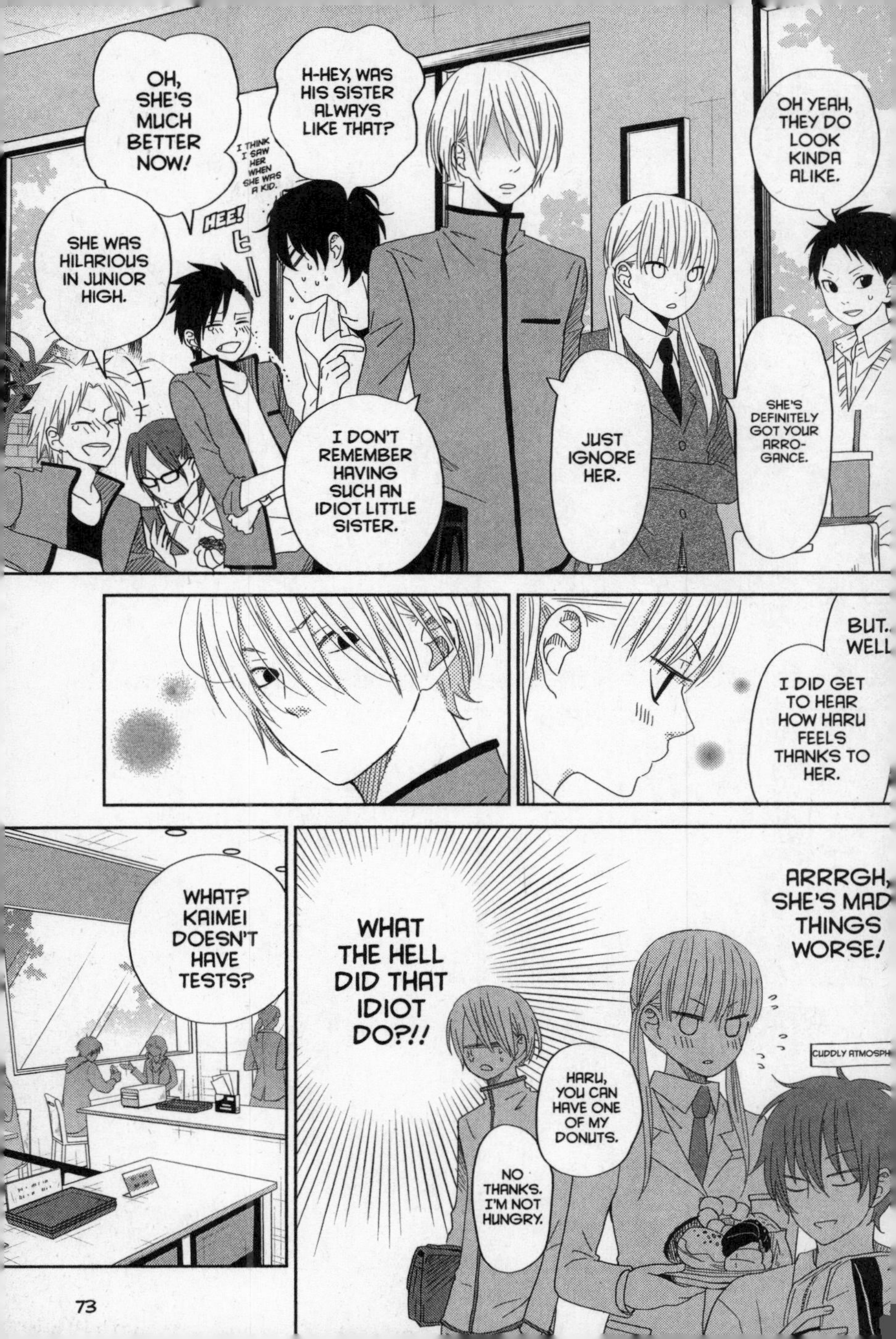
OH YEAH, THEY DO LOOK KINDA ALIKE.
SHE'S DEFINITELY GOT YOUR ARROGANCE.
JUST IGNORE HER.
I DON'T REMEMBER HAVING SUCH AN IDIOT LITTLE SISTER.
H-HEY, WAS HIS SISTER ALWAYS LIKE THAT?
I THINK I SAW HER WHEN SHE WAS A KID.
OH, SHE'S MUCH BETTER NOW!
HEE!
SHE WAS HILARIOUS IN JUNIOR HIGH.
BUT.. WELL
I DID GET TO HEAR HOW HARU FEELS THANKS TO HER.
ARRRGH, SHE'S MAD THINGS WORSE!
WHAT THE HELL DID THAT IDIOT DO?!!
CUDDLY ATMOSPH
HARU, YOU CAN HAVE ONE OF MY DONUTS.
NO THANKS. I'M NOT HUNGRY.
WHAT? KAIMEI DOESN'T HAVE TESTS?

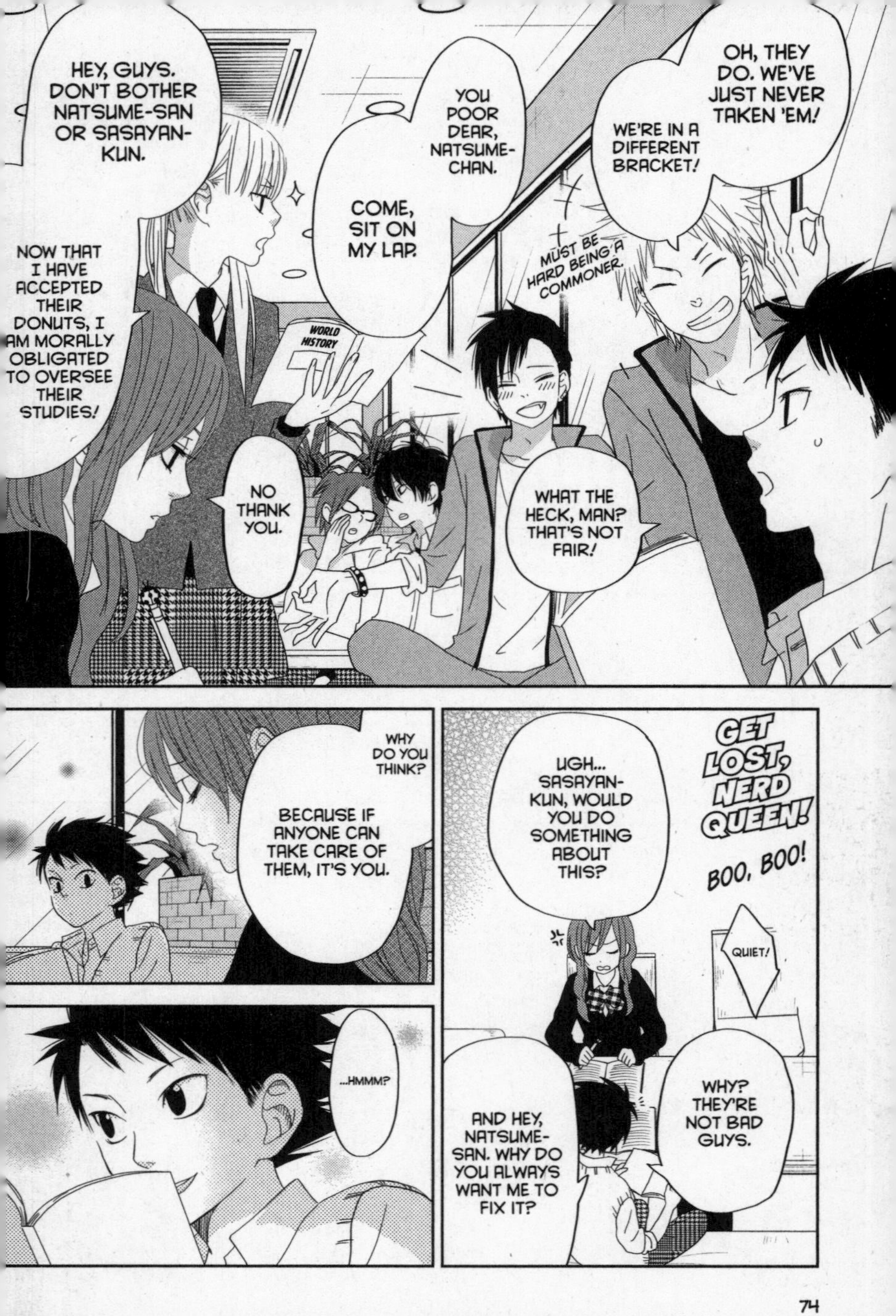
OH, THEY DO. WE'VE JUST NEVER TAKEN 'EM!
WE'RE IN A DIFFERENT BRACKET!
MUST BE HARD BEING A COMMONER.
YOU POOR DEAR, NATSUME-CHAN.
COME, SIT ON MY LAP.
NO THANK YOU.
WHAT THE HECK, MAN? THAT'S NOT FAIR!
HEY, GUYS. DON'T BOTHER NATSUME-SAN OR SASAYAN-KUN.
NOW THAT I HAVE ACCEPTED THEIR DONUTS, I AM MORALLY OBLIGATED TO OVERSEE THEIR STUDIES!
GET LOST, NERD QUEEN!
BOO, BOO!
UGH... SASAYAN-KUN, WOULD YOU DO SOMETHING ABOUT THIS?
QUIET!
WHY? THEY'RE NOT BAD GUYS.
AND HEY, NATSUME-SAN. WHY DO YOU ALWAYS WANT ME TO FIX IT?
WHY DO YOU THINK?
BECAUSE IF ANYONE CAN TAKE CARE OF THEM, IT'S YOU.
...HMMM?

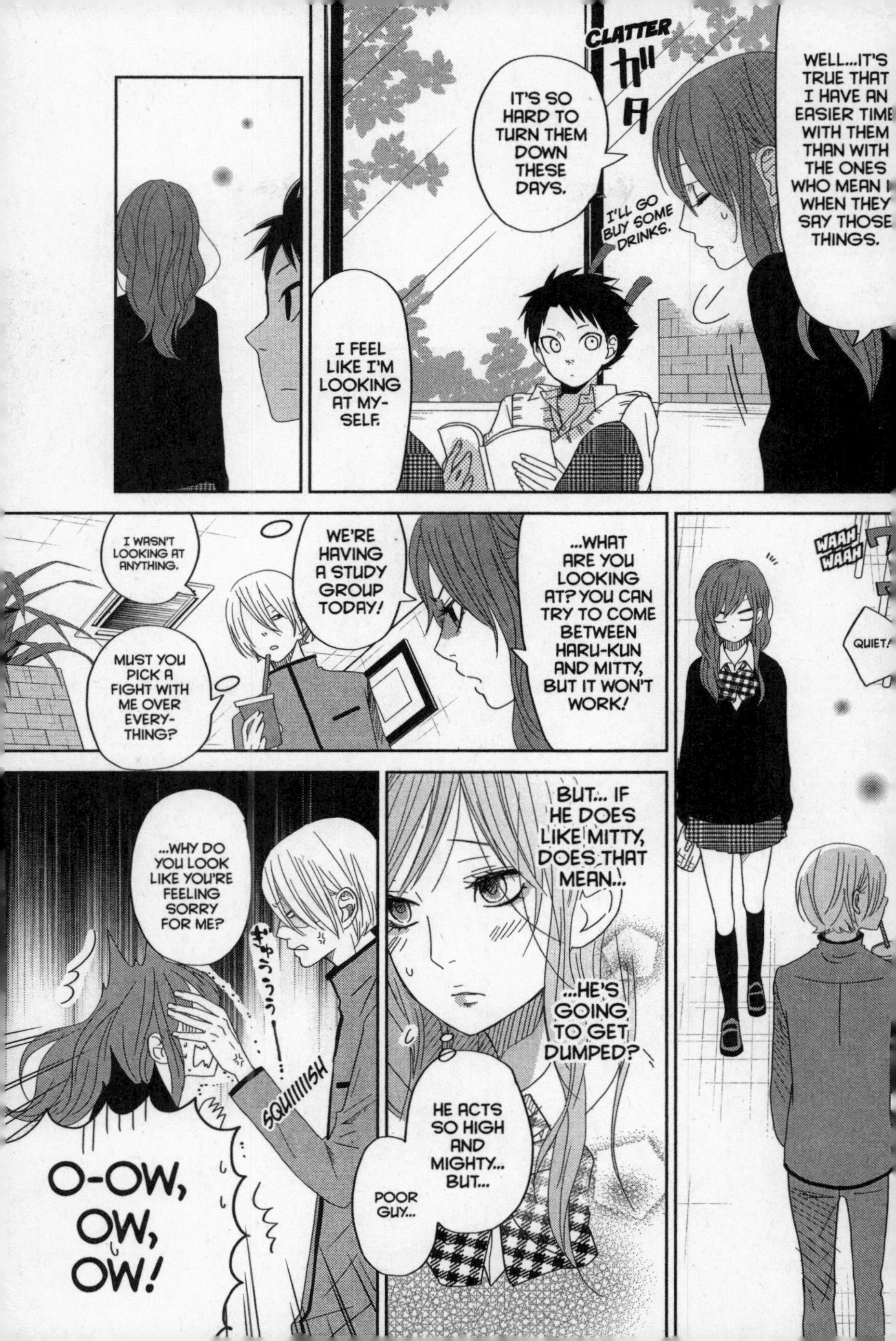
WELL...IT'S TRUE THAT I HAVE AN EASIER TIME WITH THEM THAN WITH THE ONES WHO MEAN I WHEN THEY SAY THOSE THINGS.
CLATTER
IT'S SO HARD TO TURN THEM DOWN THESE DAYS.
I'LL GO BUY SOME DRINKS.
I FEEL LIKE I'M LOOKING AT MY-SELF.
WAAH WAAH
QUIET!
...WHAT ARE YOU LOOKING AT? YOU CAN TRY TO COME BETWEEN HARU-KUN AND MITTY, BUT IT WON'T WORK!
WE'RE HAVING A STUDY GROUP TODAY!
I WASN'T LOOKING AT ANYTHING.
MUST YOU PICK A FIGHT WITH ME OVER EVERY-THING?
BUT... IF HE DOES LIKE MITTY, DOES THAT MEAN...
...HE'S GOING TO GET DUMPED?
HE ACTS SO HIGH AND MIGHTY... BUT...
POOR GUY...
...WHY DO YOU LOOK LIKE YOU'RE FEELING SORRY FOR ME?
SQUIIIISH
O-OW, OW, OW!

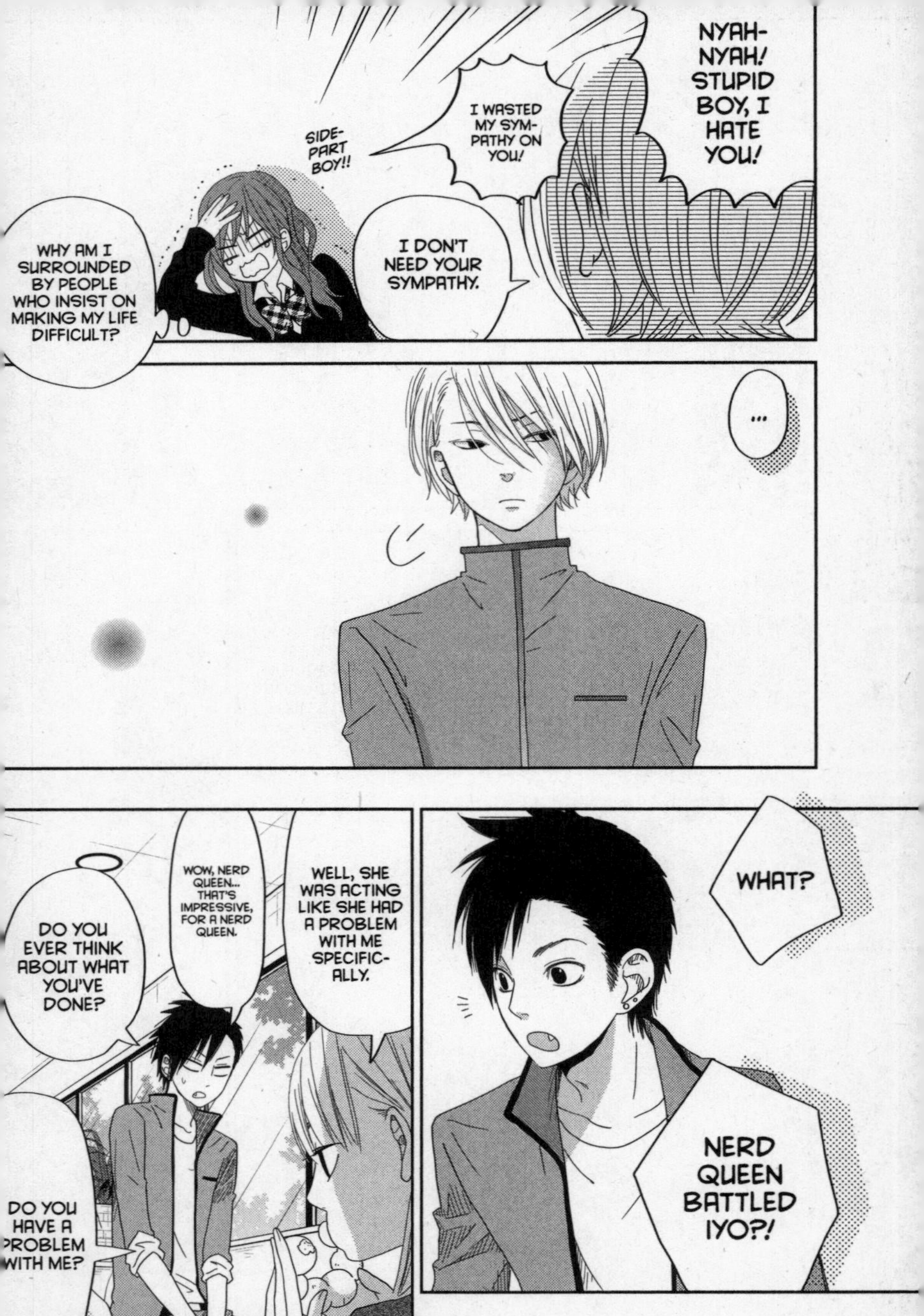
NYAH-NYAH! STUPID BOY, I HATE YOU!
I WASTED MY SYMPATHY ON YOU!
SIDE-PART BOY!!
I DON'T NEED YOUR SYMPATHY.
WHY AM I SURROUNDED BY PEOPLE WHO INSIST ON MAKING MY LIFE DIFFICULT?
...
WHAT?
NERD QUEEN BATTLED IYO?!
WELL, SHE WAS ACTING LIKE SHE HAD A PROBLEM WITH ME SPECIFICALLY.
WOW, NERD QUEEN... THAT'S IMPRESSIVE, FOR A NERD QUEEN.
DO YOU EVER THINK ABOUT WHAT YOU'VE DONE?
DO YOU HAVE A PROBLEM WITH ME?

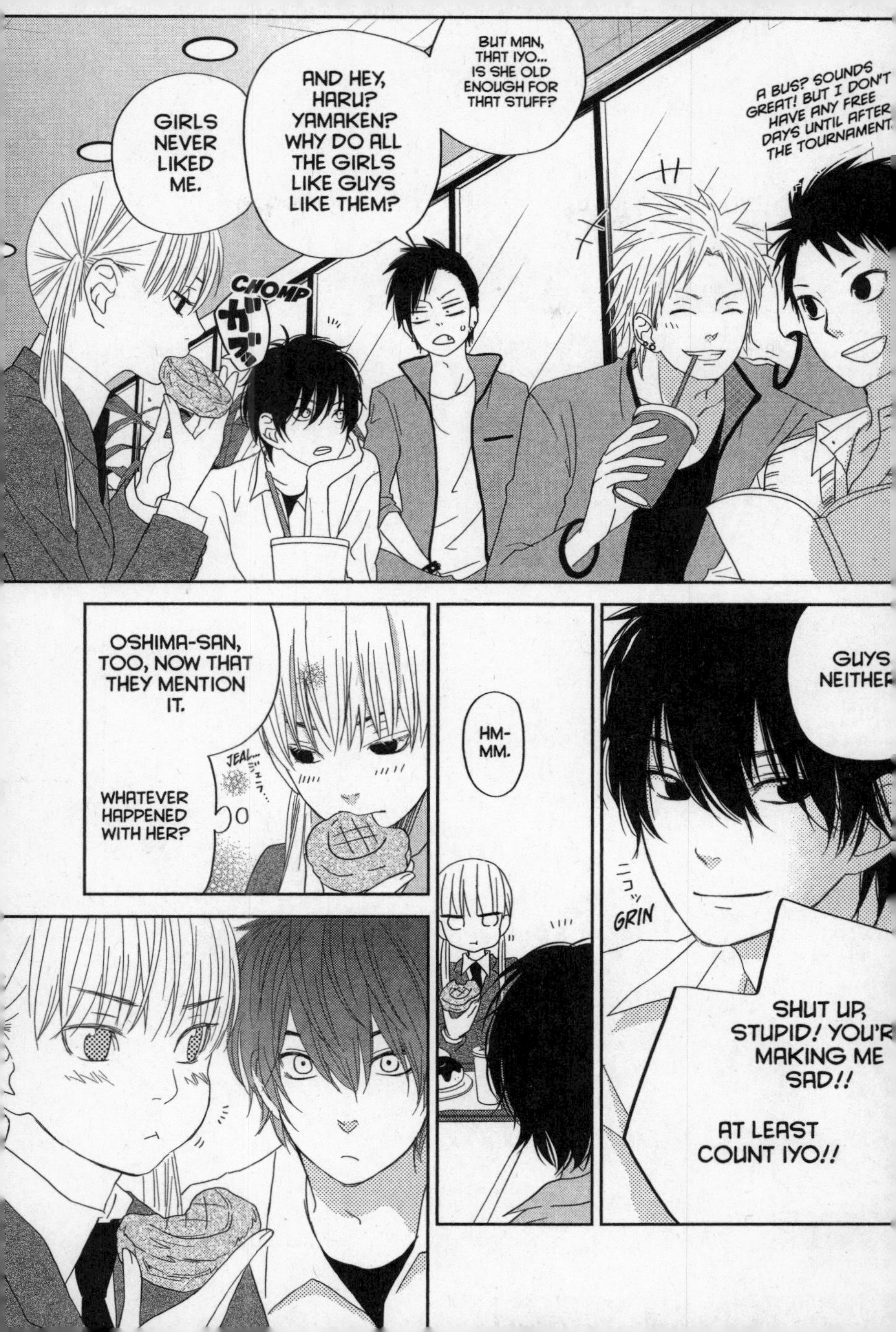

A BUS? SOUNDS GREAT! BUT I DON'T HAVE ANY FREE DAYS UNTIL AFTER THE TOURNAMENT.
BUT MAN, THAT IYO... IS SHE OLD ENOUGH FOR THAT STUFF?
AND HEY, HARU? YAMAKEN? WHY DO ALL THE GIRLS LIKE GUYS LIKE THEM?
GIRLS NEVER LIKED ME.
CHOMP
GUYS NEITHER
GRIN
SHUT UP, STUPID! YOU'R MAKING ME SAD!!
AT LEAST COUNT IYO!!
HM-MM.
OSHIMA-SAN, TOO, NOW THAT THEY MENTION IT.
JEAL...
WHATEVER HAPPENED WITH HER?

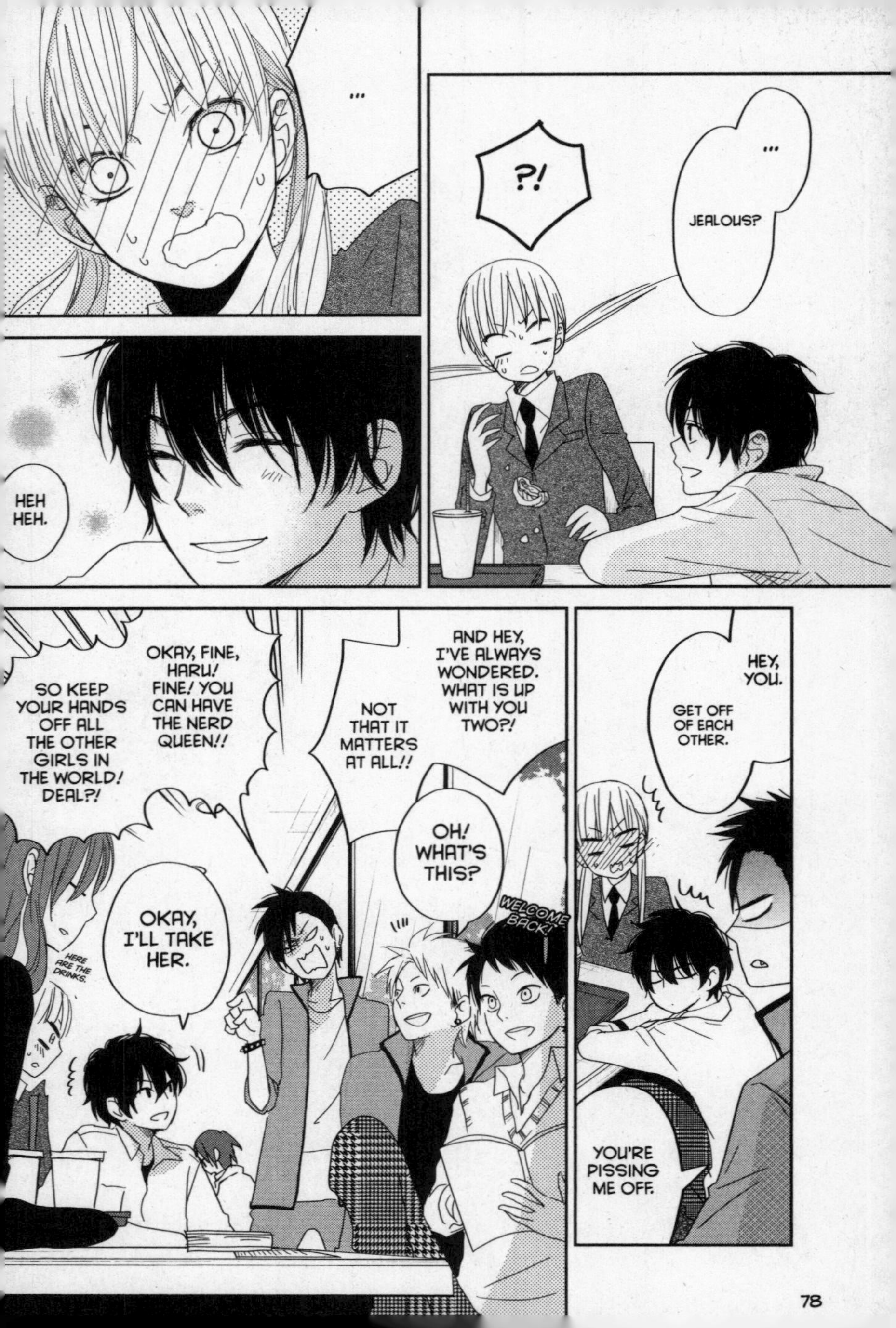
...
HEH HEH.
...
JEALOUS?
?!
HEY, YOU.
GET OFF OF EACH OTHER.
YOU'RE PISSING ME OFF.
WELCOME BACK!
OH! WHAT'S THIS?
AND HEY, I'VE ALWAYS WONDERED. WHAT IS UP WITH YOU TWO?!
NOT THAT IT MATTERS AT ALL!!
OKAY, FINE, HARU! FINE! YOU CAN HAVE THE NERD QUEEN!!
SO KEEP YOUR HANDS OFF ALL THE OTHER GIRLS IN THE WORLD! DEAL?!
HERE ARE THE DRINKS.
OKAY, I'LL TAKE HER.

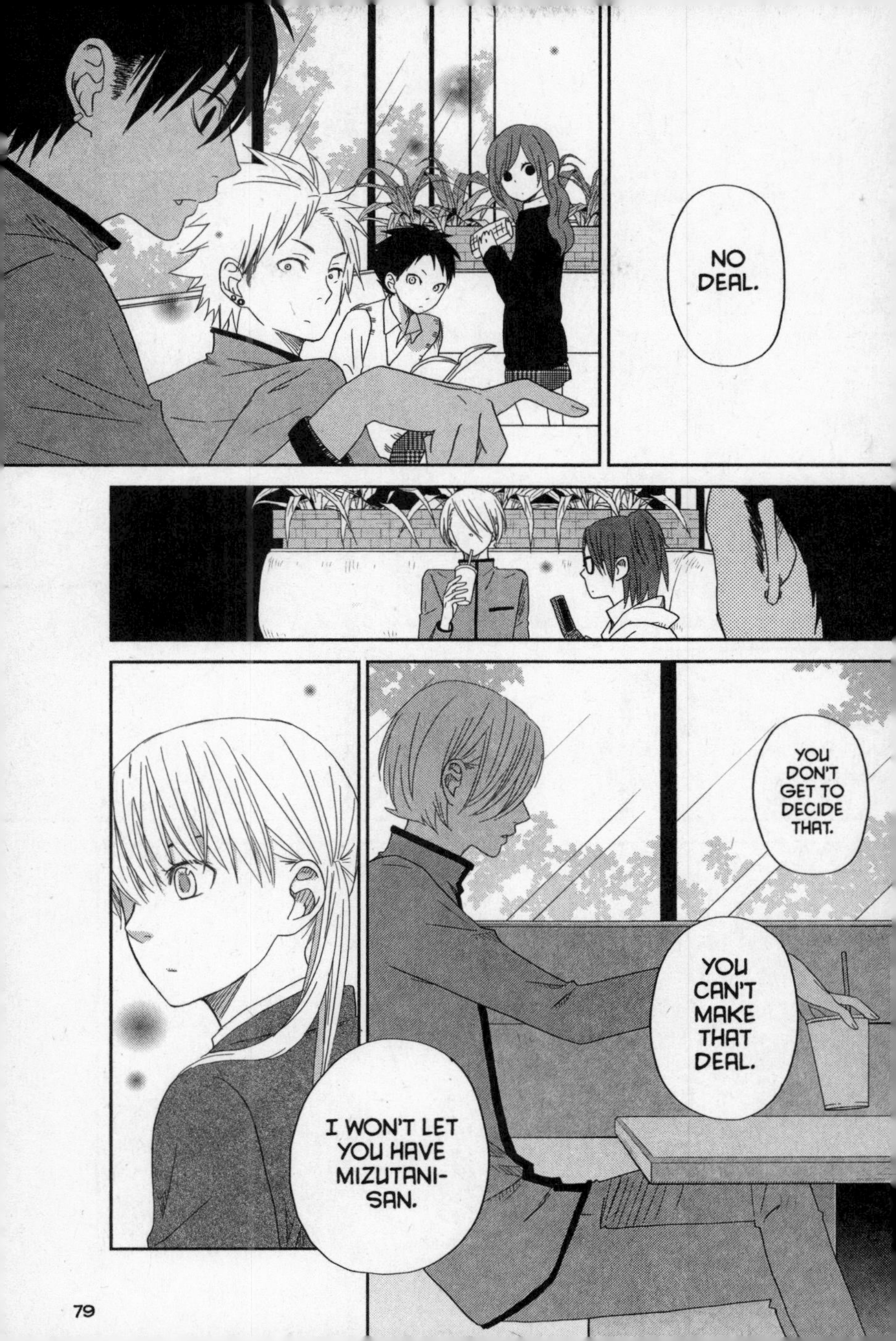
NO DEAL.
YOU DON'T GET TO DECIDE THAT.
YOU CAN'T MAKE THAT DEAL.
I WON'T LET YOU HAVE MIZUTANI-SAN.

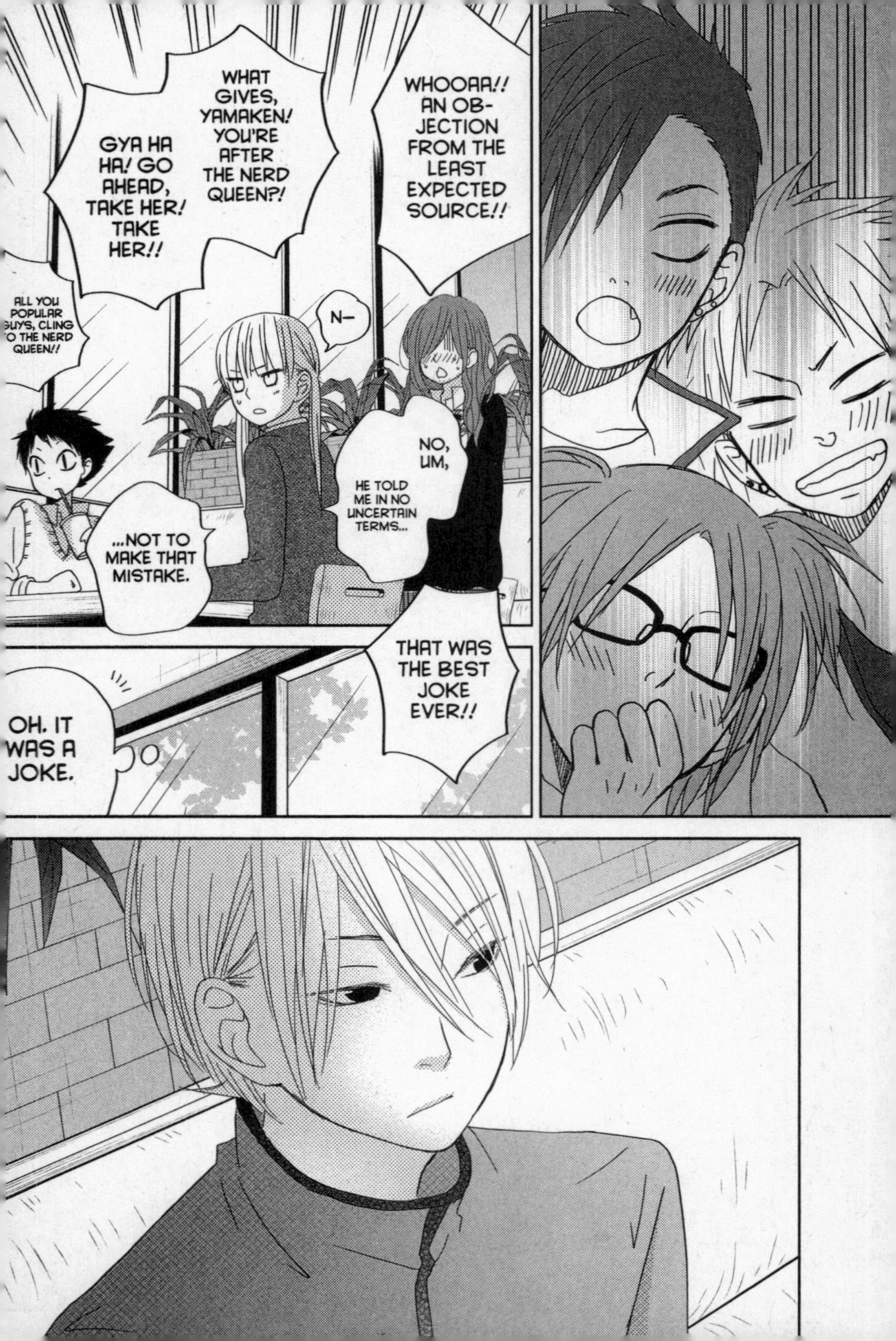
WHOOAA!! AN OB-JECTION FROM THE LEAST EXPECTED SOURCE!!
WHAT GIVES, YAMAKEN! YOU'RE AFTER THE NERD QUEEN?!
GYA HA HA! GO AHEAD, TAKE HER! TAKE HER!!
ALL YOU POPULAR GUYS, CLING TO THE NERD QUEEN!!
N—
NO, UM,
HE TOLD ME IN NO UNCERTAIN TERMS...
...NOT TO MAKE THAT MISTAKE.
THAT WAS THE BEST JOKE EVER!!
OH. IT WAS A JOKE.

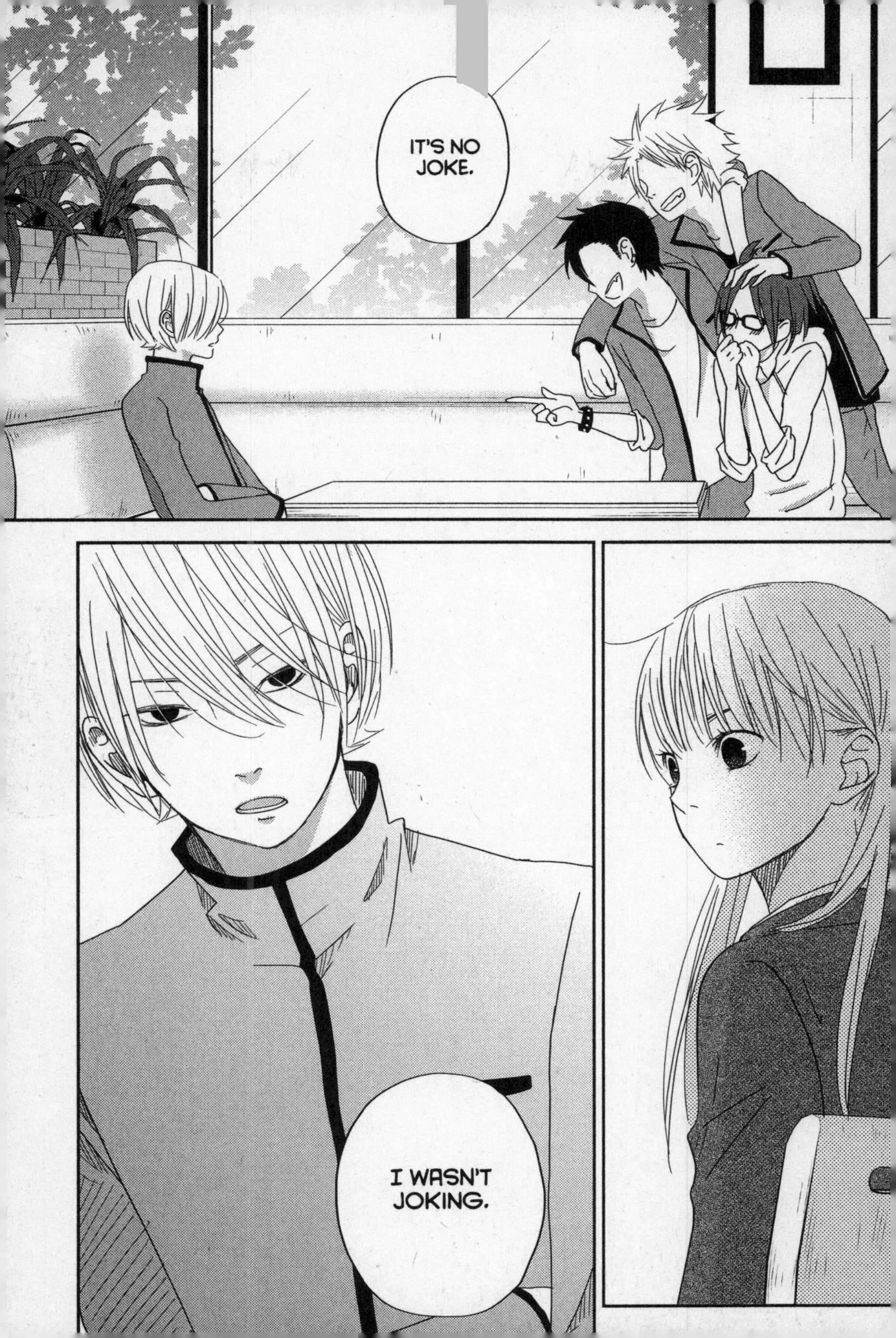
IT'S NO JOKE.
I WASN'T JOKING.

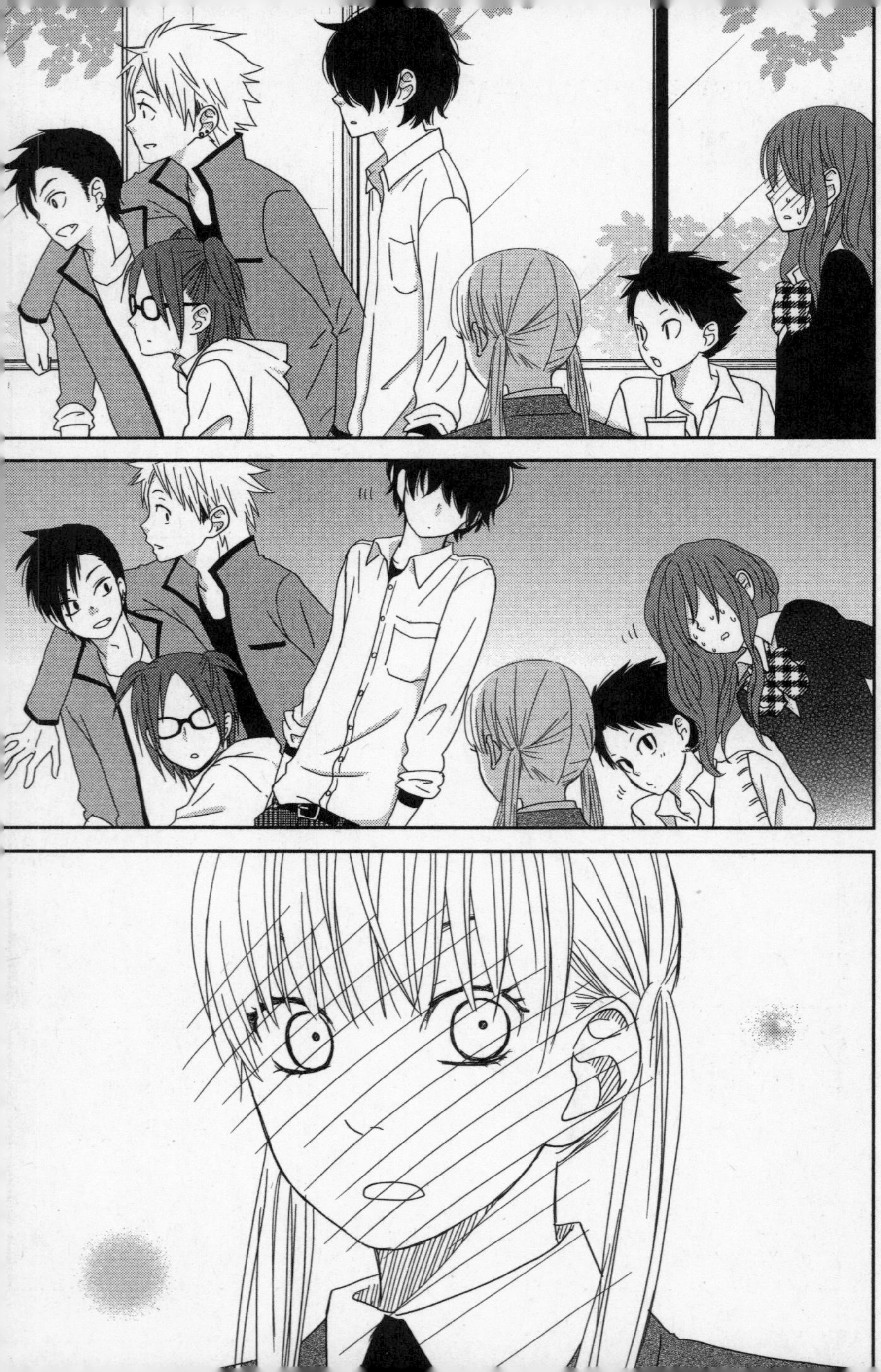

HARU-NATSU-SEMPAI

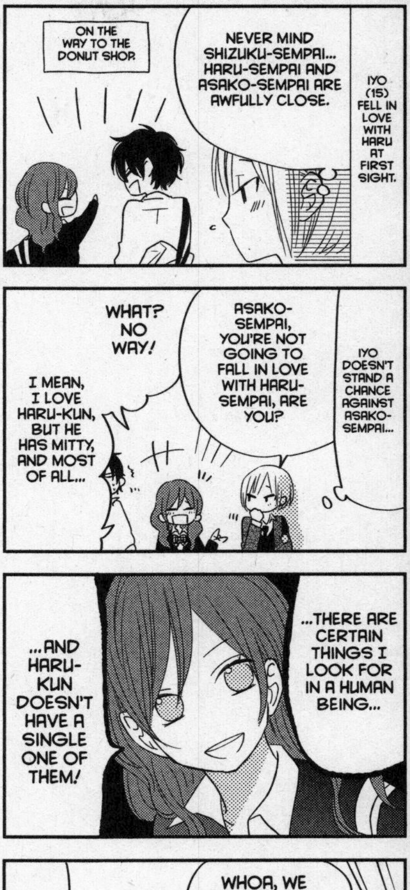
IYO (15) FELL IN LOVE WITH HARU AT FIRST SIGHT.
NEVER MIND SHIZUKU-SEMPAI... HARU-SEMPAI AND ASAKO-SEMPAI ARE AWFULLY CLOSE.
ON THE WAY TO THE DONUT SHOP.
IYO DOESN'T STAND A CHANCE AGAINST ASAKO-SEMPAI...
ASAKO-SEMPAI, YOU'RE NOT GOING TO FALL IN LOVE WITH HARU-SEMPAI, ARE YOU?
WHAT? NO WAY!
I MEAN, I LOVE HARU-KUN, BUT HE HAS MITTY, AND MOST OF ALL...
...THERE ARE CERTAIN THINGS I LOOK FOR IN A HUMAN BEING...
...AND HARU-KUN DOESN'T HAVE A SINGLE ONE OF THEM!
WHOA, WE ARE ON THE SAME WAVE-LENGTH, NATSUME!!
THANK HEAVENS.
I'M TOTALLY WITH YOU!
AH HA HA

SASAYAN AND IYO

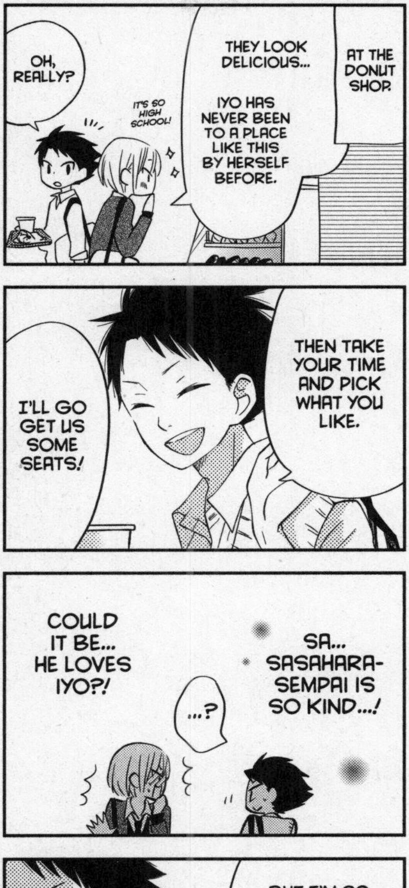
AT THE DONUT SHOP.
THEY LOOK DELICIOUS... IYO HAS NEVER BEEN TO A PLACE LIKE THIS BY HERSELF BEFORE.
IT'S SO HIGH SCHOOL!
OH, REALLY?
THEN TAKE YOUR TIME AND PICK WHAT YOU LIKE.
I'LL GO GET US SOME SEATS!
SA... SASAHARA-SEMPAI IS SO KIND...!
...?
COULD IT BE... HE LOVES IYO?!
BUT I'M SO SORRY. IYO ONLY LIKES BOYS WHO ARE TALLER THAN SHE IS...
WELL, I'LL MEET YOU AT THE TABLE.

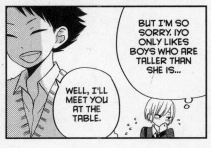

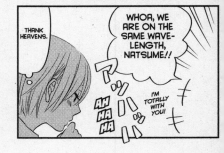

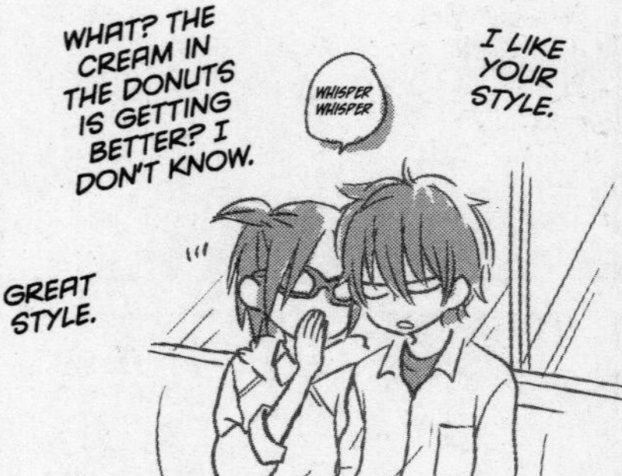
I LIKE YOUR STYLE.
WHISPER WHISPER
WHAT? THE CREAM IN THE DONUTS IS GETTING BETTER? I DON'T KNOW.
GREAT STYLE.

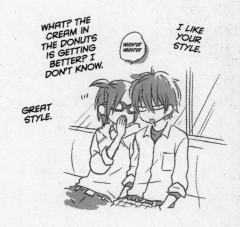

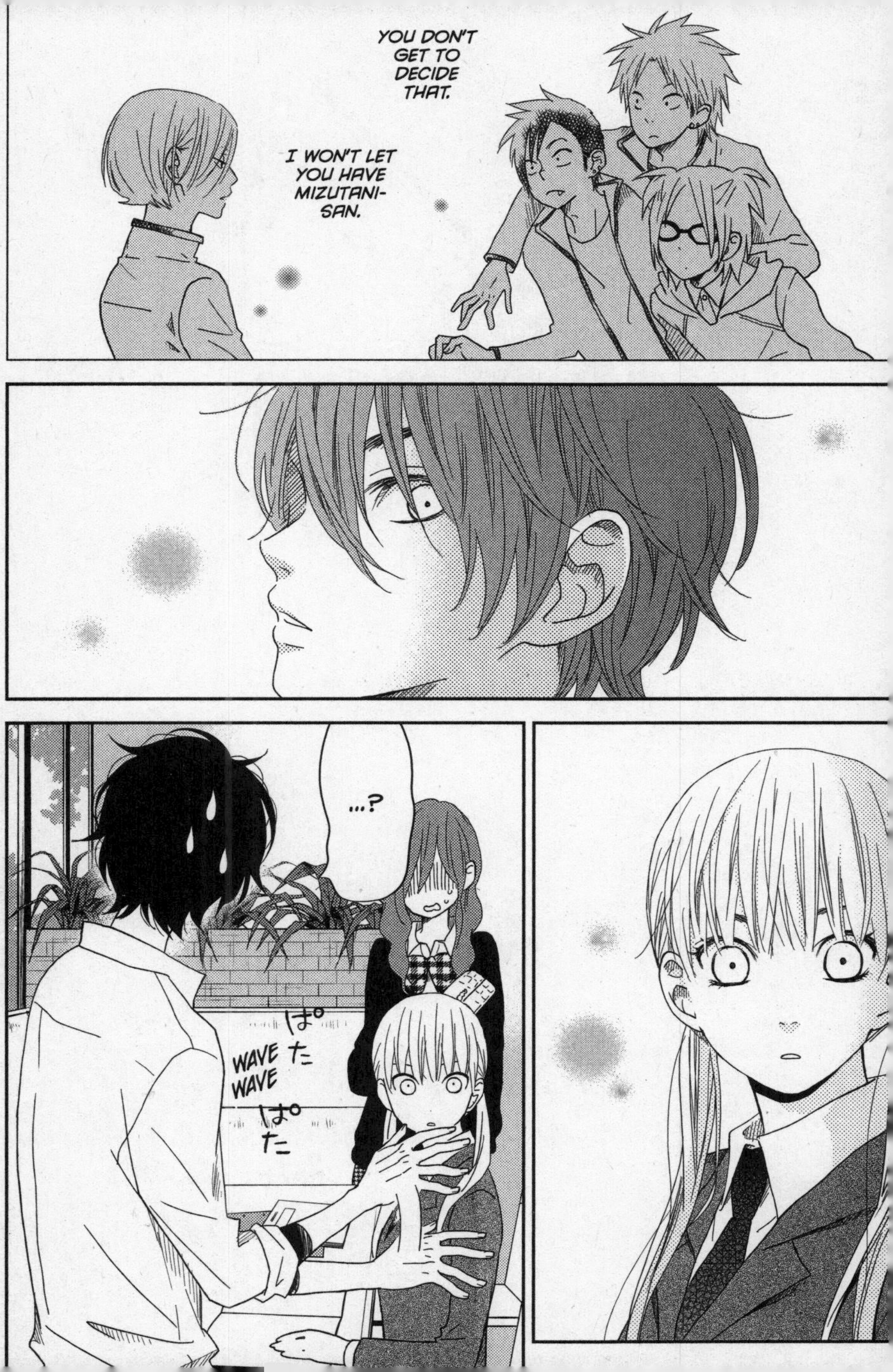
YOU DON'T GET TO DECIDE THAT.
I WON'T LET YOU HAVE MIZUTANI-SAN.
...?
ぱたぱた
WAVE WAVE

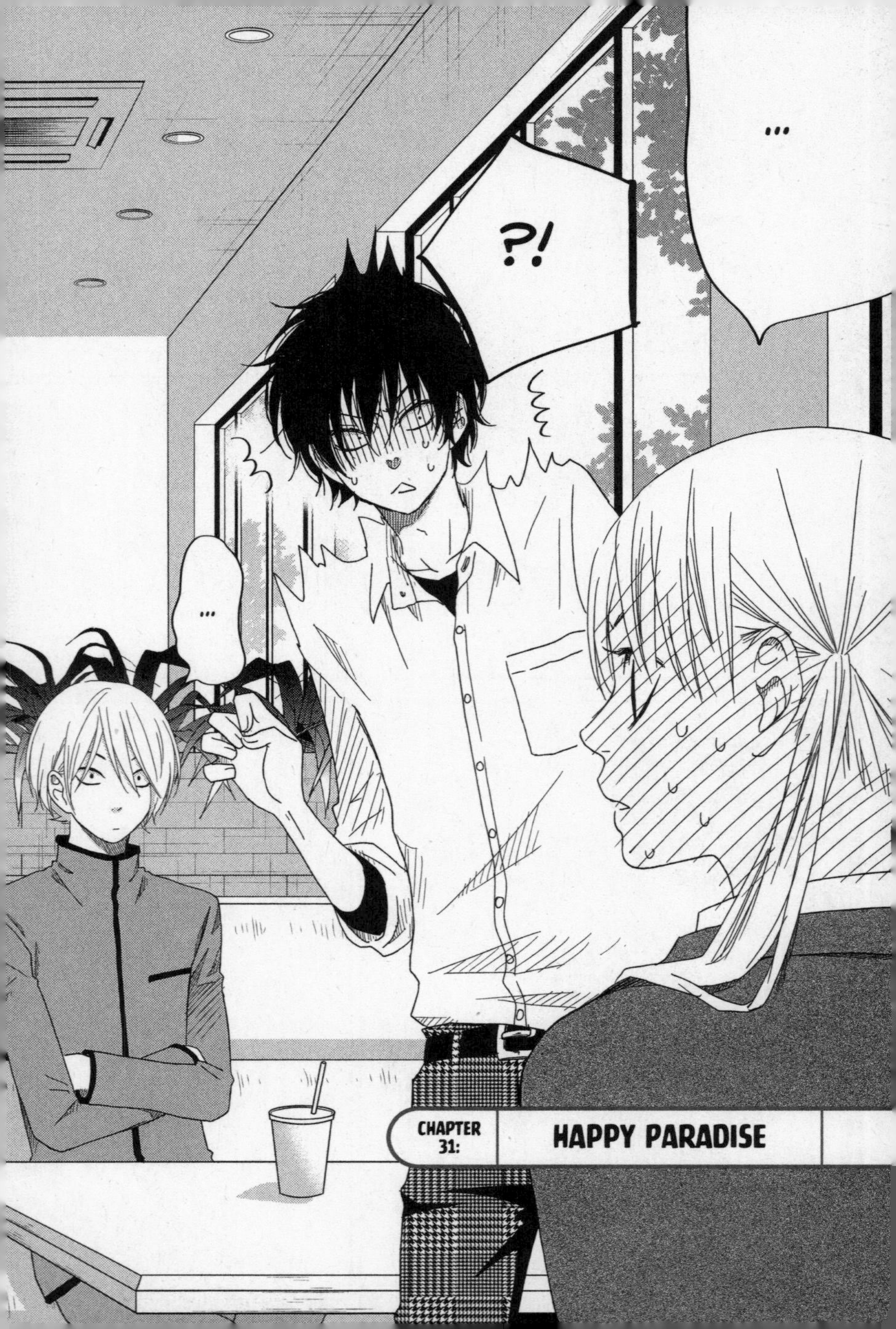
...
?!
...
CHAPTER 31:
HAPPY PARADISE

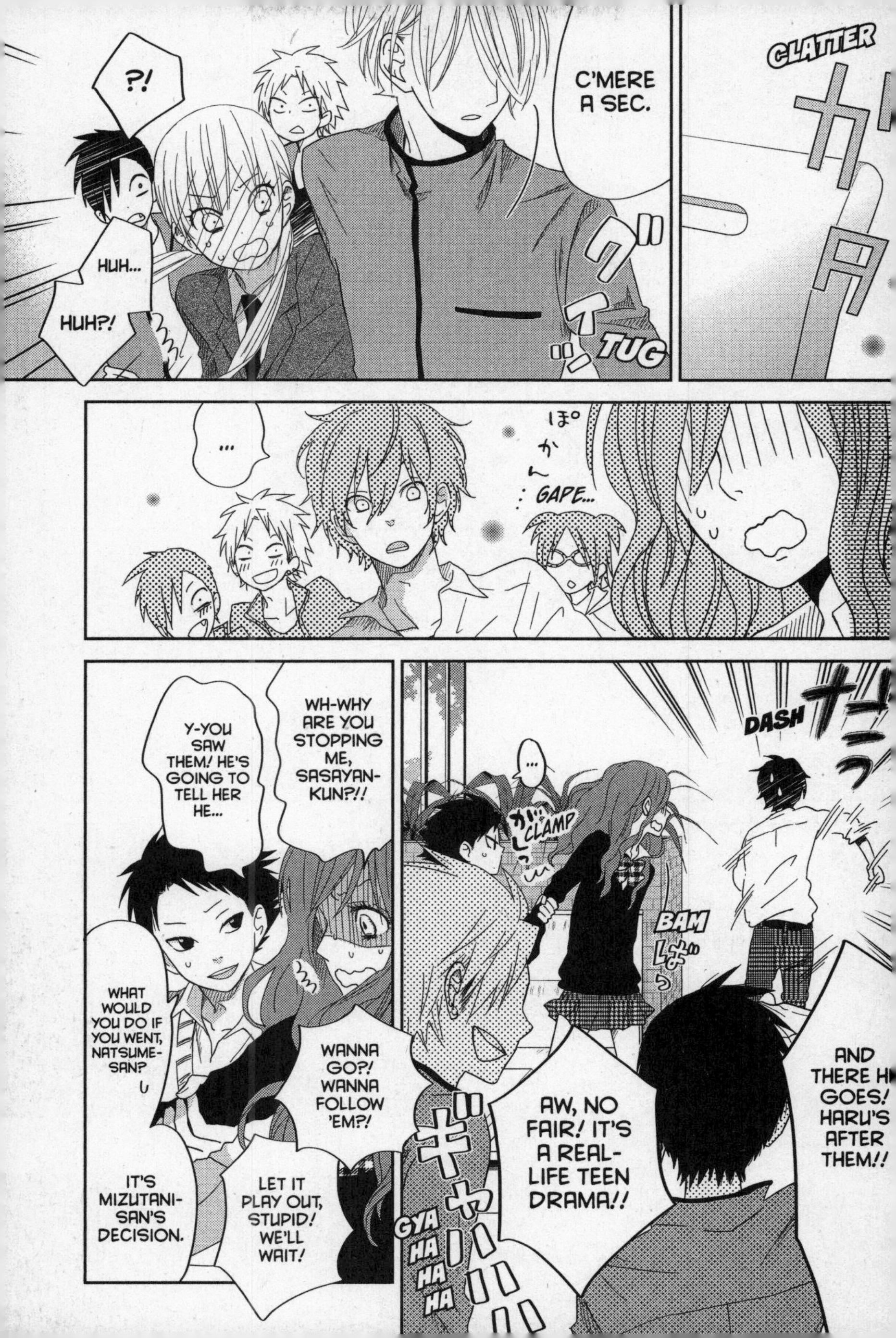
CLATTER
カタ
C'MERE A SEC.
グイ
TUG
?!
HUH...
HUH?!
...
ぽかん
GAPE...
ナコラ
DASH
AND THERE H GOES! HARU'S AFTER THEM!!
AW, NO FAIR! IT'S A REAL-LIFE TEEN DRAMA!!
...
がしっ
CLAMP
BAM
ばっ
ギャハハハ
GYA HA HA HA
WH-WHY ARE YOU STOPPING ME, SASAYAN-KUN?!!
Y-YOU SAW THEM! HE'S GOING TO TELL HER HE...
WANNA GO?! WANNA FOLLOW 'EM?!
WHAT WOULD YOU DO IF YOU WENT, NATSUME-SAN?
LET IT PLAY OUT, STUPID! WE'LL WAIT!
IT'S MIZUTANI-SAN'S DECISION.

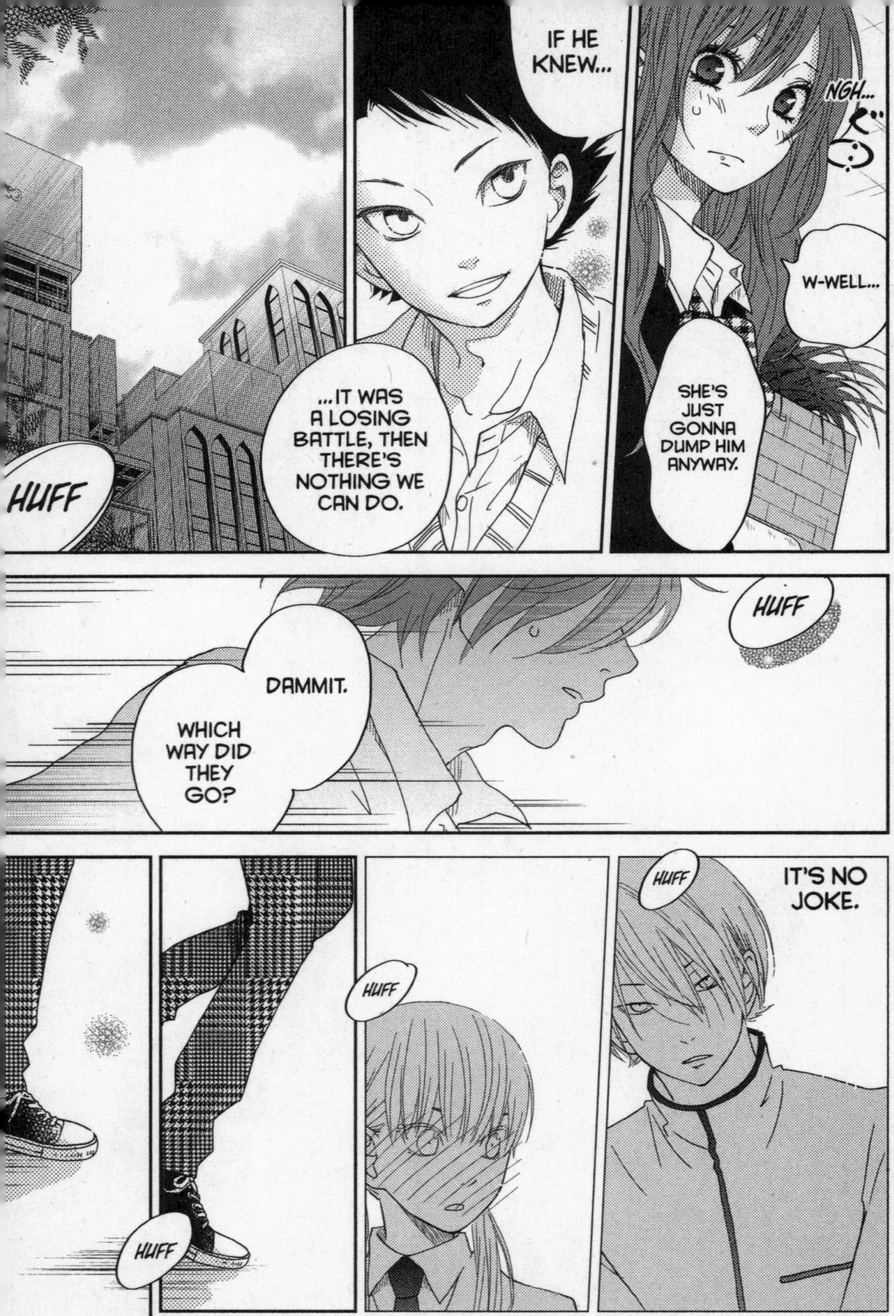
NGH...
W-WELL...
SHE'S JUST GONNA DUMP HIM ANYWAY.
IF HE KNEW...
...IT WAS A LOSING BATTLE, THEN THERE'S NOTHING WE CAN DO.
HUFF
HUFF
DAMMIT.
WHICH WAY DID THEY GO?
IT'S NO JOKE.
HUFF
HUFF
HUFF

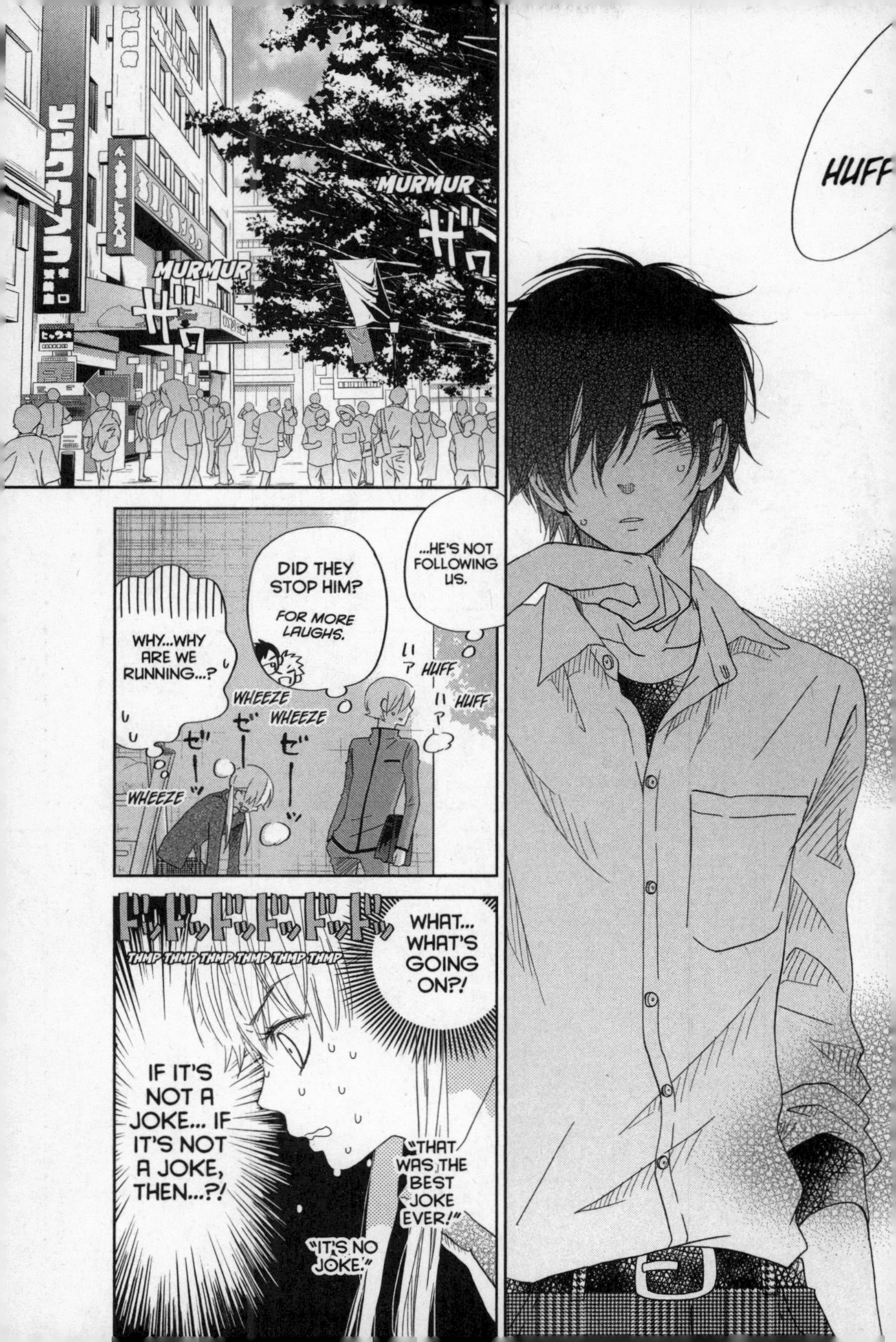
HUFF
MURMUR
MURMUR
...HE'S NOT FOLLOWING US.
DID THEY STOP HIM?
FOR MORE LAUGHS.
WHY...WHY ARE WE RUNNING...?
HUFF
HUFF
WHEEZE
WHEEZE
WHEEZE
THMP THMP THMP THMP THMP THMP
WHAT... WHAT'S GOING ON?!
IF IT'S NOT A JOKE... IF IT'S NOT A JOKE, THEN...?!
"THAT WAS THE BEST JOKE EVER!"
"IT'S NO JOKE."

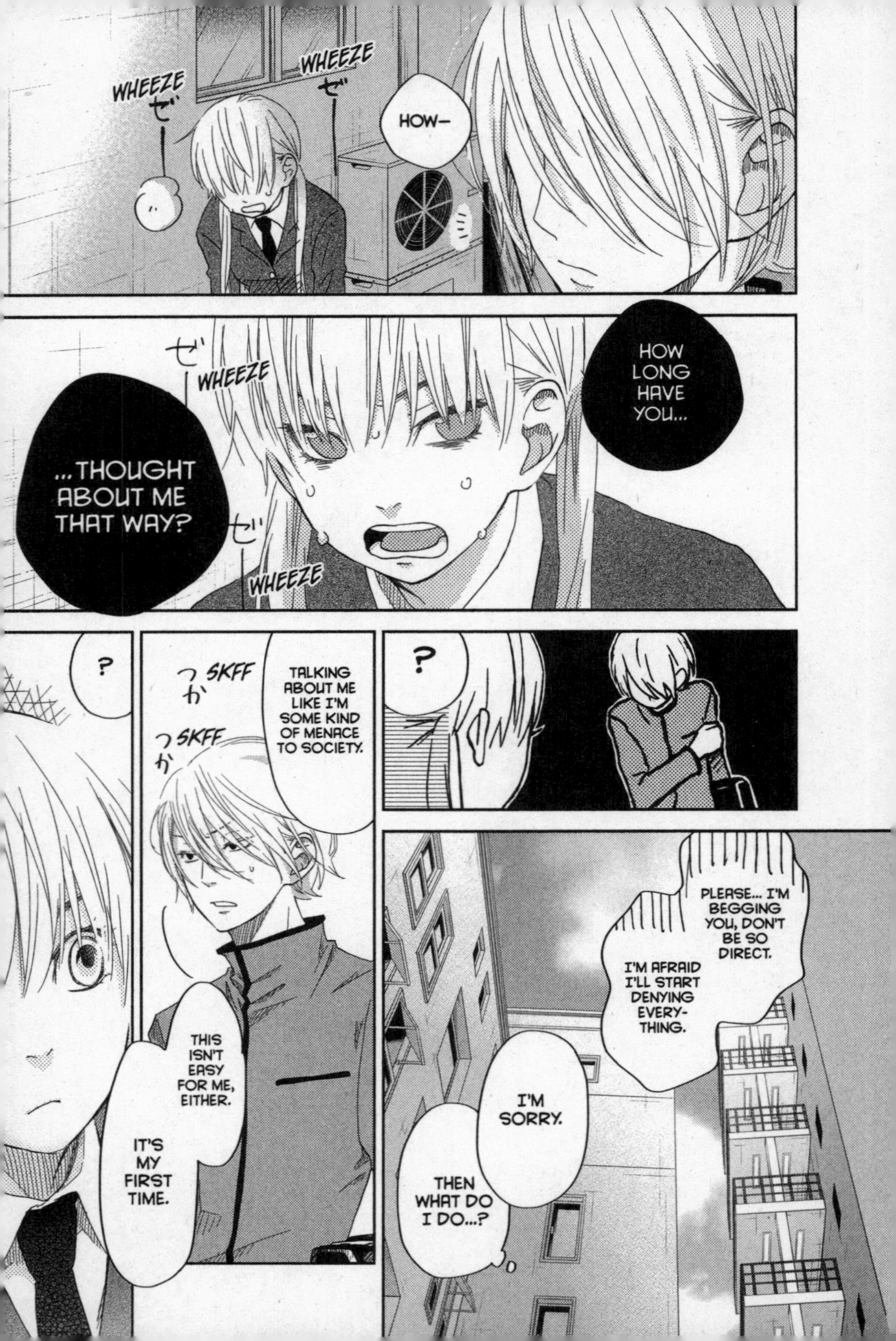
HOW–
WHEEZE
ぜ
WHEEZE
ぜ
HOW LONG HAVE YOU...
ぜ
WHEEZE
...THOUGHT ABOUT ME THAT WAY?
ぜ
WHEEZE
?
PLEASE... I'M BEGGING YOU, DON'T BE SO DIRECT.
I'M AFRAID I'LL START DENYING EVERY-THING.
I'M SORRY.
THEN WHAT DO I DO...?
つか
SKFF
つか
SKFF
TALKING ABOUT ME LIKE I'M SOME KIND OF MENACE TO SOCIETY.
THIS ISN'T EASY FOR ME, EITHER.
IT'S MY FIRST TIME.
?

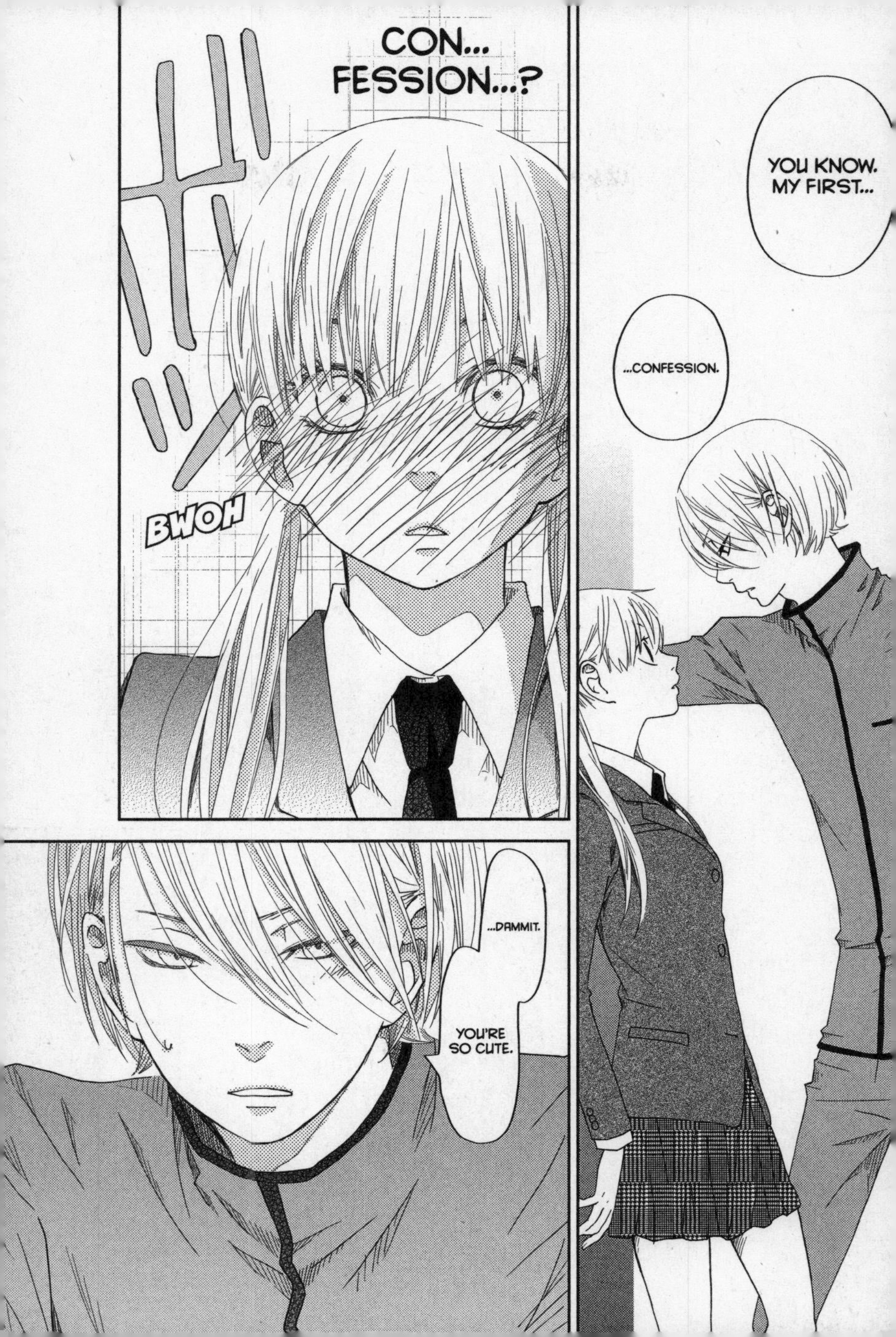
YOU KNOW. MY FIRST...
...CONFESSION.
CON... FESSION...?
BWOH
...DAMMIT.
YOU'RE SO CUTE.

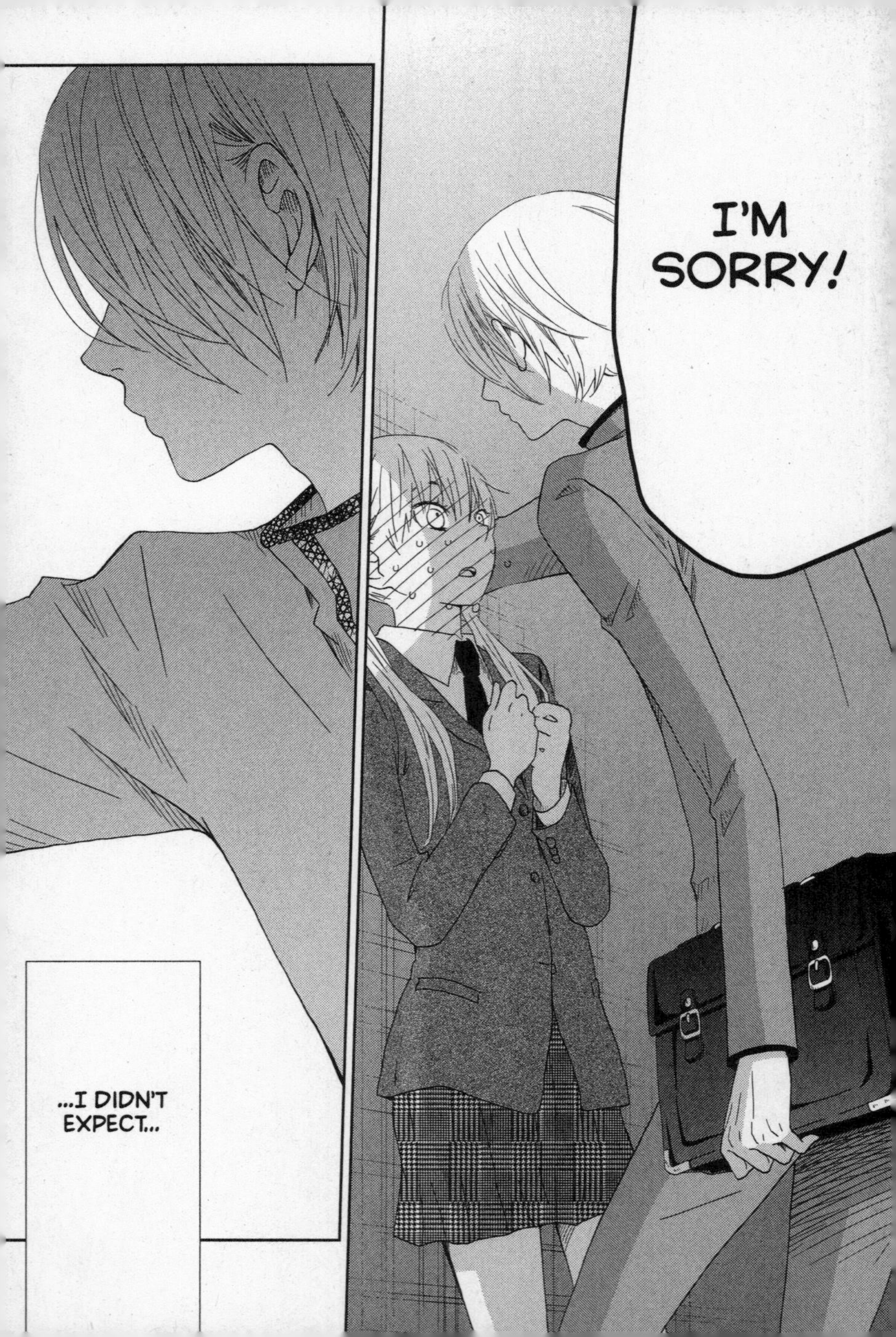
I'M SORRY!
...I DIDN'T EXPECT...

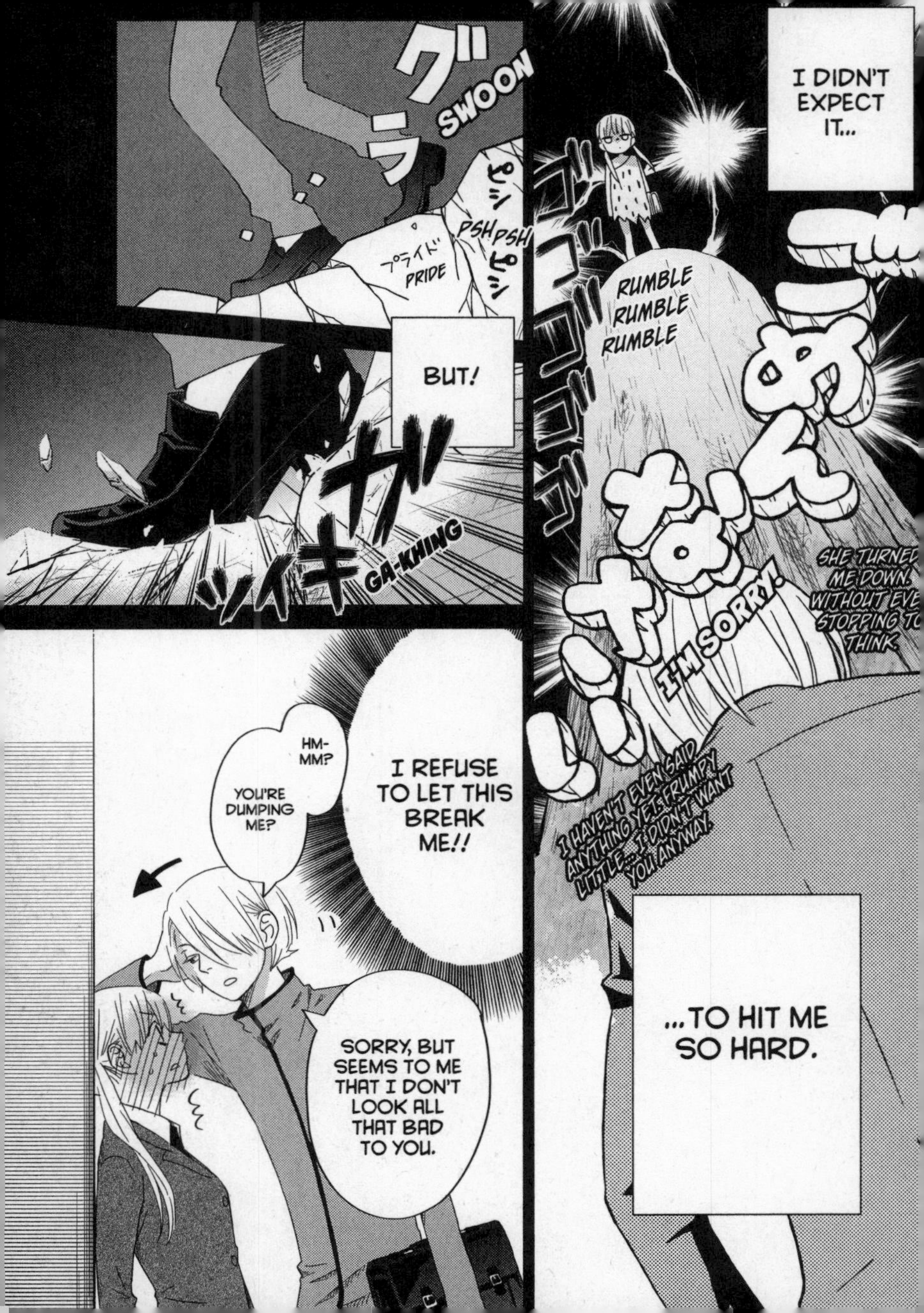
I DIDN'T EXPECT IT...
RUMBLE RUMBLE RUMBLE
ごめんなさい
I'M SORRY!
SHE TURNED ME DOWN. WITHOUT EVEN STOPPING TO THINK.
I HAVEN'T EVEN SAID ANYTHING YET. FRUMPY LITTLE... I DIDN'T WANT YOU ANYWAY.
...TO HIT ME SO HARD.
グラ
SWOON
ピシ
PSH PSH
ピシ
プライド
PRIDE
BUT!
GA-KHING
I REFUSE TO LET THIS BREAK ME!!
HM-MM?
YOU'RE DUMPING ME?
SORRY, BUT SEEMS TO ME THAT I DON'T LOOK ALL THAT BAD TO YOU.

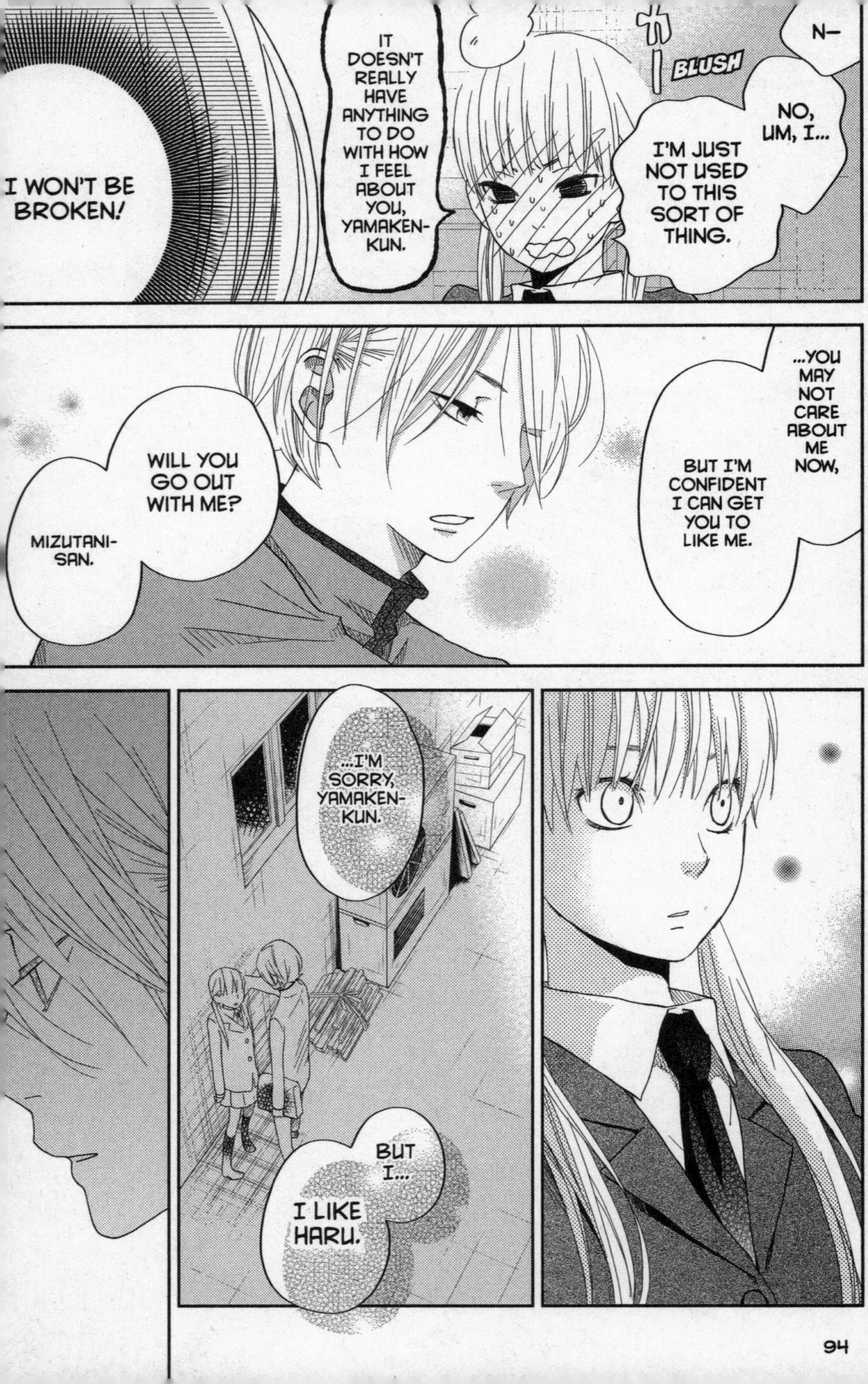
N–
NO, UM, I...
I'M JUST NOT USED TO THIS SORT OF THING.
カー
BLUSH
IT DOESN'T REALLY HAVE ANYTHING TO DO WITH HOW I FEEL ABOUT YOU, YAMAKEN-KUN.
I WON'T BE BROKEN!
...YOU MAY NOT CARE ABOUT ME NOW,
BUT I'M CONFIDENT I CAN GET YOU TO LIKE ME.
WILL YOU GO OUT WITH ME?
MIZUTANI-SAN.
...I'M SORRY, YAMAKEN-KUN.
BUT I...
I LIKE HARU.

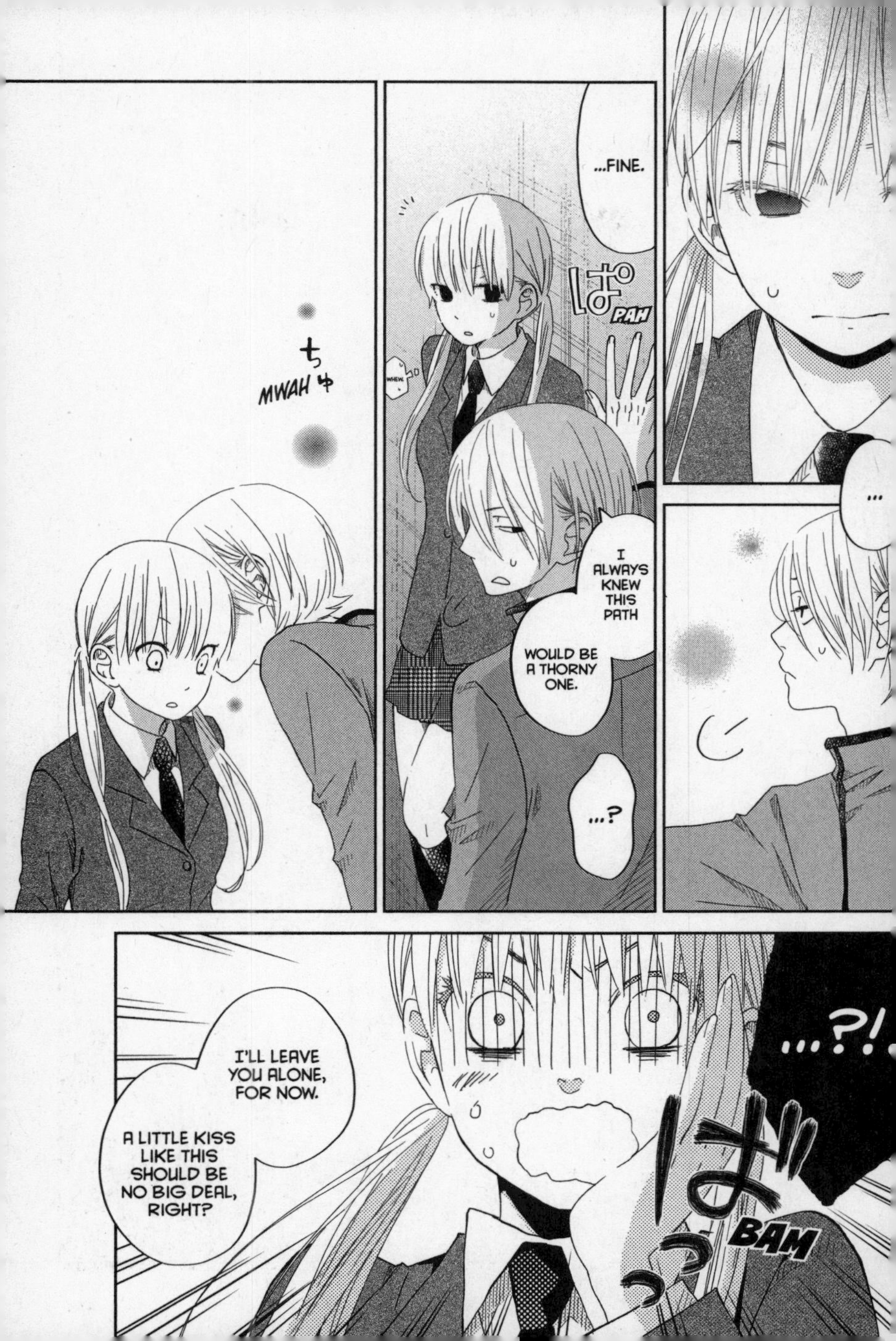
...
...FINE.
ぱ
PAH
WHEW.
I ALWAYS KNEW THIS PATH
WOULD BE A THORNY ONE.
...?
ち
MWAH
ゅ
...?!
ば
BAM
I'LL LEAVE YOU ALONE, FOR NOW.
A LITTLE KISS LIKE THIS SHOULD BE NO BIG DEAL, RIGHT?

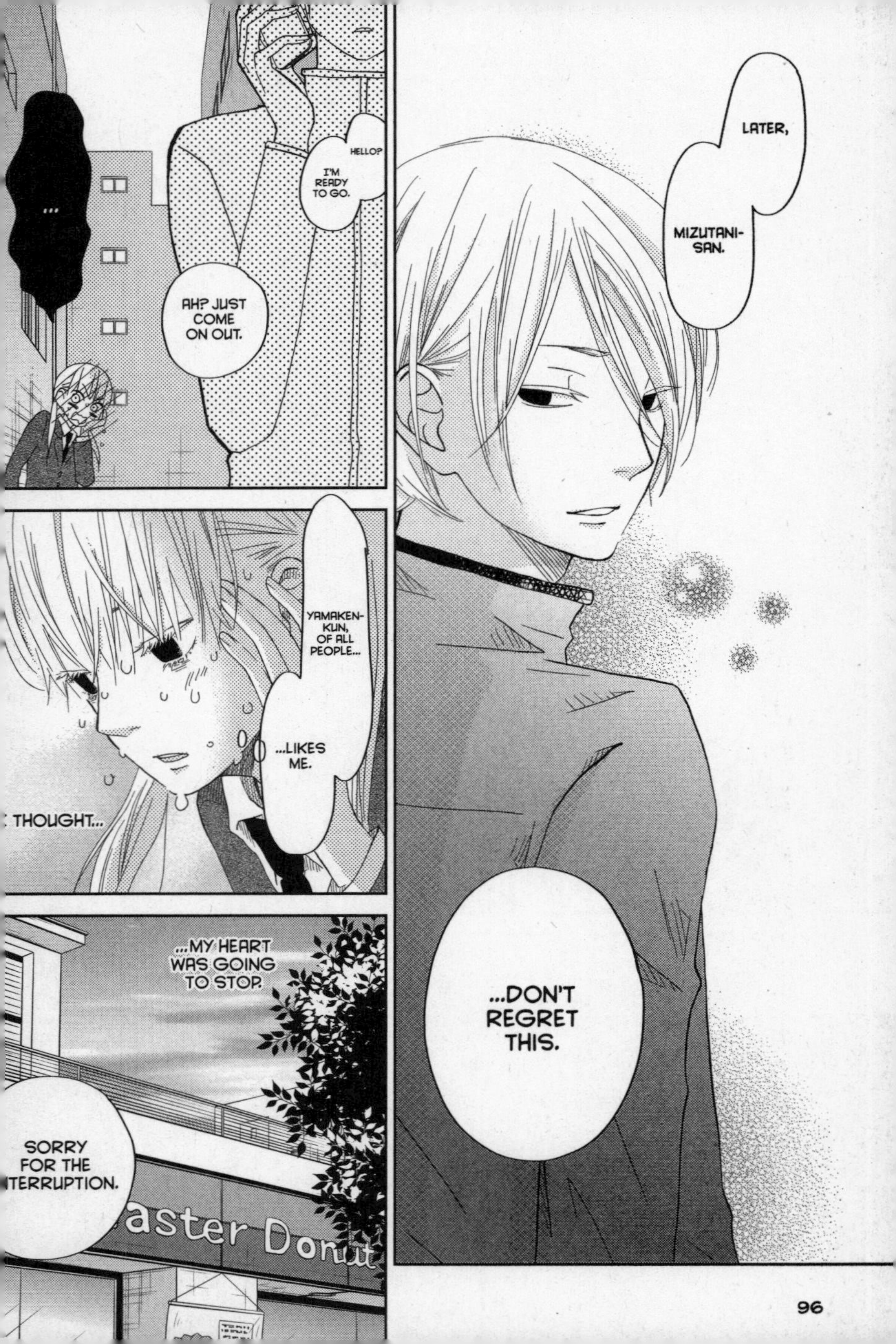
LATER,
MIZUTANI-SAN.
...DON'T REGRET THIS.
HELLO? I'M READY TO GO.
AH? JUST COME ON OUT.
...
YAMAKEN-KUN, OF ALL PEOPLE...
...LIKES ME.
THOUGHT...
...MY HEART WAS GOING TO STOP.
SORRY FOR THE TERRUPTION.
aster Donut

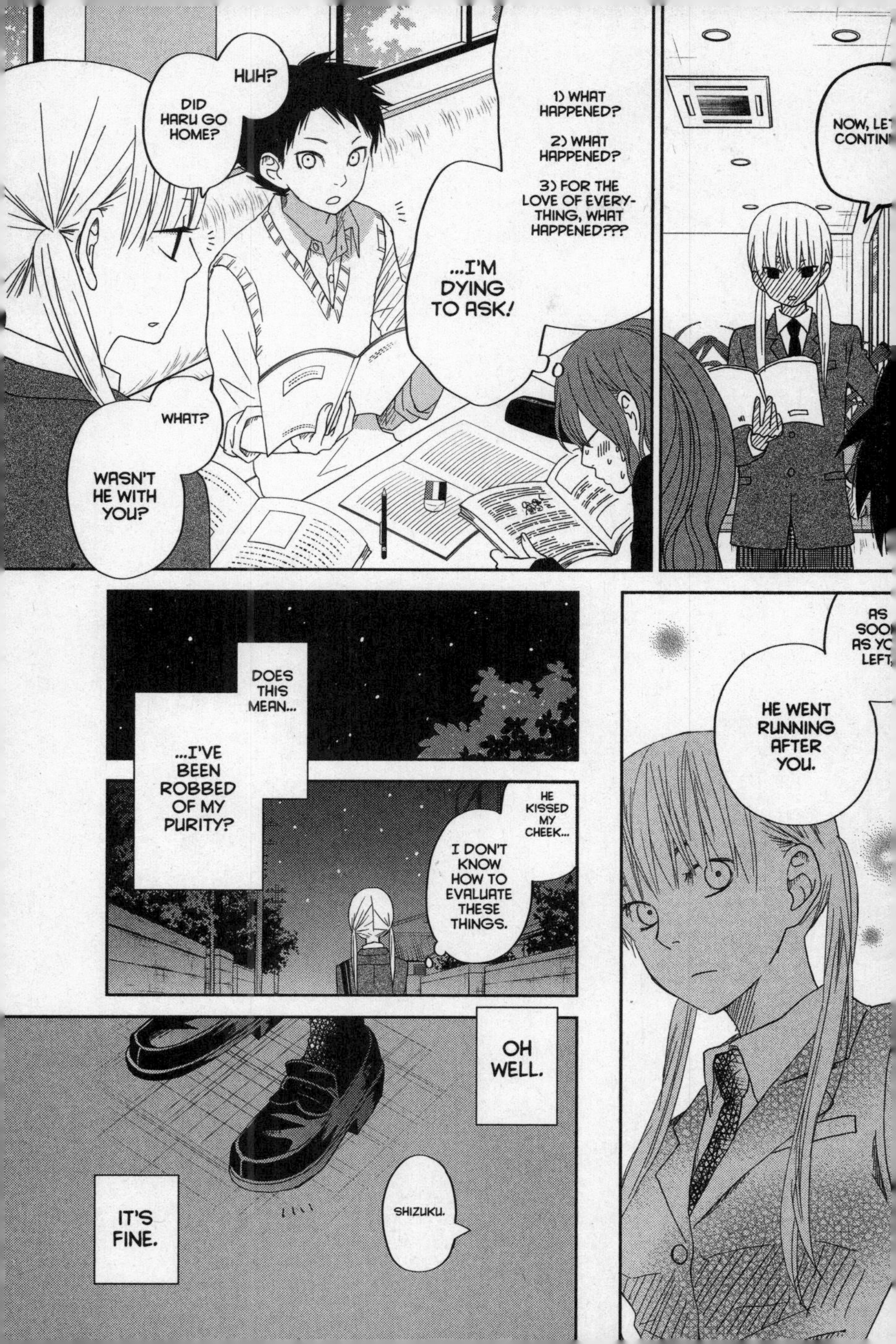

NOW, LET CONTIN
HUH? DID HARU GO HOME?
WHAT? WASN'T HE WITH YOU?
1) WHAT HAPPENED? 2) WHAT HAPPENED? 3) FOR THE LOVE OF EVERY-THING, WHAT HAPPENED???
...I'M DYING TO ASK!
AS SOO AS YO LEFT,
HE WENT RUNNING AFTER YOU.
DOES THIS MEAN...
...I'VE BEEN ROBBED OF MY PURITY?
HE KISSED MY CHEEK...
I DON'T KNOW HOW TO EVALUATE THESE THINGS.
OH WELL.
IT'S FINE.
SHIZUKU.

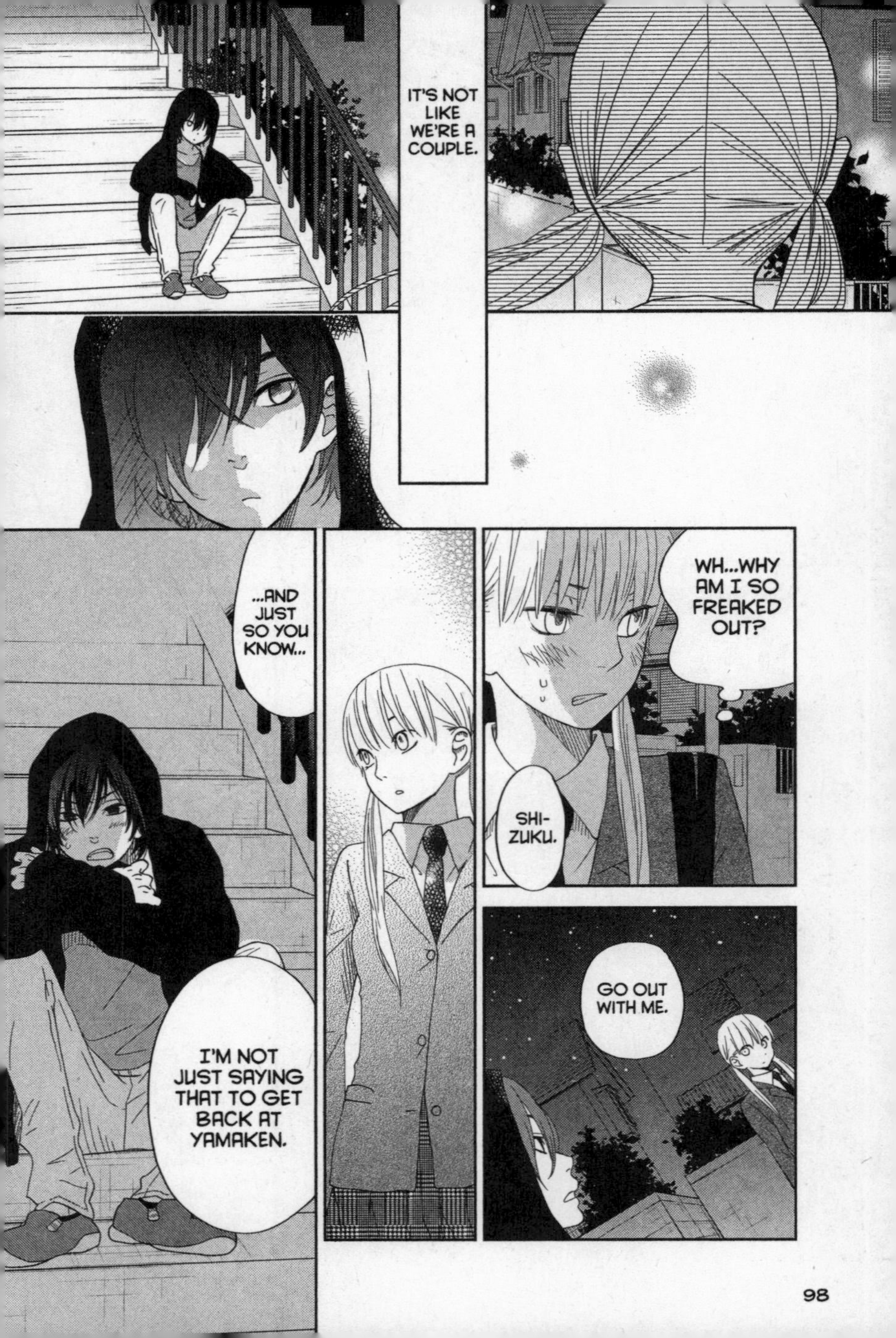
IT'S NOT LIKE WE'RE A COUPLE.
WH...WHY AM I SO FREAKED OUT?
SHI-ZUKU.
GO OUT WITH ME.
...AND JUST SO YOU KNOW...
I'M NOT JUST SAYING THAT TO GET BACK AT YAMAKEN.

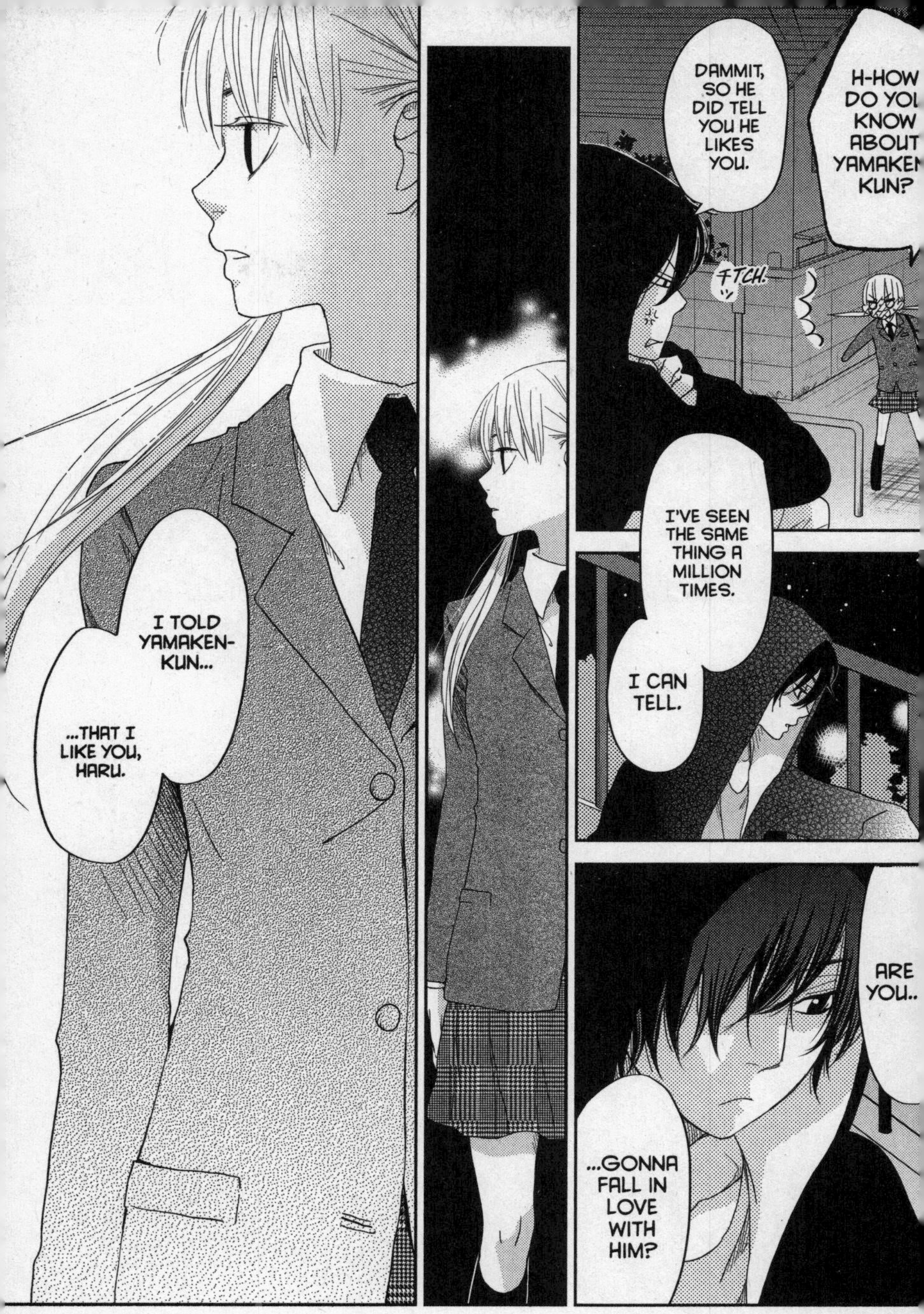
H-HOW DO YOU KNOW ABOUT YAMAKEN KUN?
DAMMIT, SO HE DID TELL YOU HE LIKES YOU.
チッ
TCH!
I'VE SEEN THE SAME THING A MILLION TIMES.
I CAN TELL.
ARE YOU..
...GONNA FALL IN LOVE WITH HIM?
I TOLD YAMAKEN-KUN...
...THAT I LIKE YOU, HARU.

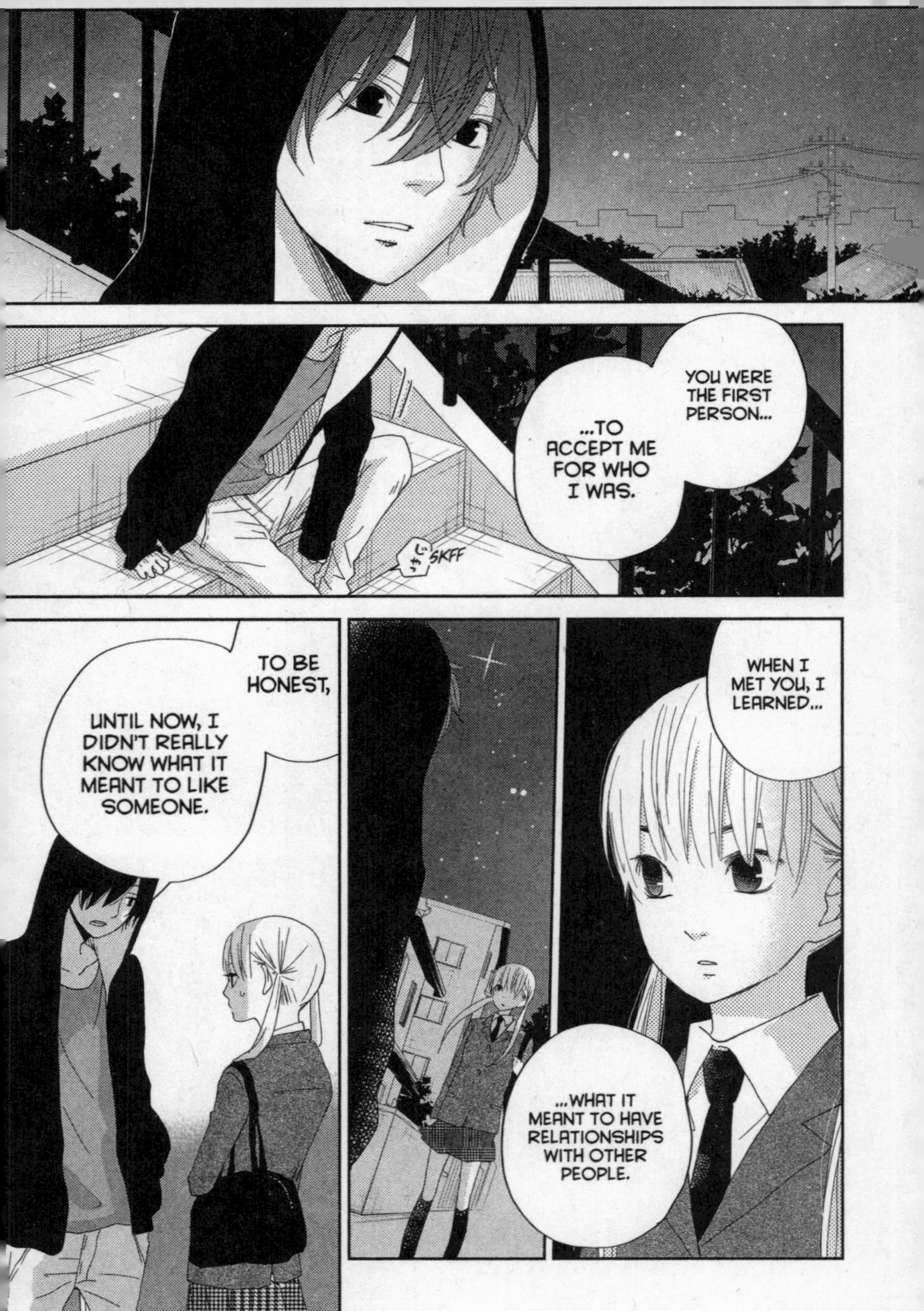
YOU WERE THE FIRST PERSON...
...TO ACCEPT ME FOR WHO I WAS.
SKFF
WHEN I MET YOU, I LEARNED...
...WHAT IT MEANT TO HAVE RELATIONSHIPS WITH OTHER PEOPLE.
TO BE HONEST,
UNTIL NOW, I DIDN'T REALLY KNOW WHAT IT MEANT TO LIKE SOMEONE.

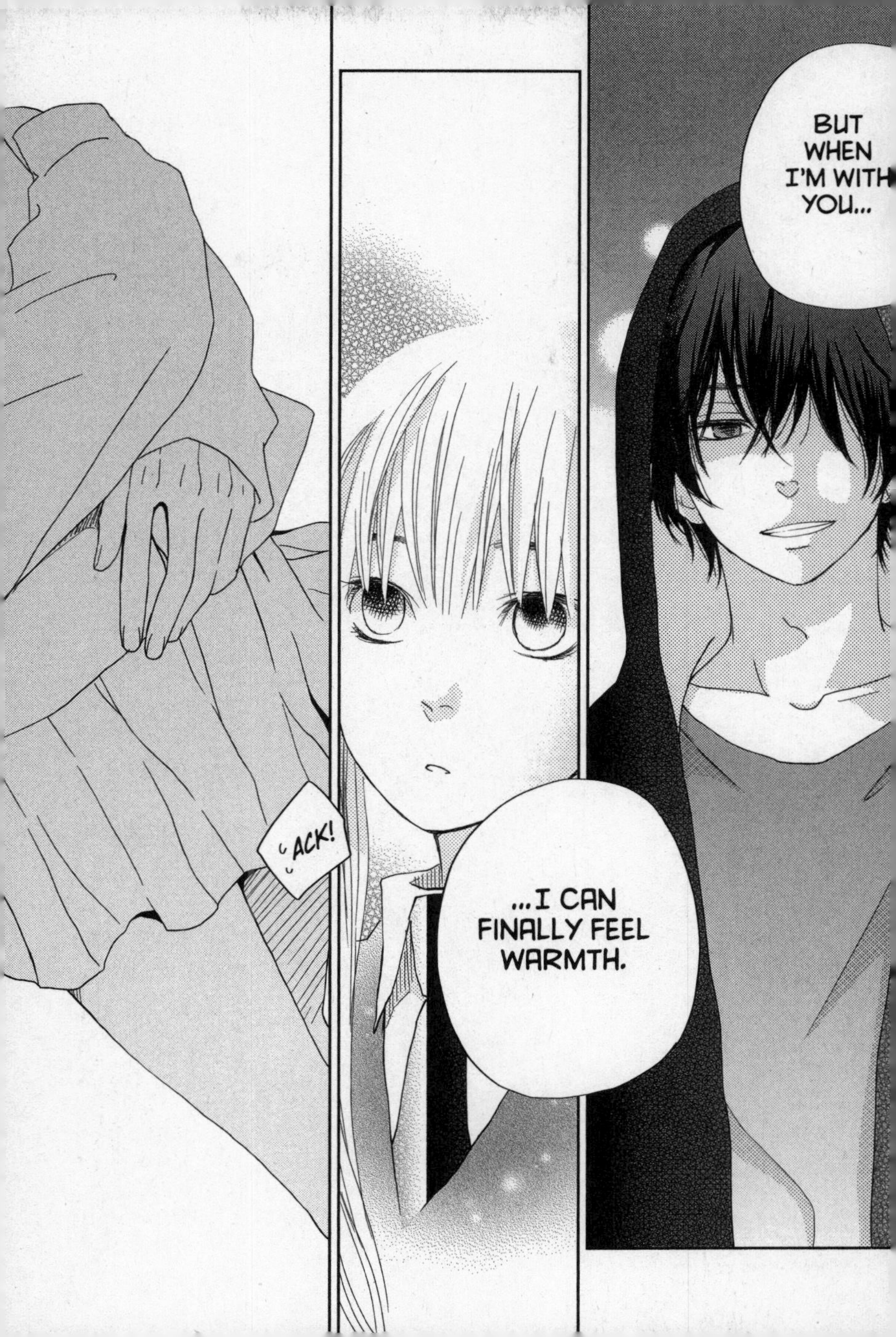
BUT WHEN I'M WITH YOU...
...I CAN FINALLY FEEL WARMTH.
ACK!

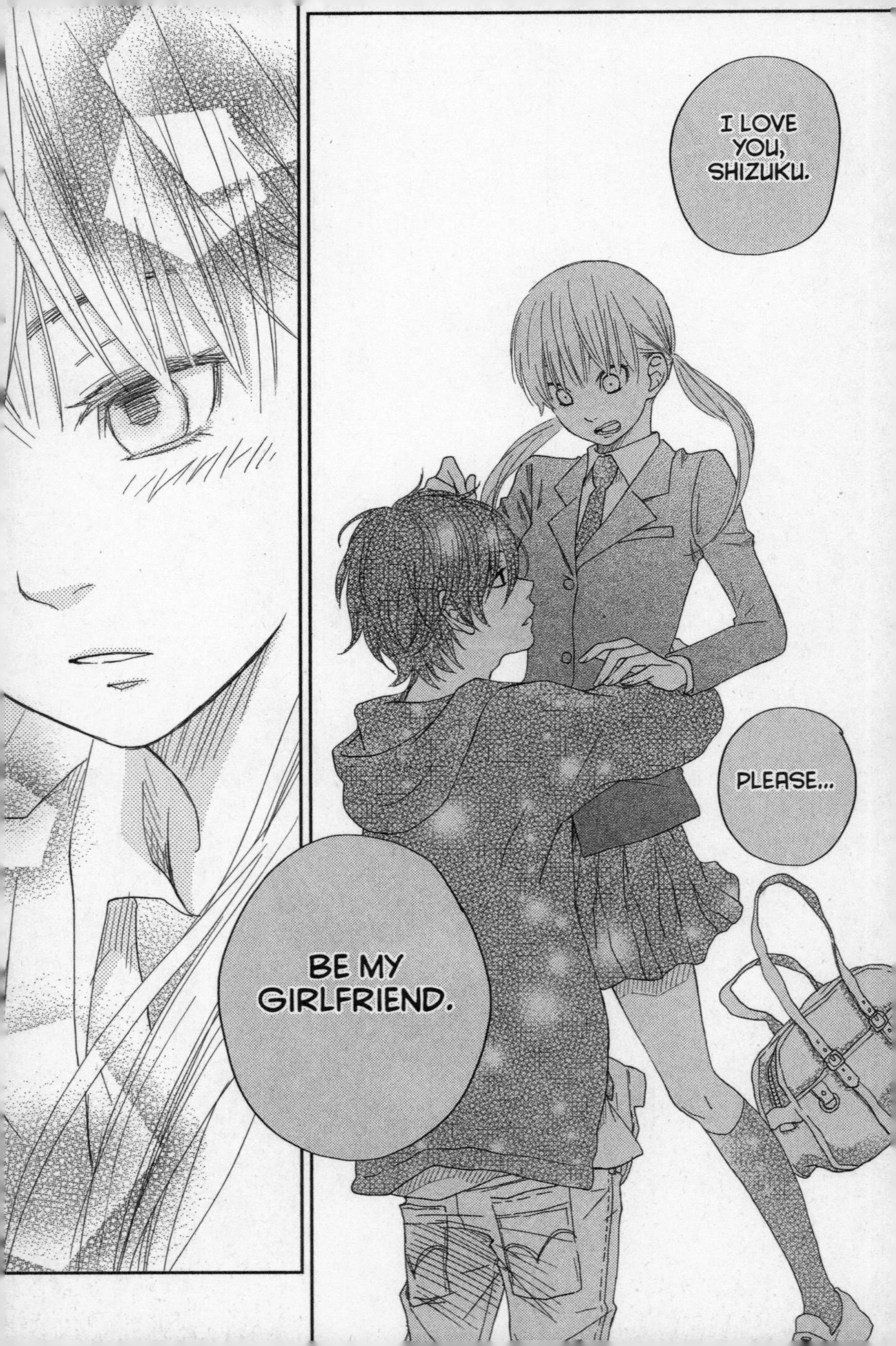
I LOVE YOU, SHIZUKU.
PLEASE...
BE MY GIRLFRIEND.

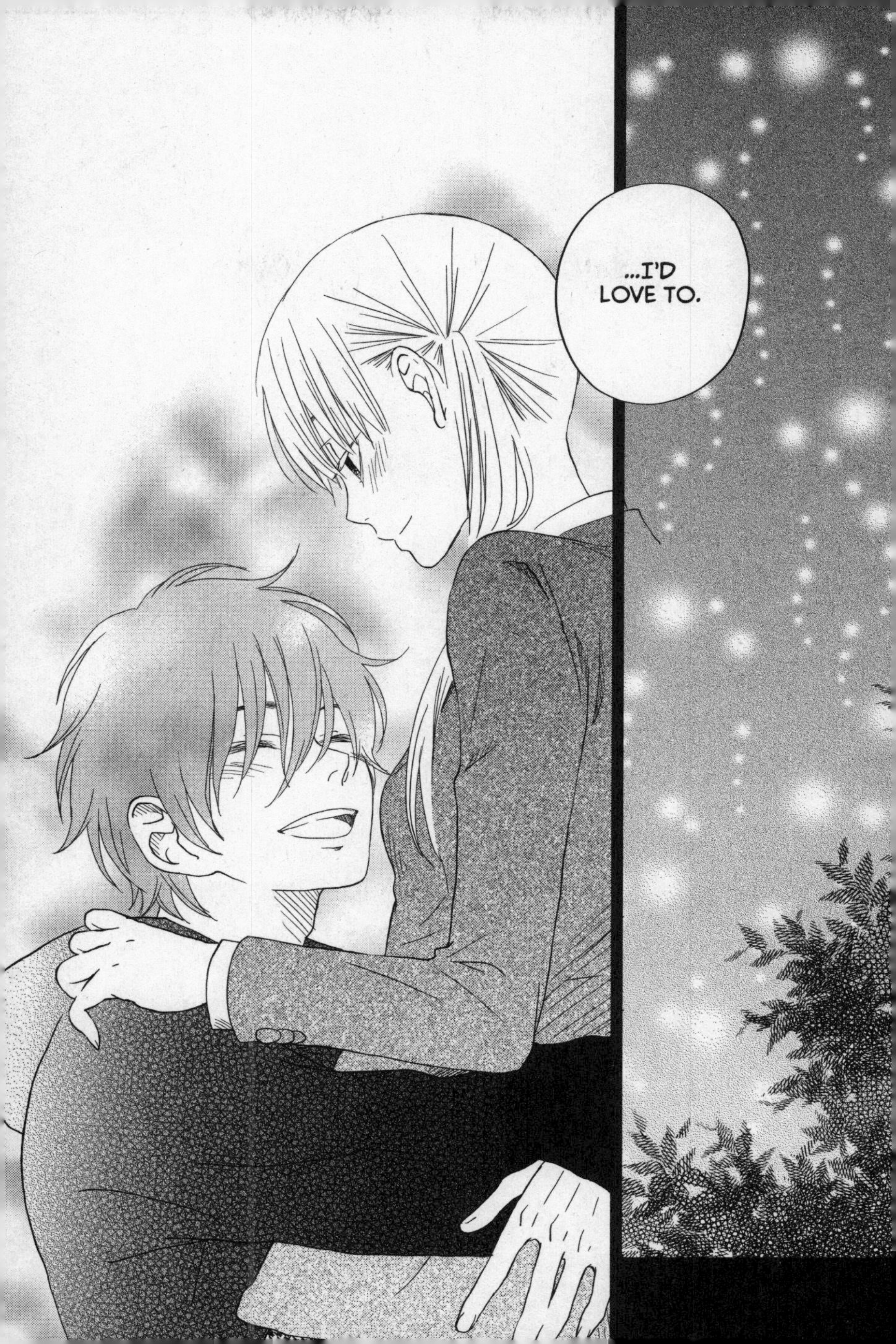
...I'D LOVE TO.

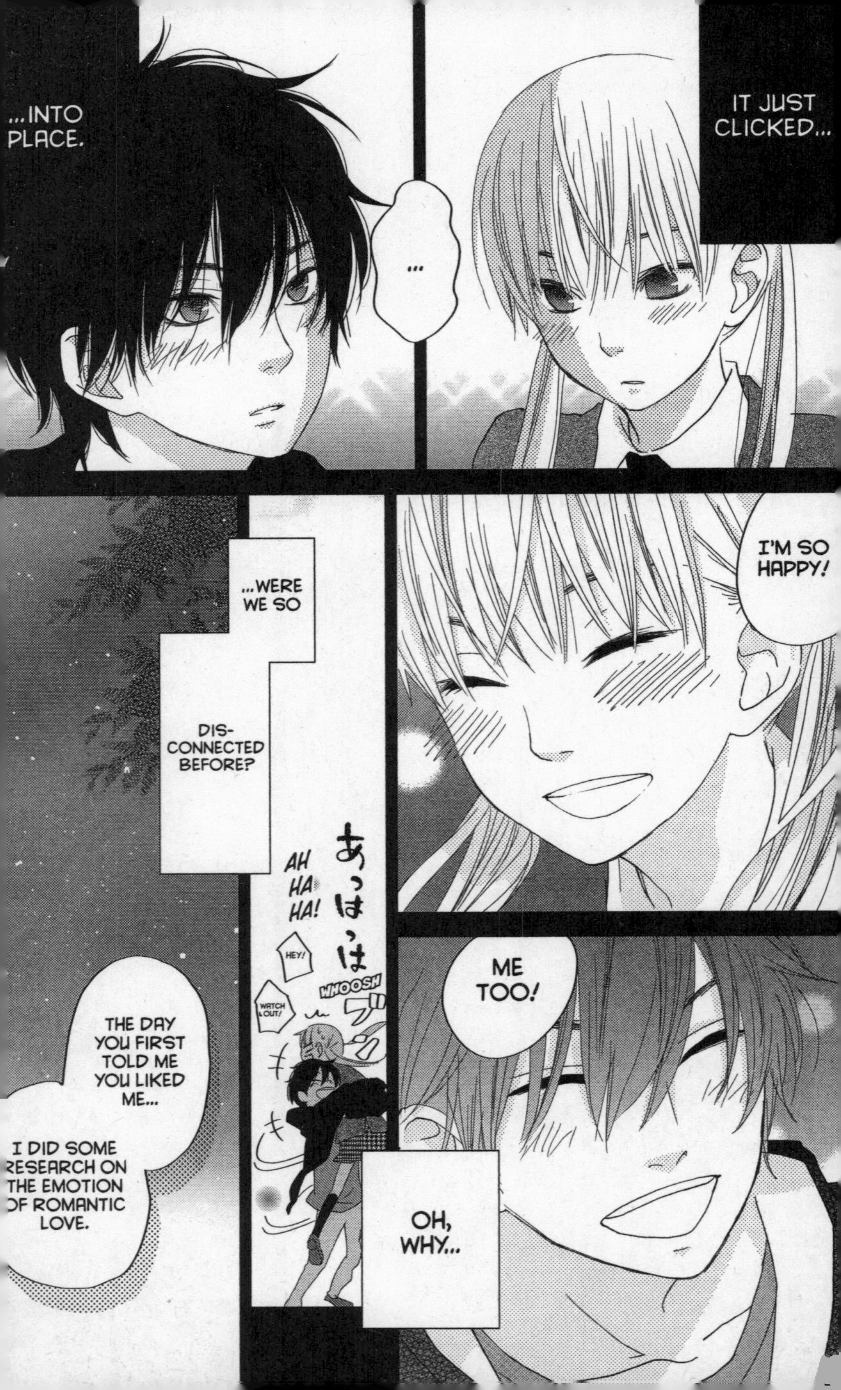
IT JUST CLICKED...
...
...INTO PLACE.
I'M SO HAPPY!
ME TOO!
OH, WHY...
...WERE WE SO
DIS- CONNECTED BEFORE?
AH HA HA!
あっはっは
HEY!
WATCH OUT!
WHOOSH
THE DAY YOU FIRST TOLD ME YOU LIKED ME...
I DID SOME RESEARCH ON THE EMOTION OF ROMANTIC LOVE.

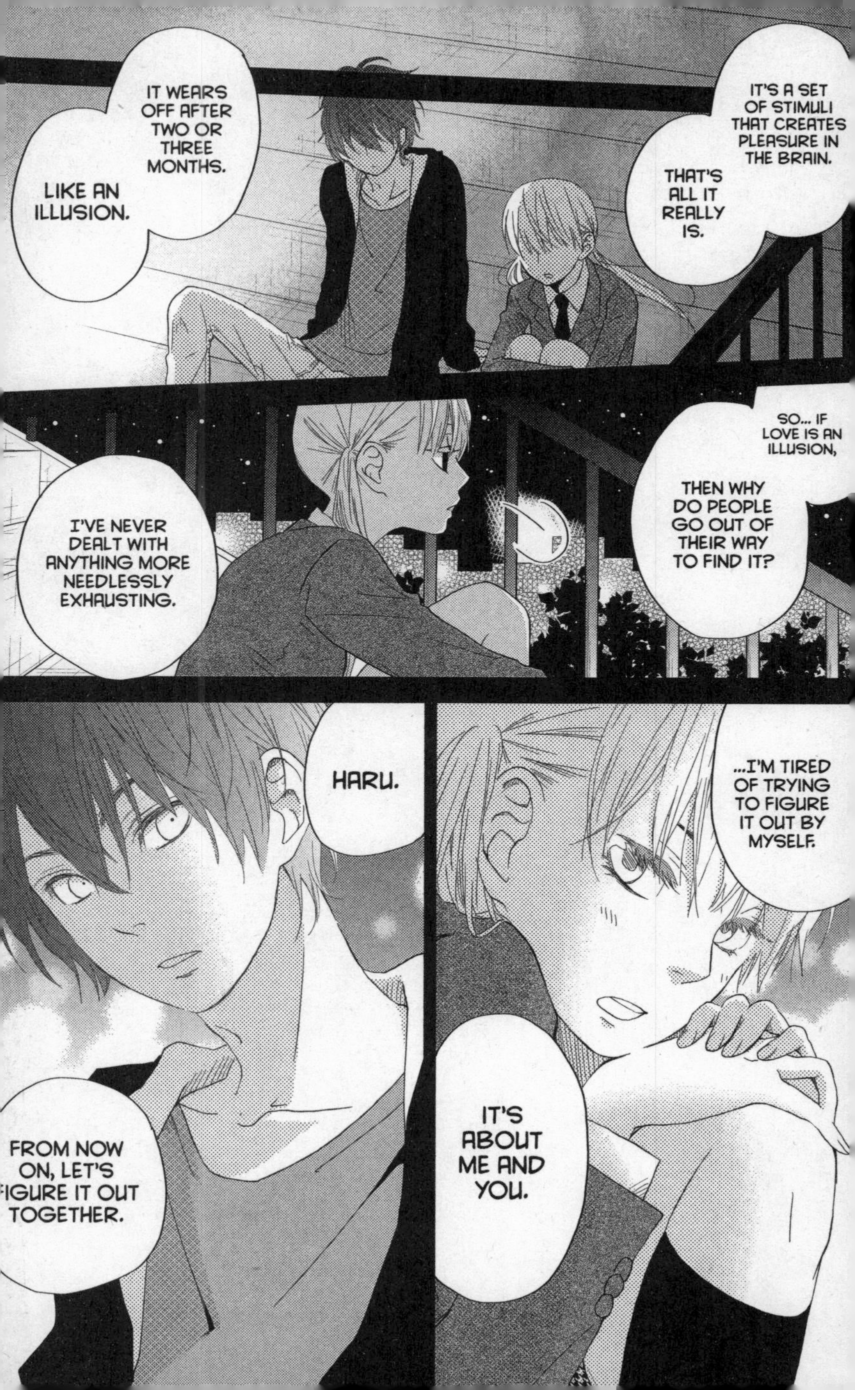
IT'S A SET OF STIMULI THAT CREATES PLEASURE IN THE BRAIN.
THAT'S ALL IT REALLY IS.
IT WEARS OFF AFTER TWO OR THREE MONTHS.
LIKE AN ILLUSION.
SO... IF LOVE IS AN ILLUSION,
THEN WHY DO PEOPLE GO OUT OF THEIR WAY TO FIND IT?
I'VE NEVER DEALT WITH ANYTHING MORE NEEDLESSLY EXHAUSTING.
...I'M TIRED OF TRYING TO FIGURE IT OUT BY MYSELF.
IT'S ABOUT ME AND YOU.
HARU.
FROM NOW ON, LET'S FIGURE IT OUT TOGETHER.

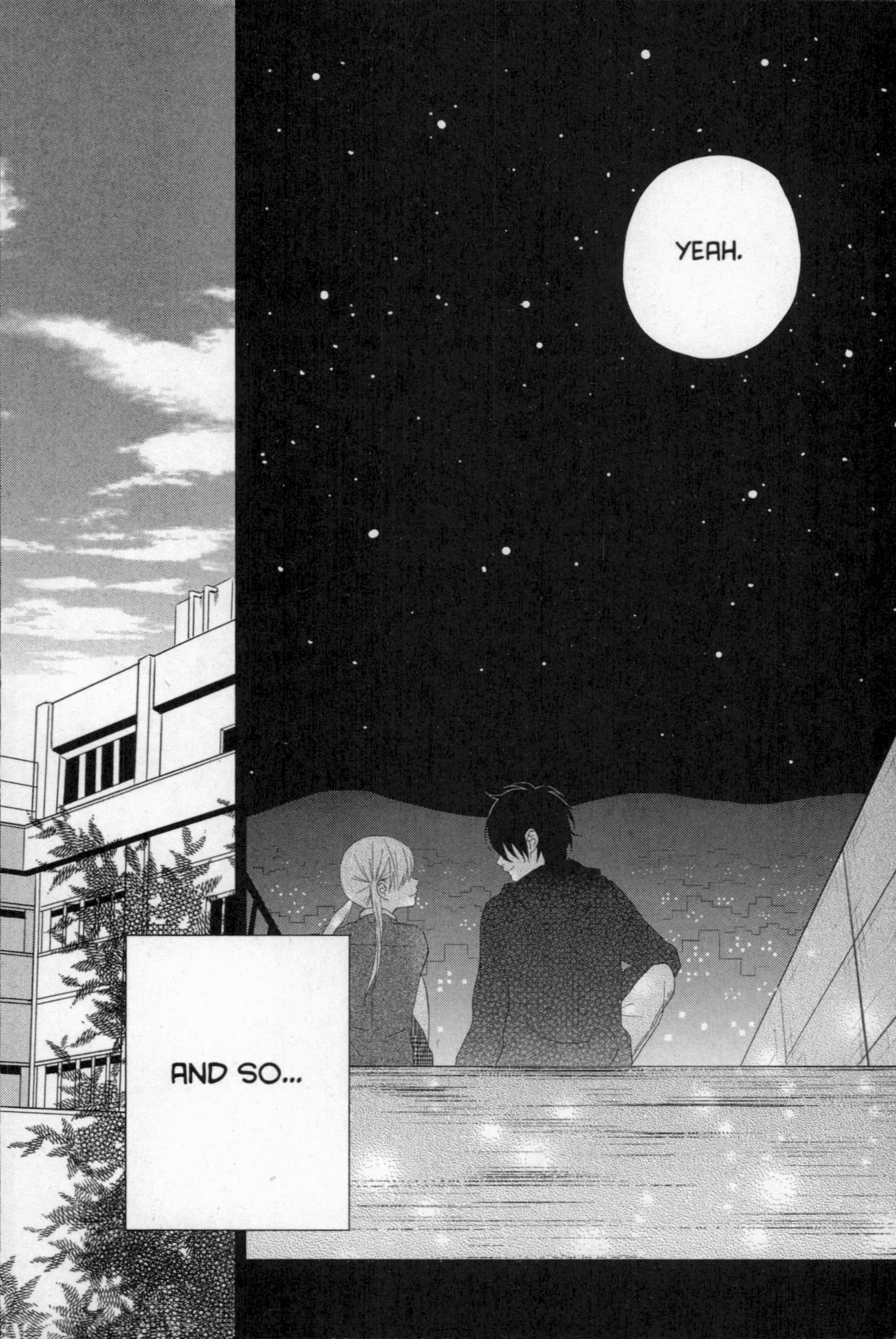
YEAH.
AND SO...

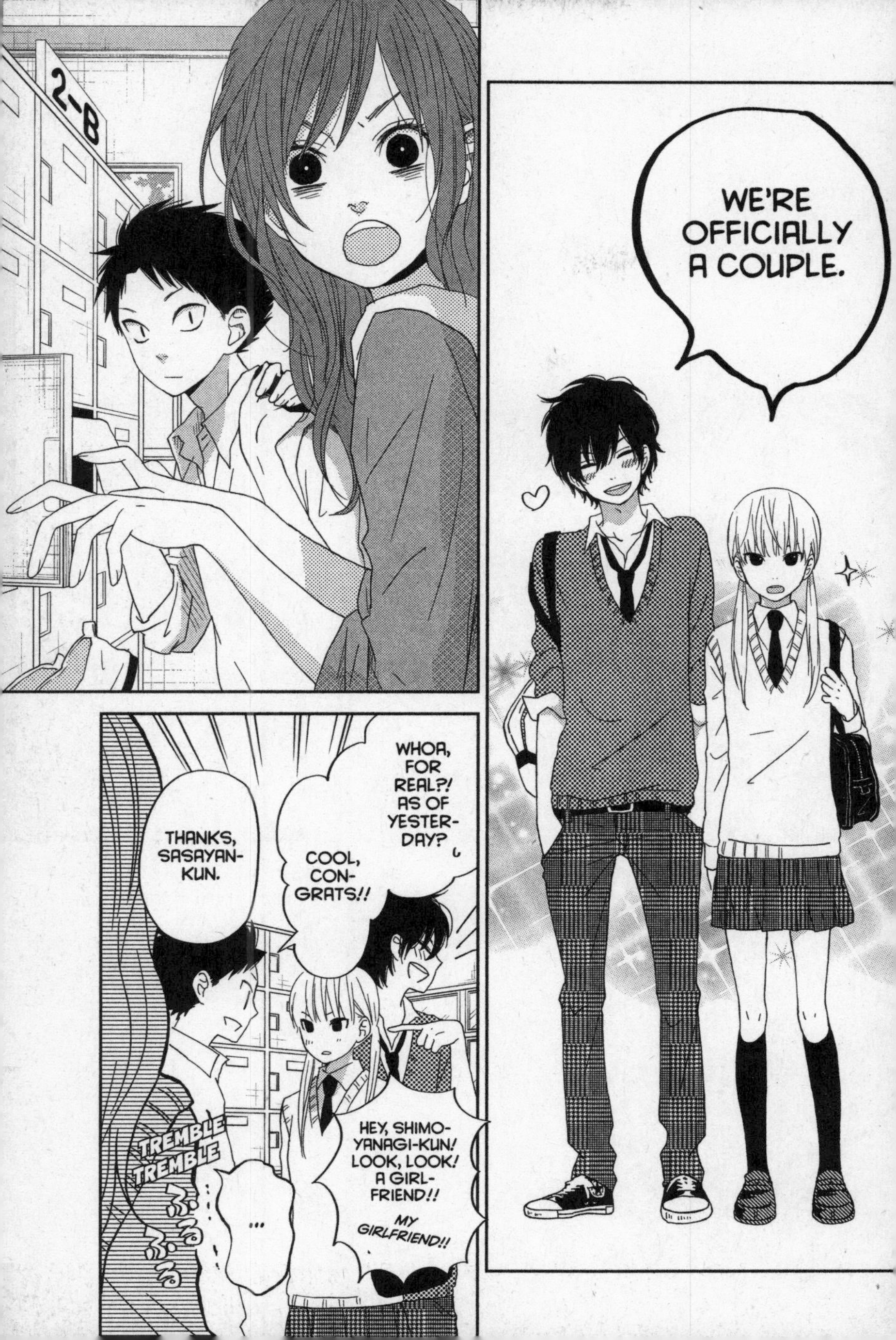
WE'RE OFFICIALLY A COUPLE.
WHOA, FOR REAL?! AS OF YESTERDAY?
COOL, CONGRATS!!
THANKS, SASAYAN-KUN.
HEY, SHIMOYANAGI-KUN! LOOK, LOOK! A GIRLFRIEND!!
MY GIRLFRIEND!!
...
TREMBLE TREMBLE

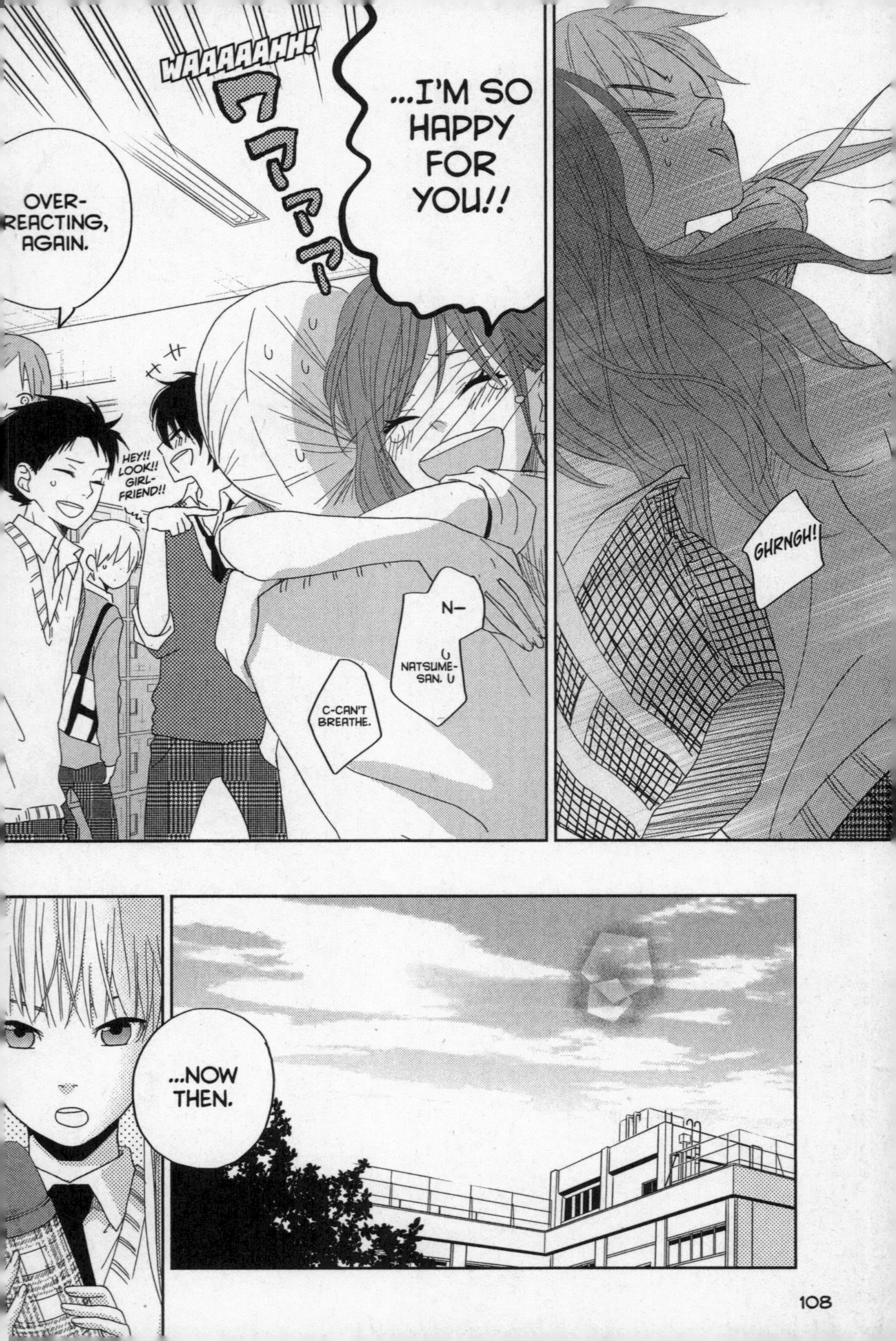
GHRNGH!
...I'M SO HAPPY FOR YOU!!
WAAAAAHH!
OVER-REACTING, AGAIN.
N— NATSUME-SAN.
HEY!! LOOK!! GIRL-FRIEND!!
C-CAN'T BREATHE.
...NOW THEN.

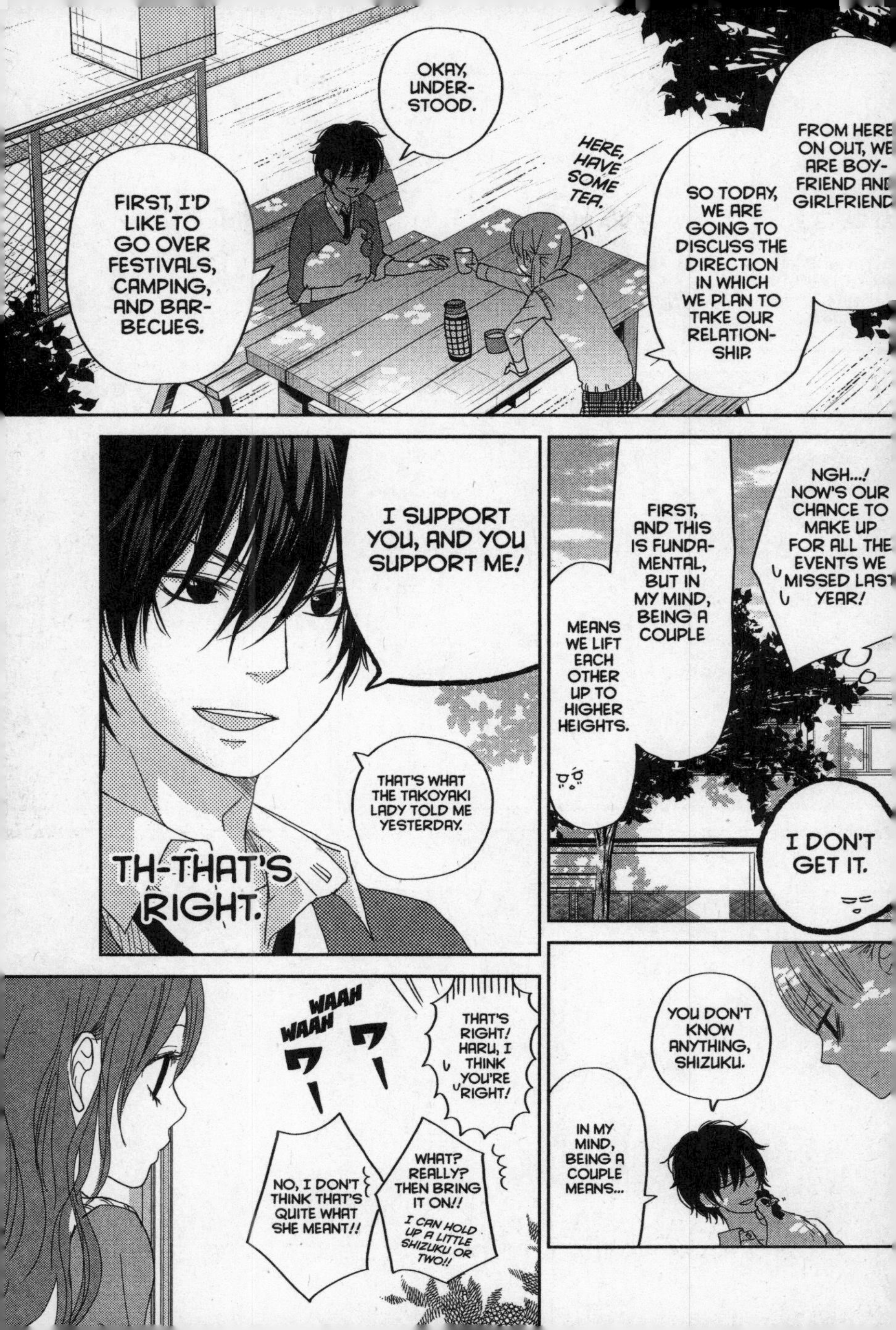
FROM HERE ON OUT, WE ARE BOYFRIEND AND GIRLFRIEND
SO TODAY, WE ARE GOING TO DISCUSS THE DIRECTION IN WHICH WE PLAN TO TAKE OUR RELATIONSHIP.
HERE, HAVE SOME TEA.
OKAY, UNDERSTOOD.
FIRST, I'D LIKE TO GO OVER FESTIVALS, CAMPING, AND BARBECUES.
NGH...! NOW'S OUR CHANCE TO MAKE UP FOR ALL THE EVENTS WE MISSED LAST YEAR!
FIRST, AND THIS IS FUNDAMENTAL, BUT IN MY MIND, BEING A COUPLE
MEANS WE LIFT EACH OTHER UP TO HIGHER HEIGHTS.
I DON'T GET IT.
I SUPPORT YOU, AND YOU SUPPORT ME!
THAT'S WHAT THE TAKOYAKI LADY TOLD ME YESTERDAY.
TH-THAT'S RIGHT.
YOU DON'T KNOW ANYTHING, SHIZUKU.
IN MY MIND, BEING A COUPLE MEANS...
THAT'S RIGHT! HARU, I THINK YOU'RE RIGHT!
WAAH WAAH
WHAT? REALLY? THEN BRING IT ON!!
I CAN HOLD UP A LITTLE SHIZUKU OR TWO!!
NO, I DON'T THINK THAT'S QUITE WHAT SHE MEANT!!

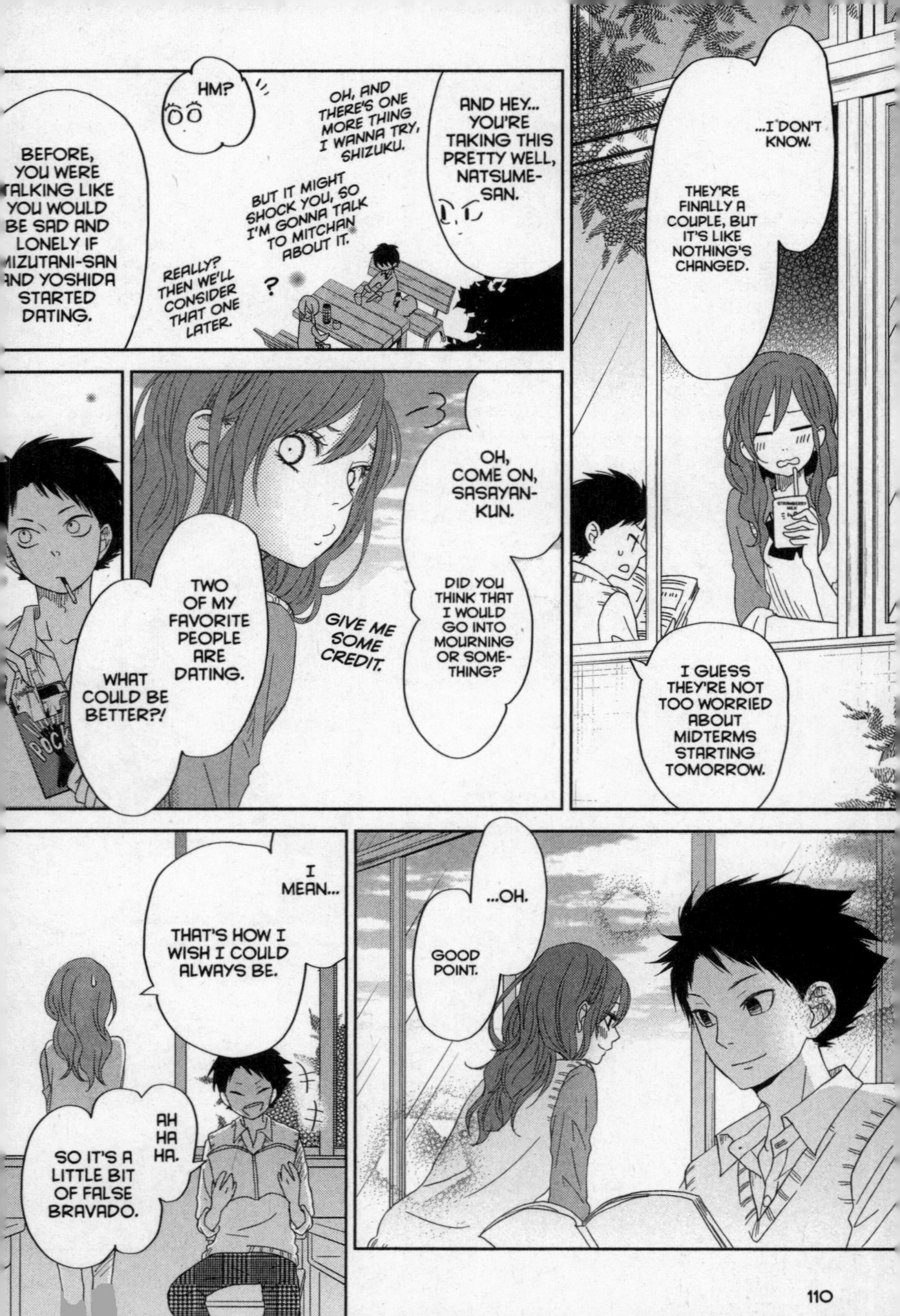
...I DON'T KNOW.
THEY'RE FINALLY A COUPLE, BUT IT'S LIKE NOTHING'S CHANGED.
I GUESS THEY'RE NOT TOO WORRIED ABOUT MIDTERMS STARTING TOMORROW.
AND HEY... YOU'RE TAKING THIS PRETTY WELL, NATSUME-SAN.
OH, AND THERE'S ONE MORE THING I WANNA TRY, SHIZUKU.
HM?
BUT IT MIGHT SHOCK YOU, SO I'M GONNA TALK TO MITCHAN ABOUT IT.
REALLY? THEN WE'LL CONSIDER THAT ONE LATER.
BEFORE, YOU WERE TALKING LIKE YOU WOULD BE SAD AND LONELY IF MIZUTANI-SAN AND YOSHIDA STARTED DATING.
OH, COME ON, SASAYAN-KUN.
DID YOU THINK THAT I WOULD GO INTO MOURNING OR SOME-THING?
GIVE ME SOME CREDIT.
TWO OF MY FAVORITE PEOPLE ARE DATING.
WHAT COULD BE BETTER?!
...OH.
GOOD POINT.
I MEAN...
THAT'S HOW I WISH I COULD ALWAYS BE.
AH HA HA.
SO IT'S A LITTLE BIT OF FALSE BRAVADO.

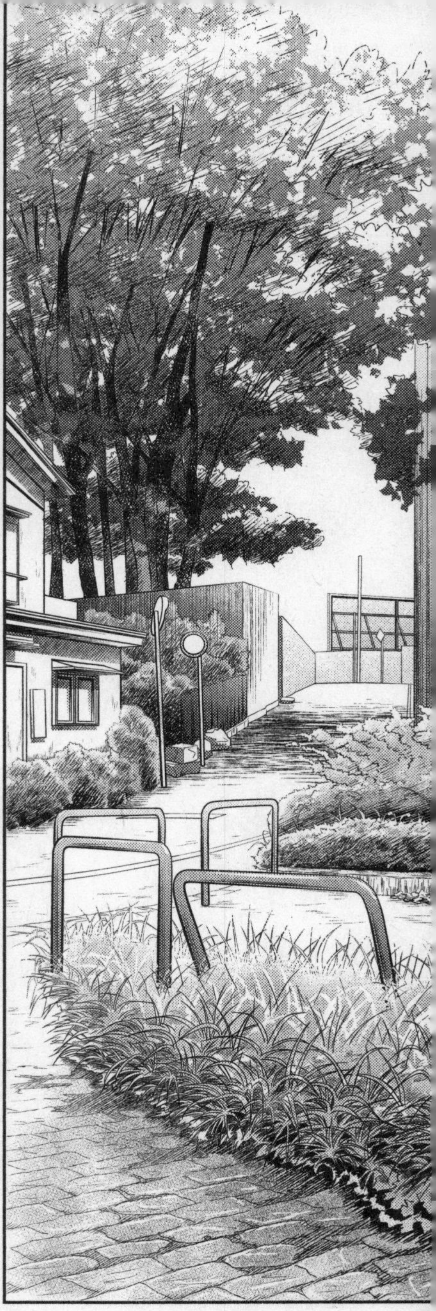

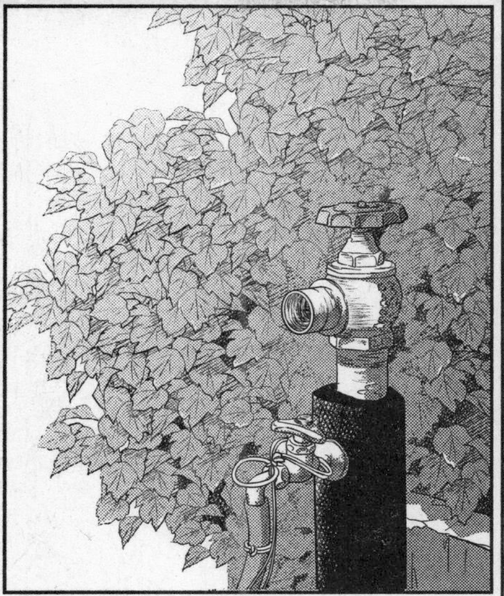

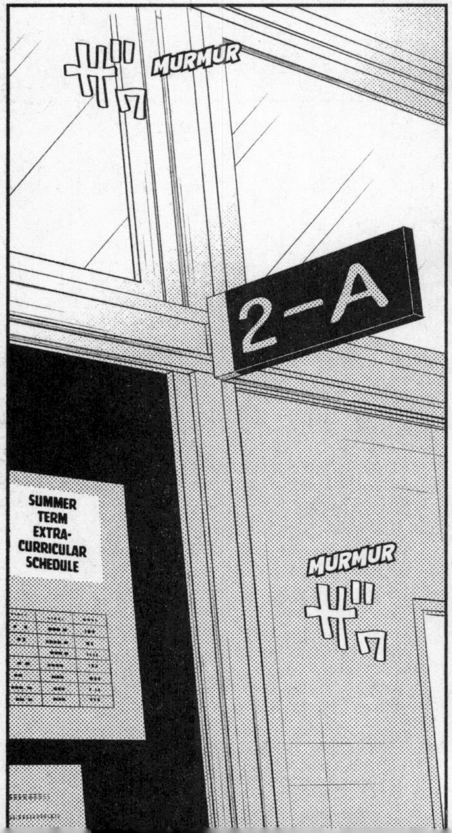
MURMUR
ザワ
2-A
SUMMER TERM EXTRA-CURRICULAR SCHEDULE
MURMUR
ザワ

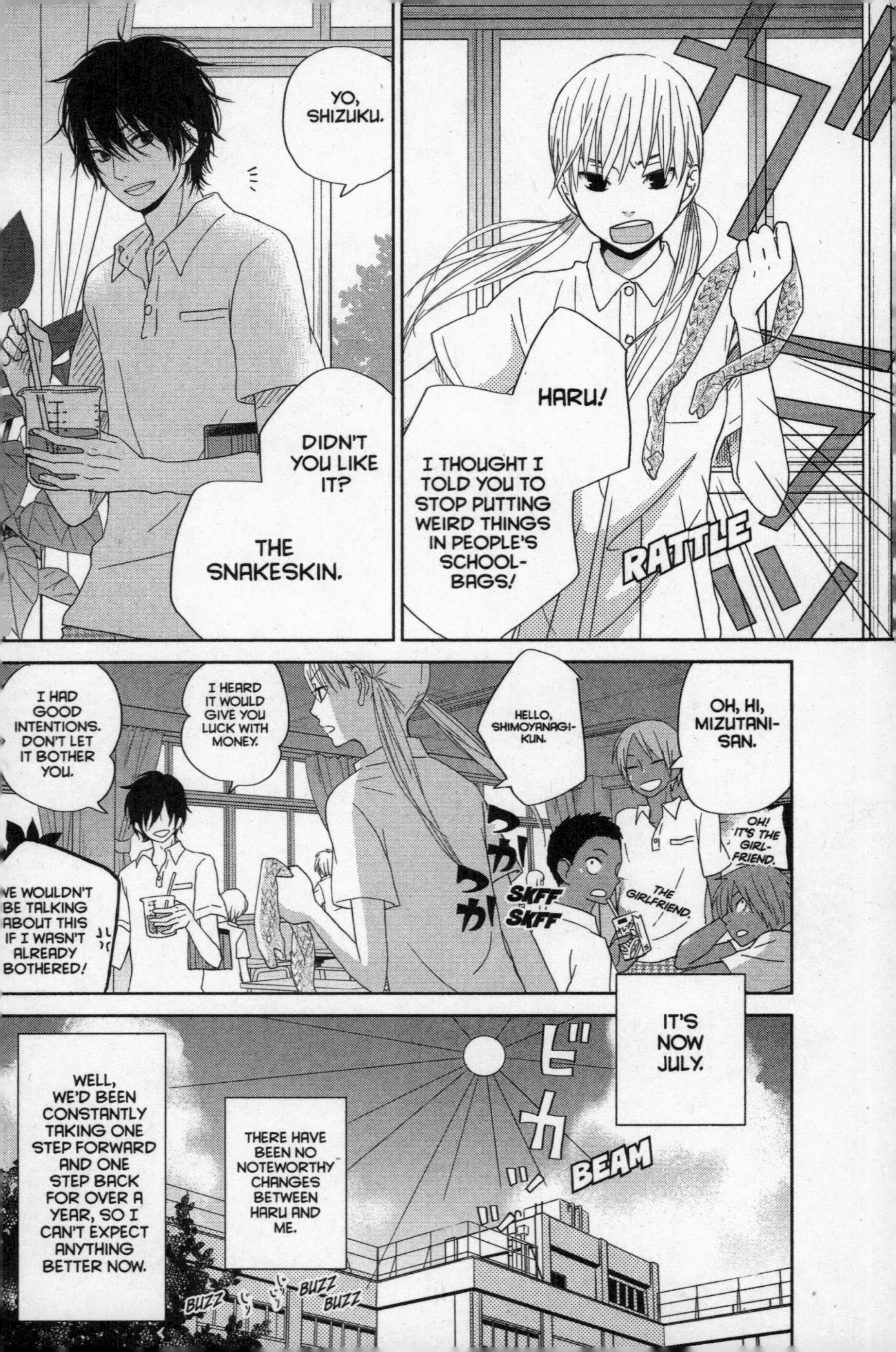
HARU!
I THOUGHT I TOLD YOU TO STOP PUTTING WEIRD THINGS IN PEOPLE'S SCHOOL-BAGS!
RATTLE
YO, SHIZUKU.
DIDN'T YOU LIKE IT?
THE SNAKESKIN.
OH, HI, MIZUTANI-SAN.
HELLO, SHIMOYANAGI-KUN.
OH! IT'S THE GIRL-FRIEND.
THE GIRLFRIEND.
SKFF SKFF
I HEARD IT WOULD GIVE YOU LUCK WITH MONEY.
I HAD GOOD INTENTIONS. DON'T LET IT BOTHER YOU.
WE WOULDN'T BE TALKING ABOUT THIS IF I WASN'T ALREADY BOTHERED!
IT'S NOW JULY.
BEAM
THERE HAVE BEEN NO NOTEWORTHY CHANGES BETWEEN HARU AND ME.
WELL, WE'D BEEN CONSTANTLY TAKING ONE STEP FORWARD AND ONE STEP BACK FOR OVER A YEAR, SO I CAN'T EXPECT ANYTHING BETTER NOW.
BUZZ BUZZ
BUZZ

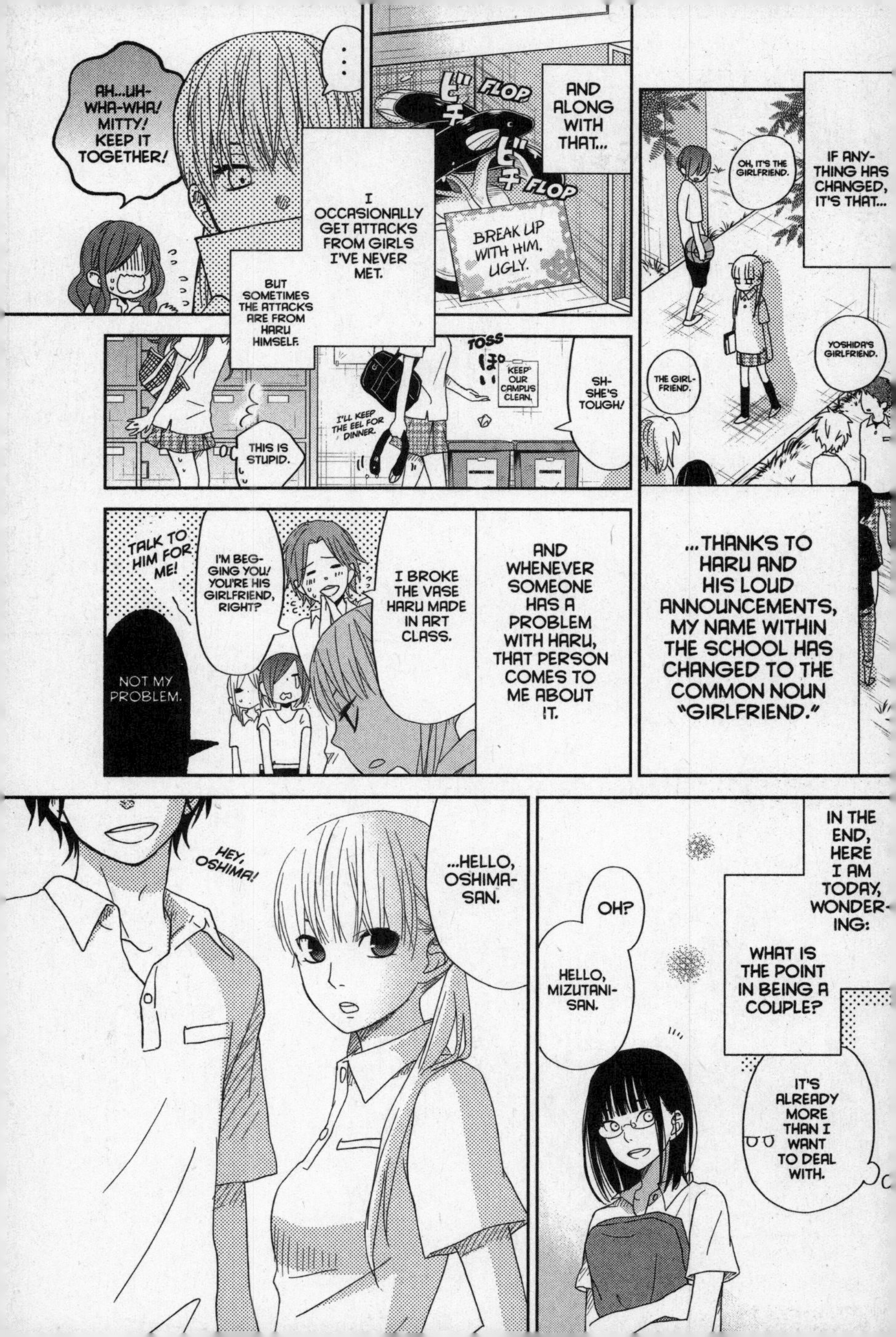
IF ANYTHING HAS CHANGED, IT'S THAT...
OH, IT'S THE GIRLFRIEND.
YOSHIDA'S GIRLFRIEND.
THE GIRLFRIEND.
...THANKS TO HARU AND HIS LOUD ANNOUNCEMENTS, MY NAME WITHIN THE SCHOOL HAS CHANGED TO THE COMMON NOUN "GIRLFRIEND."
AND ALONG WITH THAT...
FLOP
FLOP
I OCCASIONALLY GET ATTACKS FROM GIRLS I'VE NEVER MET.
BREAK UP WITH HIM, UGLY.
...
AH...UH-WHA-WHA! MITTY! KEEP IT TOGETHER!
BUT SOMETIMES THE ATTACKS ARE FROM HARU HIMSELF.
SH-SHE'S TOUGH!
TOSS
KEEP OUR CAMPUS CLEAN.
I'LL KEEP THE EEL FOR DINNER.
THIS IS STUPID.
AND WHENEVER SOMEONE HAS A PROBLEM WITH HARU, THAT PERSON COMES TO ME ABOUT IT.
I BROKE THE VASE HARU MADE IN ART CLASS.
I'M BEGGING YOU! YOU'RE HIS GIRLFRIEND, RIGHT?
TALK TO HIM FOR ME!
NOT MY PROBLEM.
IN THE END, HERE I AM TODAY, WONDERING:
WHAT IS THE POINT IN BEING A COUPLE?
IT'S ALREADY MORE THAN I WANT TO DEAL WITH.
OH?
HELLO, MIZUTANI-SAN.
...HELLO, OSHIMA-SAN.
HEY, OSHIMA!

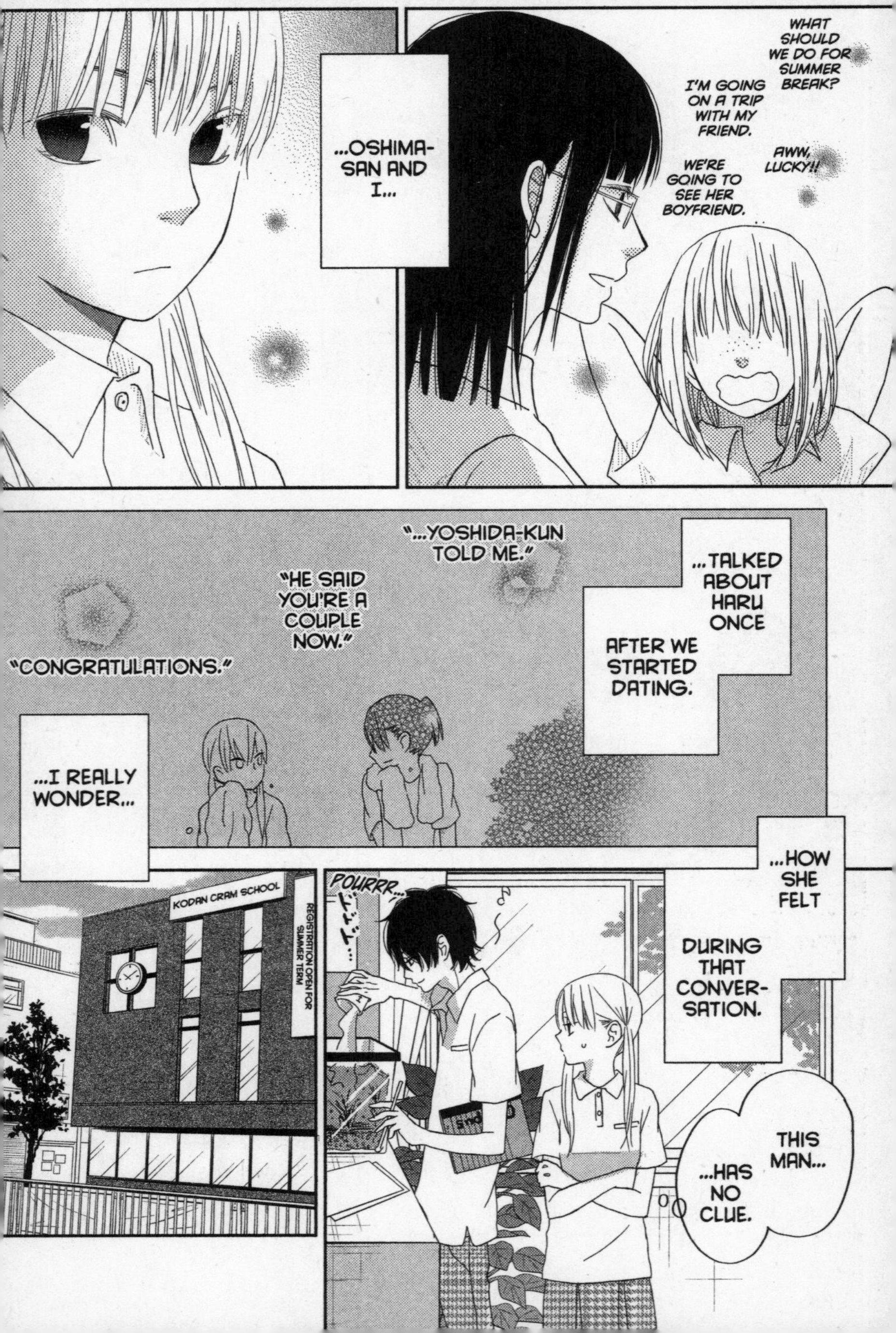
WHAT SHOULD WE DO FOR SUMMER BREAK?
I'M GOING ON A TRIP WITH MY FRIEND.
AWW, LUCKY!!
WE'RE GOING TO SEE HER BOYFRIEND.
...OSHIMA-SAN AND I...
...TALKED ABOUT HARU ONCE
AFTER WE STARTED DATING.
"...YOSHIDA-KUN TOLD ME."
"HE SAID YOU'RE A COUPLE NOW."
"CONGRATULATIONS."
...I REALLY WONDER...
...HOW SHE FELT
DURING THAT CONVERSATION.
POURRR...
THIS MAN... ...HAS NO CLUE.
KODAN CRAM SCHOOL
REGISTRATION OPEN FOR SUMMER TERM

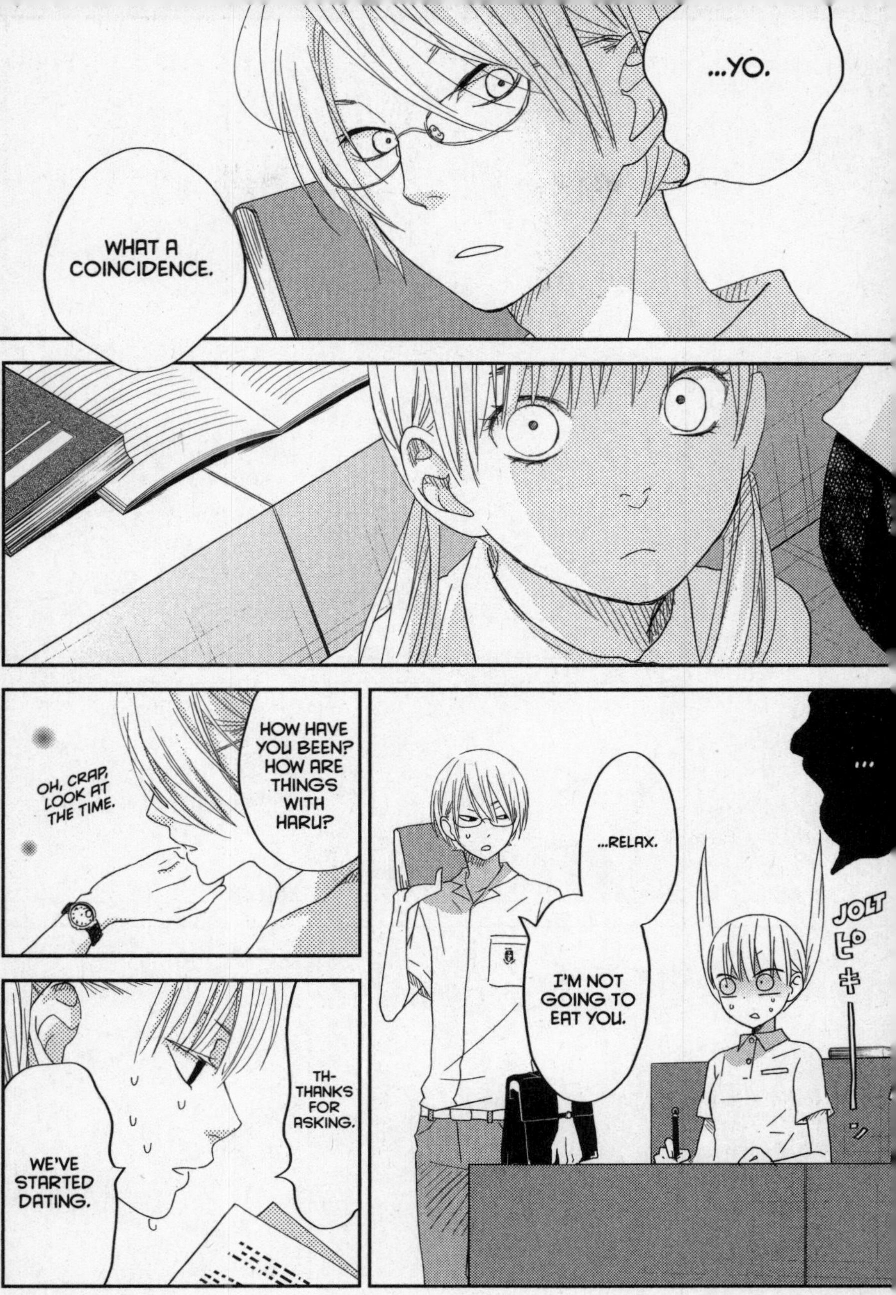
...YO.
WHAT A COINCIDENCE.
...
JOLT
...RELAX.
I'M NOT GOING TO EAT YOU.
HOW HAVE YOU BEEN? HOW ARE THINGS WITH HARU?
OH, CRAP, LOOK AT THE TIME.
TH-THANKS FOR ASKING.
WE'VE STARTED DATING.

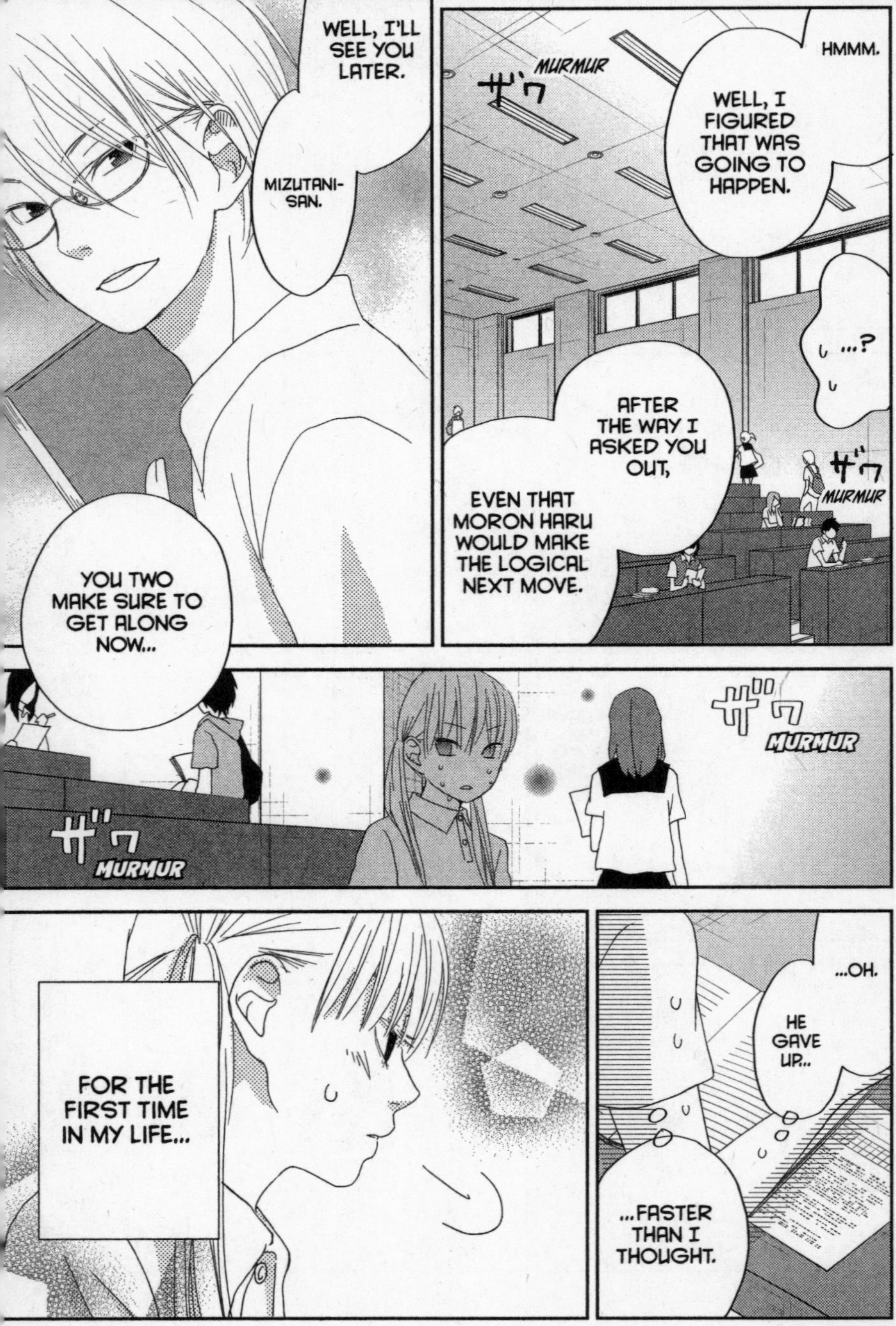
HMMM.
WELL, I FIGURED THAT WAS GOING TO HAPPEN.
ザワ
MURMUR
...?
AFTER THE WAY I ASKED YOU OUT,
EVEN THAT MORON HARU WOULD MAKE THE LOGICAL NEXT MOVE.
ザワ
MURMUR
WELL, I'LL SEE YOU LATER.
MIZUTANI-SAN.
YOU TWO MAKE SURE TO GET ALONG NOW...
ザワ
MURMUR
ザワ
MURMUR
...OH.
HE GAVE UP...
...FASTER THAN I THOUGHT.
FOR THE FIRST TIME IN MY LIFE...

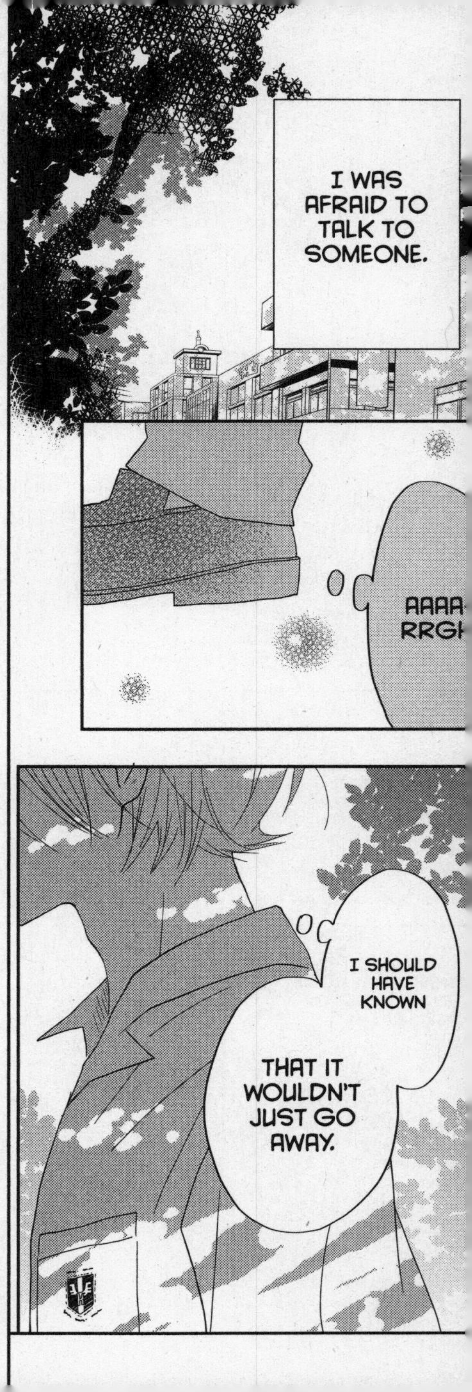
I WAS AFRAID TO TALK TO SOMEONE.
AAAA- RRG
I SHOULD HAVE KNOWN
THAT IT WOULDN'T JUST GO AWAY.

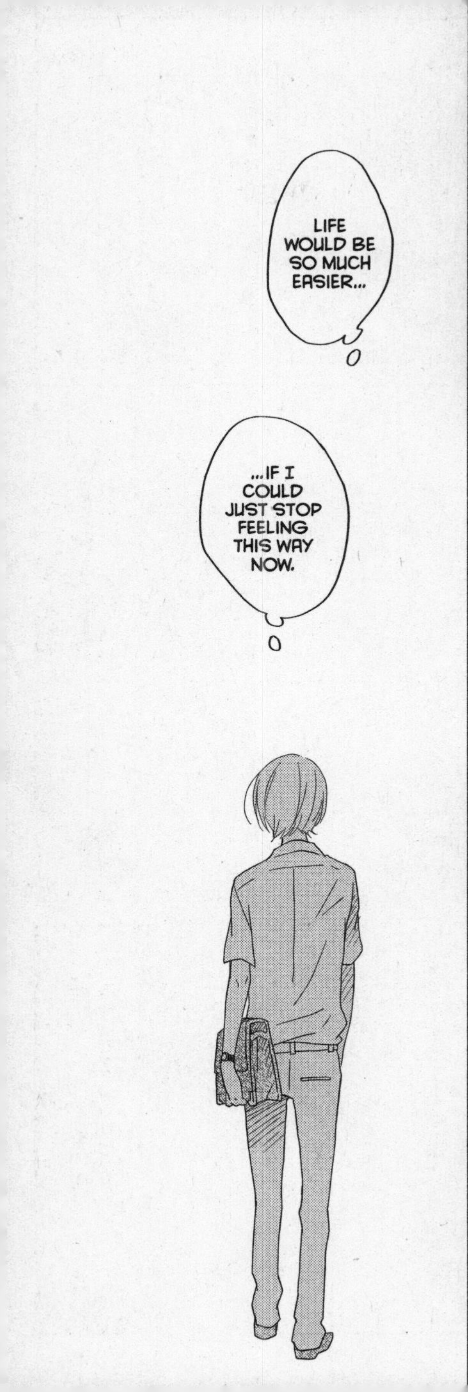
LIFE WOULD BE SO MUCH EASIER...
...IF I COULD JUST STOP FEELING THIS WAY NOW.

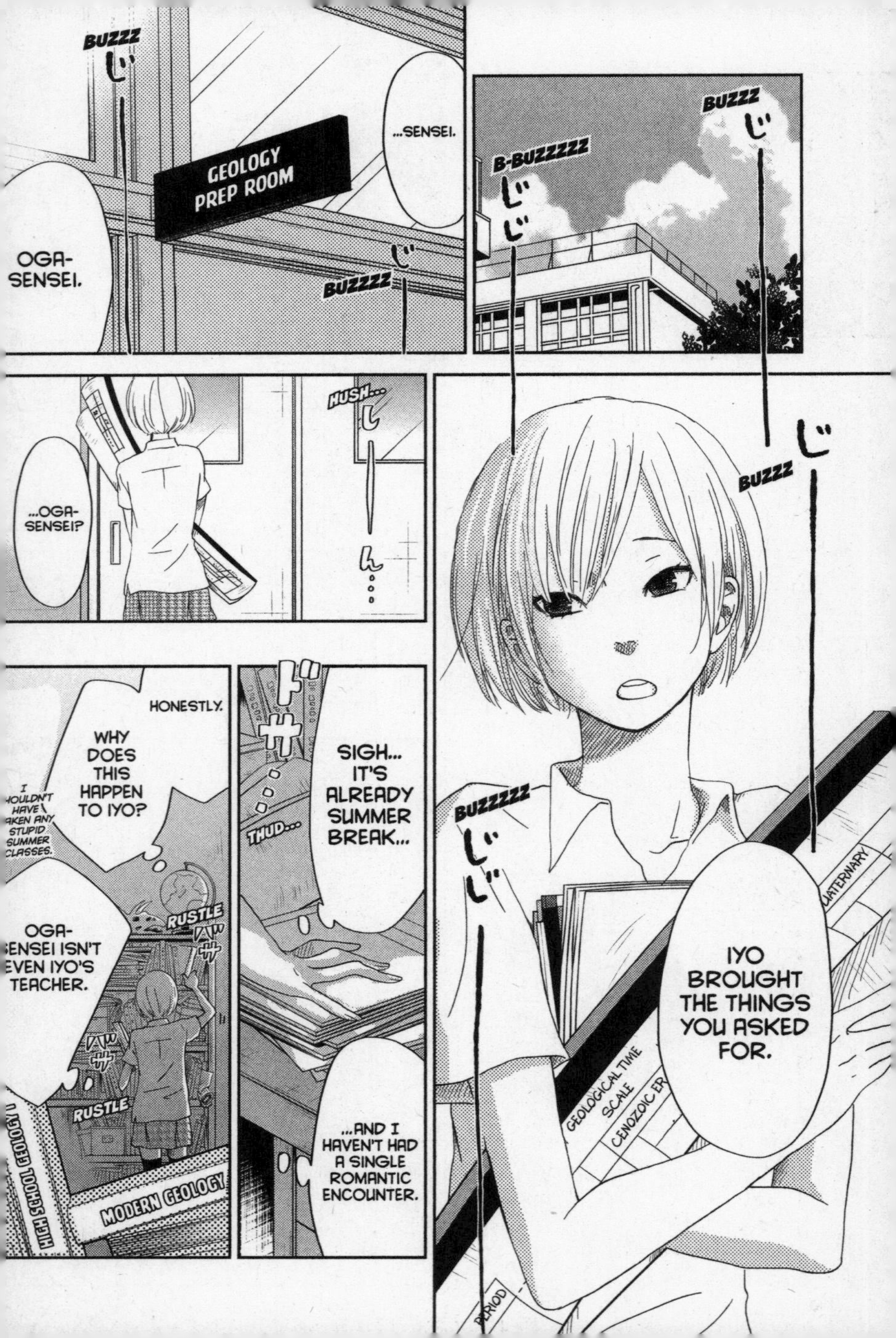
BUZZZ
じ
B-BUZZZZZ
じじじ
...SENSEI.
GEOLOGY PREP ROOM
OGA-SENSEI.
BUZZZ
じ
BUZZZZ
じ
BUZZZ
じ
IYO BROUGHT THE THINGS YOU ASKED FOR.
BUZZZZZ
じじじ
QUATERNARY
GEOLOGICAL TIME SCALE
CENOZOIC ER
PERIOD
HUSH...
じーん...
...OGA-SENSEI?
SIGH... IT'S ALREADY SUMMER BREAK...
...AND I HAVEN'T HAD A SINGLE ROMANTIC ENCOUNTER.
ドサ...
THUD...
HONESTLY.
WHY DOES THIS HAPPEN TO IYO?
I HOULDN'T HAVE AKEN ANY STUPID SUMMER CLASSES.
OGA-ENSEI ISN'T EVEN IYO'S TEACHER.
RUSTLE
バサ
バサ
RUSTLE
MODERN GEOLOGY
HIGH SCHOOL GEOLOGY I

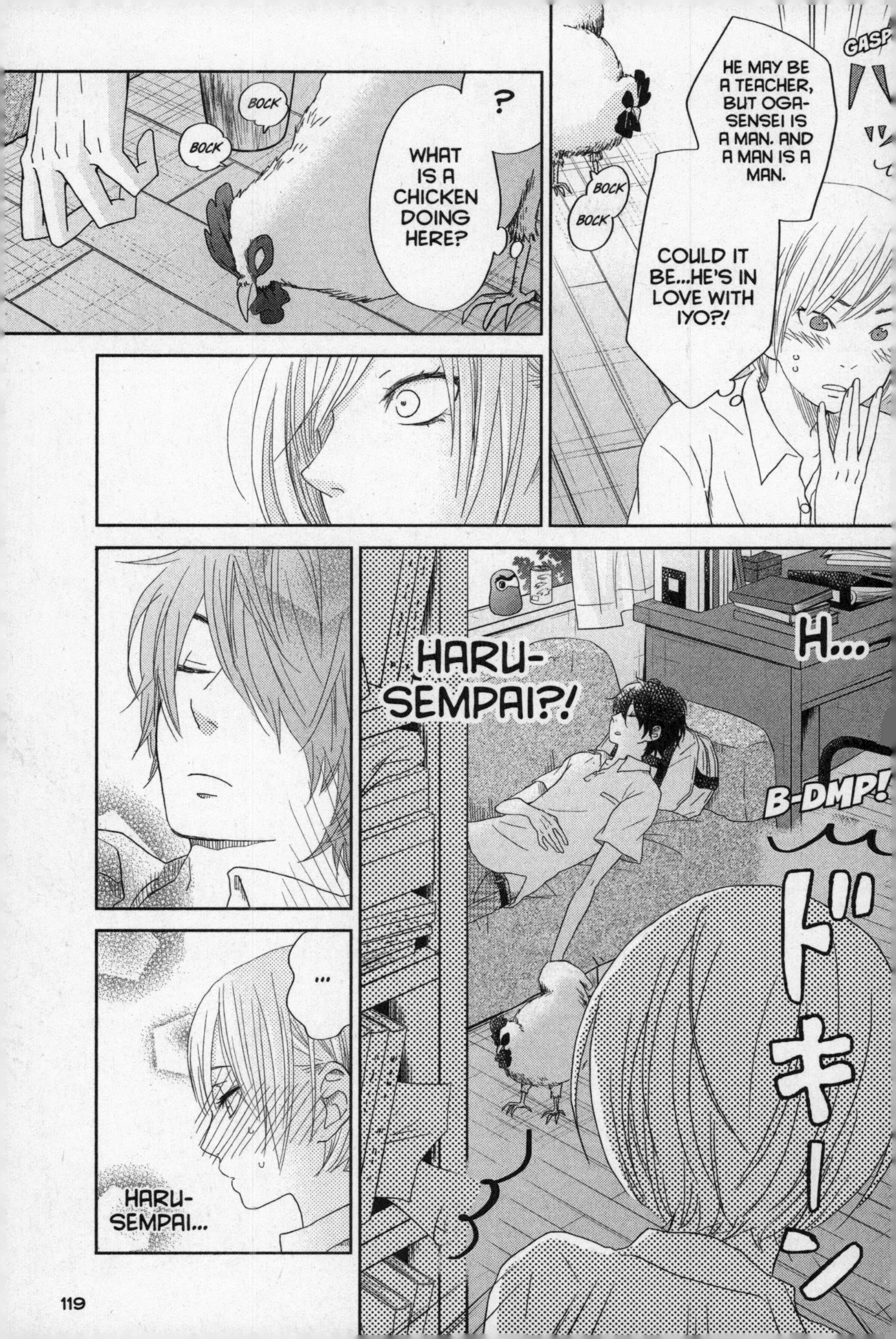
GASP
HE MAY BE A TEACHER, BUT OGA-SENSEI IS A MAN. AND A MAN IS A MAN.
COULD IT BE...HE'S IN LOVE WITH IYO?!
BOCK
BOCK
?
WHAT IS A CHICKEN DOING HERE?
BOCK
BOCK
H...
B-DMP!
HARU-SEMPAI?!
...
HARU-SEMPAI...

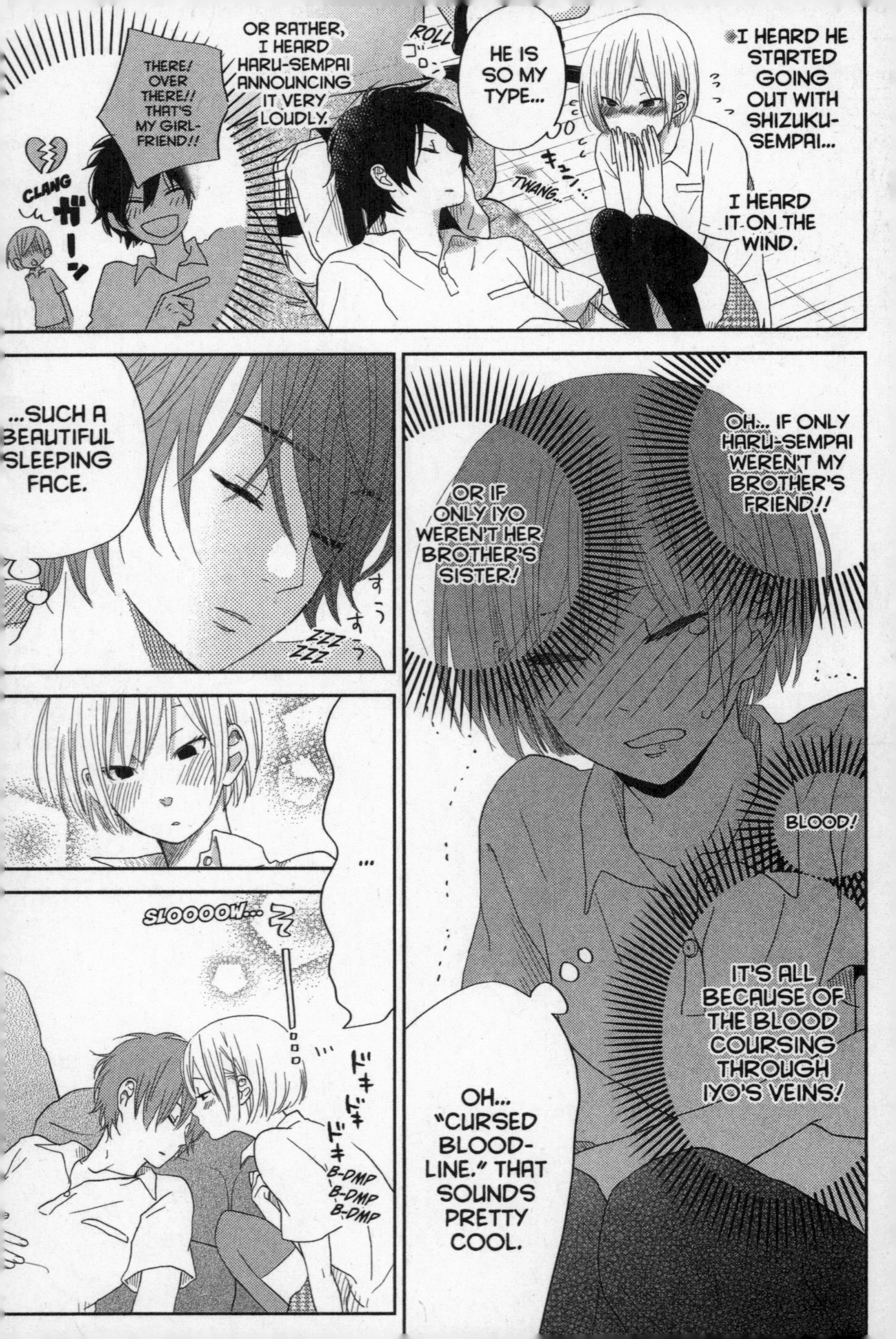
I HEARD HE STARTED GOING OUT WITH SHIZUKU-SEMPAI...
I HEARD IT ON THE WIND.
TWANG...
HE IS SO MY TYPE...
ROLL
OR RATHER, I HEARD HARU-SEMPAI ANNOUNCING IT VERY LOUDLY.
THERE! OVER THERE!! THAT'S MY GIRL-FRIEND!!
CLANG
...SUCH A BEAUTIFUL SLEEPING FACE.
ZZZ ZZZ
...
SLOOOOW...
B-DMP B-DMP B-DMP
OH... IF ONLY HARU-SEMPAI WEREN'T MY BROTHER'S FRIEND!!
OR IF ONLY IYO WEREN'T HER BROTHER'S SISTER!
BLOOD!
IT'S ALL BECAUSE OF THE BLOOD COURSING THROUGH IYO'S VEINS!
OH... "CURSED BLOOD-LINE." THAT SOUNDS PRETTY COOL.

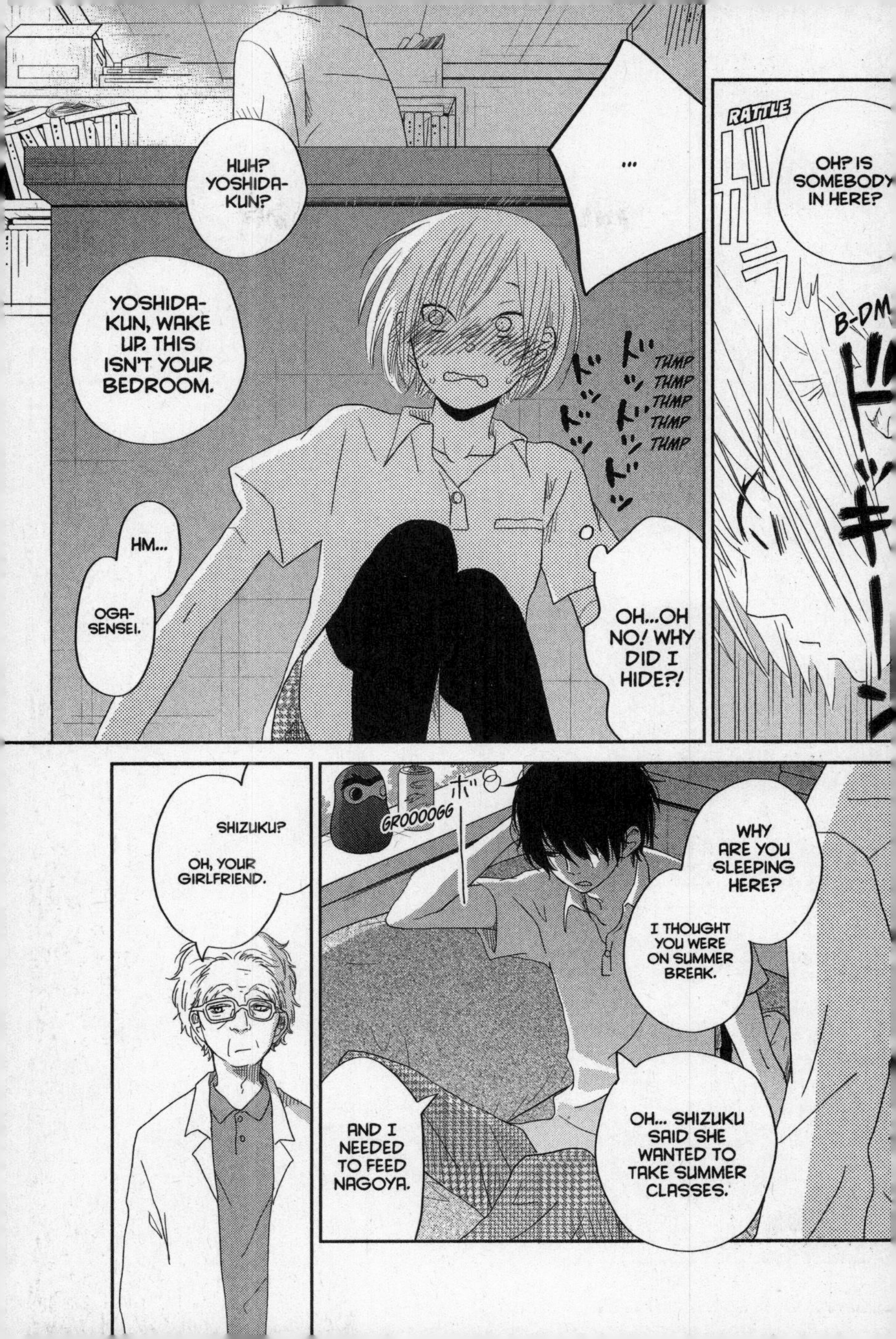
RATTLE
OH? IS SOMEBODY IN HERE?
B-DM
...
HUH? YOSHIDA-KUN?
YOSHIDA-KUN, WAKE UP. THIS ISN'T YOUR BEDROOM.
THMP THMP THMP THMP THMP
OH...OH NO! WHY DID I HIDE?!
HM...
OGA-SENSEI.
GROOOOGG
WHY ARE YOU SLEEPING HERE?
I THOUGHT YOU WERE ON SUMMER BREAK.
OH... SHIZUKU SAID SHE WANTED TO TAKE SUMMER CLASSES.
AND I NEEDED TO FEED NAGOYA.
SHIZUKU?
OH, YOUR GIRLFRIEND.

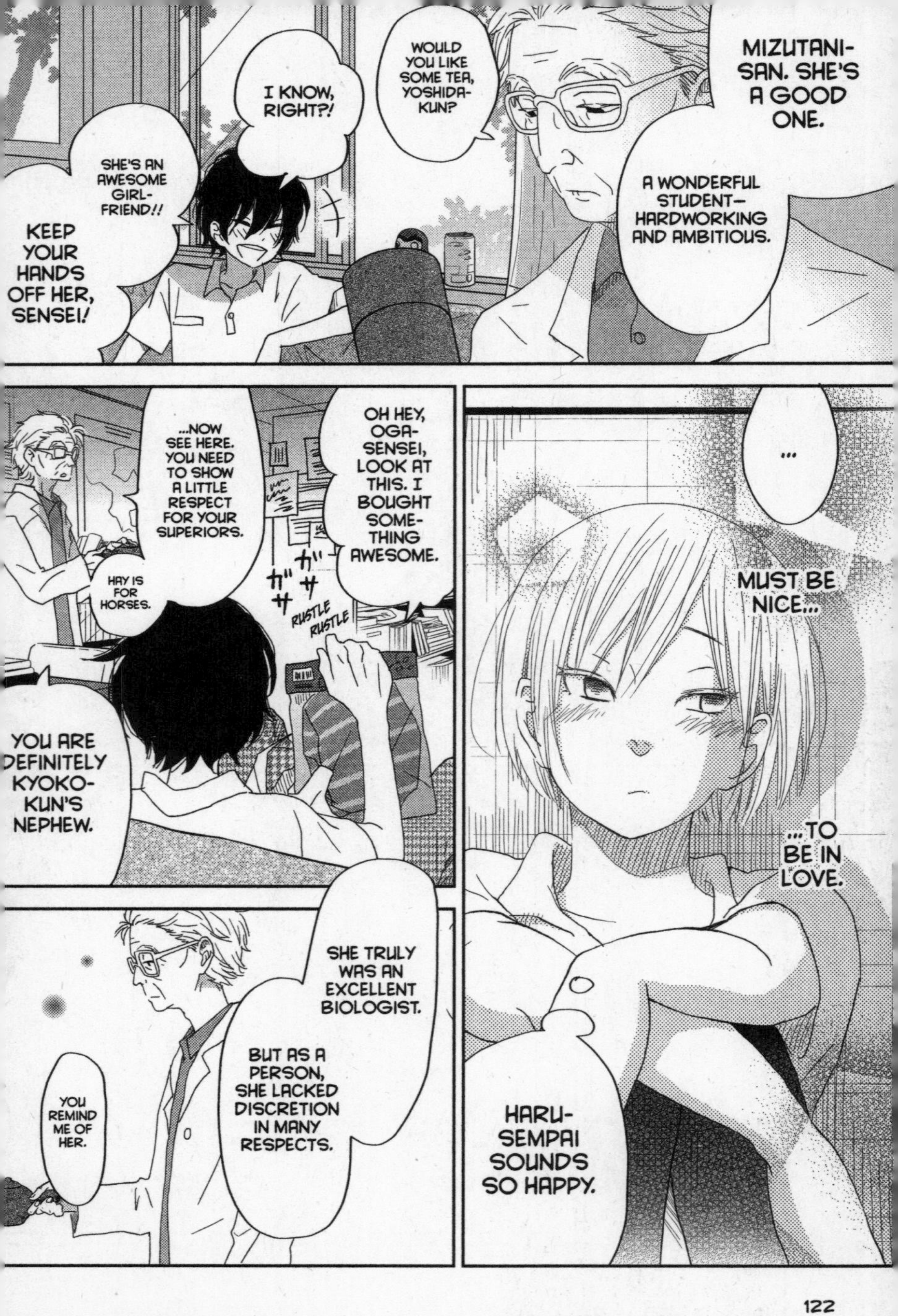
MIZUTANI-SAN. SHE'S A GOOD ONE.
A WONDERFUL STUDENT—HARDWORKING AND AMBITIOUS.
WOULD YOU LIKE SOME TEA, YOSHIDA-KUN?
I KNOW, RIGHT?!
SHE'S AN AWESOME GIRL-FRIEND!!
KEEP YOUR HANDS OFF HER, SENSEI!
...
MUST BE NICE...
...TO BE IN LOVE.
HARU-SEMPAI SOUNDS SO HAPPY.
OH HEY, OGA-SENSEI, LOOK AT THIS. I BOUGHT SOME-THING AWESOME.
...NOW SEE HERE. YOU NEED TO SHOW A LITTLE RESPECT FOR YOUR SUPERIORS.
HAY IS FOR HORSES.
ガサ ガサ
RUSTLE RUSTLE
YOU ARE DEFINITELY KYOKO-KUN'S NEPHEW.
SHE TRULY WAS AN EXCELLENT BIOLOGIST.
BUT AS A PERSON, SHE LACKED DISCRETION IN MANY RESPECTS.
YOU REMIND ME OF HER.

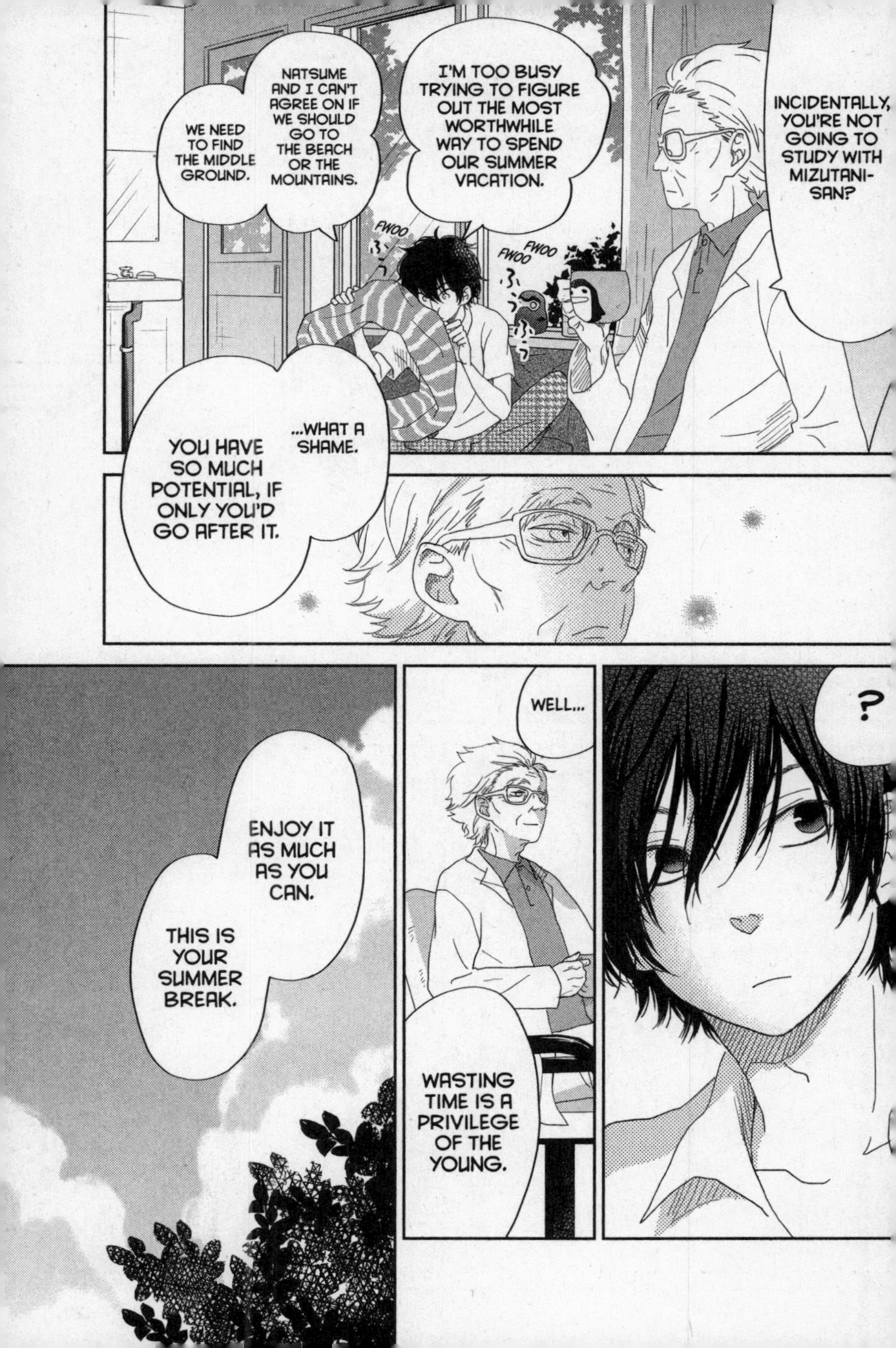
INCIDENTALLY, YOU'RE NOT GOING TO STUDY WITH MIZUTANI-SAN?
I'M TOO BUSY TRYING TO FIGURE OUT THE MOST WORTHWHILE WAY TO SPEND OUR SUMMER VACATION.
NATSUME AND I CAN'T AGREE ON IF WE SHOULD GO TO THE BEACH OR THE MOUNTAINS.
WE NEED TO FIND THE MIDDLE GROUND.
FWOO
FWOO
FWOO
...WHAT A SHAME.
YOU HAVE SO MUCH POTENTIAL, IF ONLY YOU'D GO AFTER IT.
?
WELL...
WASTING TIME IS A PRIVILEGE OF THE YOUNG.
ENJOY IT AS MUCH AS YOU CAN.
THIS IS YOUR SUMMER BREAK.

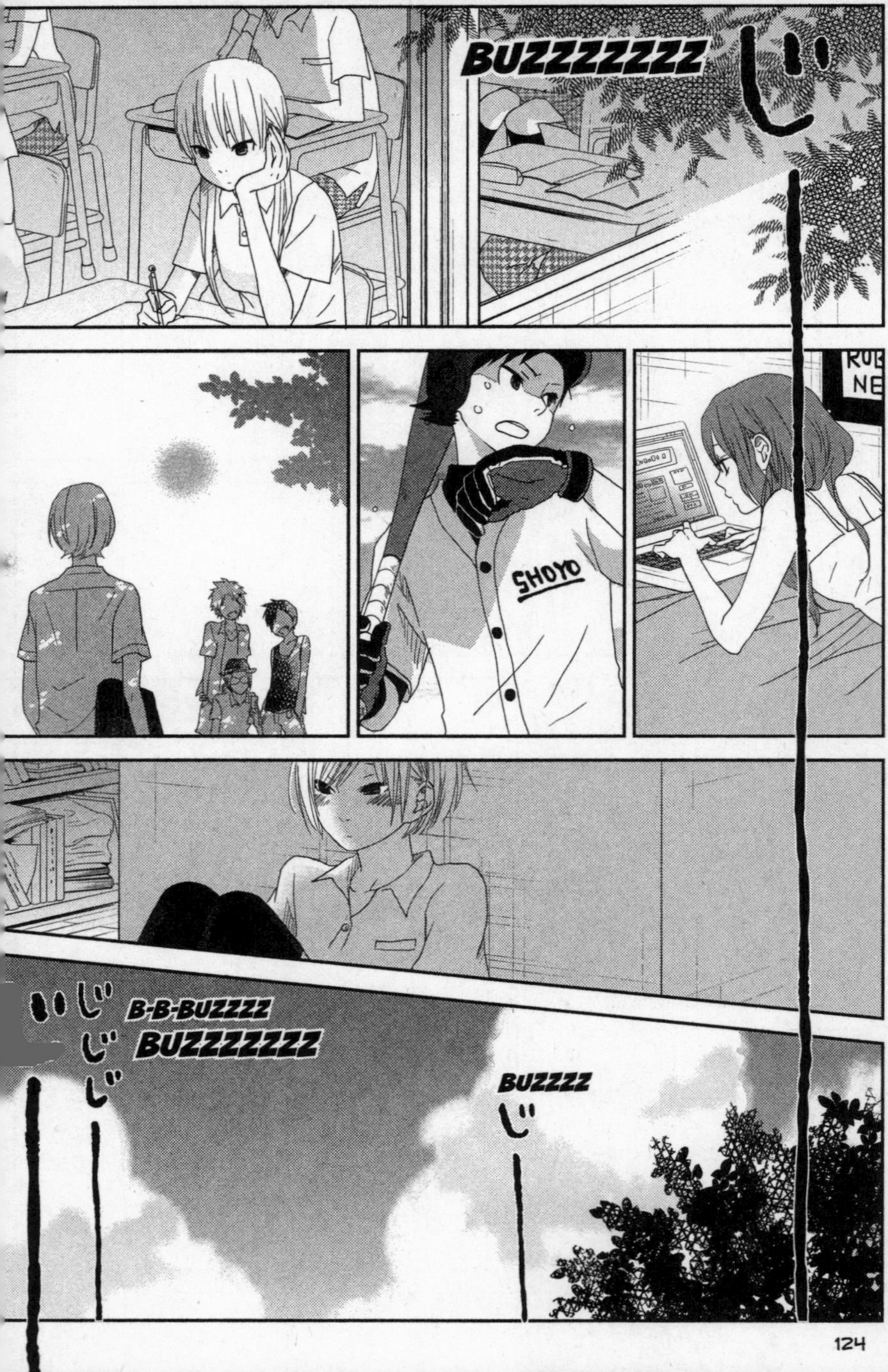
BUZZZZZZZZ
じ
SHOYO
B-B-BUZZZZ
BUZZZZZZZ
じじじ
い
BUZZZZ
じ

COUPLE ≠ FRIENDS

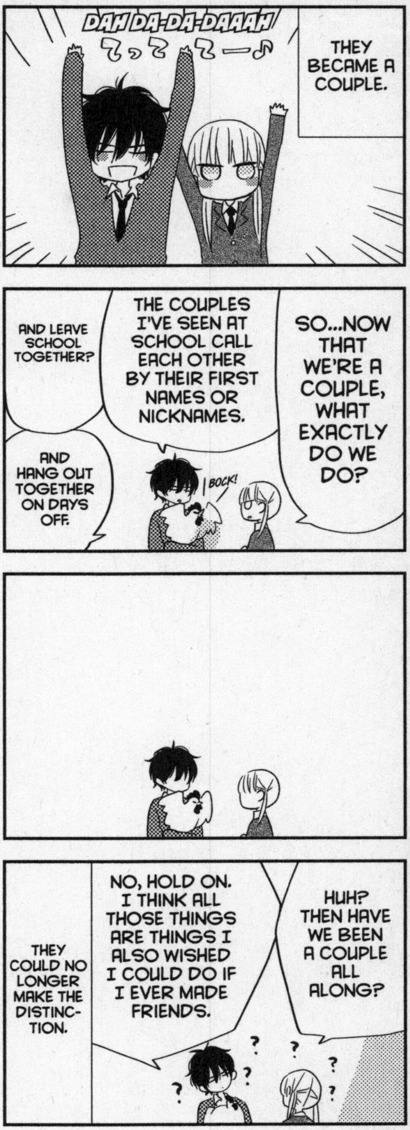
DAH DA-DA-DAAAH
THEY BECAME A COUPLE.
SO...NOW THAT WE'RE A COUPLE, WHAT EXACTLY DO WE DO?
THE COUPLES I'VE SEEN AT SCHOOL CALL EACH OTHER BY THEIR FIRST NAMES OR NICKNAMES.
AND LEAVE SCHOOL TOGETHER?
AND HANG OUT TOGETHER ON DAYS OFF.
BOCK!
HUH? THEN HAVE WE BEEN A COUPLE ALL ALONG?
NO, HOLD ON. I THINK ALL THOSE THINGS ARE THINGS I ALSO WISHED I COULD DO IF I EVER MADE FRIENDS.
THEY COULD NO LONGER MAKE THE DISTINCTION.

AFTERWARD

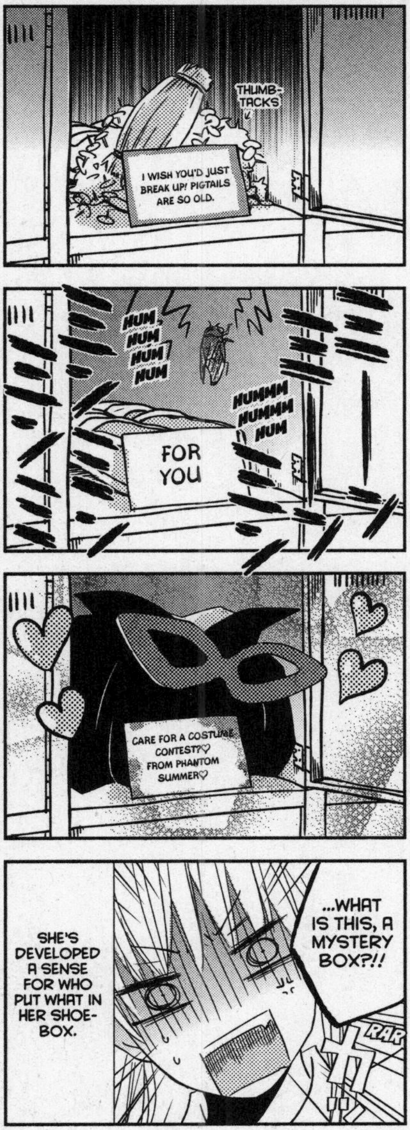
THUMB-TACKS
I WISH YOU'D JUST BREAK UP! PIGTAILS ARE SO OLD.
HUM, HUM HUM HUM
HUMMM HUMMM HUM
FOR YOU
CARE FOR A COSTUME CONTEST?♡ FROM PHANTOM SUMMER♡
...WHAT IS THIS, A MYSTERY BOX?!!
RAR
SHE'S DEVELOPED A SENSE FOR WHO PUT WHAT IN HER SHOE-BOX.

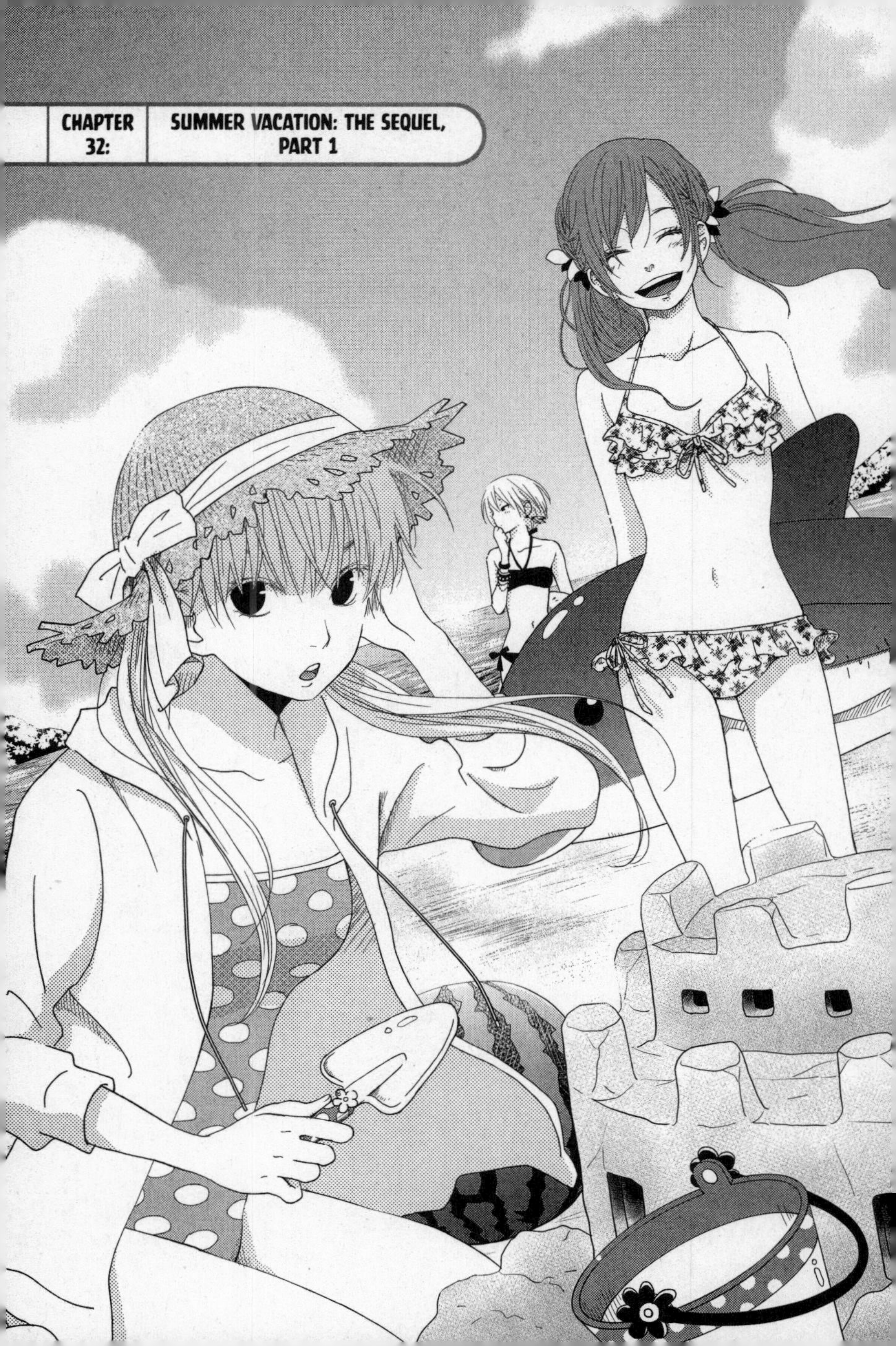
CHAPTER 32:
SUMMER VACATION: THE SEQUEL, PART 1

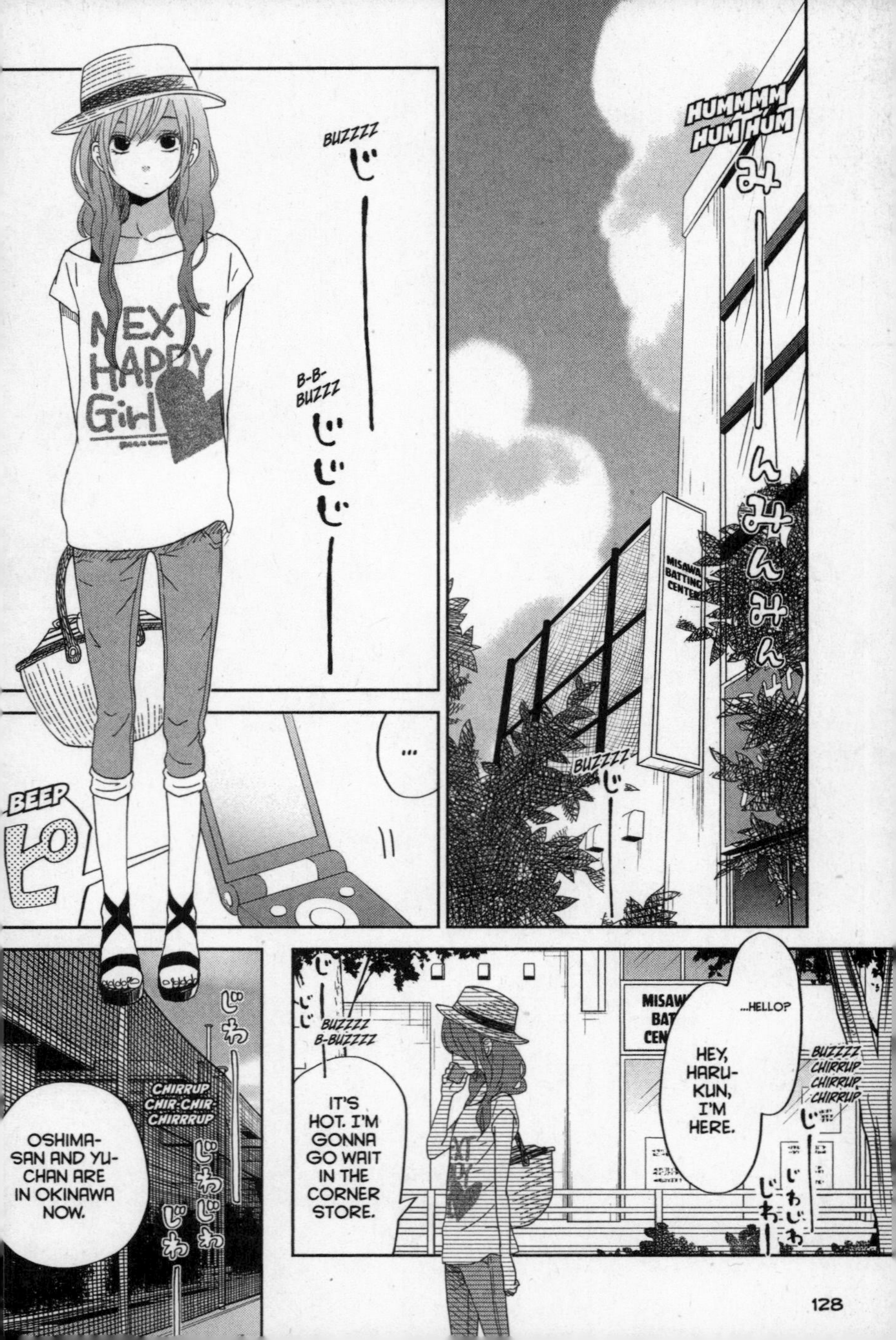
HUMMMM HUM HUM
みーんみんみんー
MISAWA BATTING CENTER
BUZZZZ
じー
BUZZZZ
じー
B-B-BUZZZ
じじじー
...
BEEP
ピ
...HELLO?
HEY, HARU-KUN, I'M HERE.
BUZZZZ CHIRRUP CHIRRUP CHIRRUP
じー
じわじわ じわー
BUZZZZ B-BUZZZZ
じー じじ
IT'S HOT. I'M GONNA GO WAIT IN THE CORNER STORE.
CHIRRUP CHIR-CHIR-CHIRRRUP
じわー
じわじわ じわー
OSHIMA-SAN AND YU-CHAN ARE IN OKINAWA NOW.

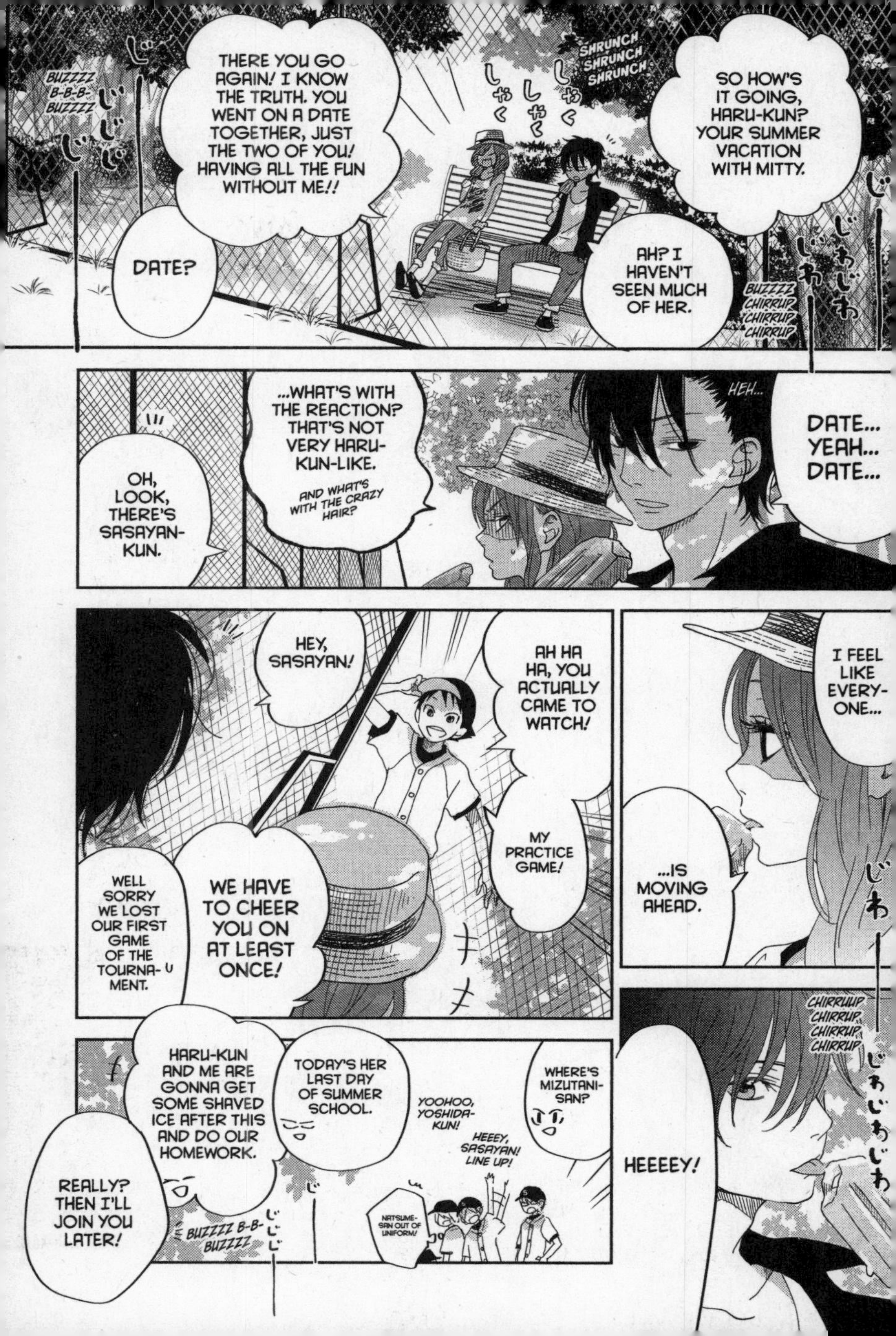
SO HOW'S IT GOING, HARU-KUN? YOUR SUMMER VACATION WITH MITTY.
BUZZZZ CHIRRUP CHIRRUP CHIRRUP
AH? I HAVEN'T SEEN MUCH OF HER.
SHRUNCH SHRUNCH SHRUNCH
THERE YOU GO AGAIN! I KNOW THE TRUTH. YOU WENT ON A DATE TOGETHER, JUST THE TWO OF YOU! HAVING ALL THE FUN WITHOUT ME!!
BUZZZZ B-B-B-BUZZZZ
DATE?
DATE... YEAH... DATE...
HEH...
...WHAT'S WITH THE REACTION? THAT'S NOT VERY HARU-KUN-LIKE.
AND WHAT'S WITH THE CRAZY HAIR?
OH, LOOK, THERE'S SASAYAN-KUN.
I FEEL LIKE EVERY-ONE...
...IS MOVING AHEAD.
AH HA HA, YOU ACTUALLY CAME TO WATCH!
HEY, SASAYAN!
MY PRACTICE GAME!
WE HAVE TO CHEER YOU ON AT LEAST ONCE!
WELL SORRY WE LOST OUR FIRST GAME OF THE TOURNA-MENT.
CHIRRUP CHIRRUP CHIRRUP CHIRRUP
HEEEEY!
WHERE'S MIZUTANI-SAN?
TODAY'S HER LAST DAY OF SUMMER SCHOOL.
HARU-KUN AND ME ARE GONNA GET SOME SHAVED ICE AFTER THIS AND DO OUR HOMEWORK.
YOOHOO, YOSHIDA-KUN!
HEEEY, SASAYAN! LINE UP!
NATSUME-SAN OUT OF UNIFORM!
REALLY? THEN I'LL JOIN YOU LATER!
BUZZZZ B-B-BUZZZZ

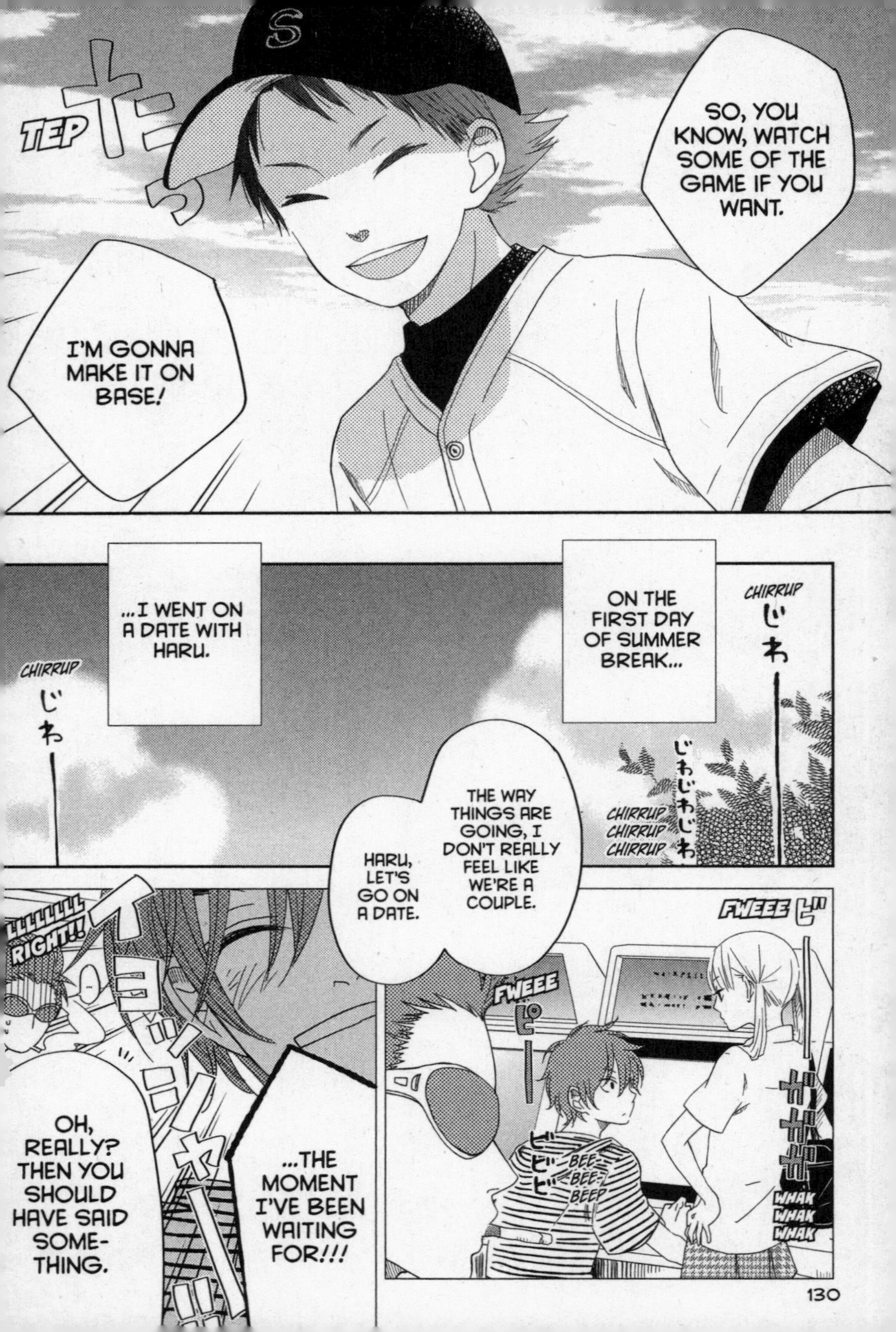
TEP
SO, YOU KNOW, WATCH SOME OF THE GAME IF YOU WANT.
I'M GONNA MAKE IT ON BASE!
CHIRRUP
ON THE FIRST DAY OF SUMMER BREAK...
...I WENT ON A DATE WITH HARU.
CHIRRUP
CHIRRUP CHIRRUP CHIRRUP
FWEEE
THE WAY THINGS ARE GOING, I DON'T REALLY FEEL LIKE WE'RE A COUPLE.
HARU, LET'S GO ON A DATE.
FWEEE
BEE-BEE-BEEP
WHAK WHAK WHAK
LLLLLLLL RIGHT!!
...THE MOMENT I'VE BEEN WAITING FOR!!!
OH, REALLY? THEN YOU SHOULD HAVE SAID SOME-THING.

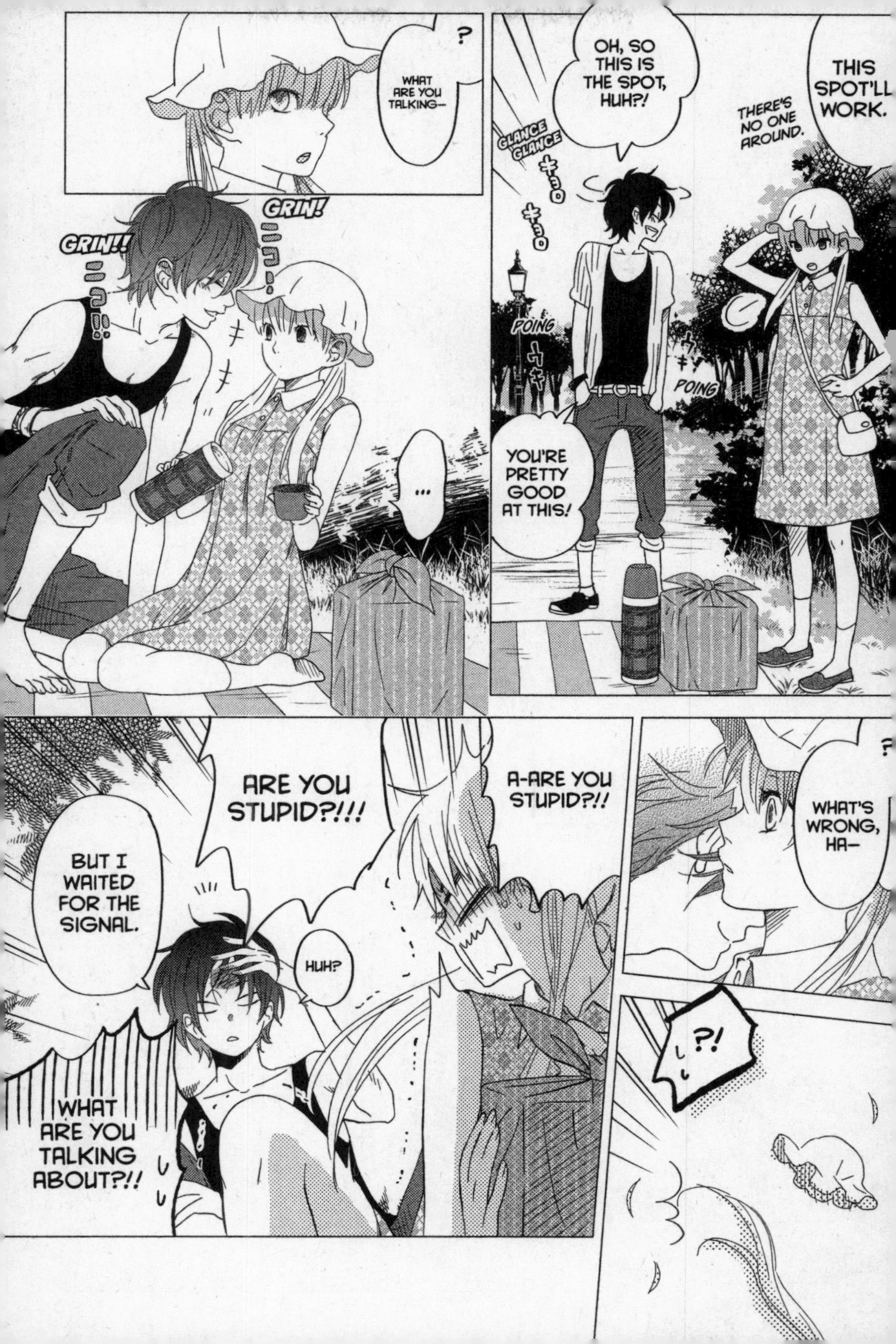
THIS SPOT'LL WORK.
THERE'S NO ONE AROUND.
OH, SO THIS IS THE SPOT, HUH?!
GLANCE GLANCE
キョロ キョロ
POING
ウキ
POING
YOU'RE PRETTY GOOD AT THIS!
?
WHAT ARE YOU TALKING—
GRIN!
GRIN!!
...
?
WHAT'S WRONG, HA—
?!
A-ARE YOU STUPID?!!
ARE YOU STUPID?!!!
BUT I WAITED FOR THE SIGNAL.
HUH?
WHAT ARE YOU TALKING ABOUT?!!

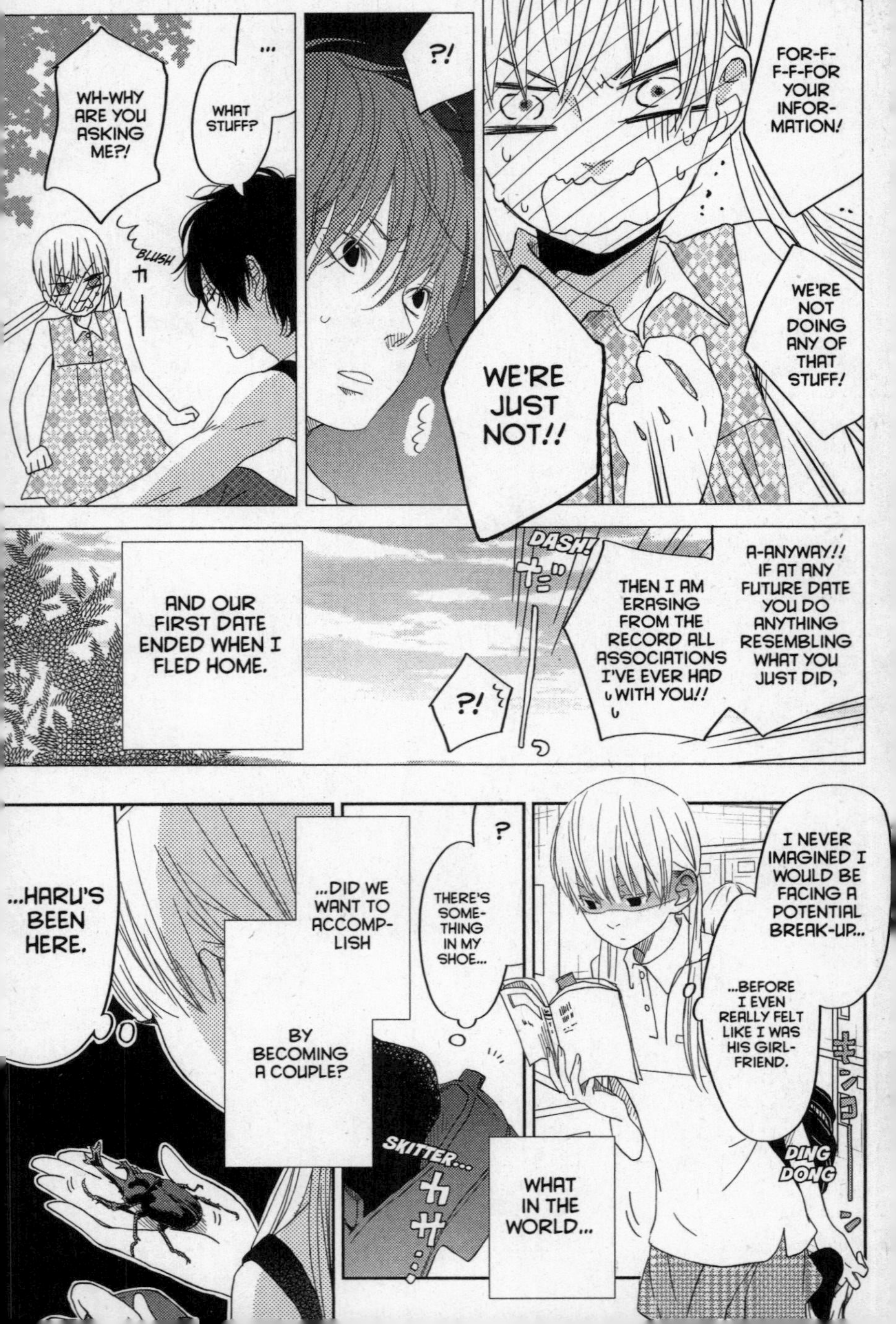
FOR-F-F-F-FOR YOUR INFORMATION!
WE'RE NOT DOING ANY OF THAT STUFF!
WE'RE JUST NOT!!
?!
...
WHAT STUFF?
WH-WHY ARE YOU ASKING ME?!
BLUSH
A-ANYWAY!! IF AT ANY FUTURE DATE YOU DO ANYTHING RESEMBLING WHAT YOU JUST DID,
THEN I AM ERASING FROM THE RECORD ALL ASSOCIATIONS I'VE EVER HAD WITH YOU!!
DASH!
?!
AND OUR FIRST DATE ENDED WHEN I FLED HOME.
I NEVER IMAGINED I WOULD BE FACING A POTENTIAL BREAK-UP...
...BEFORE I EVEN REALLY FELT LIKE I WAS HIS GIRLFRIEND.
DING DONG
WHAT IN THE WORLD...
?
THERE'S SOMETHING IN MY SHOE...
SKITTER...
...DID WE WANT TO ACCOMPLISH
BY BECOMING A COUPLE?
...HARU'S BEEN HERE.

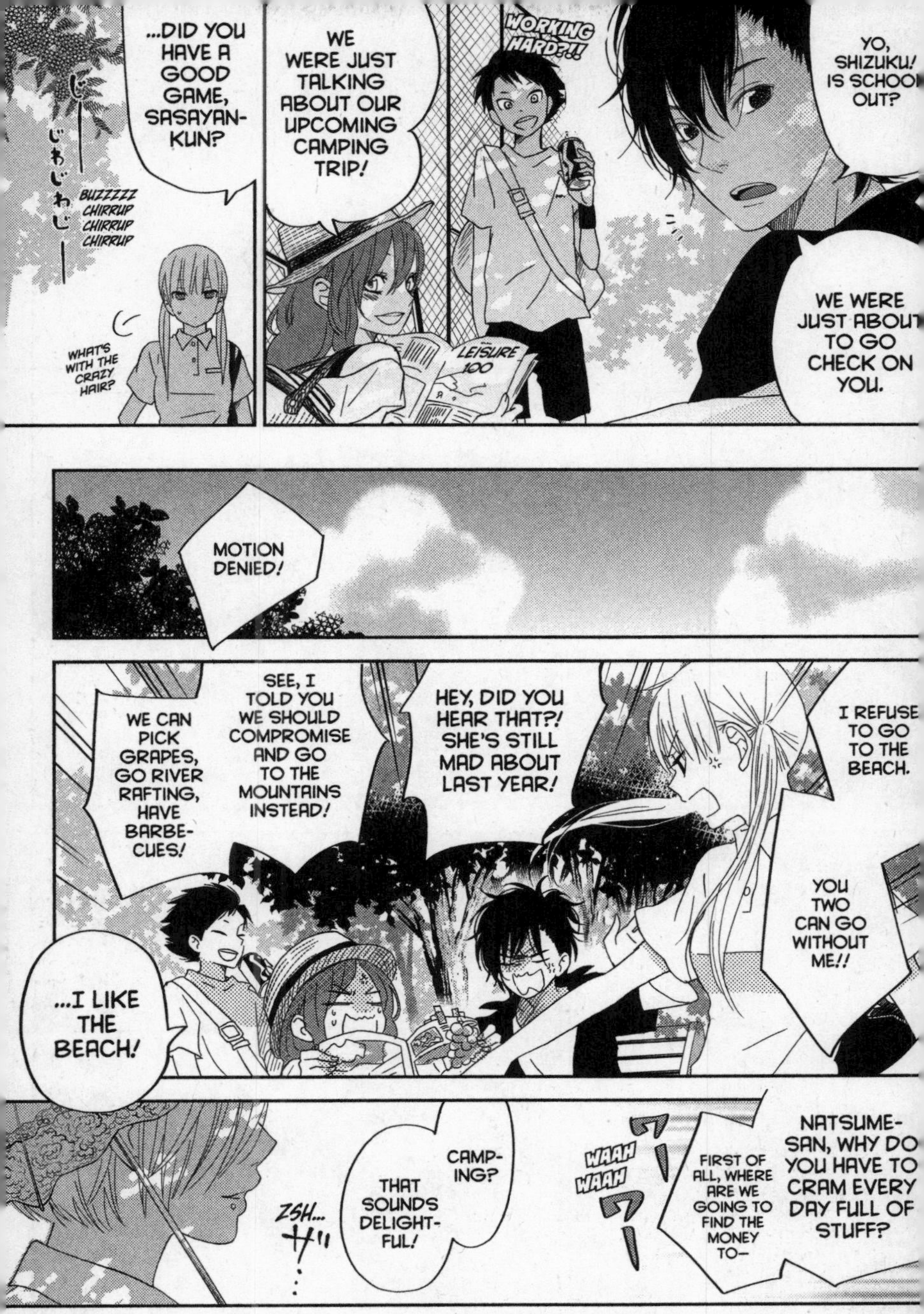
YO, SHIZUKU! IS SCHOOL OUT?
WE WERE JUST ABOUT TO GO CHECK ON YOU.
WORKING HARD?!!
WE WERE JUST TALKING ABOUT OUR UPCOMING CAMPING TRIP!
LEISURE 100
...DID YOU HAVE A GOOD GAME, SASAYAN-KUN?
じーー
じわじわじーー
BUZZZZZ CHIRRUP CHIRRUP CHIRRUP
WHAT'S WITH THE CRAZY HAIR?
MOTION DENIED!
I REFUSE TO GO TO THE BEACH.
YOU TWO CAN GO WITHOUT ME!!
HEY, DID YOU HEAR THAT?! SHE'S STILL MAD ABOUT LAST YEAR!
SEE, I TOLD YOU WE SHOULD COMPROMISE AND GO TO THE MOUNTAINS INSTEAD!
WE CAN PICK GRAPES, GO RIVER RAFTING, HAVE BARBE-CUES!
...I LIKE THE BEACH!
NATSUME-SAN, WHY DO YOU HAVE TO CRAM EVERY DAY FULL OF STUFF?
FIRST OF ALL, WHERE ARE WE GOING TO FIND THE MONEY TO—
ワー
ワー
WAAH WAAH
CAMP-ING?
THAT SOUNDS DELIGHT-FUL!
ZSH...
ザ''

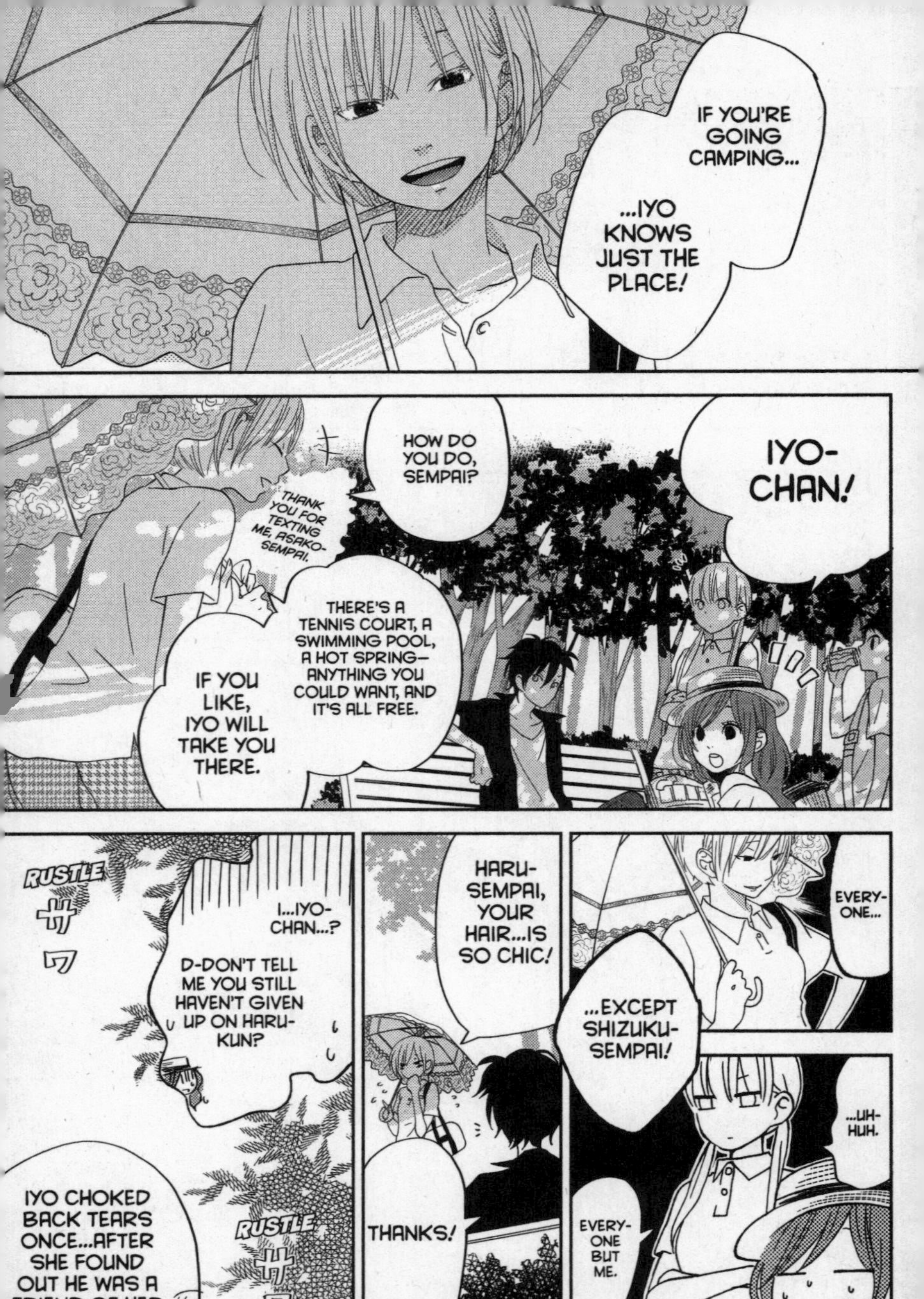
IF YOU'RE GOING CAMPING...
...IYO KNOWS JUST THE PLACE!
IYO-CHAN!
HOW DO YOU DO, SEMPAI?
THANK YOU FOR TEXTING ME, ASAKO-SEMPAI.
THERE'S A TENNIS COURT, A SWIMMING POOL, A HOT SPRING—ANYTHING YOU COULD WANT, AND IT'S ALL FREE.
IF YOU LIKE, IYO WILL TAKE YOU THERE.
EVERY-ONE...
...EXCEPT SHIZUKU-SEMPAI!
...UH-HUH.
EVERY-ONE BUT ME.
HARU-SEMPAI, YOUR HAIR...IS SO CHIC!
THANKS!
RUSTLE
サワ
I...IYO-CHAN...?
D-DON'T TELL ME YOU STILL HAVEN'T GIVEN UP ON HARU-KUN?
IYO CHOKED BACK TEARS ONCE...AFTER SHE FOUND OUT HE WAS A FRIEND OF HER BROTHER'S.
RUSTLE
サワ

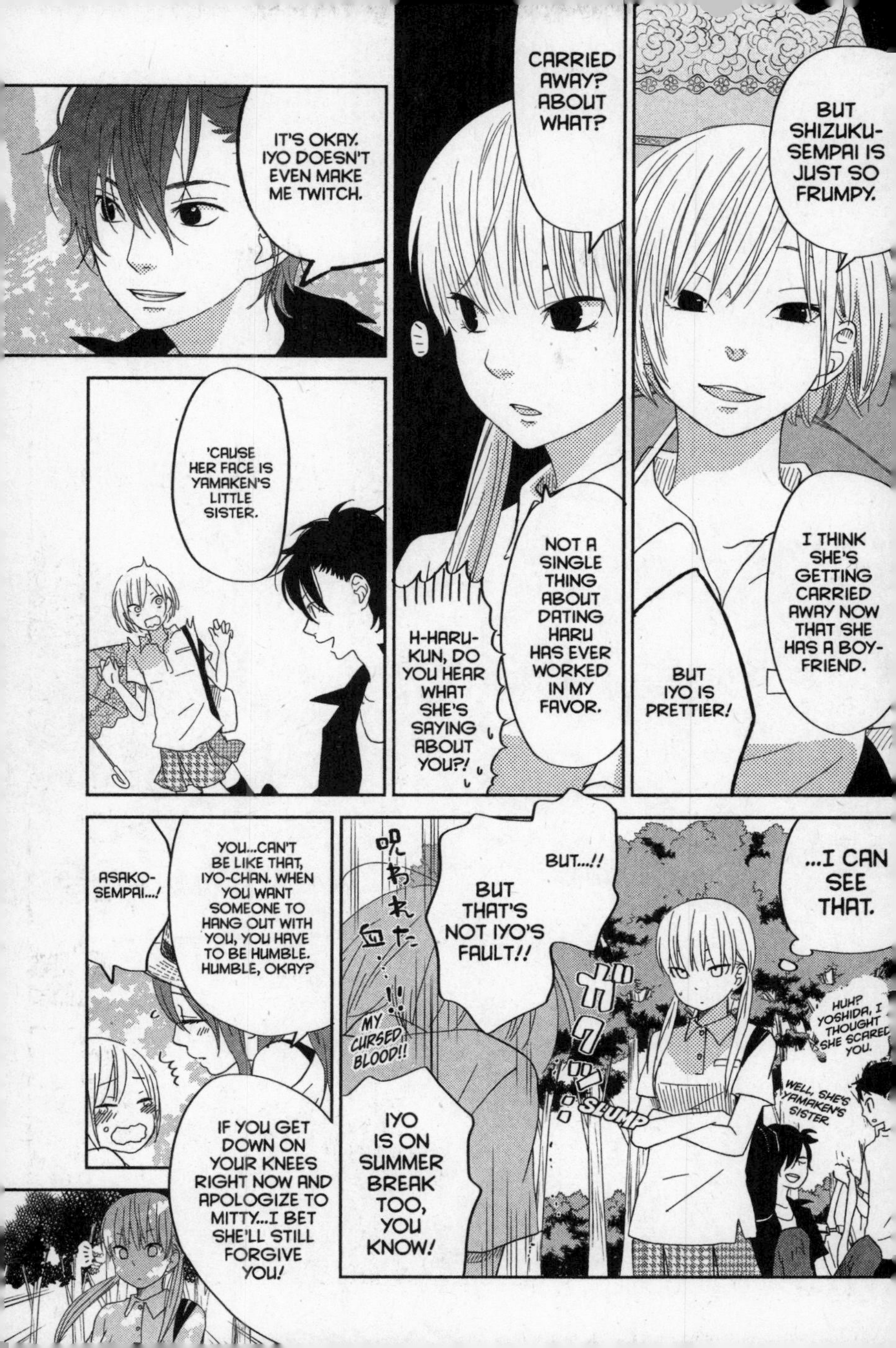
BUT SHIZUKU-SEMPAI IS JUST SO FRUMPY.
I THINK SHE'S GETTING CARRIED AWAY NOW THAT SHE HAS A BOY-FRIEND.
BUT IYO IS PRETTIER!
CARRIED AWAY? ABOUT WHAT?
NOT A SINGLE THING ABOUT DATING HARU HAS EVER WORKED IN MY FAVOR.
H-HARU-KUN, DO YOU HEAR WHAT SHE'S SAYING ABOUT YOU?!
IT'S OKAY. IYO DOESN'T EVEN MAKE ME TWITCH.
'CAUSE HER FACE IS YAMAKEN'S LITTLE SISTER.
...I CAN SEE THAT.
BUT...!!
BUT THAT'S NOT IYO'S FAULT!!
HUH? YOSHIDA, I THOUGHT SHE SCARED YOU.
WELL, SHE'S YAMAKEN'S SISTER.
ガクッ
SLUMP
呪われた血…!!
MY CURSED BLOOD!!
IYO IS ON SUMMER BREAK TOO, YOU KNOW!
YOU...CAN'T BE LIKE THAT, IYO-CHAN. WHEN YOU WANT SOMEONE TO HANG OUT WITH YOU, YOU HAVE TO BE HUMBLE. HUMBLE, OKAY?
ASAKO-SEMPAI...!
IF YOU GET DOWN ON YOUR KNEES RIGHT NOW AND APOLOGIZE TO MITTY...I BET SHE'LL STILL FORGIVE YOU!

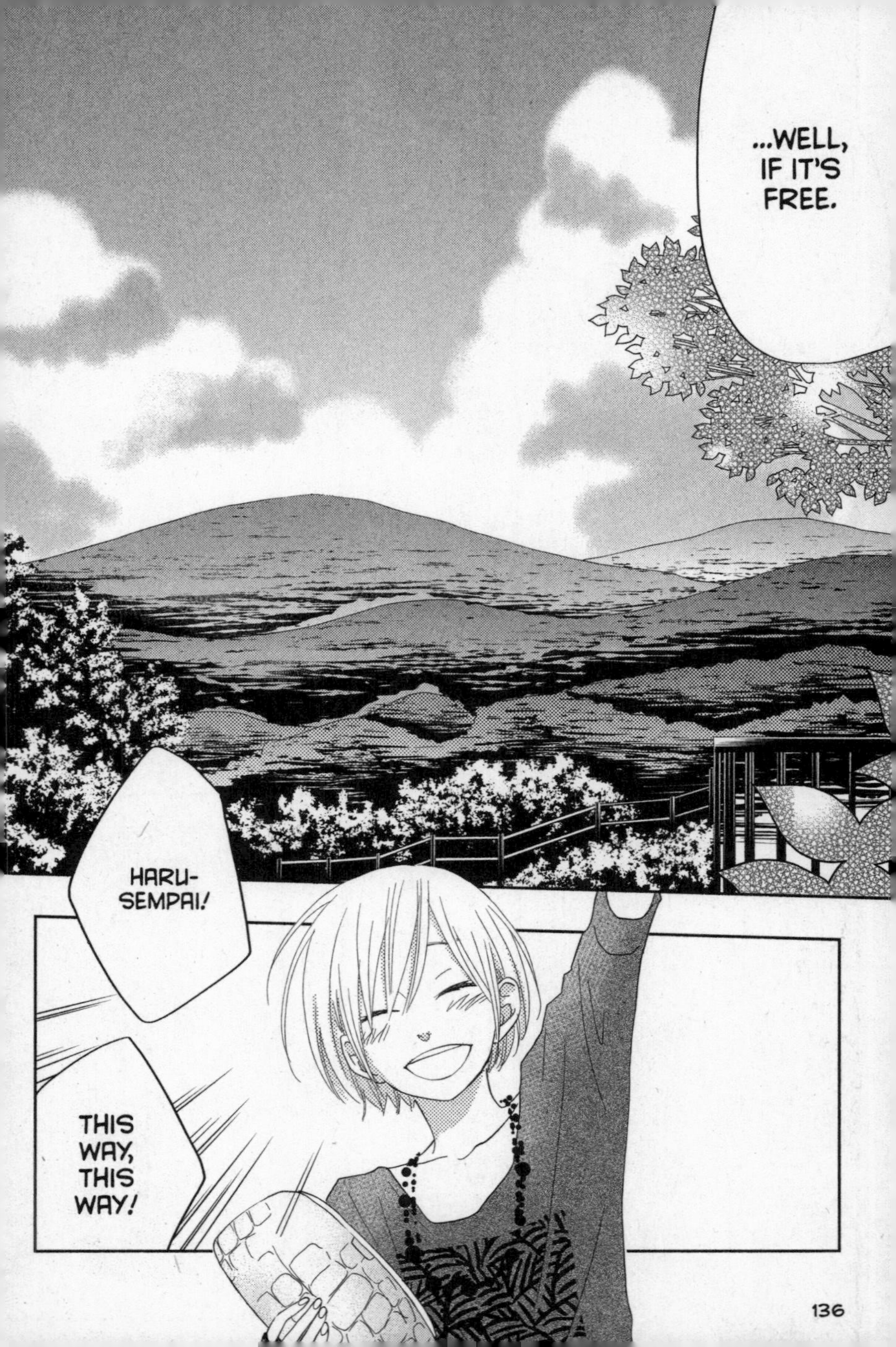
...WELL, IF IT'S FREE.
HARU-SEMPAI!
THIS WAY, THIS WAY!

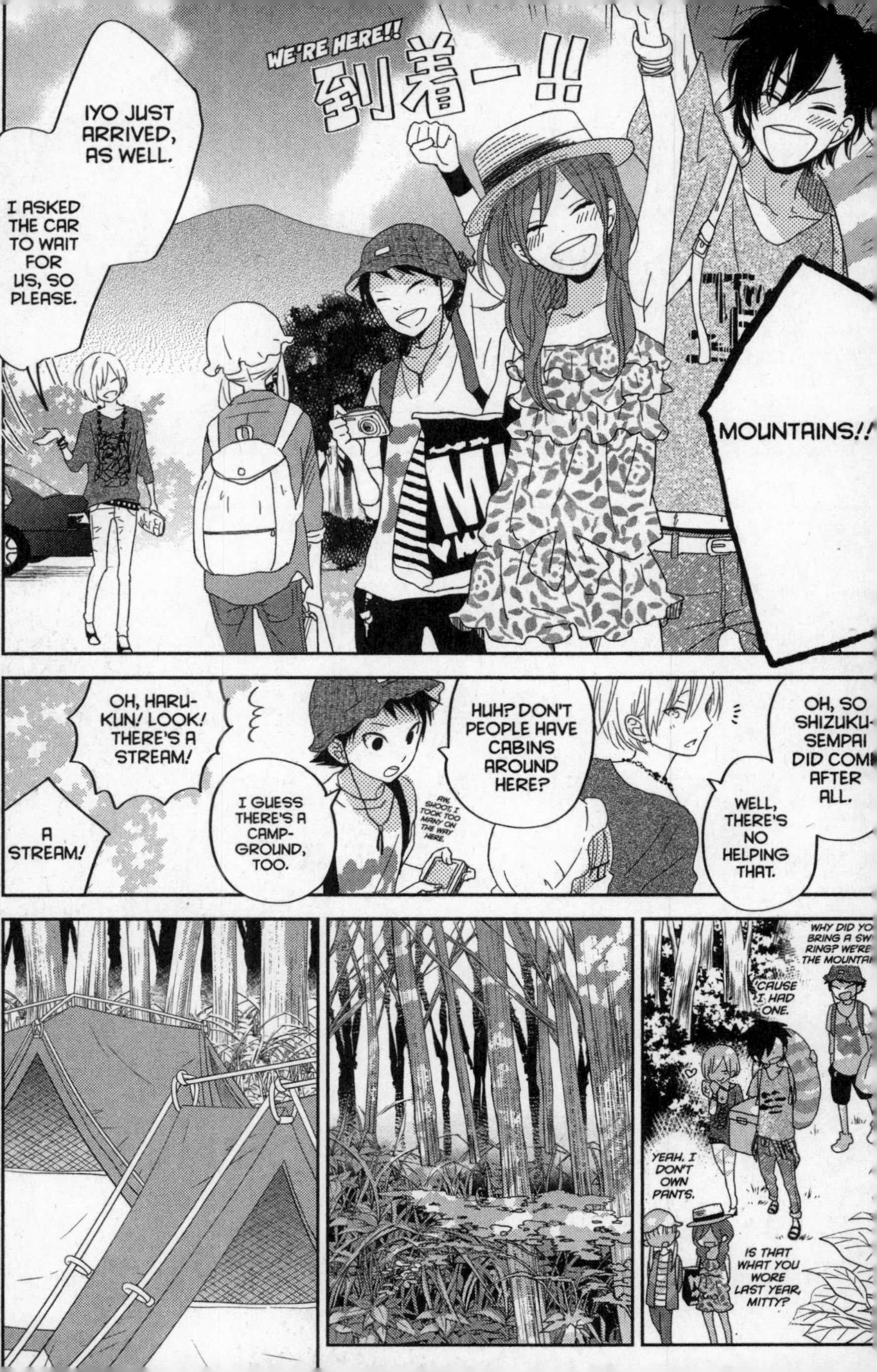
WE'RE HERE!!
到着ー!!
MOUNTAINS!!
IYO JUST ARRIVED, AS WELL.
I ASKED THE CAR TO WAIT FOR US, SO PLEASE.
OH, SO SHIZUKU-SEMPAI DID COM AFTER ALL.
WELL, THERE'S NO HELPING THAT.
HUH? DON'T PEOPLE HAVE CABINS AROUND HERE?
AW, SHOOT, I TOOK TOO MANY ON THE WAY HERE.
I GUESS THERE'S A CAMP-GROUND, TOO.
OH, HARU-KUN! LOOK! THERE'S A STREAM!
A STREAM!
WHY DID YO BRING A SW RING? WE'RE THE MOUNTAI
'CAUSE I HAD ONE.
IS THAT WHAT YOU WORE LAST YEAR, MITTY?
YEAH. I DON'T OWN PANTS.

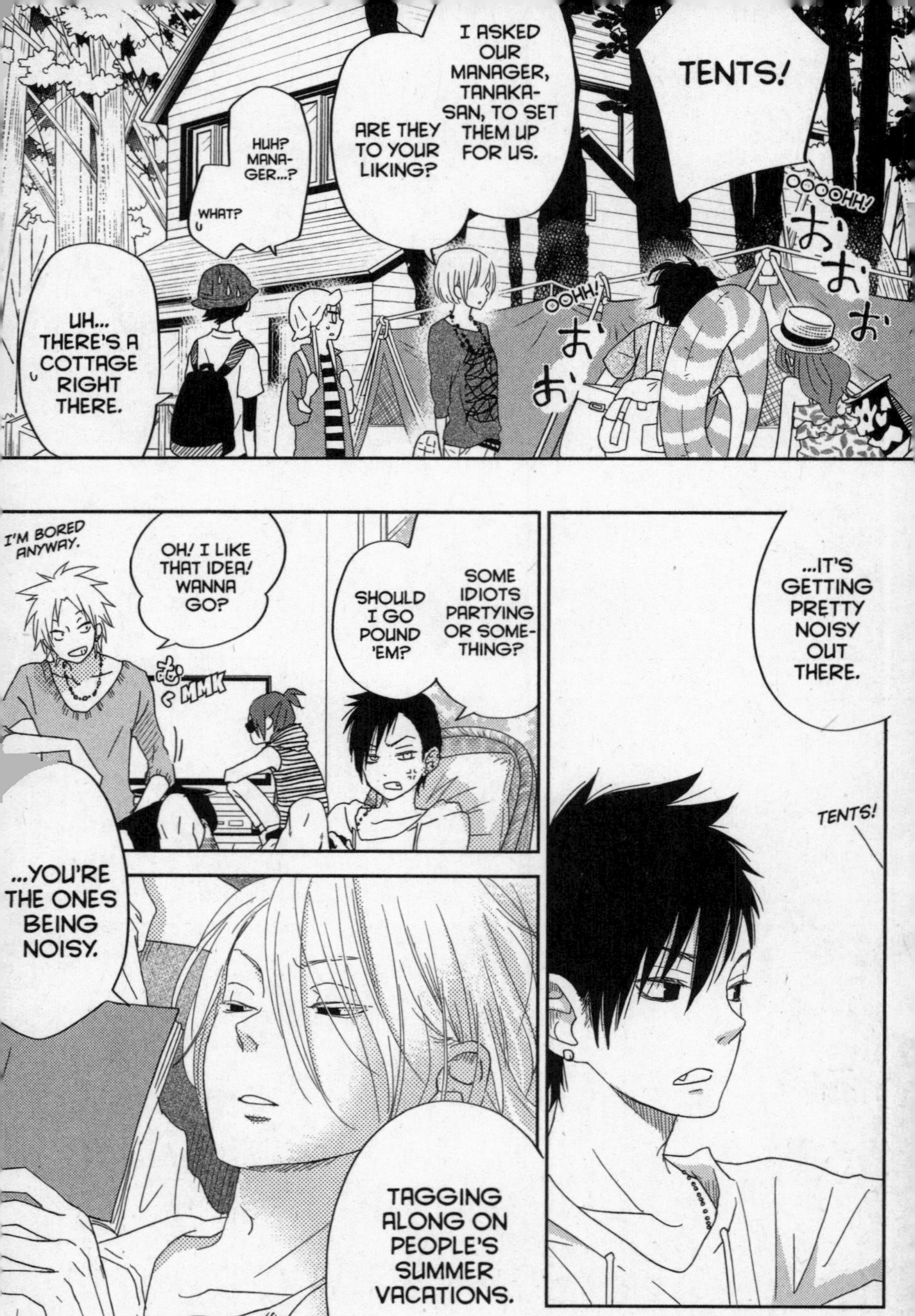
TENTS!
OOOOHH!
おおお
OOHH!
おおお
I ASKED OUR MANAGER, TANAKA-SAN, TO SET THEM UP FOR US.
ARE THEY TO YOUR LIKING?
HUH? MANA-GER...?
WHAT?
UH... THERE'S A COTTAGE RIGHT THERE.
...IT'S GETTING PRETTY NOISY OUT THERE.
TENTS!
SOME IDIOTS PARTYING OR SOME-THING?
SHOULD I GO POUND 'EM?
OH! I LIKE THAT IDEA! WANNA GO?
む MMK
I'M BORED ANYWAY.
...YOU'RE THE ONES BEING NOISY.
TAGGING ALONG ON PEOPLE'S SUMMER VACATIONS.

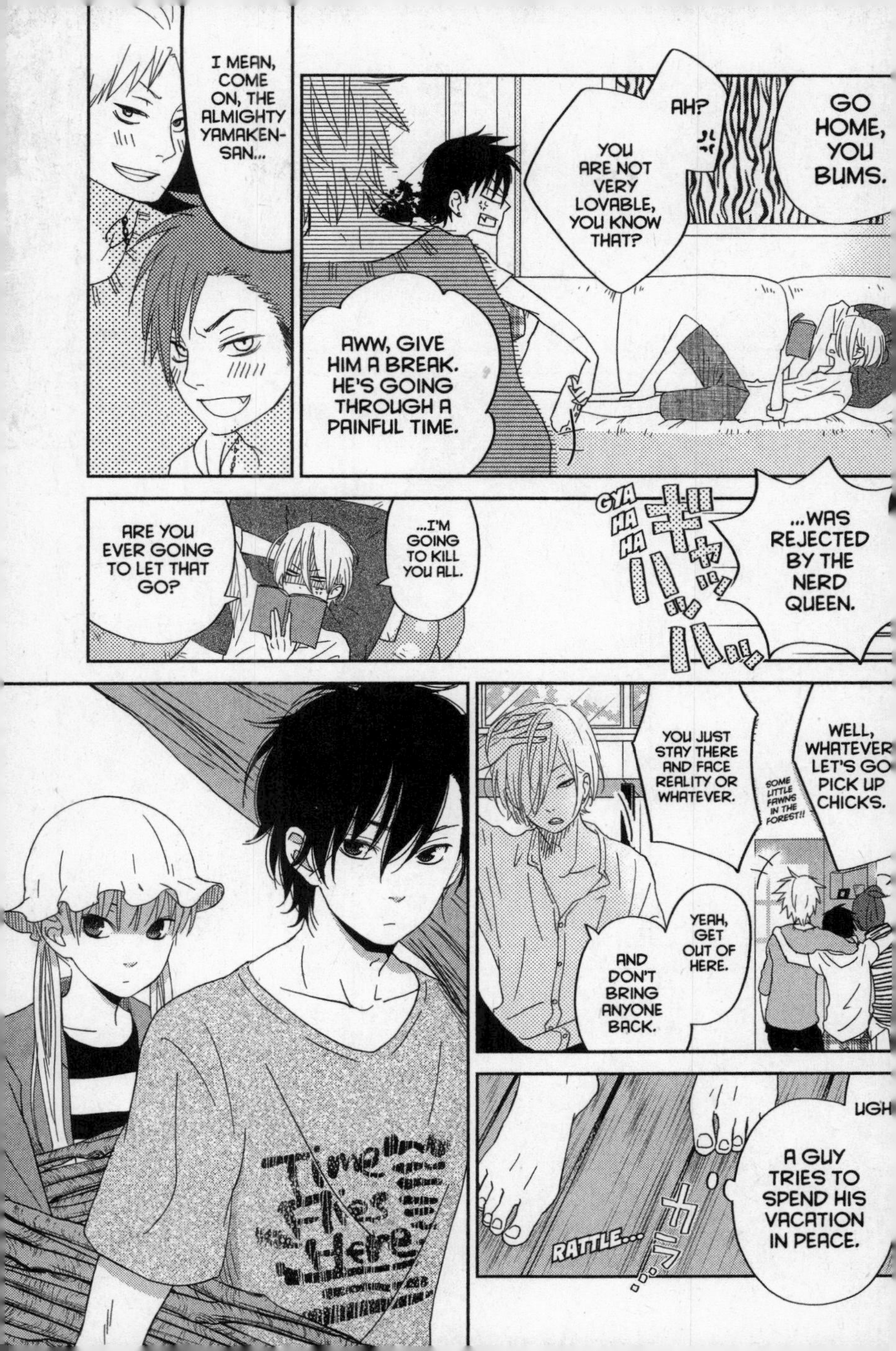
GO HOME, YOU BUMS.
AH?
YOU ARE NOT VERY LOVABLE, YOU KNOW THAT?
AWW, GIVE HIM A BREAK. HE'S GOING THROUGH A PAINFUL TIME.
I MEAN, COME ON, THE ALMIGHTY YAMAKEN-SAN...
...WAS REJECTED BY THE NERD QUEEN.
GYA HA HA
...I'M GOING TO KILL YOU ALL.
ARE YOU EVER GOING TO LET THAT GO?
WELL, WHATEVER LET'S GO PICK UP CHICKS.
SOME LITTLE FAWNS IN THE FOREST!!
YOU JUST STAY THERE AND FACE REALITY OR WHATEVER.
YEAH, GET OUT OF HERE.
AND DON'T BRING ANYONE BACK.
UGH
A GUY TRIES TO SPEND HIS VACATION IN PEACE.
RATTLE...

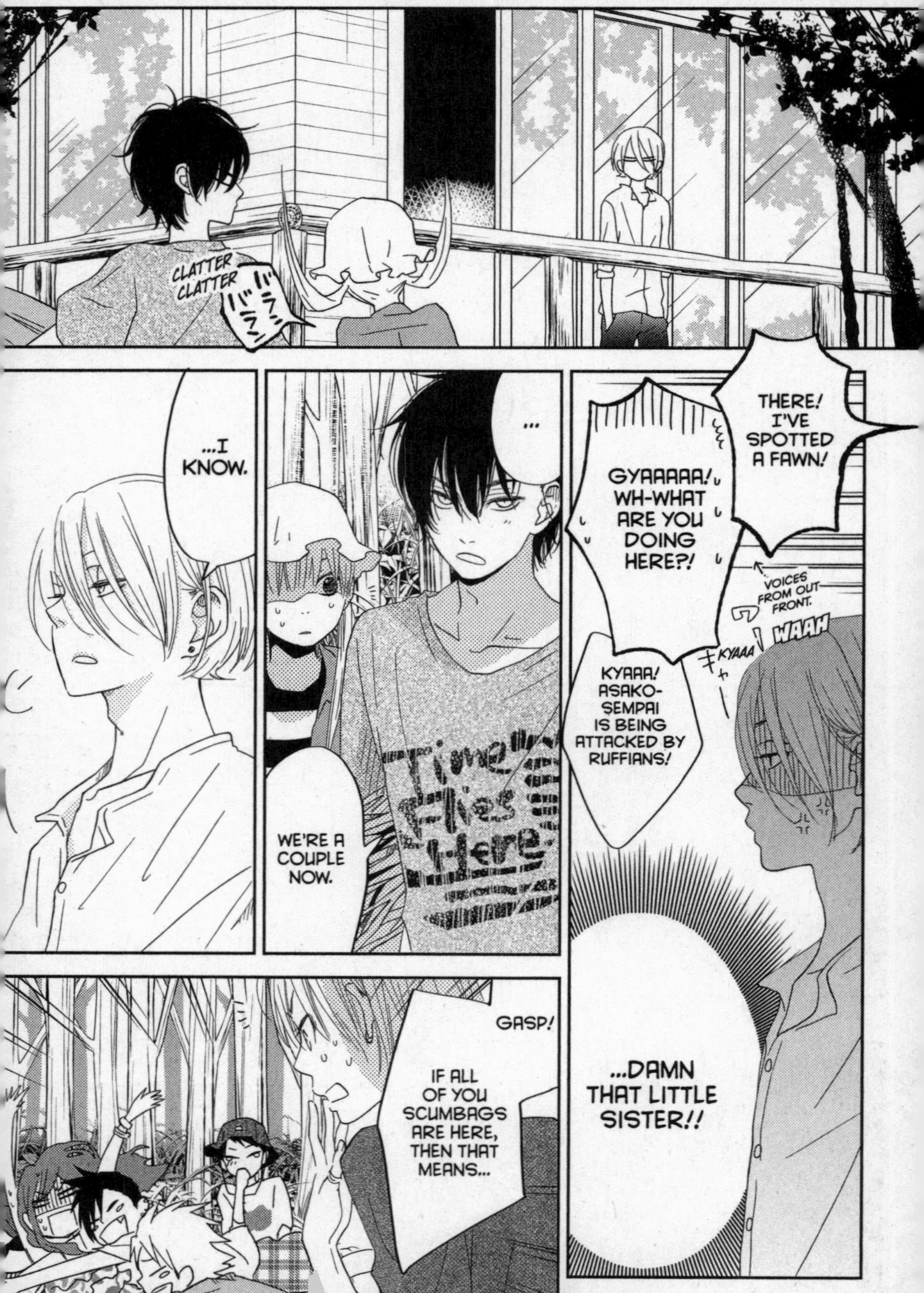
CLATTER CLATTER
バラッバラン
...
WE'RE A COUPLE NOW.
...I KNOW.
THERE! I'VE SPOTTED A FAWN!
GYAAAAA! WH-WHAT ARE YOU DOING HERE?!
VOICES FROM OUT FRONT.
WAAH
KYAAA
KYAAA! ASAKO-SEMPAI IS BEING ATTACKED BY RUFFIANS!
GASP!
IF ALL OF YOU SCUMBAGS ARE HERE, THEN THAT MEANS...
...DAMN THAT LITTLE SISTER!!

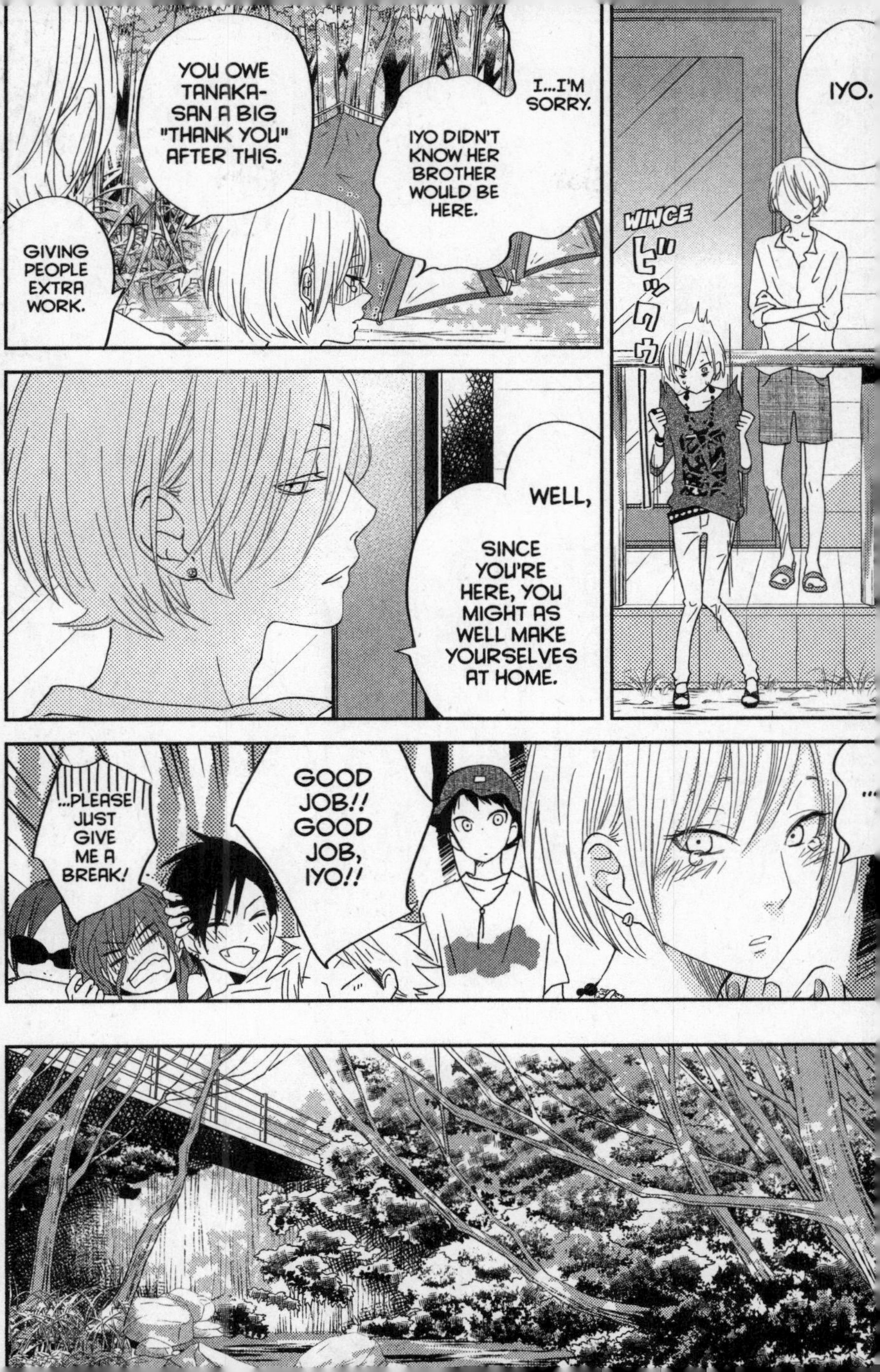
IYO.
WINCE
ビクゥ
I...I'M SORRY.
IYO DIDN'T KNOW HER BROTHER WOULD BE HERE.
YOU OWE TANAKA-SAN A BIG "THANK YOU" AFTER THIS.
GIVING PEOPLE EXTRA WORK.
WELL,
SINCE YOU'RE HERE, YOU MIGHT AS WELL MAKE YOURSELVES AT HOME.
...
GOOD JOB!! GOOD JOB, IYO!!
...PLEASE JUST GIVE ME A BREAK!

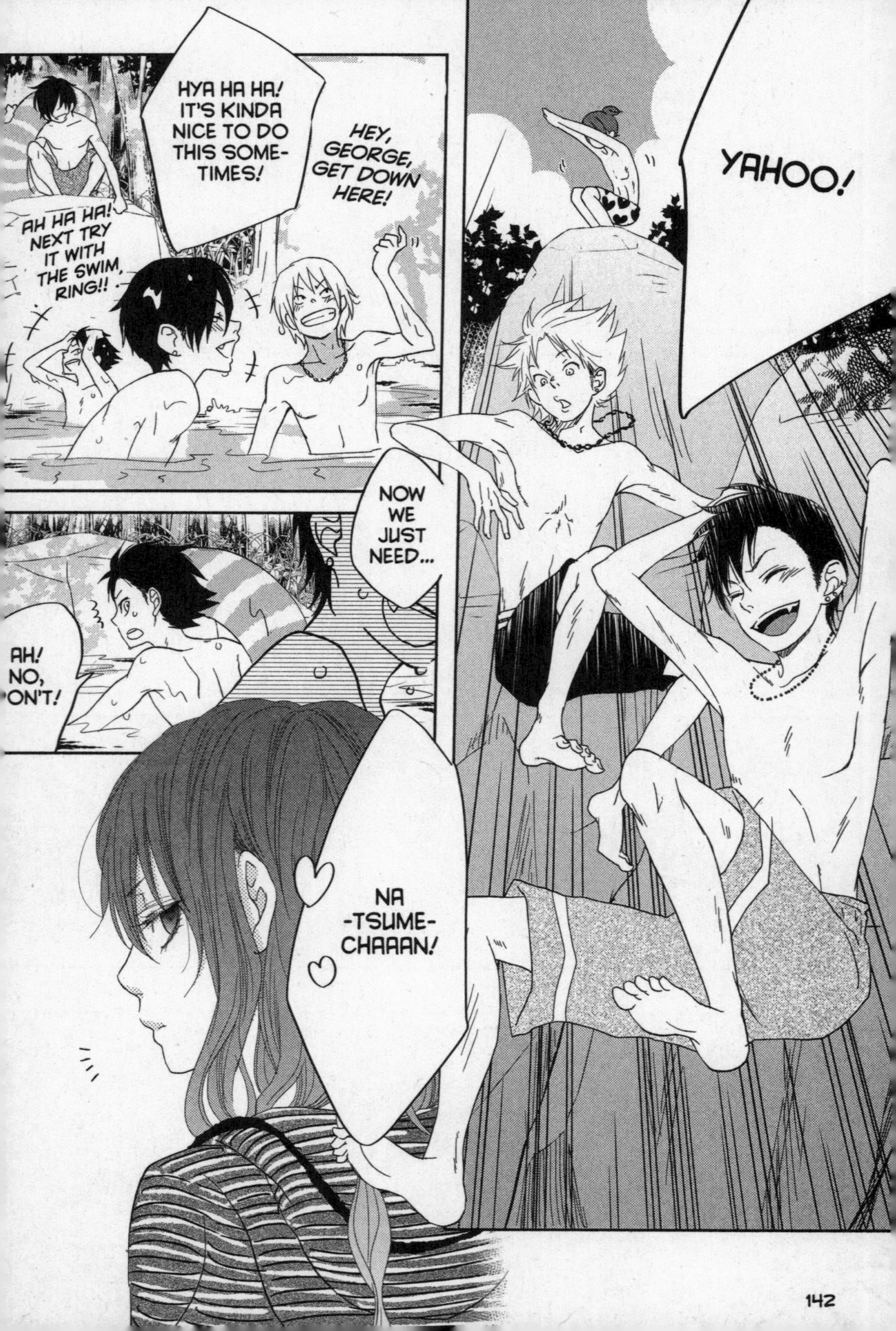
HYA HA HA! IT'S KINDA NICE TO DO THIS SOME-TIMES!
HEY, GEORGE, GET DOWN HERE!
AH HA HA! NEXT TRY IT WITH THE SWIM RING!!
YAHOO!
AH! NO, ON'T!
NOW WE JUST NEED...
NA -TSUME-CHAAAN!

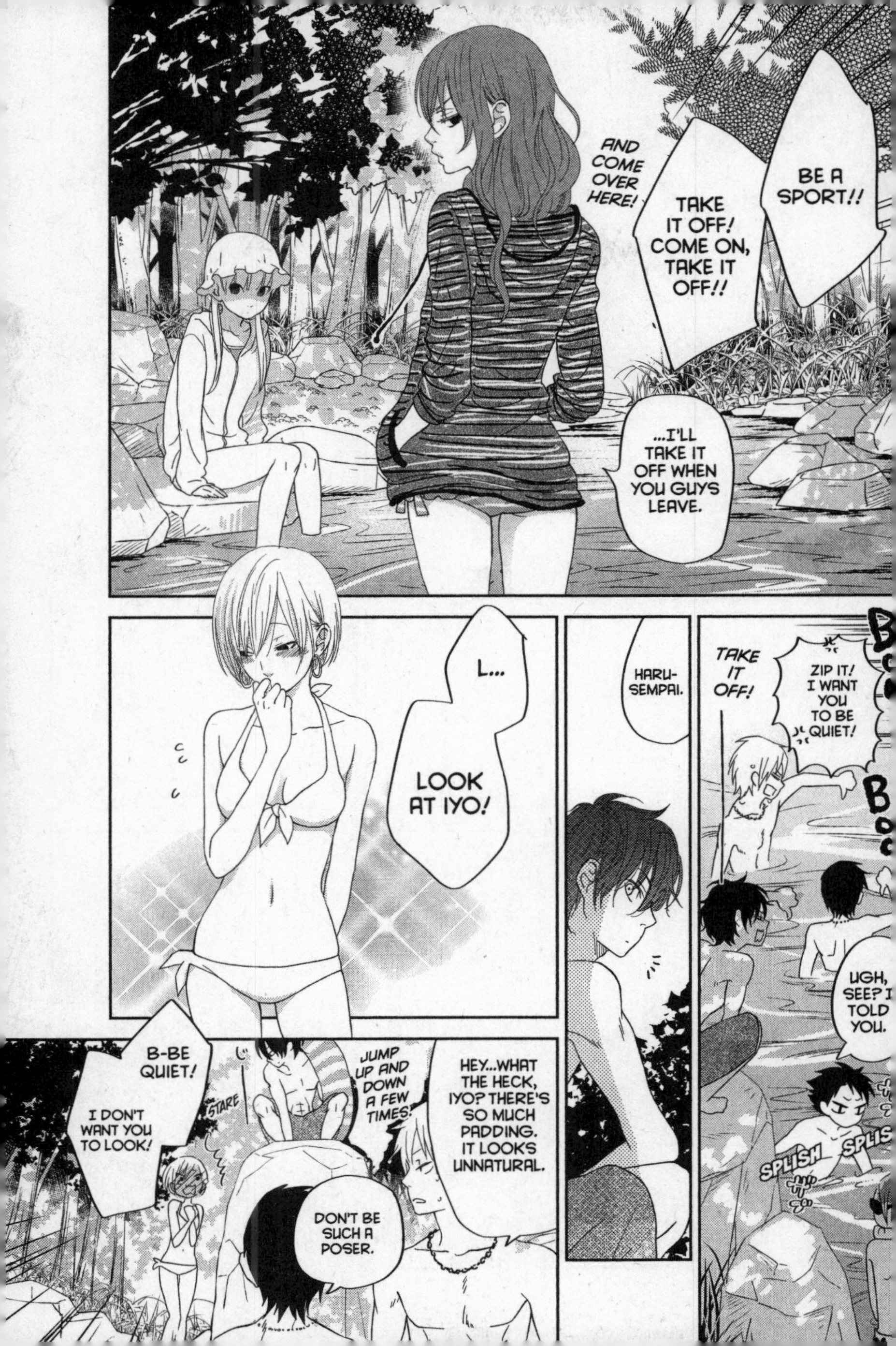
BE A SPORT!!
TAKE IT OFF! COME ON, TAKE IT OFF!!
AND COME OVER HERE!
...I'LL TAKE IT OFF WHEN YOU GUYS LEAVE.
ZIP IT! I WANT YOU TO BE QUIET!
TAKE IT OFF!
UGH, SEE? I TOLD YOU.
SPLISH
SPLISH
HARU-SEMPAI.
L...
LOOK AT IYO!
HEY...WHAT THE HECK, IYO? THERE'S SO MUCH PADDING. IT LOOKS UNNATURAL.
JUMP UP AND DOWN A FEW TIMES!
DON'T BE SUCH A POSER.
STARE
B-BE QUIET!
I DON'T WANT YOU TO LOOK!

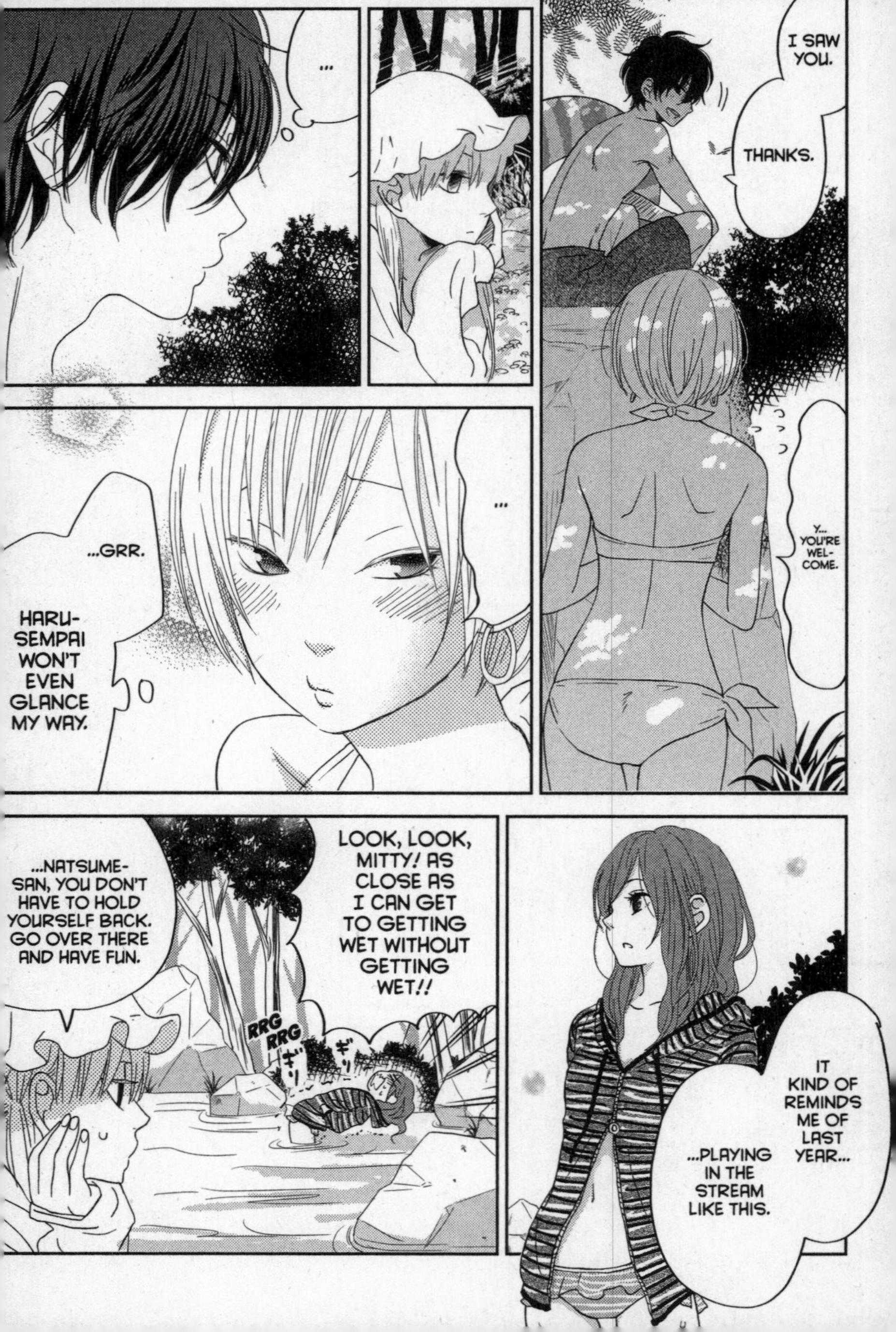
I SAW YOU.
THANKS.
Y... YOU'RE WEL-COME.
...
...
...GRR.
HARU-SEMPAI WON'T EVEN GLANCE MY WAY.
IT KIND OF REMINDS ME OF LAST YEAR...
...PLAYING IN THE STREAM LIKE THIS.
LOOK, LOOK, MITTY! AS CLOSE AS I CAN GET TO GETTING WET WITHOUT GETTING WET!!
RRG RRG
ギリ
ギリ
...NATSUME-SAN, YOU DON'T HAVE TO HOLD YOURSELF BACK. GO OVER THERE AND HAVE FUN.

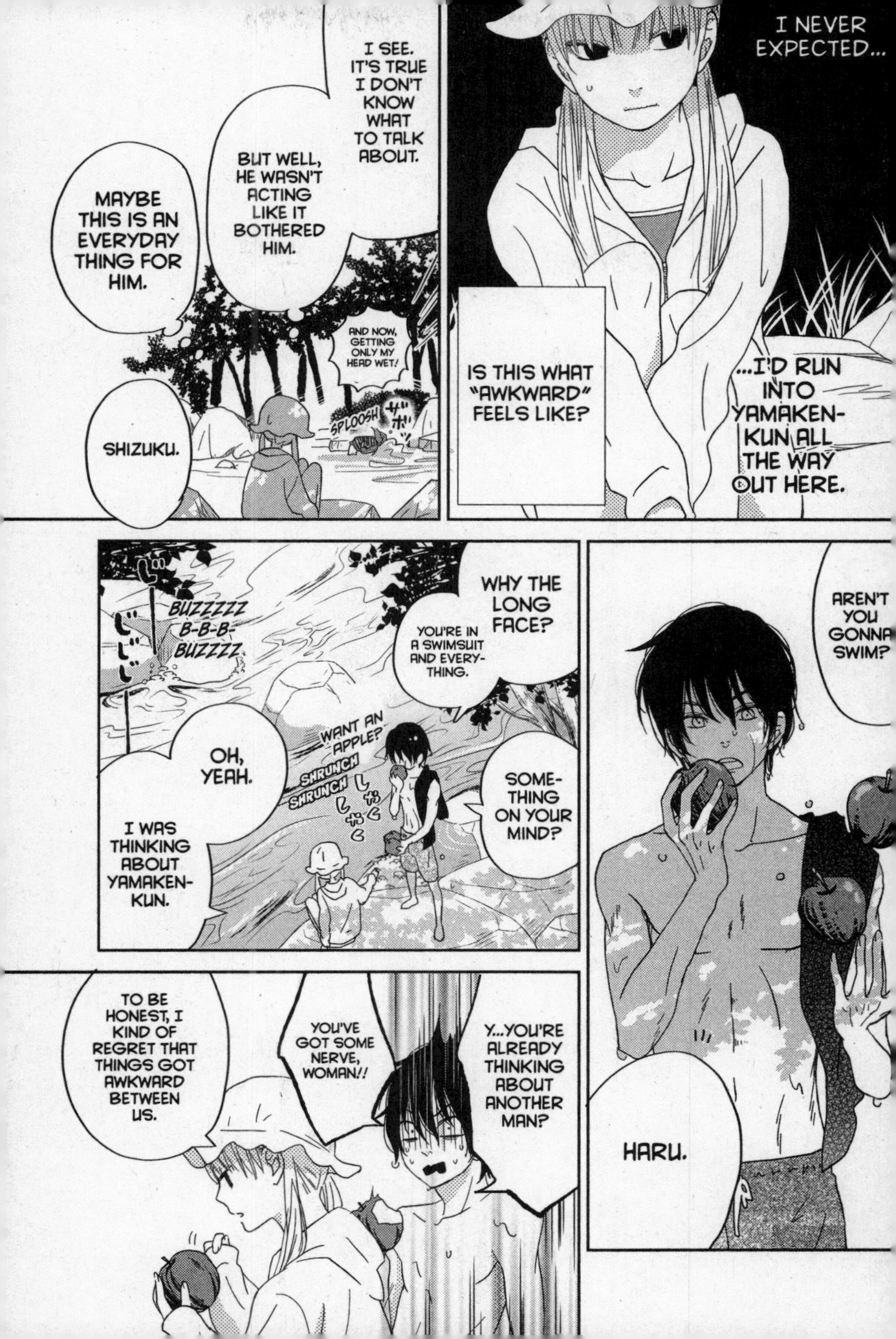

I NEVER EXPECTED...
...I'D RUN INTO YAMAKEN-KUN ALL THE WAY OUT HERE.
IS THIS WHAT "AWKWARD" FEELS LIKE?
I SEE. IT'S TRUE I DON'T KNOW WHAT TO TALK ABOUT.
BUT WELL, HE WASN'T ACTING LIKE IT BOTHERED HIM.
MAYBE THIS IS AN EVERYDAY THING FOR HIM.
AND NOW, GETTING ONLY MY HEAD WET!
SPLOOSH
SHIZUKU.
AREN'T YOU GONNA SWIM?
HARU.
WHY THE LONG FACE?
YOU'RE IN A SWIMSUIT AND EVERYTHING.
BUZZZZZ B-B-B-BUZZZZZ
WANT AN APPLE?
SHRUNCH SHRUNCH
SOMETHING ON YOUR MIND?
OH, YEAH.
I WAS THINKING ABOUT YAMAKEN-KUN.
Y...YOU'RE ALREADY THINKING ABOUT ANOTHER MAN?
YOU'VE GOT SOME NERVE, WOMAN!!
TO BE HONEST, I KIND OF REGRET THAT THINGS GOT AWKWARD BETWEEN US.

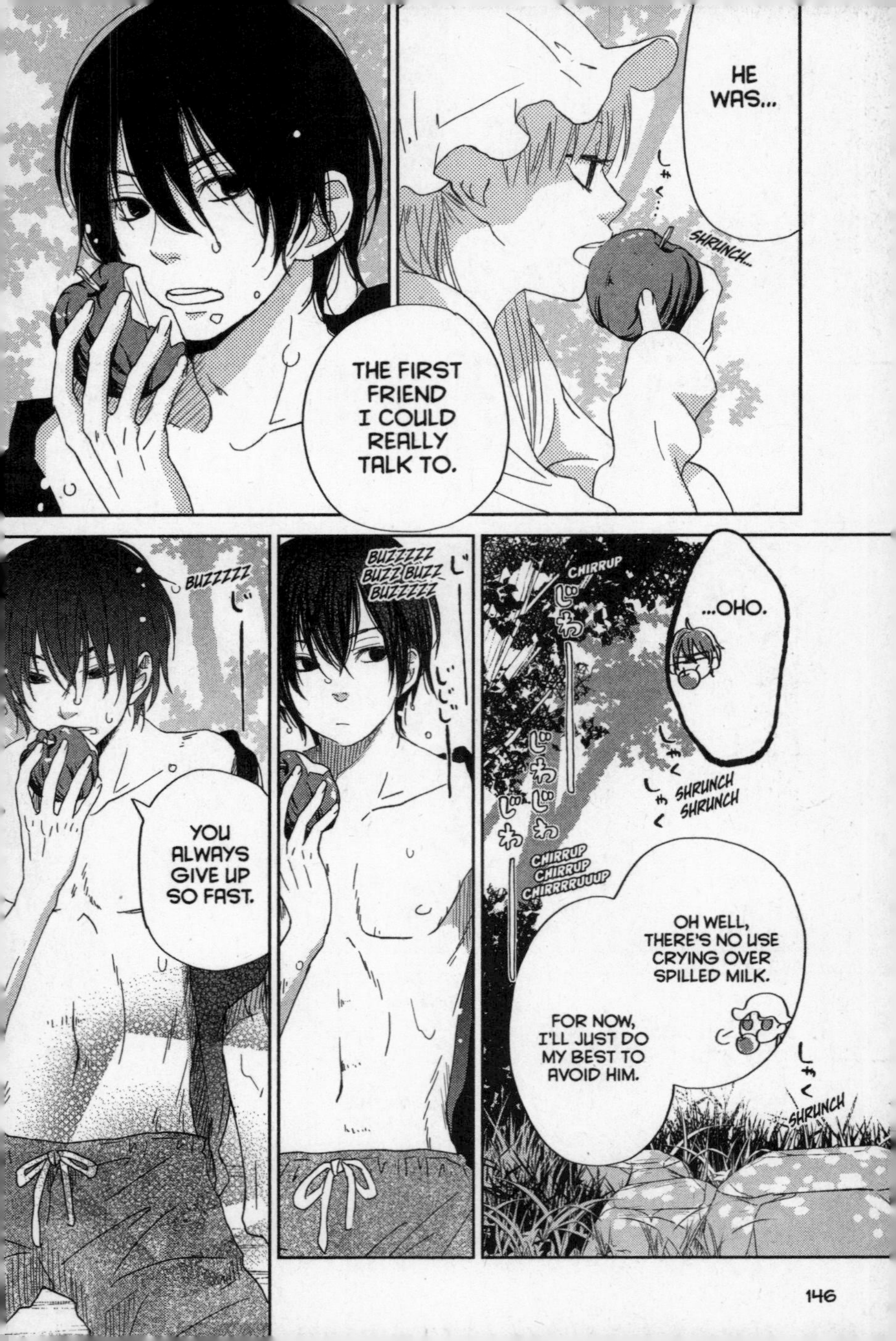

HE WAS...
しゃく…
SHRUNCH...
THE FIRST FRIEND I COULD REALLY TALK TO.
...OHO.
CHIRRUP
しゃく
しゃく
SHRUNCH SHRUNCH
CHIRRUP CHIRRUP CHIRRRRUUUP
OH WELL, THERE'S NO USE CRYING OVER SPILLED MILK.
FOR NOW, I'LL JUST DO MY BEST TO AVOID HIM.
しゃく
SHRUNCH
BUZZZZZZ BUZZ BUZZ BUZZZZZZ
じー
じじじ
BUZZZZZZ
じー
YOU ALWAYS GIVE UP SO FAST.

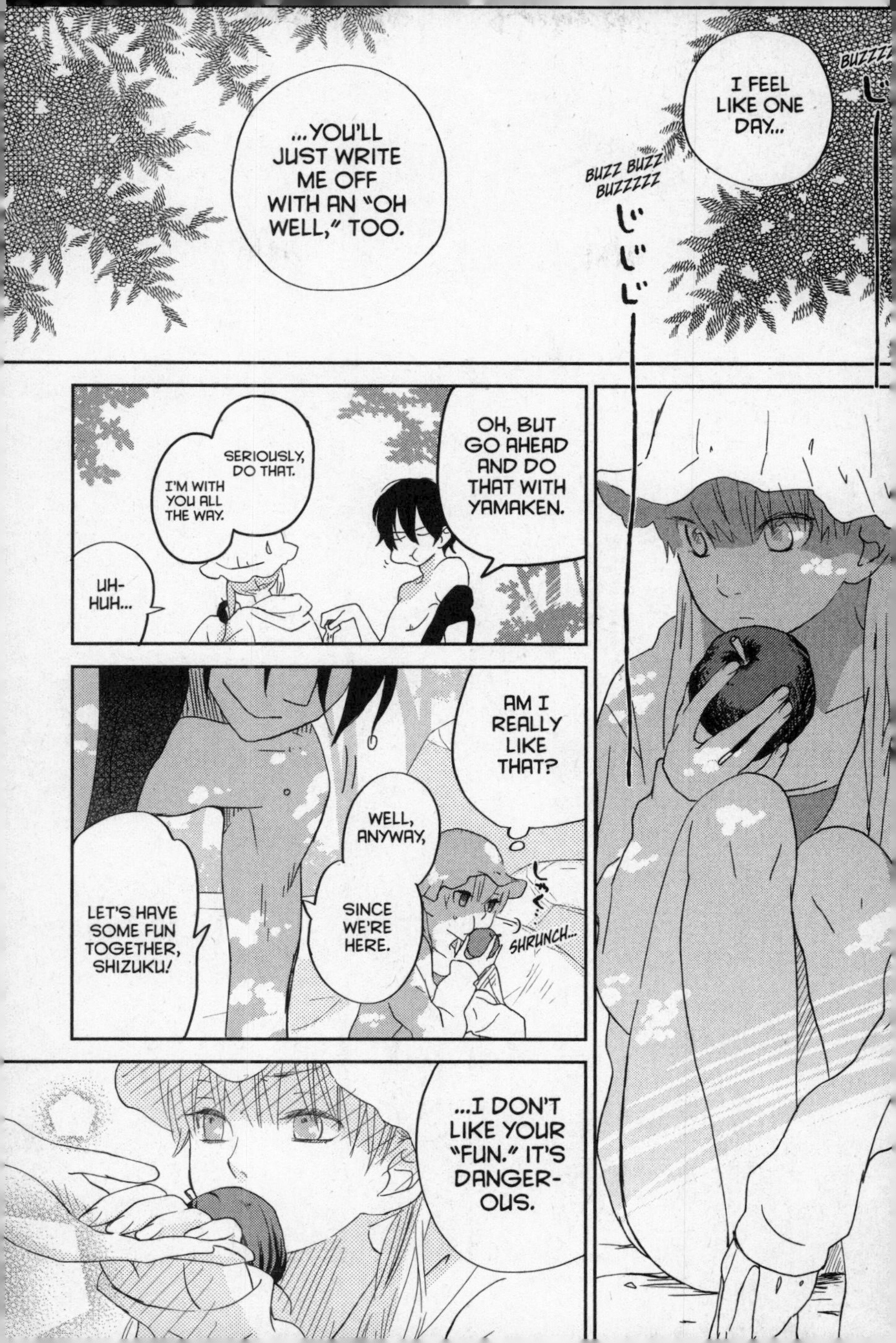
BUZZZZ
I FEEL LIKE ONE DAY...
...YOU'LL JUST WRITE ME OFF WITH AN "OH WELL," TOO.
BUZZ BUZZ BUZZZZZ
じじじ
OH, BUT GO AHEAD AND DO THAT WITH YAMAKEN.
SERIOUSLY, DO THAT.
I'M WITH YOU ALL THE WAY.
UH-HUH...
AM I REALLY LIKE THAT?
WELL, ANYWAY,
SINCE WE'RE HERE.
SHRUNCH...
LET'S HAVE SOME FUN TOGETHER, SHIZUKU!
...I DON'T LIKE YOUR "FUN." IT'S DANGER-OUS.

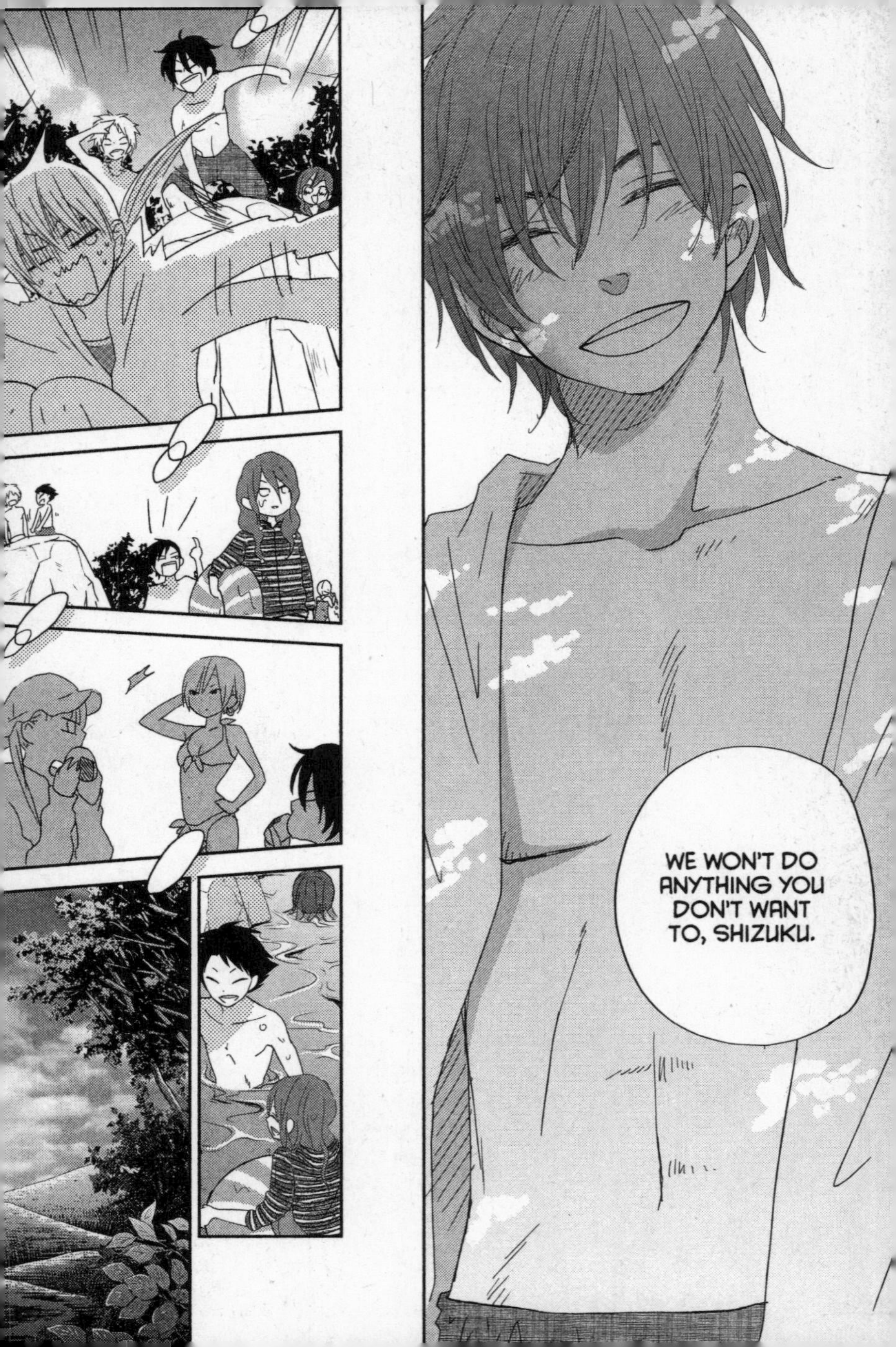
WE WON'T DO
ANYTHING YOU
DON'T WANT
TO, SHIZUKU.

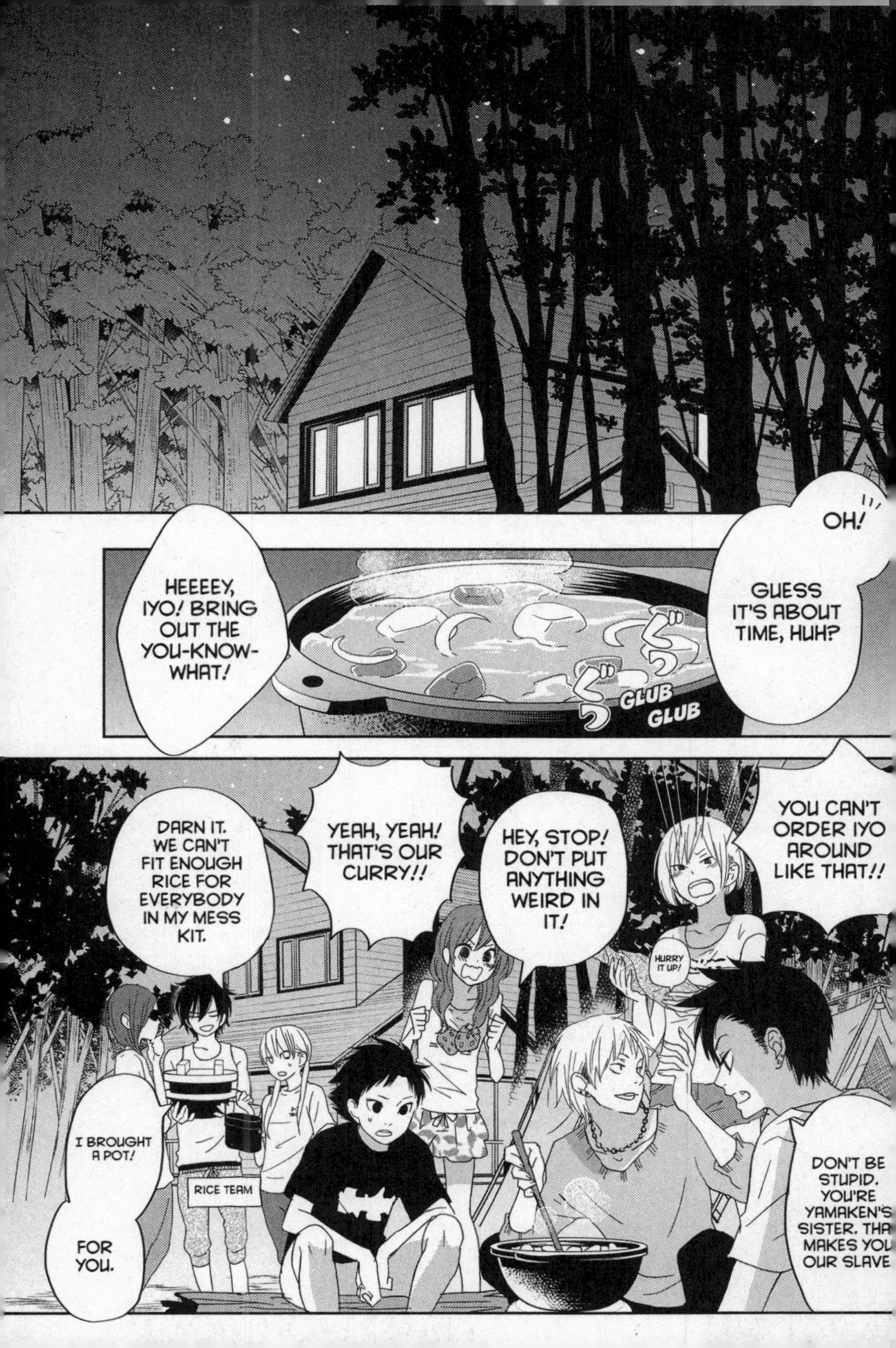
OH!
GUESS IT'S ABOUT TIME, HUH?
ぐつぐつ GLUB GLUB
HEEEEY, IYO! BRING OUT THE YOU-KNOW-WHAT!
YOU CAN'T ORDER IYO AROUND LIKE THAT!!
DON'T BE STUPID. YOU'RE YAMAKEN'S SISTER. THA MAKES YOU OUR SLAVE
HURRY IT UP!
HEY, STOP! DON'T PUT ANYTHING WEIRD IN IT!
YEAH, YEAH! THAT'S OUR CURRY!!
DARN IT. WE CAN'T FIT ENOUGH RICE FOR EVERYBODY IN MY MESS KIT.
RICE TEAM
I BROUGHT A POT!
FOR YOU.

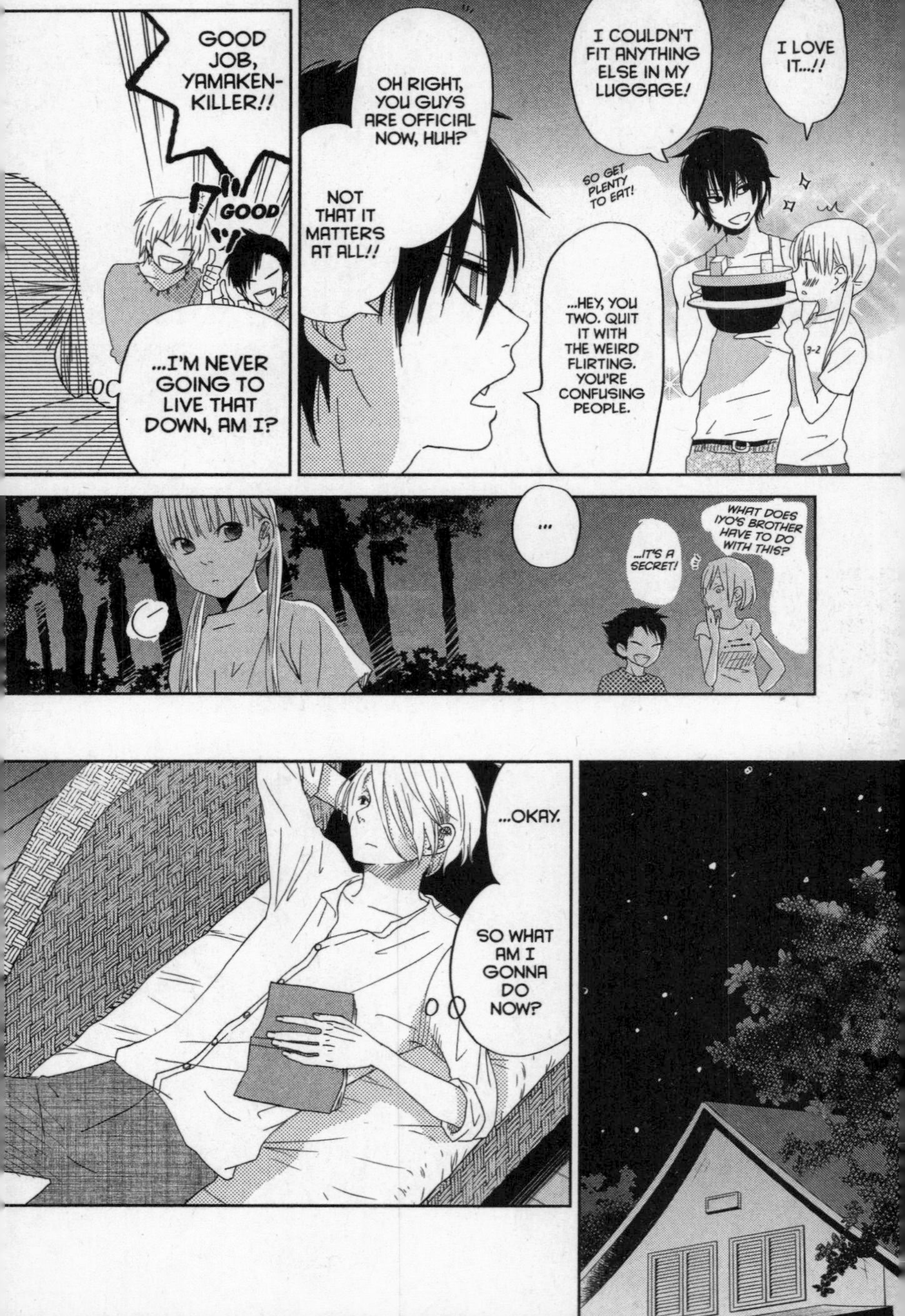
I LOVE IT...!!
I COULDN'T FIT ANYTHING ELSE IN MY LUGGAGE!
SO GET PLENTY TO EAT!
...HEY, YOU TWO. QUIT IT WITH THE WEIRD FLIRTING. YOU'RE CONFUSING PEOPLE.
OH RIGHT, YOU GUYS ARE OFFICIAL NOW, HUH?
NOT THAT IT MATTERS AT ALL!!
GOOD JOB, YAMAKEN-KILLER!!
GOOD
...I'M NEVER GOING TO LIVE THAT DOWN, AM I?
WHAT DOES IYO'S BROTHER HAVE TO DO WITH THIS?
...IT'S A SECRET!
...
...OKAY.
SO WHAT AM I GONNA DO NOW?

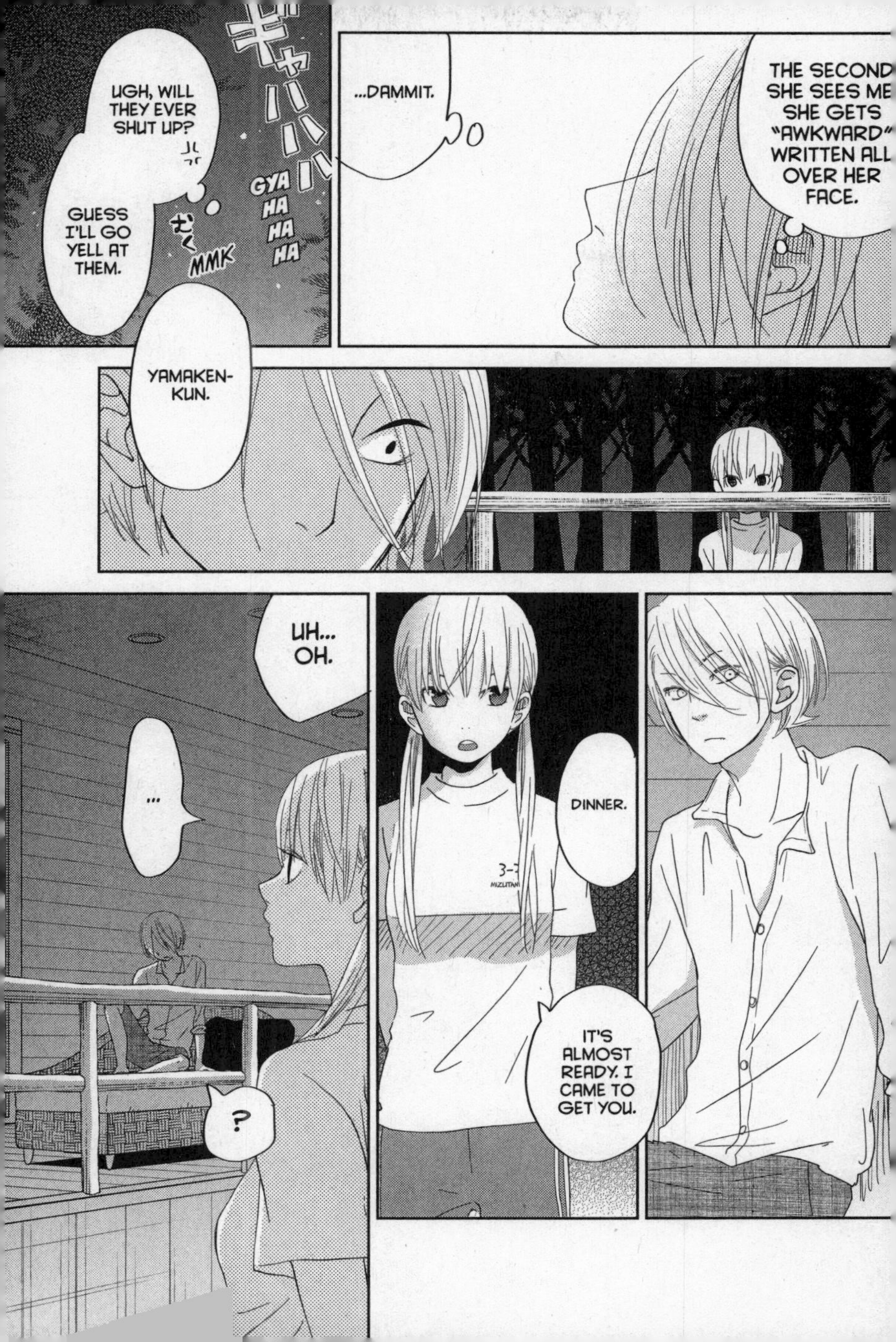
THE SECOND SHE SEES ME SHE GETS "AWKWARD" WRITTEN ALL OVER HER FACE.
...DAMMIT.
GYA HA HA HA
UGH, WILL THEY EVER SHUT UP?
MMK
GUESS I'LL GO YELL AT THEM.
YAMAKEN-KUN.
DINNER.
IT'S ALMOST READY. I CAME TO GET YOU.
UH... OH.
...
?

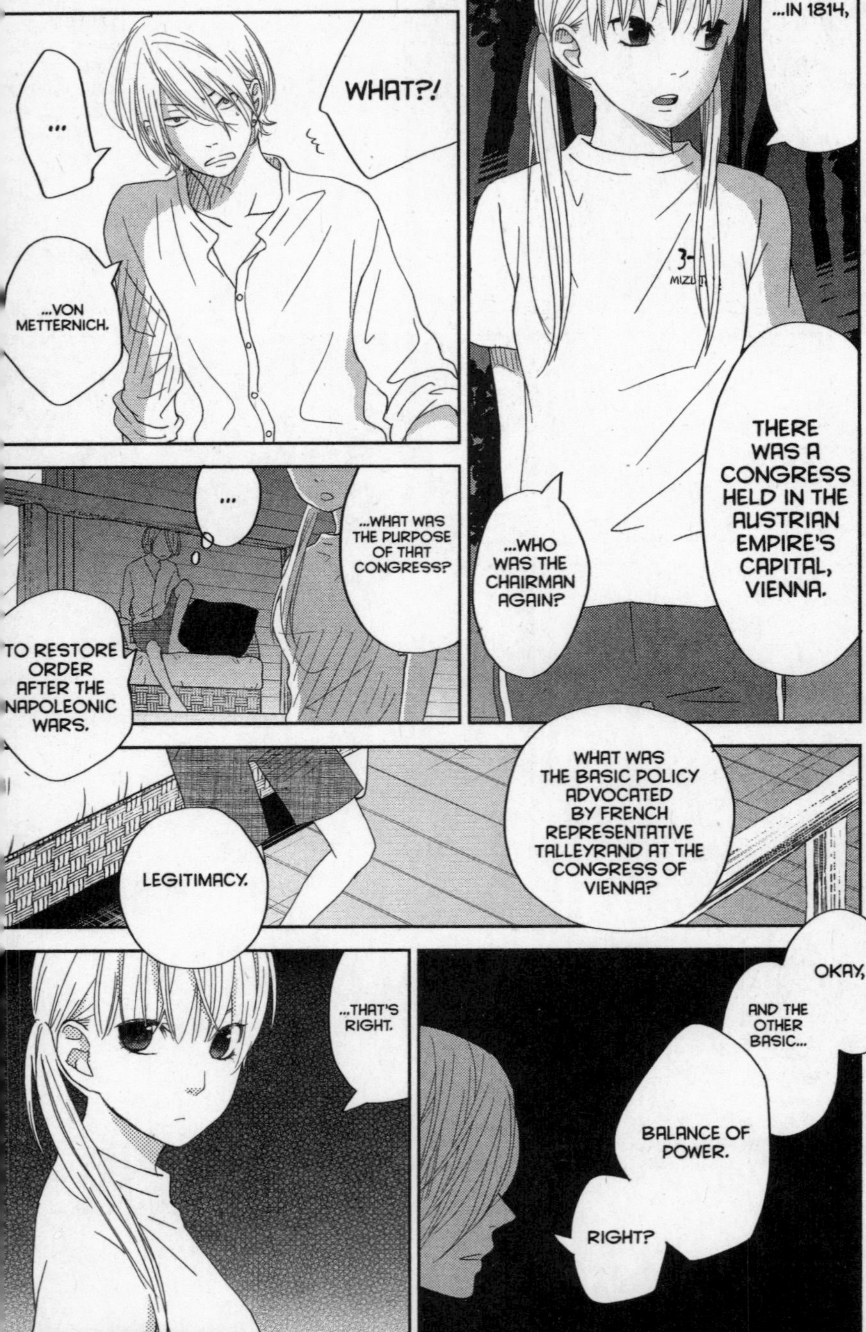
...IN 1814,
THERE WAS A CONGRESS HELD IN THE AUSTRIAN EMPIRE'S CAPITAL, VIENNA.
...WHO WAS THE CHAIRMAN AGAIN?
WHAT?!
...
...VON METTERNICH.
...
...WHAT WAS THE PURPOSE OF THAT CONGRESS?
TO RESTORE ORDER AFTER THE NAPOLEONIC WARS.
WHAT WAS THE BASIC POLICY ADVOCATED BY FRENCH REPRESENTATIVE TALLEYRAND AT THE CONGRESS OF VIENNA?
LEGITIMACY.
OKAY,
AND THE OTHER BASIC...
BALANCE OF POWER.
RIGHT?
...THAT'S RIGHT.

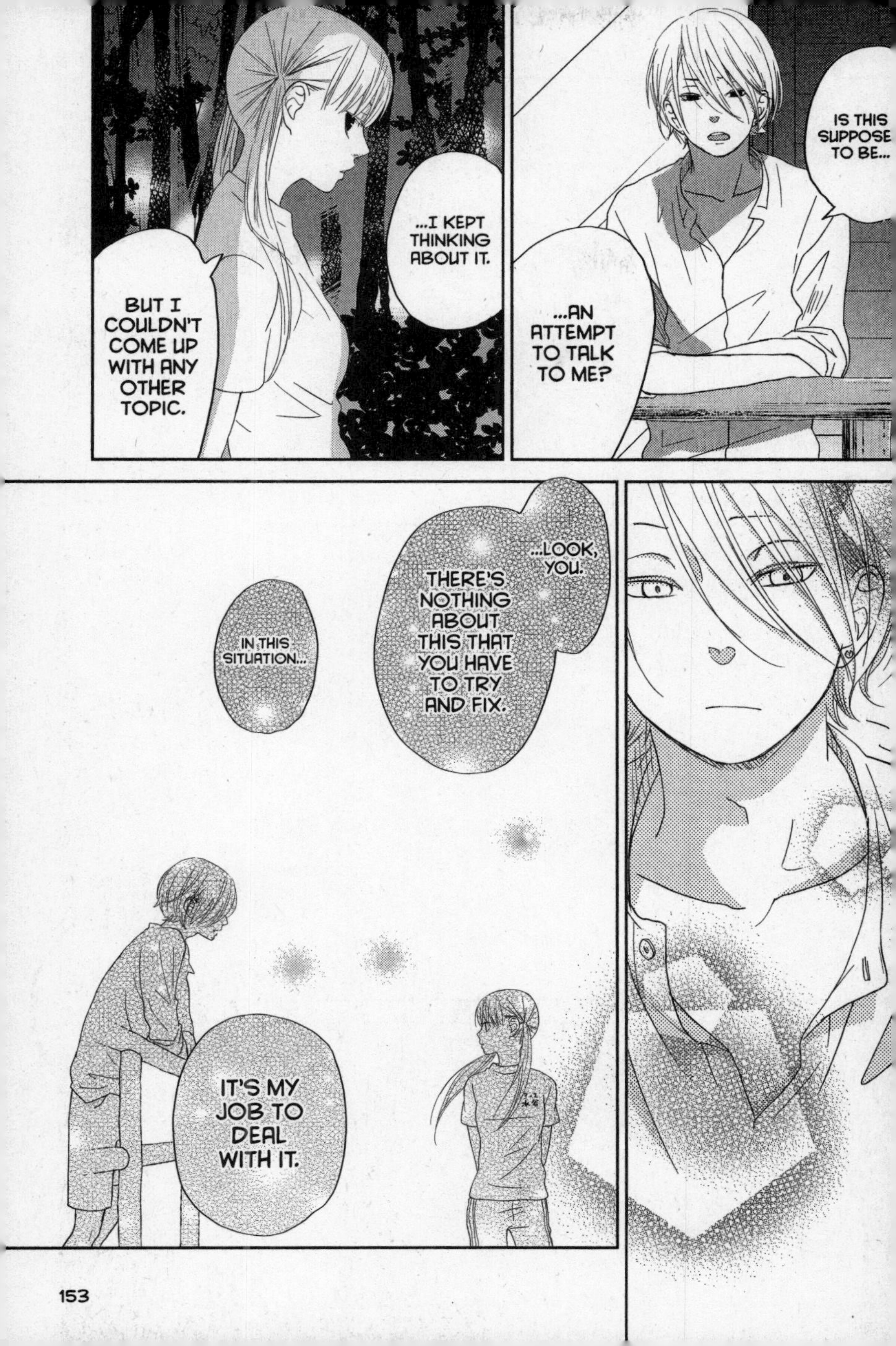
IS THIS SUPPOSE TO BE...
...AN ATTEMPT TO TALK TO ME?
...I KEPT THINKING ABOUT IT.
BUT I COULDN'T COME UP WITH ANY OTHER TOPIC.
...LOOK, YOU.
THERE'S NOTHING ABOUT THIS THAT YOU HAVE TO TRY AND FIX.
IN THIS SITUATION...
IT'S MY JOB TO DEAL WITH IT.

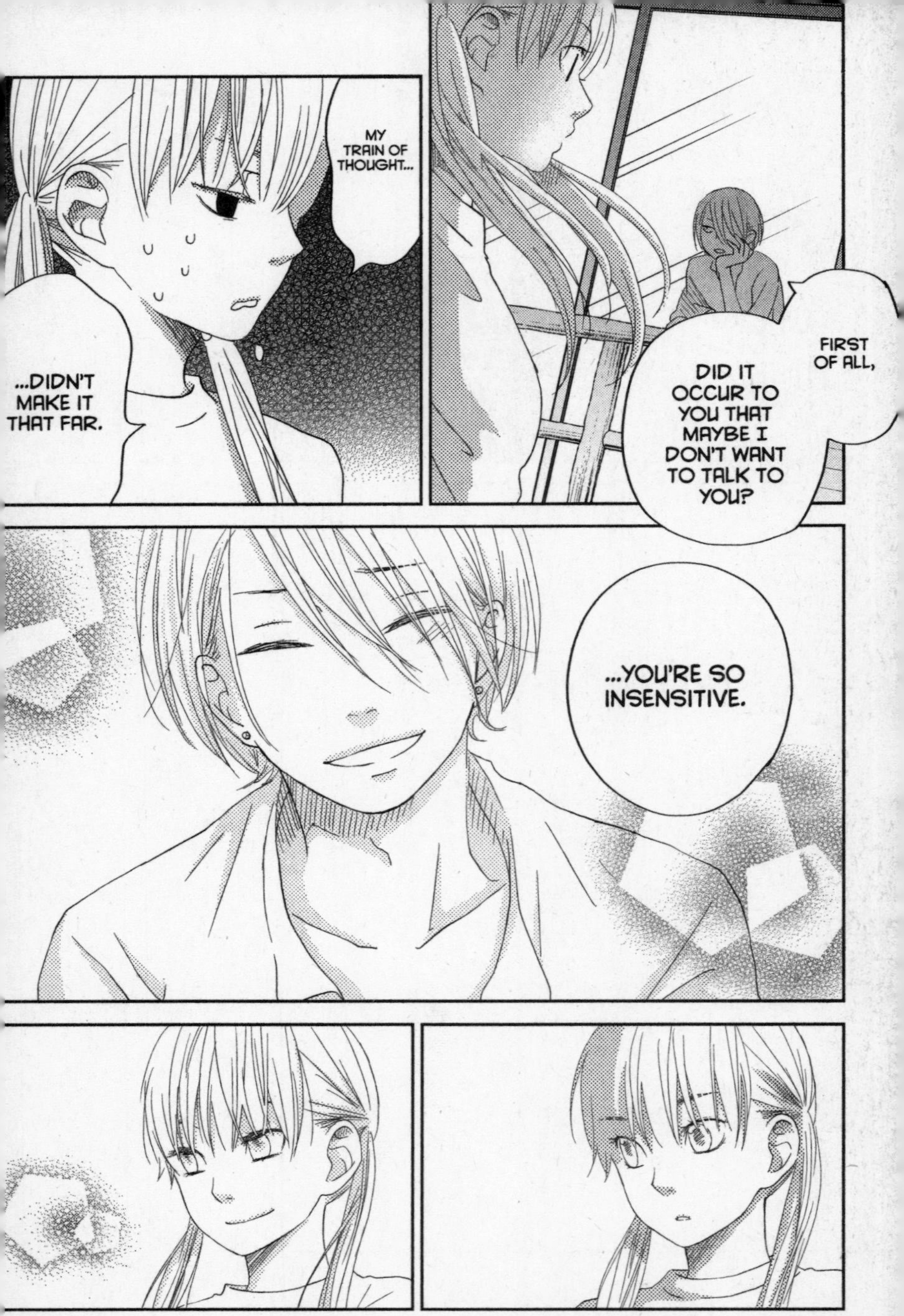
FIRST OF ALL,
DID IT OCCUR TO YOU THAT MAYBE I DON'T WANT TO TALK TO YOU?
MY TRAIN OF THOUGHT...
...DIDN'T MAKE IT THAT FAR.
...YOU'RE SO INSENSITIVE.

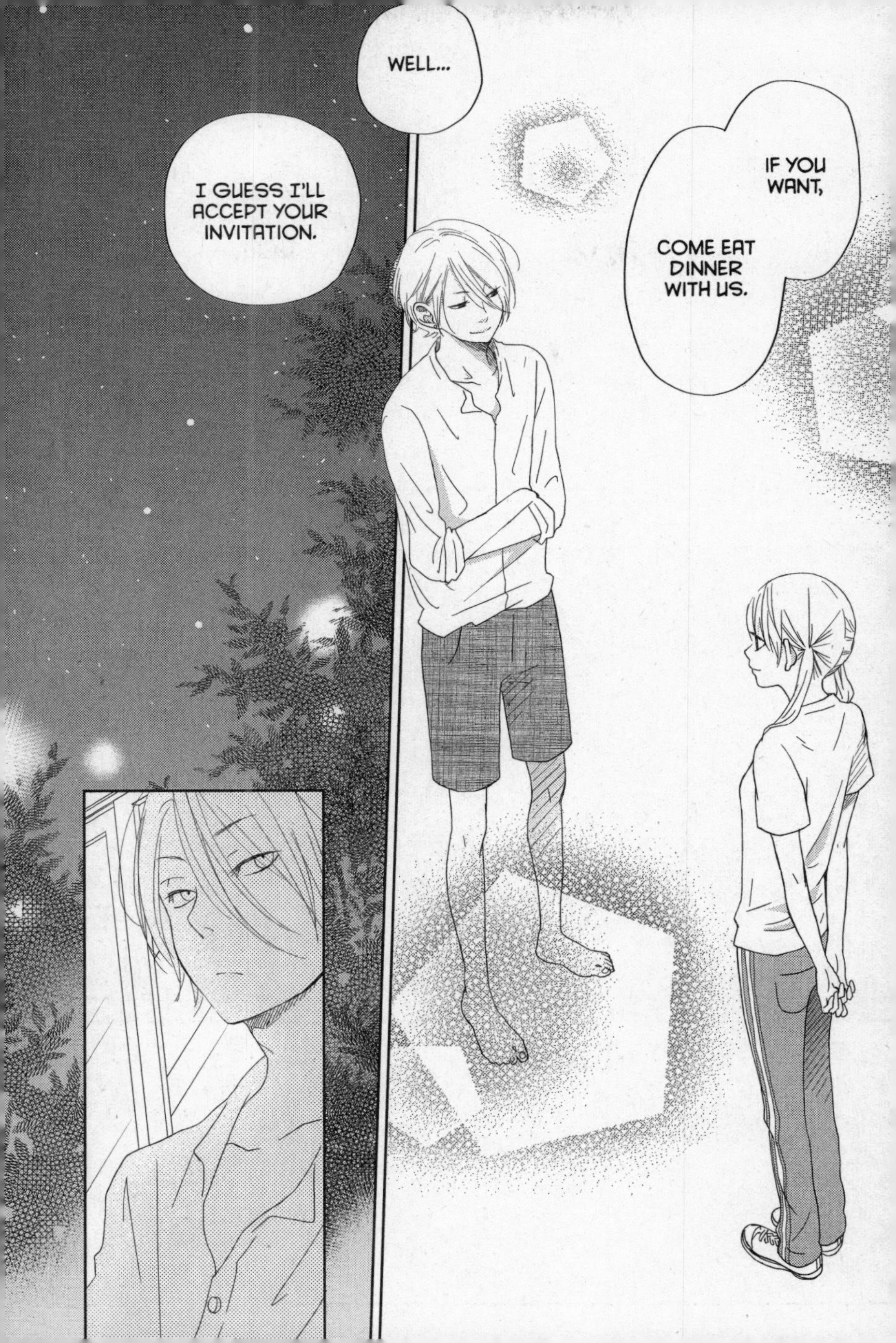
IF YOU WANT,
COME EAT DINNER WITH US.
WELL...
I GUESS I'LL ACCEPT YOUR INVITATION.

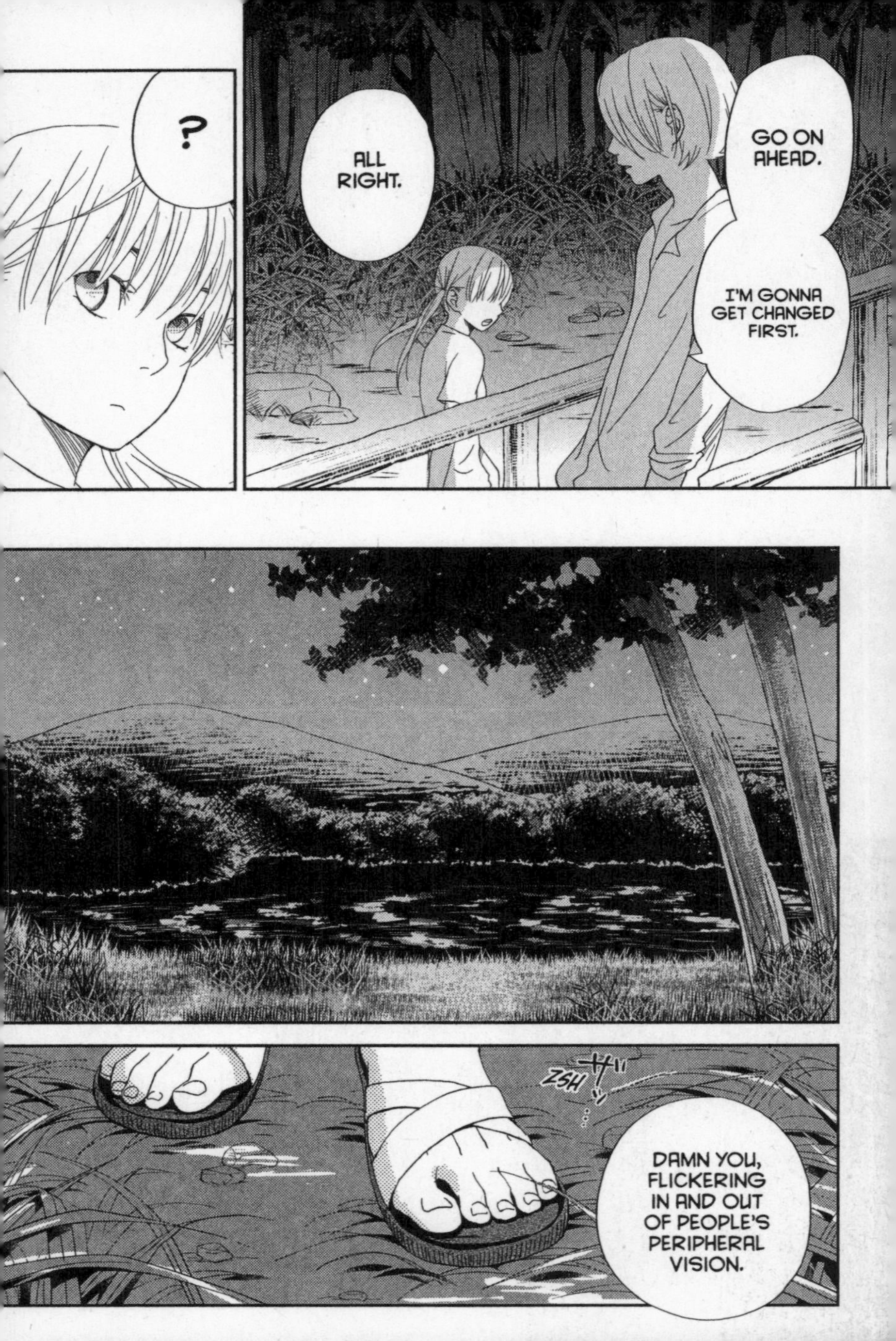
GO ON AHEAD.
I'M GONNA GET CHANGED FIRST.
ALL RIGHT.
?
ZSH
DAMN YOU, FLICKERING IN AND OUT OF PEOPLE'S PERIPHERAL VISION.

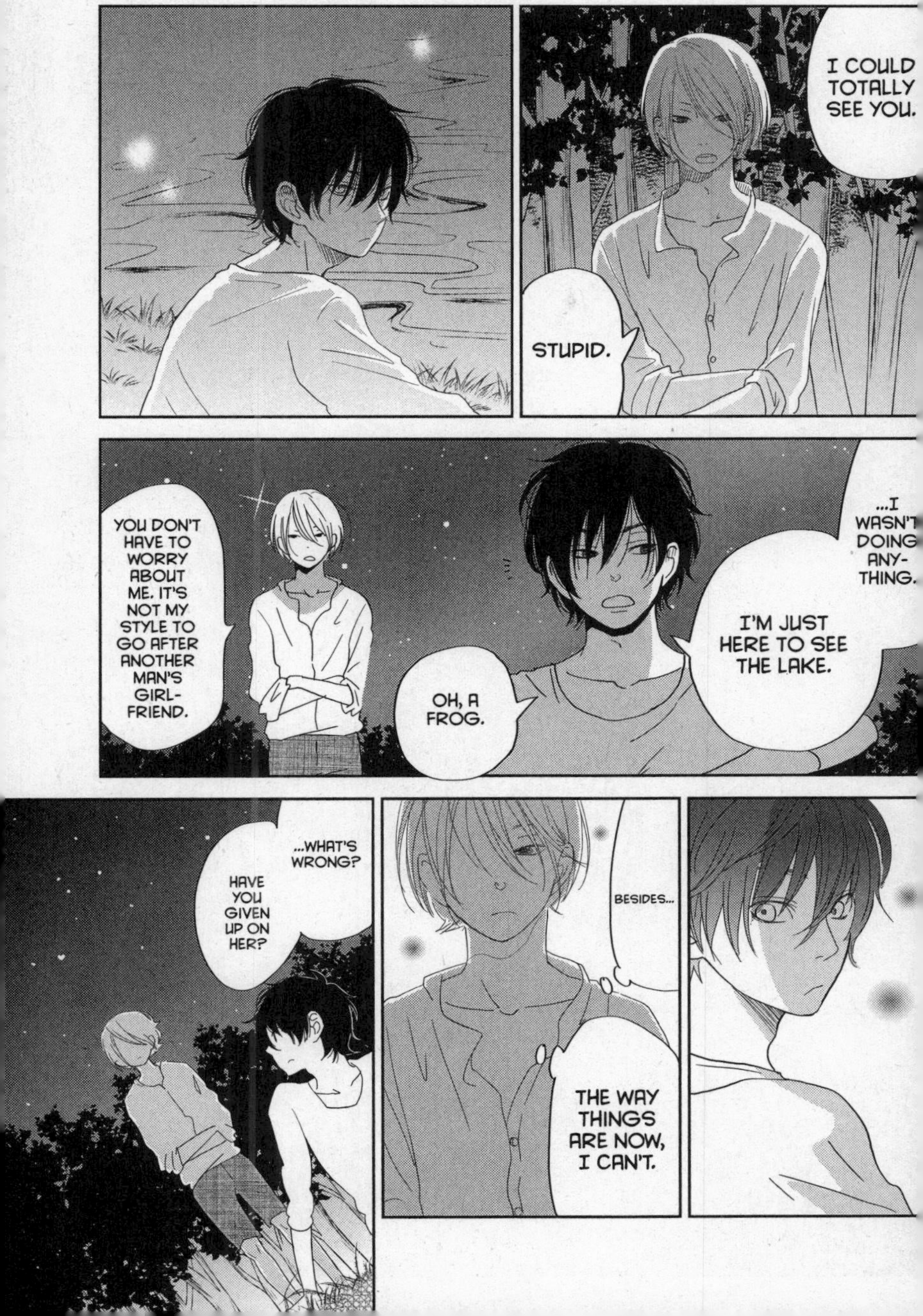
I COULD TOTALLY SEE YOU.
STUPID.
...I WASN'T DOING ANYTHING.
I'M JUST HERE TO SEE THE LAKE.
OH, A FROG.
YOU DON'T HAVE TO WORRY ABOUT ME. IT'S NOT MY STYLE TO GO AFTER ANOTHER MAN'S GIRLFRIEND.
BESIDES...
THE WAY THINGS ARE NOW, I CAN'T.
...WHAT'S WRONG?
HAVE YOU GIVEN UP ON HER?

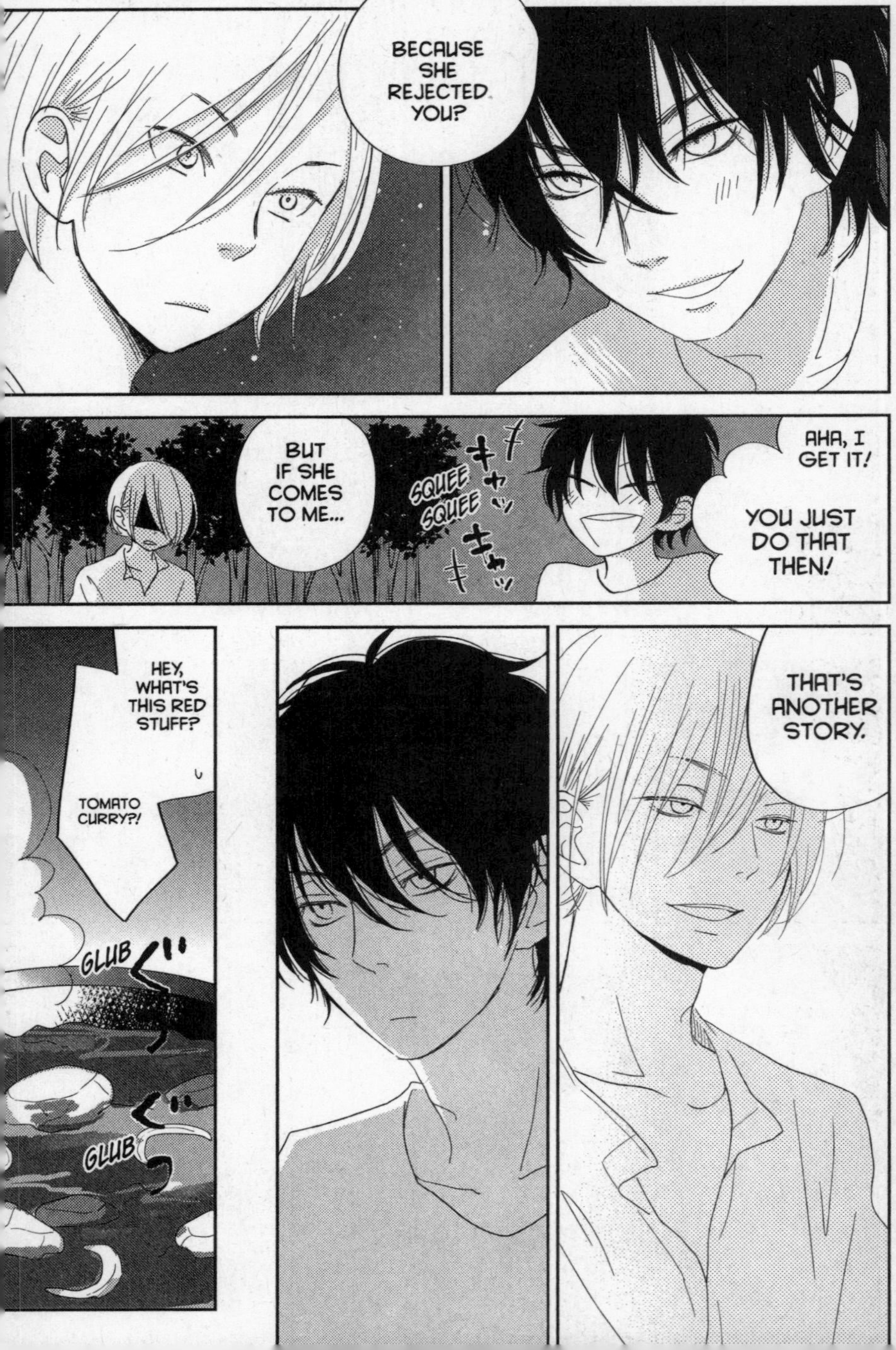
BECAUSE SHE REJECTED YOU?
AHA, I GET IT!
YOU JUST DO THAT THEN!
SQUEE SQUEE
BUT IF SHE COMES TO ME...
THAT'S ANOTHER STORY.
HEY, WHAT'S THIS RED STUFF?
TOMATO CURRY?!
GLUB
GLUB

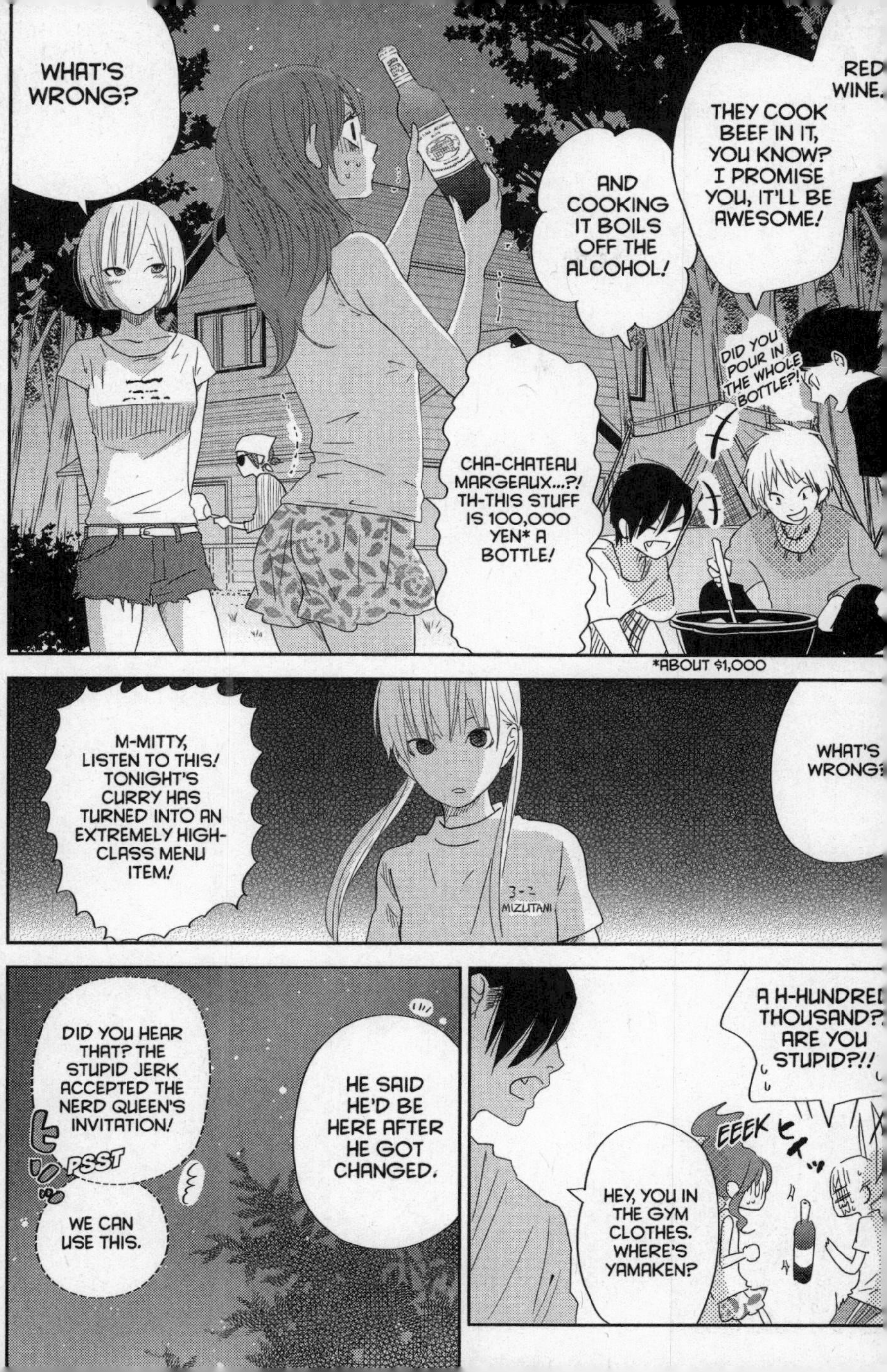
RED WINE.
THEY COOK BEEF IN IT, YOU KNOW? I PROMISE YOU, IT'LL BE AWESOME!
AND COOKING IT BOILS OFF THE ALCOHOL!
DID YOU POUR IN THE WHOLE BOTTLE?!
CHA-CHATEAU MARGEAUX...?! TH-THIS STUFF IS 100,000 YEN* A BOTTLE!
WHAT'S WRONG?
WHAT'S WRONG?
M-MITTY, LISTEN TO THIS! TONIGHT'S CURRY HAS TURNED INTO AN EXTREMELY HIGH-CLASS MENU ITEM!
3-2 MIZUTANI
A H-HUNDRED THOUSAND?! ARE YOU STUPID?!!
EEEK
ヒイッ
HEY, YOU IN THE GYM CLOTHES. WHERE'S YAMAKEN?
HE SAID HE'D BE HERE AFTER HE GOT CHANGED.
DID YOU HEAR THAT? THE STUPID JERK ACCEPTED THE NERD QUEEN'S INVITATION!
PSST
WE CAN USE THIS.

*ABOUT $1,000

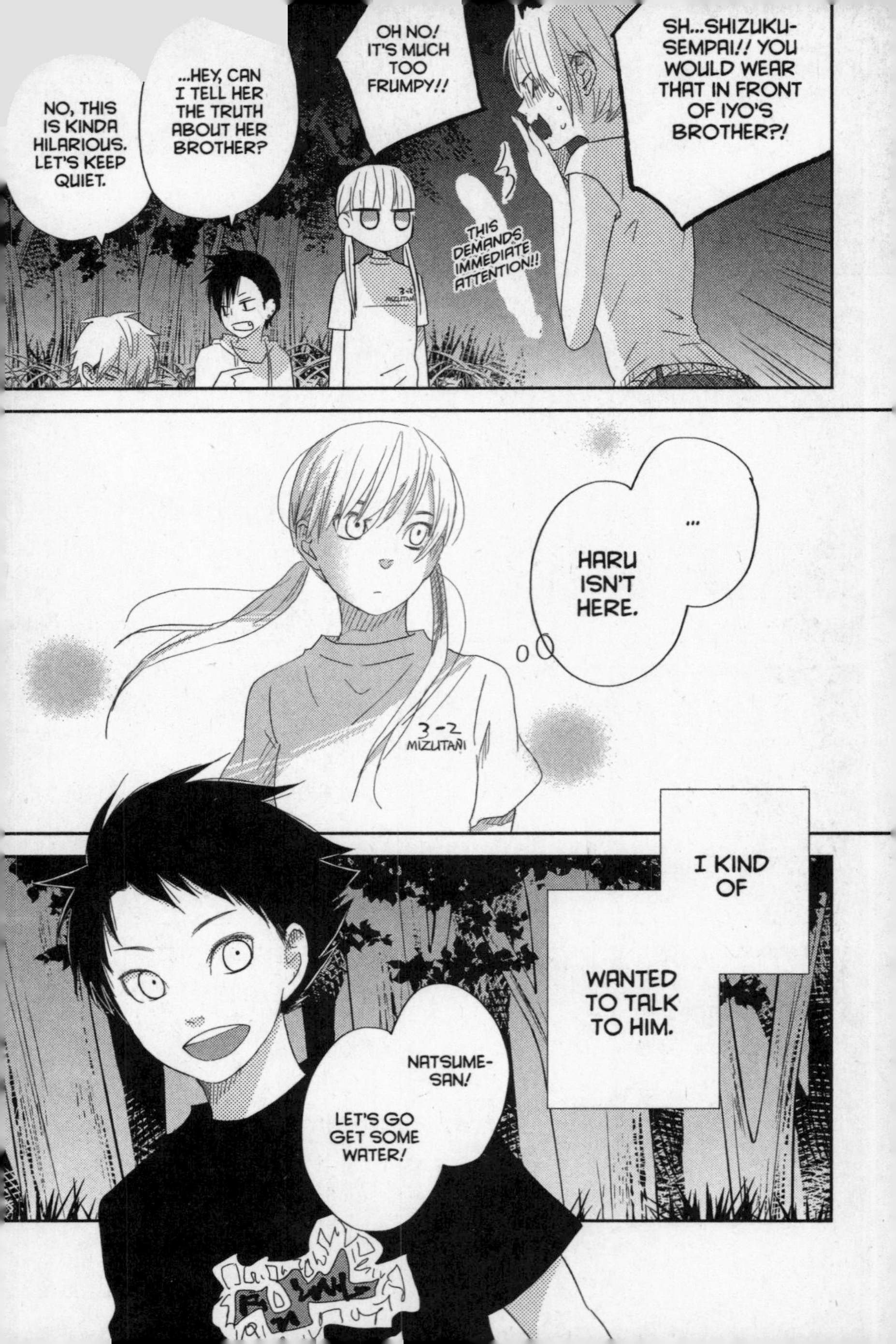
SH...SHIZUKU-SEMPAI!! YOU WOULD WEAR THAT IN FRONT OF IYO'S BROTHER?!
OH NO! IT'S MUCH TOO FRUMPY!!
THIS DEMANDS IMMEDIATE ATTENTION!!
...HEY, CAN I TELL HER THE TRUTH ABOUT HER BROTHER?
NO, THIS IS KINDA HILARIOUS. LET'S KEEP QUIET.
3-2 MIZUTANI
... HARU ISN'T HERE.
3-2 MIZUTANI
I KIND OF WANTED TO TALK TO HIM.
NATSUME-SAN! LET'S GO GET SOME WATER!

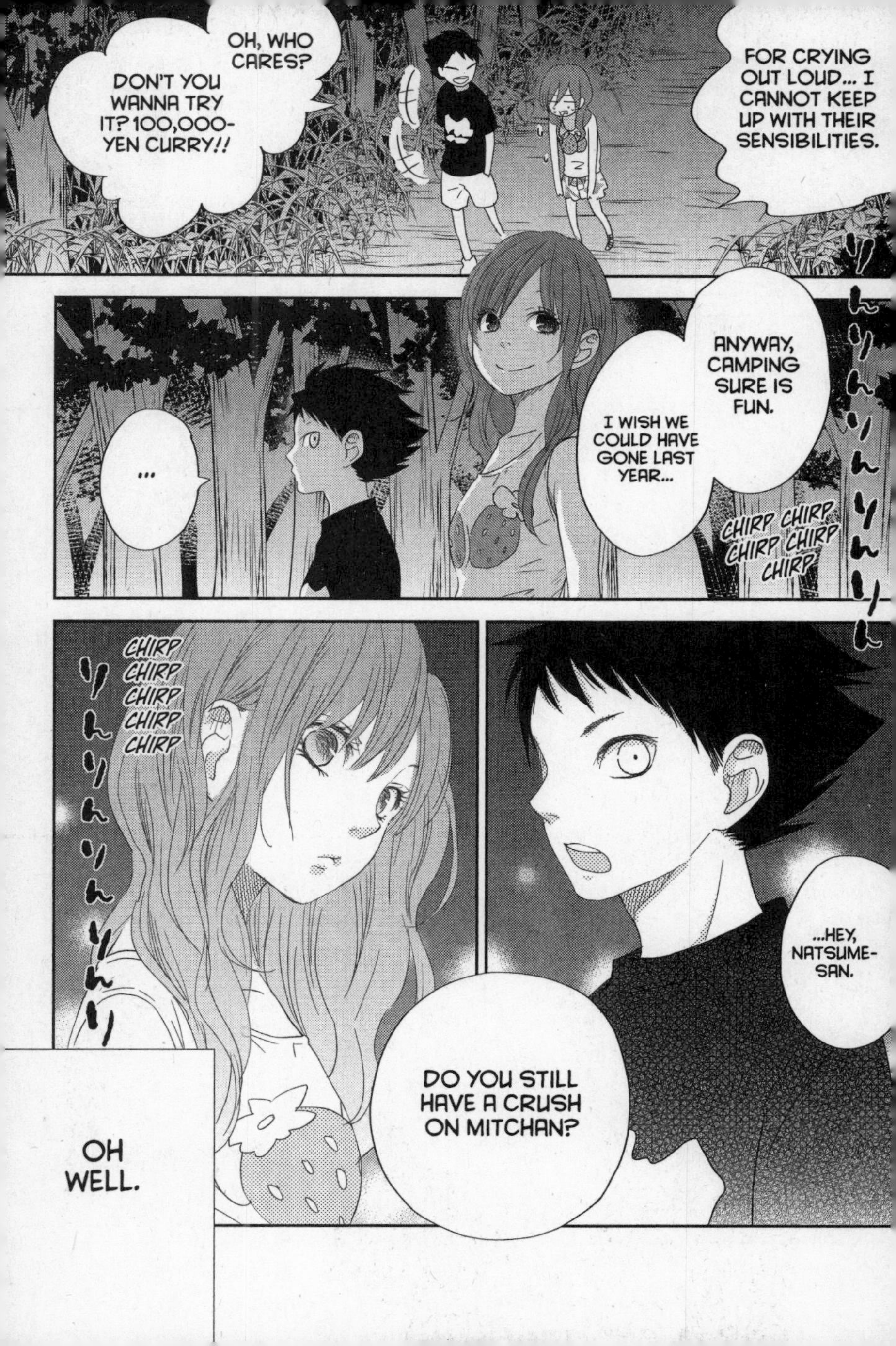
FOR CRYING OUT LOUD... I CANNOT KEEP UP WITH THEIR SENSIBILITIES.
OH, WHO CARES?
DON'T YOU WANNA TRY IT? 100,000-YEN CURRY!!
ANYWAY, CAMPING SURE IS FUN.
I WISH WE COULD HAVE GONE LAST YEAR...
CHIRP CHIRP CHIRP CHIRP CHIRP
...
...HEY, NATSUME-SAN.
DO YOU STILL HAVE A CRUSH ON MITCHAN?
CHIRP CHIRP CHIRP CHIRP CHIRP
OH WELL.

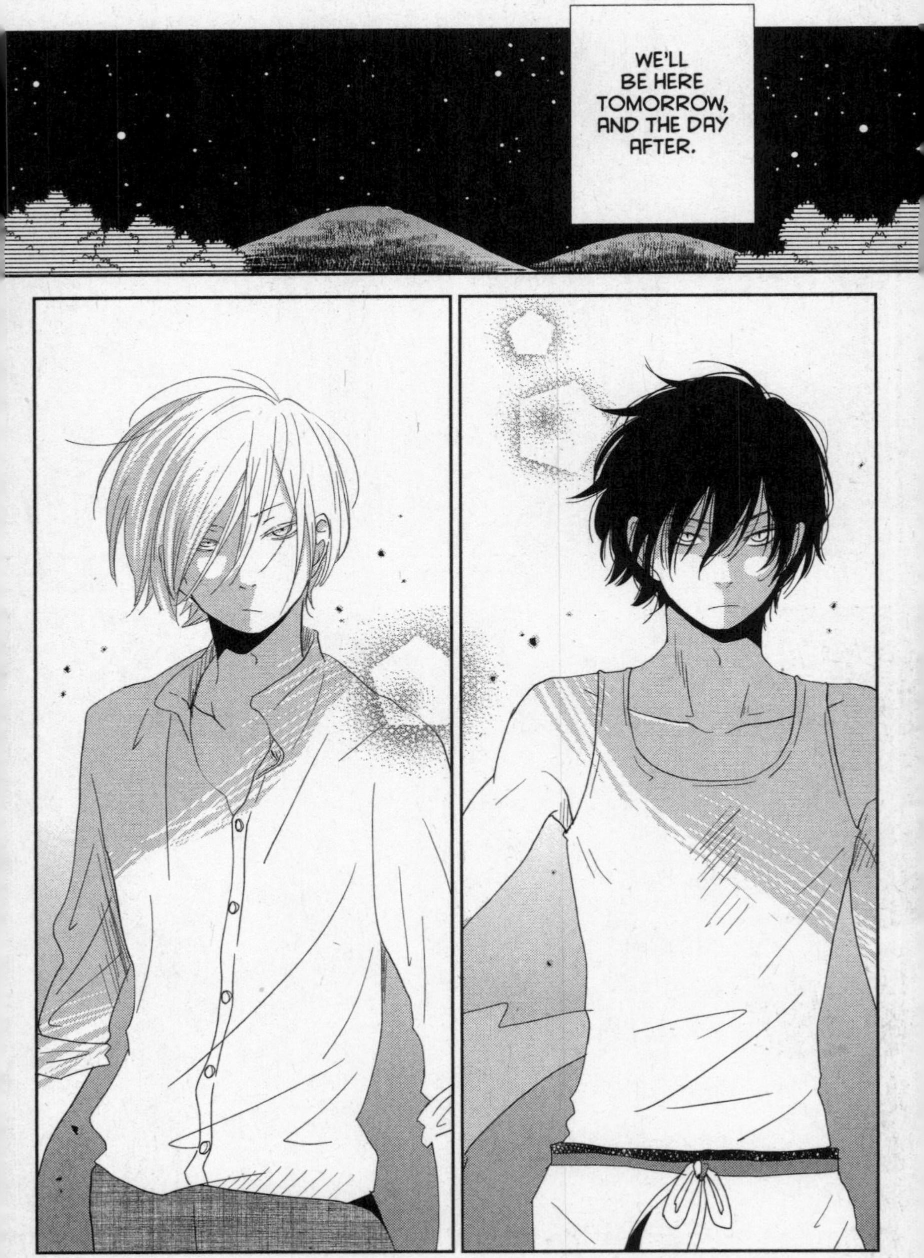
WE'LL BE HERE TOMORROW, AND THE DAY AFTER.

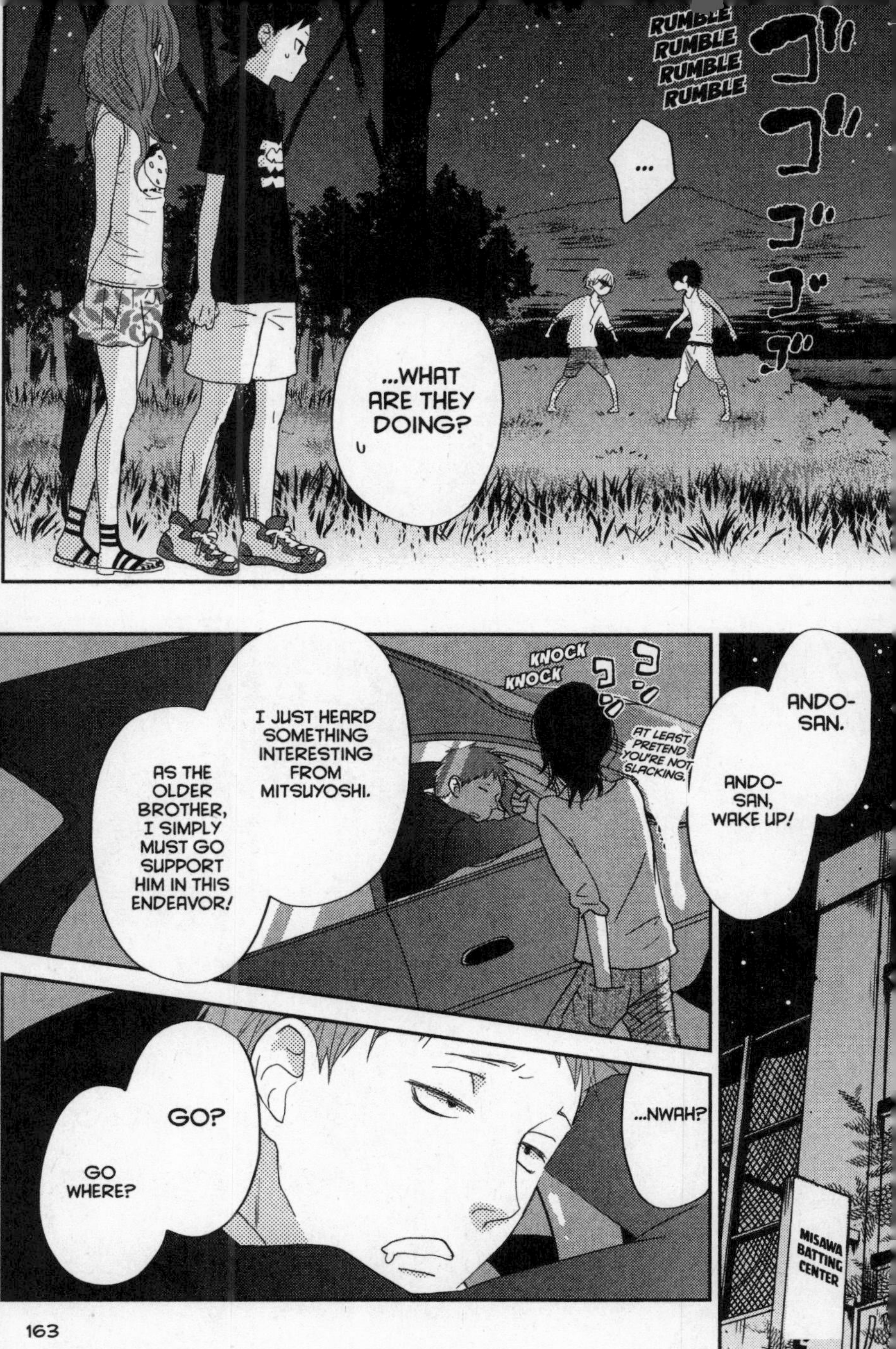
RUMBLE RUMBLE RUMBLE RUMBLE
...
...WHAT ARE THEY DOING?
ANDO-SAN.
ANDO-SAN, WAKE UP!
MISAWA BATTING CENTER
KNOCK KNOCK
AT LEAST PRETEND YOU'RE NOT SLACKING.
I JUST HEARD SOMETHING INTERESTING FROM MITSUYOSHI.
AS THE OLDER BROTHER, I SIMPLY MUST GO SUPPORT HIM IN THIS ENDEAVOR!
...NWAH?
GO?
GO WHERE?

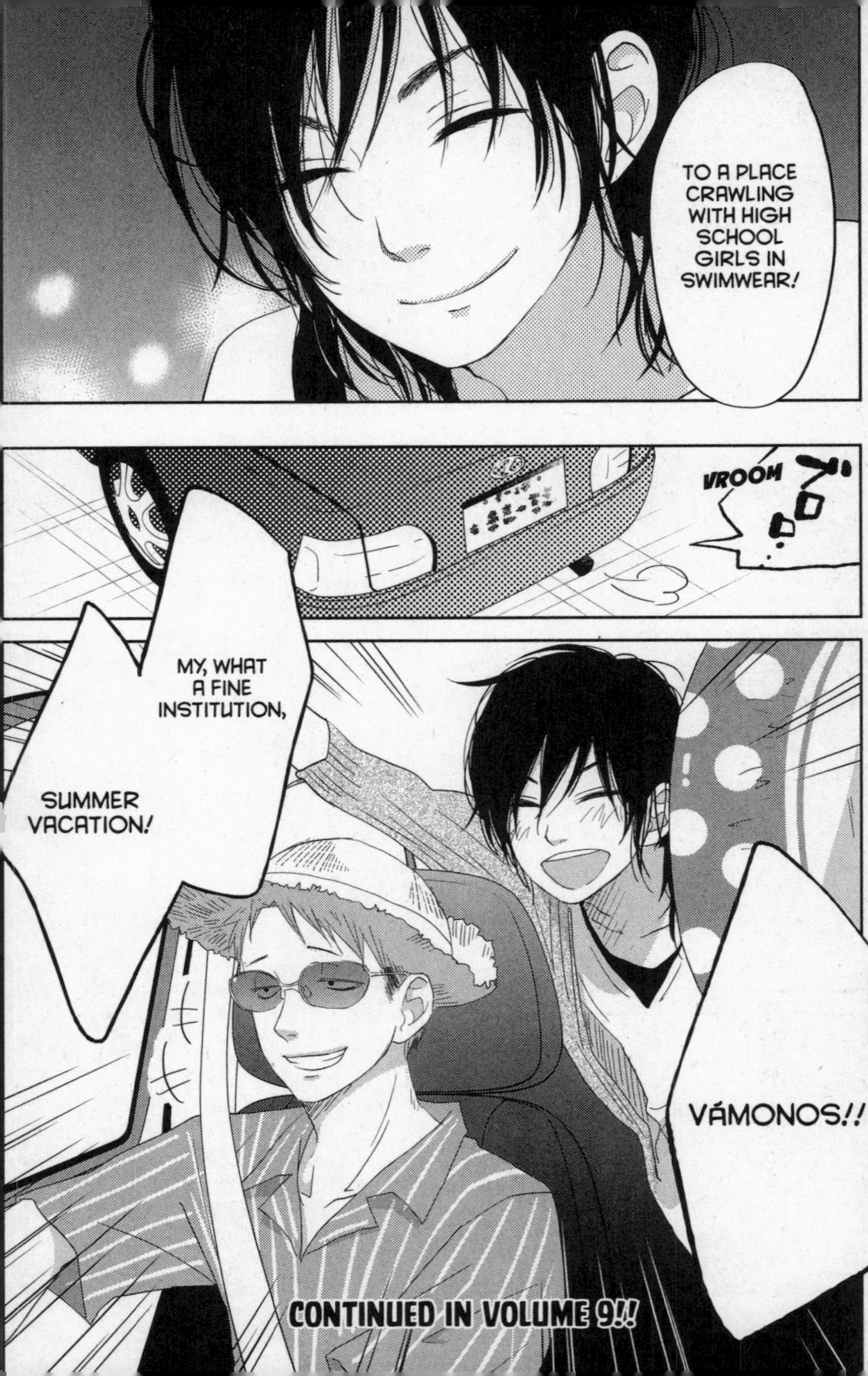
TO A PLACE CRAWLING WITH HIGH SCHOOL GIRLS IN SWIMWEAR!
VROOM
MY, WHAT A FINE INSTITUTION,
SUMMER VACATION!
VÁMONOS!!
CONTINUED IN VOLUME 9!!

DEAD OR ALIVE

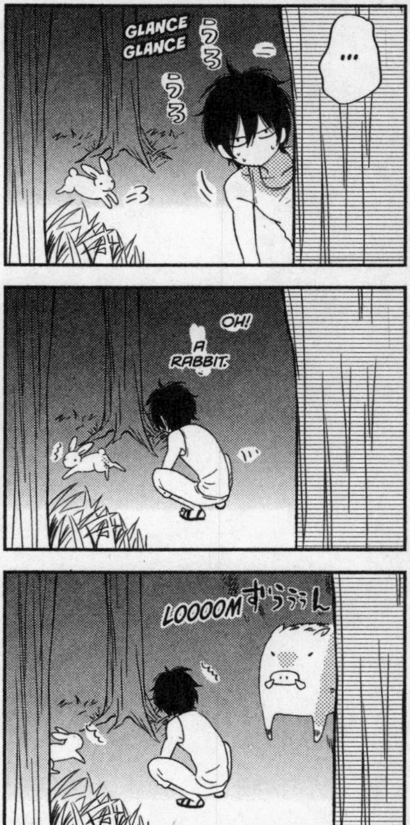
GLANCE GLANCE
うろうろ
...
OH!
A RABBIT.
LOOOOM すうううん
WAHHH うおおお
DAMMIT! HE KEEPS COMING IN AND OUT OF VIEW, THE JERK!
IT WAS DRIVING HIM OUT OF HIS MIND.
DMP DMP
ハラハラ
QUESTION 32:

DEAD OR ALIVE 2

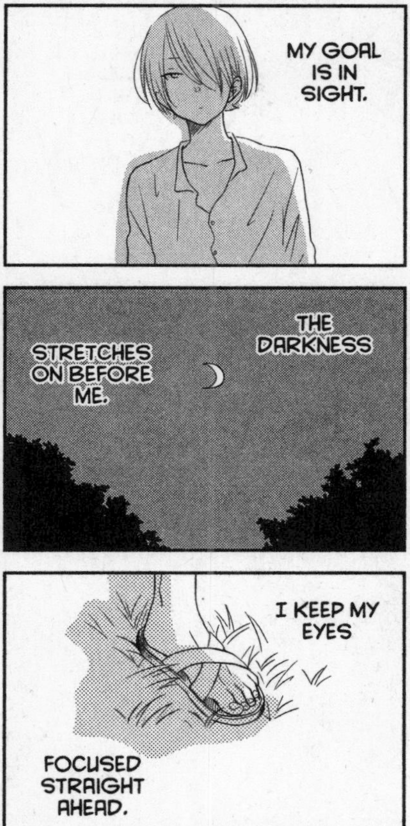
MY GOAL IS IN SIGHT.
THE DARKNESS
STRETCHES ON BEFORE ME.
I KEEP MY EYES
FOCUSED STRAIGHT AHEAD.
...I ESCAPED!!
THE GREATEST MIRACLE OF THE SUMMER.

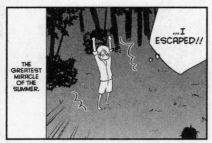

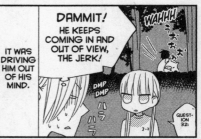

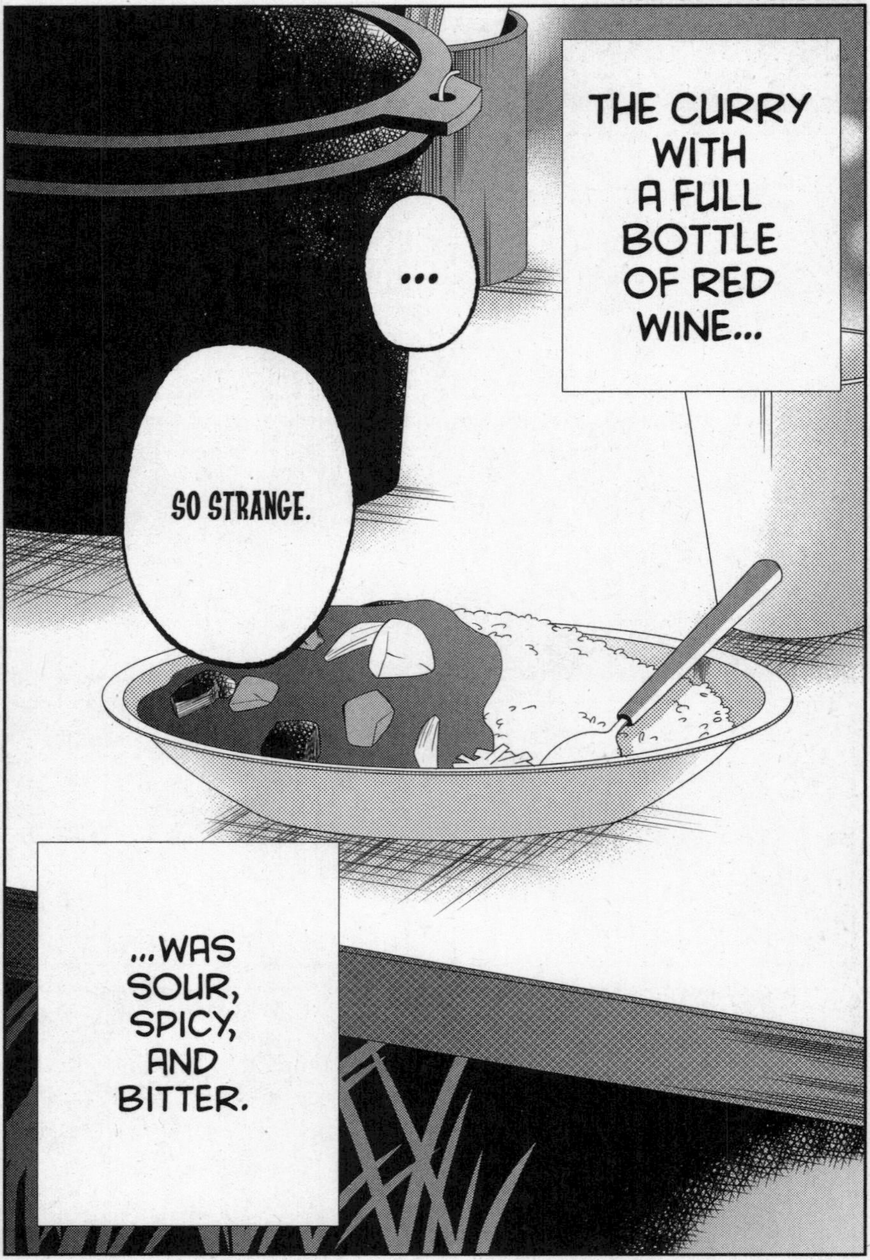
THE CURRY WITH A FULL BOTTLE OF RED WINE...
...
SO STRANGE.
...WAS SOUR, SPICY, AND BITTER.

★END OF VOLUME BONUS MANGA★ IYO'S TERRIFYING TALE

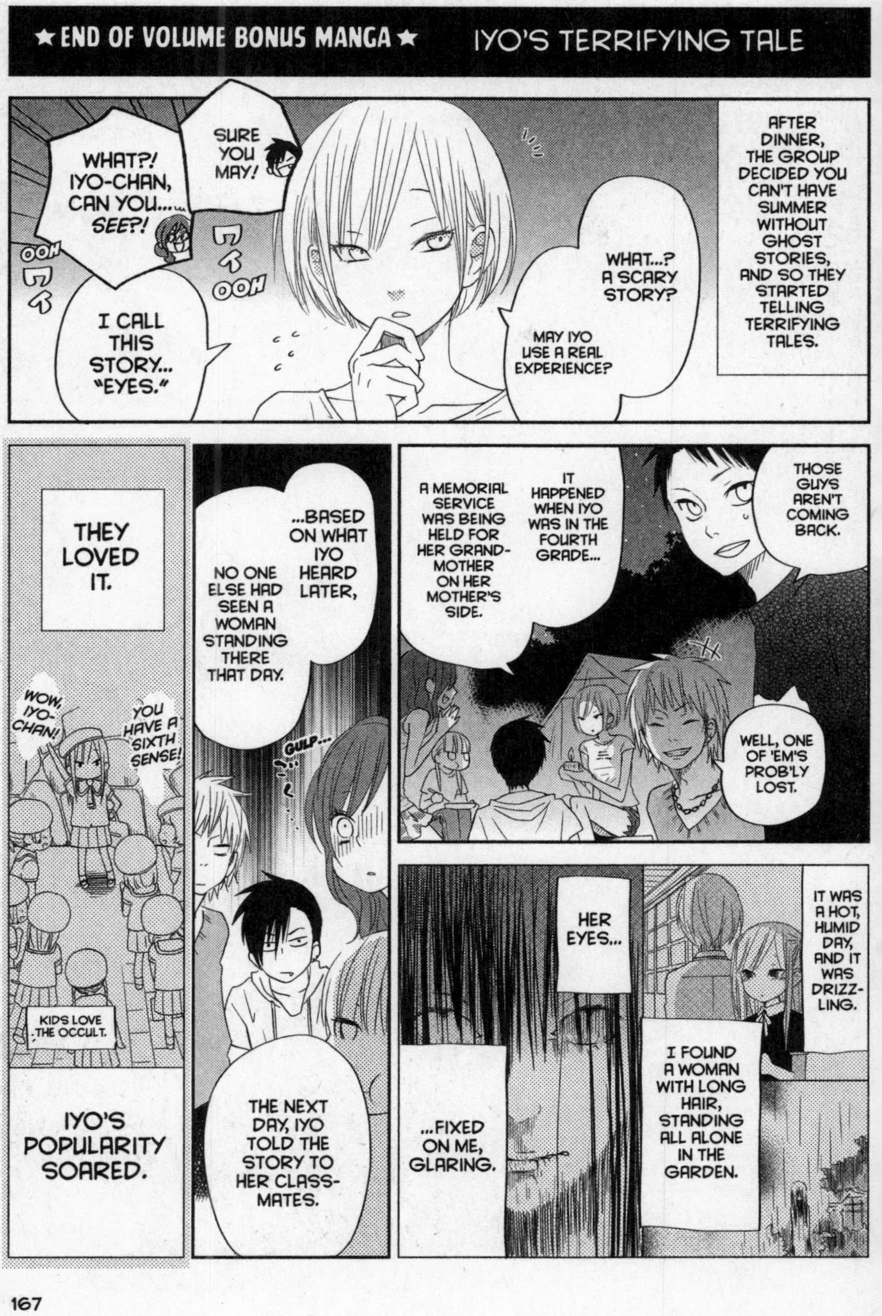
AFTER DINNER, THE GROUP DECIDED YOU CAN'T HAVE SUMMER WITHOUT GHOST STORIES, AND SO THEY STARTED TELLING TERRIFYING TALES.
WHAT...? A SCARY STORY?
MAY IYO USE A REAL EXPERIENCE?
SURE YOU MAY!
WHAT?! IYO-CHAN, CAN YOU... SEE?!
OOH
OOH
I CALL THIS STORY... "EYES."
THOSE GUYS AREN'T COMING BACK.
IT HAPPENED WHEN IYO WAS IN THE FOURTH GRADE...
A MEMORIAL SERVICE WAS BEING HELD FOR HER GRAND-MOTHER ON HER MOTHER'S SIDE.
WELL, ONE OF 'EM'S PROB'LY LOST.
IT WAS A HOT, HUMID DAY, AND IT WAS DRIZZ-LING.
I FOUND A WOMAN WITH LONG HAIR, STANDING ALL ALONE IN THE GARDEN.
HER EYES...
...FIXED ON ME, GLARING.
...BASED ON WHAT IYO HEARD LATER,
NO ONE ELSE HAD SEEN A WOMAN STANDING THERE THAT DAY.
GULP...
THE NEXT DAY, IYO TOLD THE STORY TO HER CLASS-MATES.
THEY LOVED IT.
YOU HAVE A SIXTH SENSE!
WOW, IYO-CHAN!
KID'S LOVE THE OCCULT.
IYO'S POPULARITY SOARED.

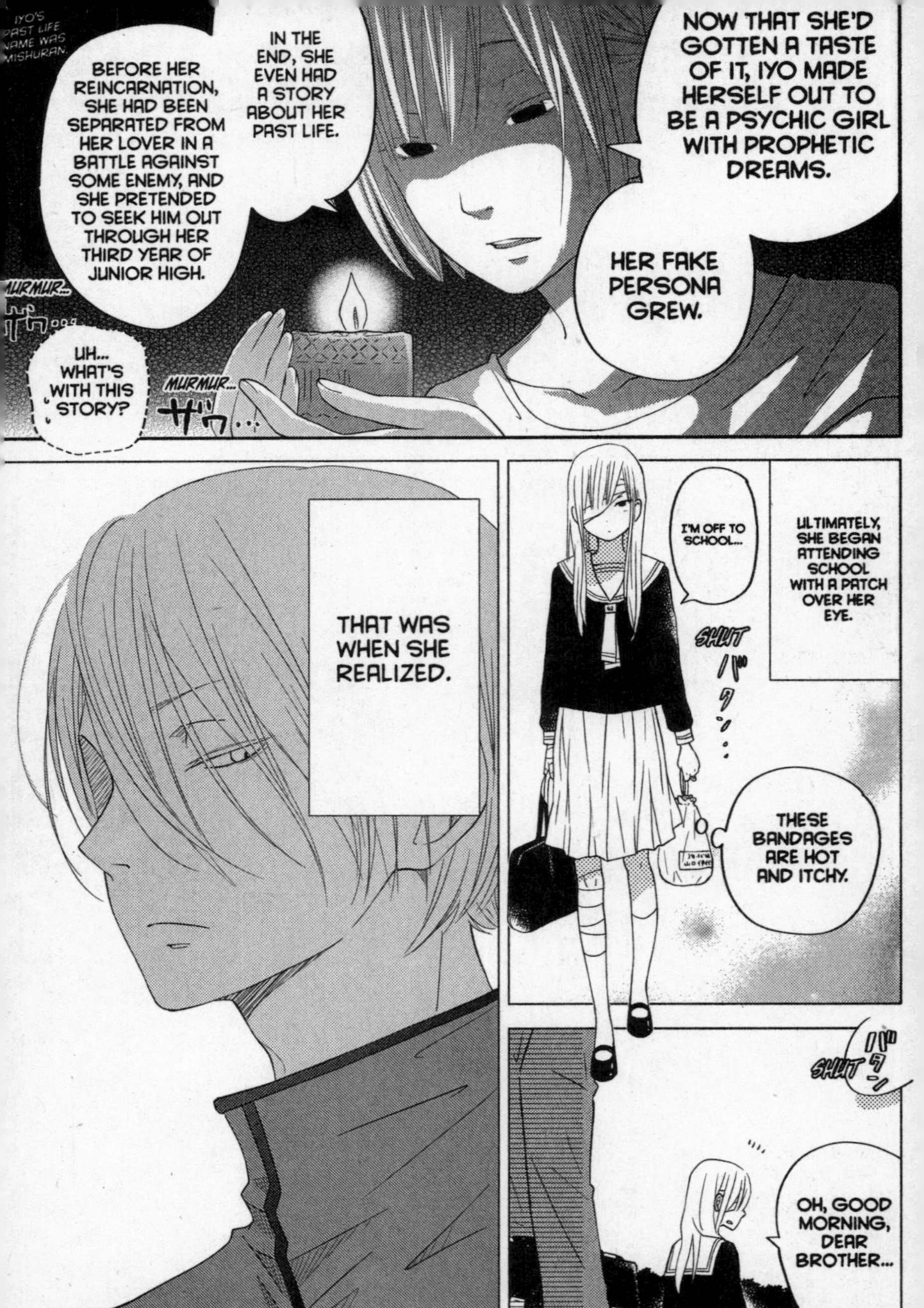
NOW THAT SHE'D GOTTEN A TASTE OF IT, IYO MADE HERSELF OUT TO BE A PSYCHIC GIRL WITH PROPHETIC DREAMS.
HER FAKE PERSONA GREW.
IN THE END, SHE EVEN HAD A STORY ABOUT HER PAST LIFE.
BEFORE HER REINCARNATION, SHE HAD BEEN SEPARATED FROM HER LOVER IN A BATTLE AGAINST SOME ENEMY, AND SHE PRETENDED TO SEEK HIM OUT THROUGH HER THIRD YEAR OF JUNIOR HIGH.
IYO'S PAST LIFE NAME WAS MISHURAN.
MURMUR...
ザワ...
MURMUR...
ザワ...
UH... WHAT'S WITH THIS STORY?
ULTIMATELY, SHE BEGAN ATTENDING SCHOOL WITH A PATCH OVER HER EYE.
I'M OFF TO SCHOOL...
SHUT
バタン
THESE BANDAGES ARE HOT AND ITCHY.
SHUT
バタン
OH, GOOD MORNING, DEAR BROTHER...
THAT WAS WHEN SHE REALIZED.

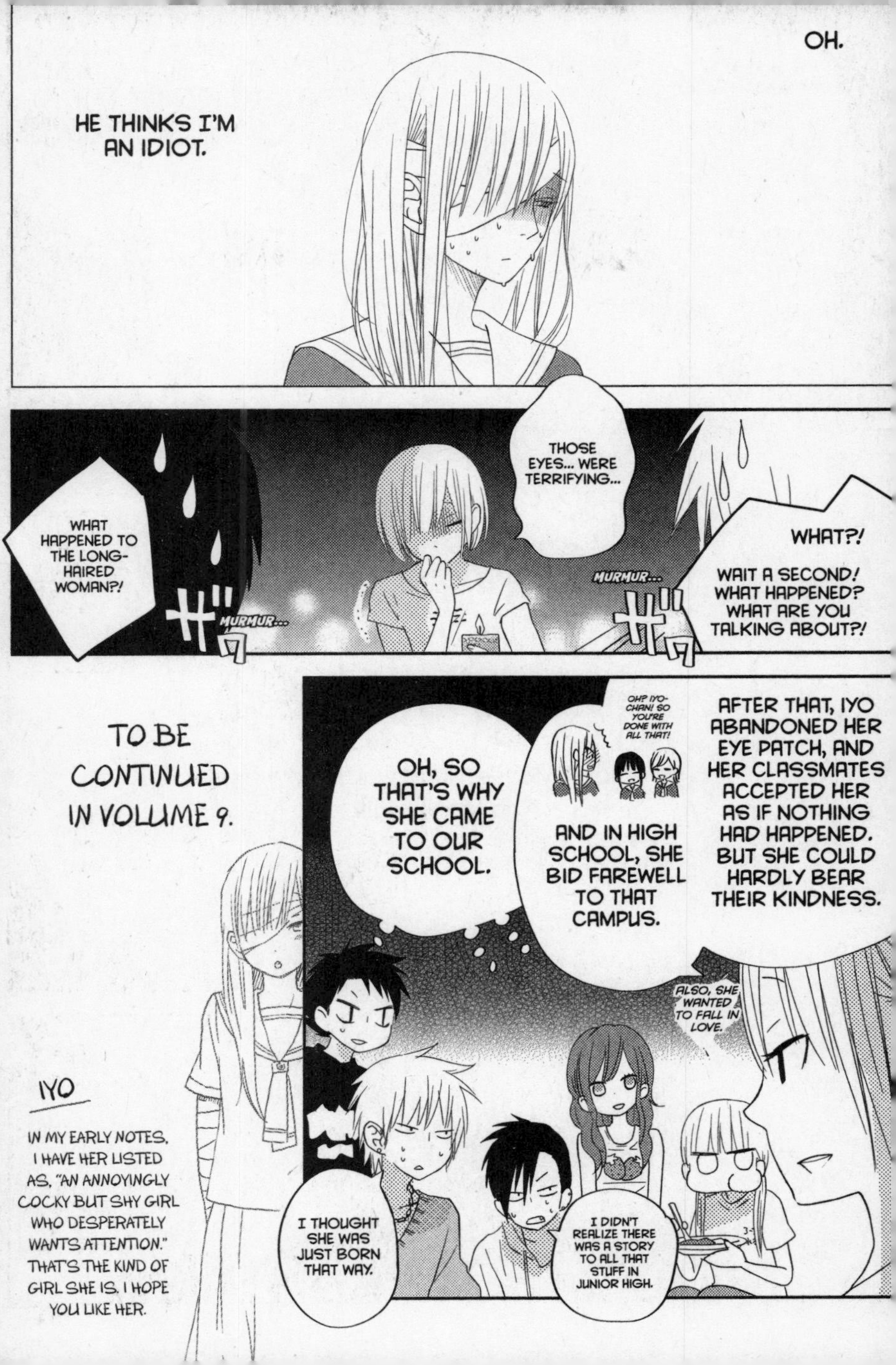
OH.
HE THINKS I'M AN IDIOT.
WHAT?!
WAIT A SECOND! WHAT HAPPENED? WHAT ARE YOU TALKING ABOUT?!
MURMUR...
THOSE EYES... WERE TERRIFYING...
MURMUR...
WHAT HAPPENED TO THE LONG-HAIRED WOMAN?!
AFTER THAT, IYO ABANDONED HER EYE PATCH, AND HER CLASSMATES ACCEPTED HER AS IF NOTHING HAD HAPPENED. BUT SHE COULD HARDLY BEAR THEIR KINDNESS.
OH? IYO-CHAN! SO YOU'RE DONE WITH ALL THAT!
AND IN HIGH SCHOOL, SHE BID FAREWELL TO THAT CAMPUS.
OH, SO THAT'S WHY SHE CAME TO OUR SCHOOL.
ALSO, SHE WANTED TO FALL IN LOVE.
I DIDN'T REALIZE THERE WAS A STORY TO ALL THAT STUFF IN JUNIOR HIGH.
I THOUGHT SHE WAS JUST BORN THAT WAY.
TO BE CONTINUED IN VOLUME 9.
IYO
IN MY EARLY NOTES, I HAVE HER LISTED AS, "AN ANNOYINGLY COCKY BUT SHY GIRL WHO DESPERATELY WANTS ATTENTION." THAT'S THE KIND OF GIRL SHE IS. I HOPE YOU LIKE HER.

C O M M E N T

Robico

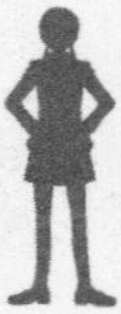

This is volume eight. I did kind of get the feeling that when they changed classes in the last volume, the *tonari no* (next to me) in the Japanese title *Tonari no Kaibutsu-kun* (The Monster Next to Me) didn't really apply anymore, but I can't just take it off, so please continue to enjoy *My Little Monster*, still known in Japan as The Monster Next to Me.

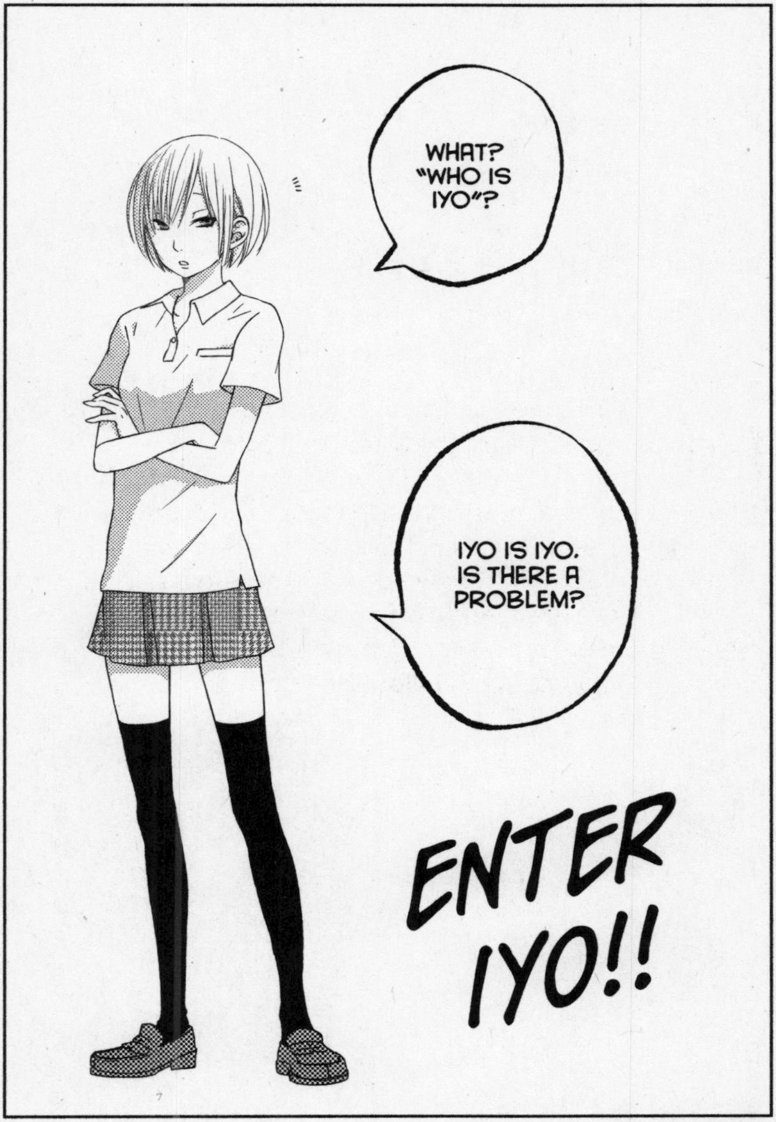
WHAT? "WHO IS IYO"?
IYO IS IYO. IS THERE A PROBLEM?
ENTER IYO!!

ROBICO

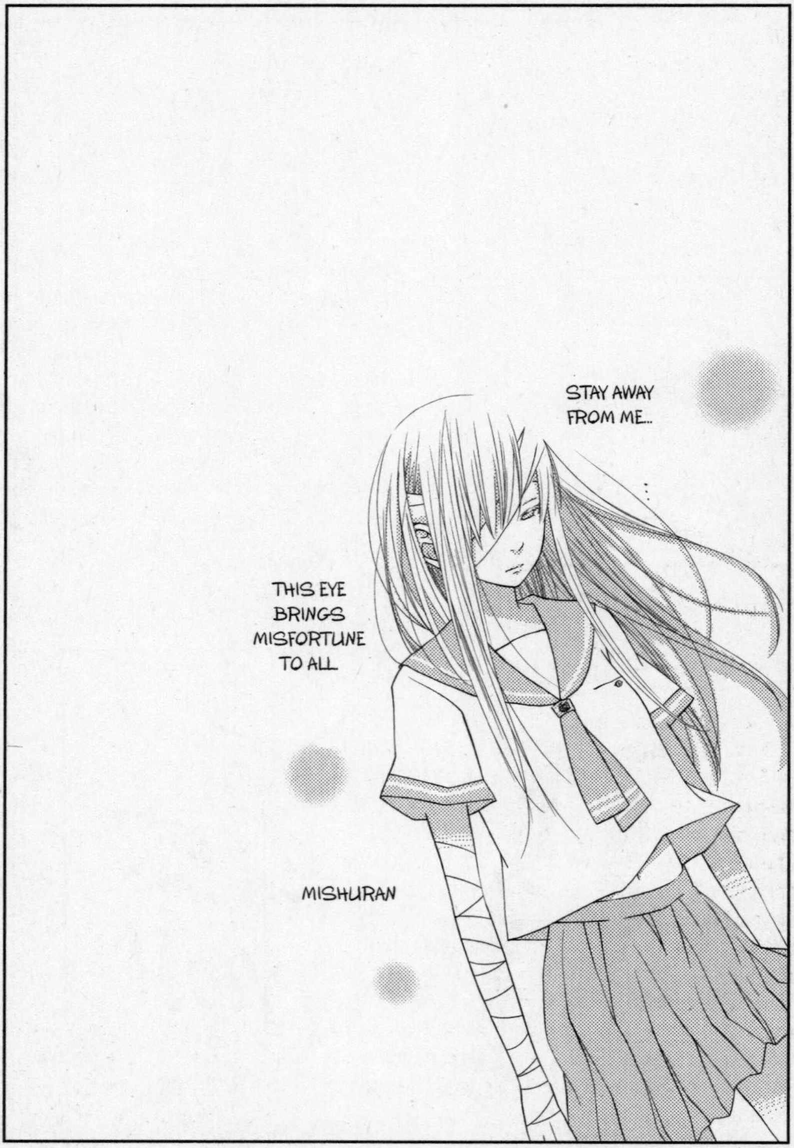
STAY AWAY FROM ME...
THIS EYE BRINGS MISFORTUNE TO ALL
MISHURAN

ROBICO

My Little Monster 08 Translation Notes

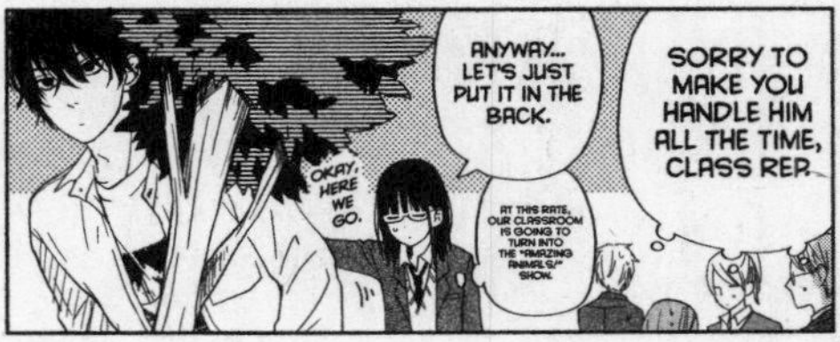
SORRY TO MAKE YOU HANDLE HIM ALL THE TIME, CLASS REP.
ANYWAY... LET'S JUST PUT IT IN THE BACK.
AT THIS RATE, OUR CLASSROOM IS GOING TO TURN INTO THE "AMAZING ANIMALS!" SHOW.
OKAY, HERE WE GO.

Amazing Animals!, page 17
Oshima is referencing a TV show called *Dobutsu Kiso Tengai*, also known as "Amazing Animals!" As one might guess from the context, the show features all kinds of animals doing amazing tricks.

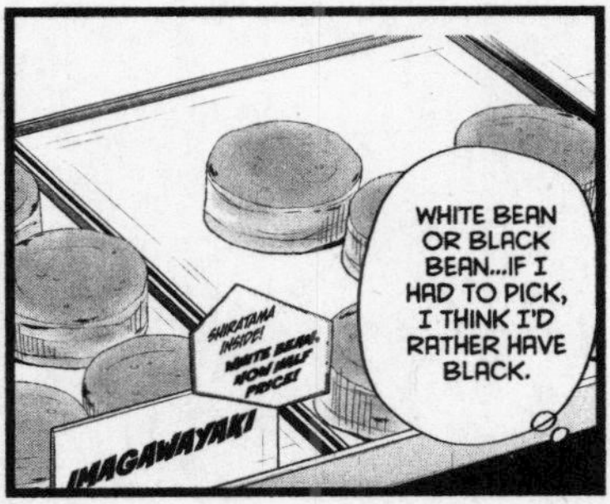
WHITE BEAN OR BLACK BEAN...IF I HAD TO PICK, I THINK I'D RATHER HAVE BLACK.
SHIRATAMA INSIDE!
IMAGAWAYAKI

Imagawayaki, page 45
Imagawayaki is a Japanese dessert, consisting of sweet bean paste (or some other filling) sandwiched between two layers of cooked batter. This particular shop offers fillings of black bean paste, made from black soybeans, or white bean paste, made from navy beans. The white bean Imagawayaki comes with the added bonus of having shiratama (sweet dumplings made from rice flour) inside the filling.

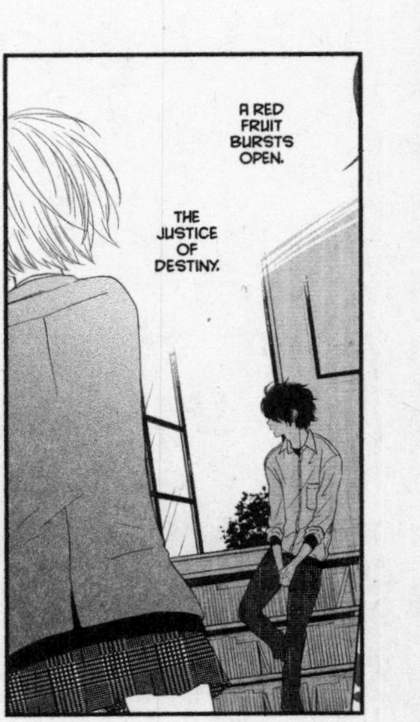
A RED FRUIT BURSTS OPEN.
THE JUSTICE OF DESTINY.

A red fruit bursts open, page 63
This is a reference to a children's novel, *Akai Mi Hajiketa* (Red Fruit Bursts Open), by Keiko Nagita. It is a collection of stories about different children going through different circumstances. The bursting of the red fruit is a metaphor for something like an aha moment—when each child realizes something important. An important thing realized by one of the children is that she is in love. Her particular story is included in Japanese language arts textbooks, and so the expression "the red fruit bursts open" has come to be synonymous with falling in love. As for what Iyo means by "the justice of destiny," the reader's guess is as good as the translators'.

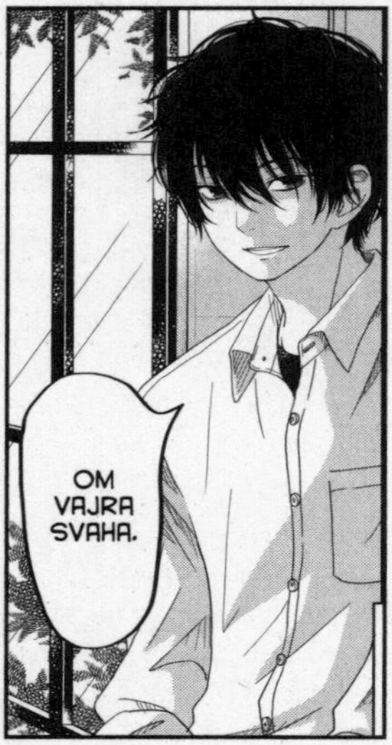
OM VAJRA SVAHA.

Om vajra svaha, page 64
This is sort of a Buddhist mantra, and may or may not be a real one. "Om" is a mystical word signifying the beginning of a mantra, and "svaha" signifies the end of one. "Vajra" means diamond and has symbolic significance in Buddhism. Haru and Asako don't seem like the types to be discussing religious matters, so most likely they were trying to remember a chant used in an anime that they saw, or that they read in a manga.

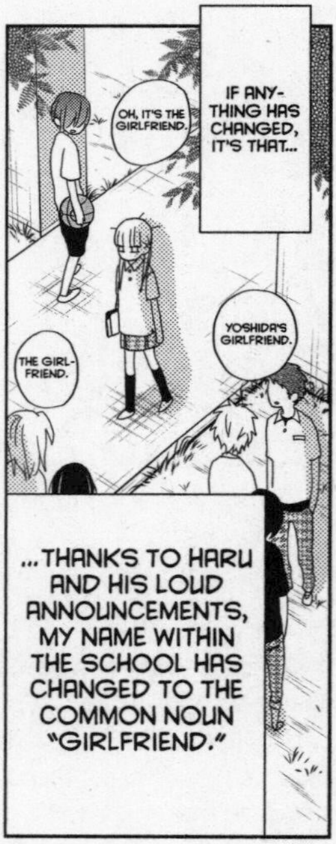
IF ANYTHING HAS CHANGED, IT'S THAT...
OH, IT'S THE GIRLFRIEND.
YOSHIDA'S GIRLFRIEND.
THE GIRLFRIEND.
...THANKS TO HARU AND HIS LOUD ANNOUNCEMENTS, MY NAME WITHIN THE SCHOOL HAS CHANGED TO THE COMMON NOUN "GIRLFRIEND."

Girlfriend, page 113
In Japanese, Shizuku observes that her name has changed to something even lower than a common noun—a third-person pronoun. The Japanese word for girlfriend is kanojo, which also means "she" or "her," so when she walks around campus, it can easily sound like everyone is saying, "It's her!"

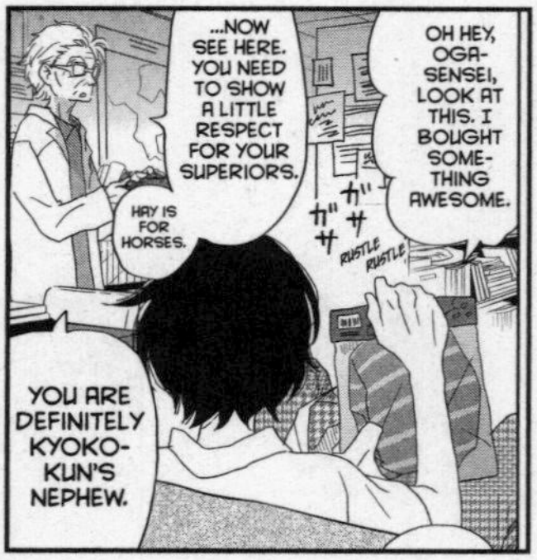
OH HEY, OGA-SENSEI, LOOK AT THIS. I BOUGHT SOMETHING AWESOME.
...NOW SEE HERE. YOU NEED TO SHOW A LITTLE RESPECT FOR YOUR SUPERIORS.
HAY IS FOR HORSES.
ガサ ガサ
RUSTLE RUSTLE
YOU ARE DEFINITELY KYOKO-KUN'S NEPHEW.

Hay is for horses, page 122
This is translators' way of having Oga-sensei correct the way Haru speaks to his teachers. In the Japanese version, he tells Haru to use the polite Japanese speech pattern that one would reasonably expect a student to use when addressing a teacher. As the reader may have guessed, Haru doesn't think to use such formalities.

A Kodansha Comics Trade Paperback Original.

My Little Monster volume 8 copyright © 2011 Robico
English translation copyright © 2015 Robico

All rights reserved.

Published in the United States by Kodansha Comics, an imprint of Kodansha USA Publishing, LLC, New York.

Publication rights for this English edition arranged through Kodansha Ltd., Tokyo.

First published in Japan in 2011 by Kodansha Ltd., Tokyo, as *Tonari no Kaibutsu-kun*, volume 8.

ISBN 978-1-61262-992-6

Printed in the United States of America.

www.kodanshacomics.com

9 8 7 6 5 4 3 2 1

Translator: Alethea Nibley & Athena Nibley
Lettering: Paige Pumphrey